Human MONSTERS

PUBLISHER
Denis Kitchen

ART DIRECTOR
Amie Brockway

DESIGNER
Douglas Bantz

EDITORS
Dave Schreiner and Chris Couch

ASSISTANT EDITOR
Kate Carey

VP, DEPUTY PUBLISHER
Judith Hansen

VP, PRODUCTION
Jim Kitchen

VP, BUSINESS AFFAIRS AND OPERATIONS
Scott Hyman

SALES AND MARKETING DIRECTOR
Jamie Riehle

SALES MANAGER
Gail "Ziggy" Zygmont

CUSTOMER SERVICE MANAGER
Karen Lowman

MANAGING EDITOR
Michele Boudreau

VP, CHIEF FINANCIAL OFFICER
Dean Zirolli

WAREHOUSE MANAGERS
John Wills and Vic Lisewski

Library of Congress Cataloging-in-Publication Data
Turner, George, 1925–
　　　Human monsters : the bizarre psychology of movie villains / by George E. Turner and Michael H. Price ; introduction by Fay Wray.
　　　p.　　　cm.
　　　Includes indes.
　　　ISBN 0-87816-377-8 (soft cover)
　　　1. Villains in motion pictures. I. Price, Michael H., 1947–
II. Title.
PN1995.9.V47T87　　　1995　　　9540772
791.43'6520692—dc20　　　　CIP

Human
MONSTERS
The Bizarre Psychology of
Movie Villains

George E. Turner and Michael H. Price

SELECTIONS

1. The Great Gabbo (1929) 17

2. Svengali (1931) 21

3. Guilty Hands (1931) 25

4. The Unholy Garden (1931) 28

5. The Hatchet Man (1932) 31

6. Behind the Mask (1932) 33

7. Mystery Ranch (1932) 35

8. The Old Dark House (1932) 37

9. The Mask of Fu Manchu (1932) 41

10. Secrets of the French Police (1932) 46

11. Murders in the Zoo (1933) 49

12. I Cover the Waterfront (1933) 52

13. The Mystery of Mr. X (1934) 54

14. The Black Cat (1934)..57

15. The Love Captive (1934) 63

16. The Man With Two Faces (1934) 65

17. Smoking Guns (1934) 68

18. The Man Who Reclaimed His Head (1934) 71

19. The Mystery of Edwin Drood (1935) 74

20. Mark of the Vampire (1935) 78

21. Let 'Em Have It (1935)..81

22. Show Them No Mercy (1935)..84

23. The Walking Dead (1936) 87

24. Trouble For Two (1936) 91

25. Sweeney Todd, the Demon Barber of Fleet Street (1936) 93

26. Broken Blossoms (1936) 96

27. Uncivilized (Pituri) (1936) 98

28. Blake of Scotland Yard (1937)...101

29. Island of Doomed Men (1940) 103

30. Stranger on the Third Floor (1940) 105

31. Dark Eyes of London (The Human Monster) (1940) 108

32. The Ape (1940) 112

33. The Mad Doctor (1941) 115

34. Among the Living (1941) 119

35. Who Is Hope Schuyler? (1942) 122

36. The Man Who Wouldn't Die (1942) 124

37. Moontide (1942) 126

38. The Night Has Eyes (Terror House) (1942) 128

39. The Leopard Man (1943) 130

40. The Seventh Victim (1943) 134

41. Bluebeard (1944) 138

42. The Soul of a Monster (1944) 141

43. The Mad Ghoul (1944) 145

44. Dark Waters (1944) 147

45. The Missing Juror (1944) 150

46. Guest in the House (Satan in Skirts) (1944) 153

47. The Great Flamarion (1945) 156

48. Jealousy (1945) 158

49. The Madonna's Secret (1946) 160

50. Dragonwyck (1946) 162

51. Decoy (1946) 165

52. The Dark Mirror (1946) 167

53. So Dark the Night (1946) 169

54. The Locket (1946) 171

55. Ivy (1947) 174

56. The Queen of Spades (1947) 177

57. The Sign of the Ram (1948) 180

58. Behind Locked Doors (The Human Gorilla) (1948) 183

59. Obsession (The Hidden Room) (1949) 185

60. M (1951) 188

FOREWORD by Fay Wray

What station I may hold in the history of Hollywood shall, I suppose, forever be identified with films of the ilk that George Turner and Mike Price have assembled for discussion in this book. The "ilkiest" of the lot of course, is *King Kong*. But that one has been amply discussed elsewhere—and examined in especially satisfying detail in a book called *The Making of King Kong*, which Mr. Turner and my friend Orville Goldner wrote sixteen years ago.

I am most appreciative that Mr. Turner has seen fit not to limit his attention to Kong alone in his continuing survey of my career. He and Mr. Price devoted considerable effort to the rediscovery of one assignment—a movie I did with Melvyn Douglas and Lionel Atwill, *The Vampire Bat*, in 1933 — for their 1979 book, *Forgotten Horrors*. And true to their title, even I had practically forgotten *The Vampire Bat!* Their researches served to correct my mistaken belief that it had been a Universal Pictures production. While my memory of shooting *The Vampire Bat* at Universal proved accurate, it took *Forgotten Horrors* to bring back to me that this film had been an independent production by Majestic Pictures on rented Universal sets. So long as I am digressing, I must take modest issue with the title of that first book of Mr. Turner's and Mr. Price's: such pictures may well have been Forgotten — but Horrors? I do wish that a gentler term, like fantasies perhaps, could come into popular usage. Now, I was glad to see Mr. Turner soften the punch somewhat with a more dignified title for his collection of essays, *The Cinema of Adventure, Romance & Terror*, where he devoted a chapter to *The Most Dangerous Game*, a picture on which I worked with many of the people who would become our *King Kong* "family." But then, Mr. Price tells me he and Mr. Turner are planning to call this new book *Human Monsters*, a return to the sensational after a brush with dignity! Well, it is their book, after all. And once again I am proud to be a part of a Turner-Price book, particularly in the company of some distinguished pictures—as well as, I suppose, some not so distinguished. The picture of mine they have selected for this outing is *The Unholy Garden*, an adventurous fantasy (I emphasize fantasy) which I believed to have been thoroughly forgotten. As ever, I find it reassuring and pleasantly surprising to find writers so concerned with investigating the bigger picture of film history.

Fay Wray

INTRODUCTION

O ur crime journalism days seemed safely behind us when George Turner and I first knuckled down to researching the esence Hollywood villainy. That is Hollywood villainy as opposed to the real-world variety, which was in uncomfortably close quarters with us where we had both grown up and pursued much of our kindred careers.

We recognized, of course, the affinity between the fiction of evil and the fact of evil, and said as much in the notes we had begun compiling as a foundation for the present book. We had taken to heart, more from experience than from passive assent, Joseph Conrad's argument that "Men alone are quite capable of all wickedness," and we were aware that among the movies we had chosen to study, many had taken explicit cues from the bad people of history and the headlines.

George and I were more or less comfortably ensconced at a Texas newspaper, where we held forth as editorial art director (Turner) and business/financial editor, then city editor (myself), our assignments ranging agreeably far from our backgrounds in police reporting, suspect sketching, and courtroom portraiture.

George's pen and ink drawings from witnesses' observations had brought about the capture of a handful of murder suspects and any number of people wanted for rape and armed robbery. I had covered a ghastly variety of police cases, including the abduction and slaying of a state legislator's teen-aged daughter—whose killer owed his capture to a Turner sketch.

All of which plays impressively enough on the front page, but takes a toll on the human spirit unless the reporter is the classic frustrated cop of journalistic legend. One must enjoy looking for trouble and finding same to get much of a charge out of front line crime reportage, and George and I had seen so much evil, at inadvertently close range, since our respective childhoods, that we knew better than to perceive policework as a glamour gig.

George's first encounter with criminality came in 1930, when as a child approaching grammar school age in Amarillo, Texas, he chanced upon the horrifying aftermath of the what became known as A.D. Payne car bomb case. Thirty odd years later, George retold that grisly episode for the historical journal, *Southwest Heritage*, and then in 1992 he and I developed an illustrated version, with the artist Lamberto Alvarez, for *Heavy Metal* magazine.

I was born in 1947, by which time George had seen a genial roommate from his college days lapse into a brief career of extortion and murder by torture; he observed a sweet natured neighbor lady fall into a lethal rage; and as a new journalist had helped cover the mutilation slaying of Tex Thornton, the celebrated explosives expert whose choice of drinking companions left much to be desired.

My own childhood years in Amarillo—an extraordinarily violent town, which even today retains both the nihilistic lawlessness and the fascist vigilante spirit that characterized the Texas oil and cattle booms of the early twentieth century—were overshadowed by an ominous Shunned House just down the street. This was a residence which once belonged to my maternal grandparents, but now it was ill famed as the last dwelling place of the despicable Sam Gasway, executed for the rape of a neighbor girl. Sam Gasway, once regarded as the most chivalrous of citizens, had been turned over to the police by another neighbor, a Baptist minister whose son was a playmate of mine. This playmate grew up to become a horse thief and a bank robber.

And they say this stuff only happens in the movies.

⇢ THE SOLACE OF CINEMA AND REAL WORLD INTRUSIONS UPON SAME ⇠

Fortunately, both George's childhood and my own were leavened by a fascination with motion pictures. He in his adolescence and I in mine, would spend hours in the cinema, taking notes, screening favorite films repeatedly, and looking forward to the day when a career might be forged from this passion.

When finally we met as fellow journalists in 1968, it turns out we might as well have been brothers born in separate generations. The interest in movies was still more a pastime than a business, but we determined to intensify our involvement.

We began to find right direction with the 1975 publication of the book coauthored with Orville Goldner, *The Making of King Kong.* The Turner-Price book *Forgotten Horrors* had wrapped by 1977 and awaited release, and with the sequel called Human Monsters of the Movies, we felt grateful to begin writing about crime as a function of the cinema. Our police reporting dues seemed paid in full.

But no sooner had we decided on the content of this project than a senior editor, a Junior G-man-type with sanctimonious, adventurous delusions, decided that I should tackle a couple of investigative projects that would involve some human monsters of the real world. All of a sudden, the menacing souls of *Guilty Hands, I Cover the Waterfront,* and even *The Man Who Reclaimed his Head*—to cite a few of the pictures herein—became more identifiably real for their resemblance to the miscreants whose activities this assignment involved.

There was the New Mexico-based pornographer whose forays into Texas were taken as a personal affront by our church-deacon editor. My small team of reporters and photographers, deployed to the field while the editor held court in the office he had christened his "war room," wound up having our lives threatened unless we laid off a story that wasn't much of a story to begin with. (The big scoop proved to be a Texas comptroller's bust on grounds that the porno entrepreneur had neglected to register as an out-of-state corporation.)

And there was the matter of the oil lease scam—reams of documents, hinted at in a vaguely tantalizing tip, that I found myself under orders to locate in a backwoods West Texas courthouse, then to pore over until they yielded the revelation that some prominent lawyer/portico had misappropriated a hefty sum in petroleum royalties.

My crusading editor had bragged it about that our sheet was on the point of nailing a big shot—before simple arithmatic demonstrated that the statute of limitations had long since passed. No story here, just the sad understanding that fountain-pen banditry had been committed with impunity.

In orchestrating this non-news extravaganza, of course, the editor had conveniently attached my name to the boast, paving the way for a couple of years' worth of threatening harassments—anonymous, naturally, but hardly a mystery as to the source.

Journalism was growing less pleasurable by the moment. My promotion to city editor in 1977 seemed a safe enough holding pattern. Unfortunately it coincided with the selection of our burg as the trial venue for a blood and money cause celebre known as the Cullen Davis Murder Case.

George and I toughed that one out as a team: I supervised the field reporter coverage, George produced a portfolio of widely published courtroom scenes—and we decided to jump ship as soon as things calmed down. George lit a shuck out of Texas; I stayed put but began planting greener pastures that finally began taking root around 1980.

✦ THE BOOK TAKES SHAPE ✦

Does it take everybody this long to write a book about the movies? And is every film-history book so intimidatingly intertwined with real world parallels? Or is it just us?

We've called *Human Monsters* a done deal on several occasions since the first manuscript was completed in 1978. By which time our paths had diverged drastically—George to a new career in Hollywood, myself to a holding pattern in public relations and college administration, then back to the newspaper racket—and we've kept tampering with this book until the time felt right to publish.

Broadening interests have dictated the removal of some chapters (revised and fattened up for *American Cinematographer* magazine during George's hitch there as editor) and the addition of others. We are fortunate to have Fay Wray's newly composed introduction and the eloquent afterword by Vincent Price, who during visits spanning almost twenty years, proved to be a generous font of cinematic information as well as also a distant cousin.

And inevitably, true crime intrudes on our discussions of cinematic trespasses. Just as George and I were wrapping our chapter-by-chapter revisions for this edition in 1990, a New Jersey publisher contracted me to develop an encyclopedia of serial-murder cases to be published in card-portfolio form. This assignment resulted in the Bloody Visions series of trading card sets from Shel-Tone Publications, a recurring collection whose key impact upon my own work has been to serve notice that fiction isn't half so malicious or debauched as fact. If Peter Kurten, the despised "Vampire of Dusseldorf" was not the grim inspiration for Fritz Lang's *M*, then certainly Kurtain's murderous debaucheries anticipated that breakthrough picture in many particulars.

M figures largely in this book, though not in the form of the famous Lang original. It is in the Americanized remake that George and I have chosen to discuss—a mid-century production that is by turns forgotten or unfairly dismissed as an insignificant copy.

For that matter, all the films here are long overdue for fresh consideration. Their binding concern is a near complete avoidance of the fantastic—even 1935's *Mark of the Vampire* is rooted in mundane circumstances—and yet each movie has its monster, a creature that seems as unremarkably human as the family down the street.

✦ ABOUT THE SELECTIONS ✦

Mr. Poe's imp of the perverse gave literature such choice human monsters as Iago, who laid his creation to "an evil god," Emily Bronte's haunted Gypsy,

Heathcliff, in Wuthering Heights, Richard Connell's man-stalking Zaroff of The Most Dangerous Game; ruthless archcriminals epitomized by Conan Doyle's Professor Moriarty and Sax Rohmer's Fu Manchu; Danny, the baby-faced guardian of the ominous hatbox in Emlyn Williams' Night Must Fall —and many another master at holding the public in the thrall of unease.

Extravagant and far removed from reality though some of these characters seem, the most effective of them are traced largely from real-life counterparts; often, in fact, dictates of taste and even dramatic license have required that they be toned down. Few such fictitious exploits are half so depraved or bizarre as the factual exploits of Gilles de Rais, Vlad Tepes, Countess Erzebet Bathory, Jack the Ripper, David Berkowitz, the Boston Strangler, Dr. Cream, Scorpio, Burke & Hare, the Texarkana Sniper, Kate Bender or Alistair Crowley. In a world that has spawned the Inquisition, Lyndon Johnson's own private Vietnam, the Third Reich, and Murder, Incorporated—to say nothing of those benighted Payne and Gasway households in whose neighborhood George Turner and I grew up—most human monsters of fiction are safely within the bounds of realism.

Our selection hinges as vitally upon the genres the films represent and the cinematic history they reflect as upon their central characterizations. In the choosing, we have sought to display both the definitive and the neglected. To illustrate: *Behind Locked Doors, Behind the Mask*, and *Island of Doomed Men*—all thoroughly ignored except as convenient objects of stylish sneers—examine the sadistic abuse of authority with remarkable insight. *The Ape* couches an outlandish premise in a reasonable anticipation of Dr. Salk's assault on polio and frames those oddly matched elements with a vivid depiction of provincial American pettiness and intolerance. *Svengali* is the study of mesmerism applied for cruel purposes, run a close second by *The Love Captive. Uncivilized*, a fascinating Australian production, comments profoundly upon the civilization of savagry: vice versa for *I Cover the Waterfront*. British behavior appears all the more so in contrast with the innocent beauty in both *Moontide* and the little-known talking film remake of *Broken Blossoms*. Touching yet chilling portrayals of haunted genius are delivered in *The Soul of a Monster* and *The Madonna's Secret*, films that also betray, on the one hand, the powerful influence of Val Lewton's formula for conveying terror via understatement and, on the other, the artistry of a studio which was more commonly action oriented. Moral outrage, as a rule mishandled on film as mere tantrum throwing, is given dignity and genuine shock value in *The Hatchet Man*.

Show Them No Mercy and *Let 'Em Have It* are gangster films—but gangster films with a difference, demonstrating the horror engendered by the public enemy, rather than the fun and games of outlawry. Bruce Cabot's portrayals in both are, we insist, the equal of anything set forth by more celebrated crime stars such as Edward G. Robinson, James Cagney, Humphrey Bogart, and Richard Widmark.

Sympathy for the human monster seems justified at times because the victim is hardly so worthy as the one plotting his demise. The deserving object of afflictions in *Obsession* is a wife stealer; in *The Great Flamarion*, a nagging, woman; in *Guilty Hands*, a scoundrel whose doom is desirable to the end of improving the species. A scorecard would prove useful now and again to help distinguish malicious heroes from righteously indignant villains. Lionel Atwill in *The Man Who Reclaimed His Head*, deserves to loose his Claude Rains' bayonet, and Boris Karloff's insults and injuries to Bela Lugosi in *The Black Cat* earn him nothing as much as the privilege of being skinned alive. Even the psychopaths of *Murder in the Zoo* and *The Missing Juror* are right in their own minds, for nobody wants to be perceived as the bad guy.

The female miscreant, relatively rare in the 1930s selections, is dominant in the '40s batch, representing the fundamental tone of the psychological thriller genre that flourished during and following the Second World War. The likes of *Guest in the House, Ivy, Jealousy,* and *The Night Has Eyes* derived from and paced this segment of the industry.

In sum, this grouping amounts to the makings of a "dream" film festival for the movie buff intrigued by vamps, scamps, schemers, outright evildoers, and villains in spite of themselves. George and I had made obscurity a requisite for inclusion in our previous collection of essays on film, *Forgotten Horrors: Early Talkie Chillers from Poverty Row.* No such condition applies here, for we can not resist the temptation to cast additional light on such well known items as *The Old Dark House, The Black Cat, Svengali* and two of Val Lewton's justly revered films, *The Seventh Victim* and *The Leopard Man.*

❖ THE RE-DISCOVERY IMPERATIVES ❖

Among the lesser known pictures—the likes of *The Hatchet Man, Trouble For Two* and *Secrets of the French Police*—many face renewed opportunity to reach an appreciative audience. These three examples represent, respectively, the legacies of Old Hollywood's Warner Bros., MGM and RKO Radio Studios. An MGM nitrate conversion program, begun during the 1960s, has seen the transfer of every MGM title from chemically unstable nitrate film stock to virtually imperishable safety stock. In an underacknowledged follow-through development, modeled after the MGM preservation project and picking up where it left off, Turner Entertainment Company (no kin to George) has generated definitive safety film editions of such MGM gems as *Gone With the Wind* and *The Wizard of Oz*—recapturing the grandeur of those pictures' 1939 release prints—and meanwhile enabled the transfer to safety stock of the entire pre-1948 Warner Bros. library.

With its purchase of the RKO library in 1988, Turner Entertainment continued that formidable task of rescuing the movies' master elements from the inexorable decay of nitrocellulose film stock. This costly archival commitment has been conveniently ignored in the controversy involving Turner Entertainment's role in the computer-coloring of video tape masters struck from various recognized classic motion pictures. We'll include ourselves out of that argument except to suggest that preservation carries more weight than colorization.

In this gallery of seminal and transcendent "heavy" portrayals may be found the ancestors of such enduring latter-twentieth century performances as Angela Lansbury's show of vicious mom-ism in *The Manchurian Candidate* (1962), Chuck Connors' and Charlton Heston's truculent frontier hoodlums in *The Big Country* (1958), Bill Paxton's deceptively amusing sadist in *Weird Science* (1985), Michael Berryman's cannibalistic desert rat in *The Hills Have Eyes* (1977), Joe Spinell's deadly big city recluse in *Maniac* (1980), and Rod Steiger's evil-eye surgeon in *The Kindred* (1987). Much as these more recent examples distinguish motion pictures that range wildly in terms of quality, our *Human Monsters* entries are chosen more for their vivid performances than for any categorically high merits on a scale of filmmaking artistry.

Some of these films we consider excellent in every respect, some merely good, some seriously flawed, but even the lesser entries contain elements that set them quite apart from the run of the mill, and all are noteworthy for their exploration of what Coleridge called "the motive-hunting of a motiveless malignity."
—Fort Worth
1995

Acknowledgements

To the following friends, acquaintances, correspondents and colleagues—too many of whom are no longer among us—we wish to express our gratitude for vital information, assistance and encouragement:

Robert Armstrong, Mischa Auer, William Bakewell, Jim Bannon,

Robert Benchley, William "Billy" Benedict, Joseph Biroc, ASC; Robert

Bloch, DeWitt Bodeen, Oscar "Budd" Boetticher, Ron Borst, David and

Jan Bowser, Hilyard Brown, Richard Bush, Bruce Cabot, Louis Calhern, Gene A. Clardy, Daniel B. Clark, ASC; Mae Clarke, Charles G. Clarke, ASC; Ray Corrigan, Maury Coats, Stanley Cortez, ASC; Reginald Denny, André de Toth, Andy Devine, Edward Dmytryk, Melvyn Douglas, Linwood G. Dunn, ASC; John Gallaudet, Lee Garmes, ASC; Dorothy Goldner, Dr. Orville Goldner, George T. Grader, Loyal Griggs, ASC; Burnett Guffey, ASC; Ron Haver, John Hall, Alice Harbaugh, Vernon Harbin, Paul Hogan, John Howard, James Wong Howe, ASC; I. Stanford Jolley, Boris Karloff, Sam Katzmam, Albert Keller, ASC; Ted Kent, ACE; Donald Kerr, Richard Kidwell, Hans J, Koenekamp, ASC; Milton Krasner, ASC; Ernest Laszlo, ASC; Charles Laughton; Francis Lederer, Sheldon Leonard, Paul Lerpae, ASC; Joseph A. Lewis, Peter Lorre, Joseph Losey, Ida Lupino, Marian Marsh, Thom and Jane Marshall, Archie Marshek, ACE; John P. McCarthy Jr., Susan Metcalf, Don Moore, Robert Montgomery, Carmel Myers, Ed Neal, Ronald Neame, Edgar Norton, L. William O'Connell, ASC; Gene O'Donnell, Henry O'Neill, Barbara Pepper, Vincent Price, Lucien Prival, Vivian Salazar, J. Ben Sargent, Joe and Dorothy Sargent, Harry Semels, Yahoo Serious, Kurt (Curtis) Siodmak, Kenneth Strickfaden, Murray Spivack, Larry D. Springer, Judy Tolk, Fred and Mary Kate Tripp, Allan R. Turner, Thomas Tutwiler, ASC; Shirley Ulmer, Theodor von Eltz, George Waggner, Pierre Watkin, Harold Wellman, ASC; Lyle Wheeler; Carroll and Susan Wilson, Martha Winterhalter, Fay Wray, Maris Wrixon.

Special thanks to Christina Price and Jean Wade Turner.

Grateful acknowledgments are also due to the following firms and agencies and their representatives, who have embellished their professional duties with genuine comradeship:

The Academy of Motion Picture Arts and Sciences

The American Society of Cinematographers (ASC)

The American Society of Composers, Anthors & Publishers, Sara Kerber, index department

Columbia Pictures Entertainment, Inc.

George Eastman House

Eastman Kodak Company

The Samuel Goldwyn Company

The Hoblitzelle Theatre Arts Library, Humanities Research Center, the University of Texas at Austin

The Library of West Texas State University at Canyon

Los Angeles County Museum of Art

MGM

Paramount Pictures

Republic Pictures Corporation

RKO Radio Pictures, Inc.

The Screen Directors Guild

The Screen Writers Guild

The Texas Commission on the Arts & Humanities

Turner Entertainment Company

Twentieth Century Fox Film Corporation

UCLA Film Archives

Universal Pictures

Warner Bros., Inc.

The Great Gabbo

1929   Sono-Art/World Wide Pictures
Presented by Henry D. Meyer and Nat Cordish
Released by Sono-Art/World Wide Pictures by arrangement with Harry H. Thomas
Director: James Cruze
Producer: James Cruze Productions, Ltd.
Continuity and Dialogue: Hugh Herbert
Story: Ben Hecht
Photography: Ira H. Morgan
Art Director: Robert E. Lee
Musical Director: Howard Jackson
Songs: *The New Step, I'm in Love with You, The Web of Love, I'm Laughing, The Ga-Ga Bird, Ickey,* and *Every Now and Then,* Paul Titsworth, Lynn Cowan, Donald McNamee and King Zanee.
Choreography: Maurice L. Kusell
Sound Supervisor: Helmar Bergman
Costumes: Andre-Ani
Production Manager: Vernon Keays
Running Time: 90 Minutes

Cast: Erich von Stroheim (Gabbo), Betty Compson (Mary), Donald Douglas (Frank), Margie "Babe" Kane (Comedienne), Harry Ross (Performer)

Synopsis: Gabbo is a coldly perfectionistic, egocentric ventriloquist who performs on the vaudeville circuits with his dummy, Otto, and a pretty assistant, Mary. Mary loves Gabbo and understands that he is capable of expressing tenderness only through Otto. Spurning Mary's affection, Gabbo drives her away after he berates her when she drops a tray during his act. Gabbo becomes a star on Broadway with the Manhattan Revue. Here he encounters Mary and her new singing-and-dancing partner, Frank. Comprehending at last his love for Mary, Gabbo woos her through Otto and assumes that she will return to him. When he learns that Mary and Frank are married, his mind snaps and he rushes onstage during a musical number, raves insanely, and smashes Otto. When Mary tries to comfort him, he doesn't recognize her. Dragging Otto, Gabbo wanders aimlessly into the street.

"Talkies" proved an apt term for motion pictures made during the early days of the industry's plunge into audio synchronization. Top heavy with sound over sight, the new technology promised a great deal more than it was able to deliver. The novelty it afforded moviegoers of 1928-1930 was paltry compensation for restraints the microphone placed on the camera. Talk was practically all that most of the early sound pictures had going for them: if a screen story lacked emotional impact or intellectual stimulus, then neither camera nor cutting room could do much to help. One musical drama from the period, James Cruze's *The Great Gabbo* bears up strikingly well today in terms of story and bravura performance—and moreover tells much about how filmmakers, hobbled by microphone cables, sought to overcome the purely documentary function to which sound had temporarily reduced the camera.

While the Ben Hecht-Hugh Herbert screen treatment is gripping enough to have worked as a photographed stage play, it is clear that cinematographer Ira H. "Joe" Morgan held still only when there was no other choice. Although lengthy takes of story exposition rely on actor-director strengths, a willingness to experiment and an impatience with the sanctions of sound are evident throughout. Insertions of footage depicting laughter and applause are more interruption than complement and serve only to demonstrate the forced compatibility of lens and microphone. More effective is the use of superimposition, heralding the climax with a chaotic mingling of visual

The Great Gabbo - Gabbo (Erich von Stroheim) is intolerant of the clumsiness of his assistant, Marie (Betty Compson).

The Great Gabbo – *Gabbo communicates with Marie through his dummy, Otto.*

imagery underscored by shouts and orchestral dissonance.

Gabbo's lure for audiences today (it is popular with film societies and film students) is as Erich von Stroheim's talking-picture debut—a seething, yet never menacing, portrayal of gathering madness. No longer considered affordable as a director, Stroheim's bent for extravagance having alienated the studios, he plainly contributed more than his depiction of a haunted artist who "talks to that [dummy] and . . . takes it seriously." The Stroheim-style exposition, integrated sub-plot and all, may be attributable to producer-director James Cruze, who practiced a similarly deliberate approach and asked for suggestions from what he called a "community council" of cast and crew members following the first recitation of the script. It has long been rumored that Stroheim actually directed the picture; there is little doubt that Stroheim, a frustrated experimenter with ideas budgets often could not bear, at least took advantage of Cruze's receptiveness.

Cruze (*1884-1942*) entered the movies as an actor, his roles including a 1912 version of *Dr. Jekyll and Mr. Hyde* and heroic characters in Thanhauser serials. He then became a director of remarkable versatility, as adept at slapstick (Fatty Arbuckle comedies) as at spectacle (*The Covered Wagon,* 1923), and fluent in sophisticated humor (*Ruggles of Red Gap* and the self-parodic *Hollywood,* both 1925). Upon completion of his Paramount contract in 1928, Cruze organized his own company with offices in Hollywood on Santa Monica Boulevard. By March 1929, he had acquired spacious sound-film production facilities with the purchase of the I. E. Chadwick Studios on North Gower Street, where he turned out several short subjects as a prelude to an ambitious lineup starting with *The Great Gabbo.* Cruze adapted readily to the demands of sound, which had in fact caused an intimidating if fleeting de-evolution of moviemaking to a primitive state. After *Gabbo,* Cruze was responsible for such strong efforts as *I Cover the Waterfront* (1933), *David Harum* and *Helldorado* (both 1934), and *Sutter's Gold* (1937). His career was seriously hampered by a chronic drinking problem.

None of *Gabbo's* weaknesses—most stemming from the microphone undermining production confidence—is crippling. An understanding of the technology of the time explains why the players often appear self-conscious, why their dialogue is sometimes hindered by a muffled tone, and why long exchanges go unrelieved by close-ups. Cameras were confined to stationary Celotex-windowed booths known as "iceboxes," which prevented the camera's whir from registering on the soundtrack but sacrificed motion. A centrally positioned, hidden microphone (boom-miking out of camera range had yet to be perfected) could capture voices faithfully only if the players spoke directly into it. The fear of botching synchronization by post-production intercutting evidently kept Cruze from blocking drawn-out conversations into shorter takes.

One such sequence illustrates both the awe in which filmmakers held the new technology and Stroheim's professed distaste for memorizing dialogue: The actor scrambles "now" and "more" into "nor," then recovers his line and proceeds. Why Cruze allowed this blot on his reputation as a perfectionist defies an answer, although a retake would have demanded more work by far than a simple patch.

Near-lavish production numbers, incorporating the Gershwinesque orchestral jazz that was all the rage in 1929 impart welcome motion and propel the story. One tune, *I'm Laughing,* explores the value of laughter as anaesthesia for the ventriloquist's emotional pain, but then is distorted into cruel self-contradiction as Gabbo, his depression decaying into hysteria, charges off-cue into the finale of his own show, screaming, "I can laugh!" Ziegfeld-type production spectacle merges with expressionism in a sequence for which the stage is strung with a vast spiderweb. This dominant prop, a metaphor for the tangled emotions of Gabbo's love interest (played by Betty Compson, Cruze's wife during 1927-29), is as important dramatically as it is scenically.

Between stanzas of their vocal duet, Compson and Donald Douglas argue violently about the feelings she harbors for Gabbo. To compound the participatory feeling, there are realistic scenes of backstage hustle-and-bustle as performers grumble about Gabbo's pomposity and hurry to change costumes.

Story development also hinges on the secondary tale of a struggling show-business man and wife who knew Gabbo "when" and track his fall by eavesdropping, reading trade paper accounts, and at last observing his breakdown from the audience. This is a Stroheim trademark, used with the honeymooners in *Blind Husbands* (1919) and with the junk dealer's household in *Greed* (1925).

Ben Hecht had originated Gabbo as a Stroheim-like character in his short story *The Rival Dummy*, a flashback account framed by a present-day description of Gabbo as a down-and-out eccentric. The film builds upon this likeness, investing Gabbo with Stroheim's own superstitiousness as well as his militaristic formality masking a fragile self-esteem. He is established as a tyrant who drives away his lover, but then gradually lets surface an excitably childlike tenderness that deteriorates briefly to violence and finally withdrawn apathy. In depicting the loss of control, the camera work contributes as much as the acting and the direction through the expert superimposition of stage-review excerpts and a close-up of Stroheim's contorted face. Happy expressionist-deco sets become nightmarish as their context darkens, a quality intensified by the juxtaposition and mingling of musical fragments and dialogue. One prominent stage fixture, a huge revolving spiral of the sort used in the German Expressionist films of the 1920s to connote chaos or insanity, dominates this passage.

The use of Gabbo's dummy, Otto, as an outlet for feelings the ventriloquist wishes to mask, anticipates loosely the most memorable passage of Ealing Studios' acclaimed anthology film, *Dead of the Night* (Great Britain; 1945),

The Great Gabbo - *Marie's new lover, Frank (Don Douglas), is jealous of Gabbo's attentions.*

of an Alfred Hitchcock television episode of the 1950s, *The Glass Eye*, and of Richard Attenborough's *Magic* (1978). Unlike these descendants, all of which were calculated to shock or horrify, *The Great Gabbo* is purely a tragic study of a deteriorating mind. Otto's falsetto voice is given a Viennese accent that nearly matches Stroheim's own, but there is a serious discrepancy: Otto addresses the Betty Compson character as "Mary," but Stroheim pronounces the name "Ma-ree;" in much the same way, he would lend an unfortunately laughable note to *As You Desire Me* (1932) by referring to Greta Garbo's Maria as "Ma-rear."

The ventriloquial routines are entertaining in a broadly cornball way; in one based upon the famed act of Marshall Montgomery, Otto speaks while Gabbo smokes, drinks and dines.

Cinematographer "Joe" Morgan (1889-1960) had become a cameraman in 1911. He spent the 1920s on glossy, expensive productions but by the 1930s found himself relegated to the quick-and-cheap Poverty Row companies. He spent much of the 1940s as a portrait photographer, then shot numerous Sam Katzman serials and *Jungle Jim* features; a heart attack forced his retirement in 1956.

Gabbo does not showcase Morgan's skills at their best—the new technology was too restrictive. Lighting usually is so generalized as to deny the theme its dramatic possibilities, and the static camera misses many possibilities for enhancement of the spoken situations. The stage production sequences were shot in Multicolor, a process that rendered the screen garish in a film of otherwise subdued visual effect. The bipack two-color system enabled extraction of tones from orange and blue,

resembling the later and better known Cinecolor. (Even Technicolor was a two-color process at the time, its range of hues deriving from red and green elements.) Other Multicolor films include *Fox Movietone Folies* (1929) and the animated cartoon *Goofy Goat* (1931). The company's chief owner and vice president was Howard Hughes, who used the Multicolor plant in Hollywood as his California headquarters after the process was discontinued in 1932. (Surviving prints of *The Great Gabbo* are entirely in black-and-white.)

Stroheim dominates the cast with ease. Betty Compson's bittersweet portrayal provides a realistic ballast for Gabbo's paranoia; her displays of spurned romantic affection, motherly concern, and unwitting cruelty are uniformly convincing. Pauline Stark had been announced for the role, but Compson applied pressure to Cruze and got it. Unfortunately her rather strident voice did not record well, and her days of stardom in the talkies were few. A lovely portrait of Compson in better days figures as a significant prop in *Invisible Ghost* (1941), in which she

plays a haggard intruder whose appearance drives Bela Lugosi to a murderous rage. As the jealous husband who resents Compson's kindliness towards Stroheim, light-opera veteran Donald Douglas proves better as a singer than an actor.

Initially appealing as a curiosity, *The Great Gabbo* delivers a fascinating story and characterization to match. The most stock-still camerawork must be accepted as a matter of historical reality (audiences of the time, spoiled to the fluid photography of the late silents, faced a similar caveat.) What the camera could not capture through motion, however, is sometimes brought to life through artful composition. In a poignant closing scene that comes near reconciling sight with sound, the lens has the last word: as the microphone picks up Stroheim's receding footfalls, the camera captures a scene of horrid desolation. At ground level, Gabbo ambles past the scene of his rise and fall while, above, a theater handyman removes, letter by letter, THE GREAT GABBO from the marquee.

The Great Gabbo - *Gabbo has to be restrained when he suffers a breakdown on stage.*

Svengali

1931   Warner Bros. Pictures, Inc.
The Vitaphone Corporation
Director: Archie Mayo
Screenplay: J. Grubb Alexander
From the George du Maurier novel *Trilby*
Photography: Barney McGill
Art Director: Anton Grot
Film Editor: William Holmes
Gowns: Edward Luick
Technical Effects: Fred W. Jackman and Hans F. Koenekamp
Music: The Vitaphone Orchestra conducted by David Mendoza
Composition and Arrangement: David Mendoza
Additional Music: Arthur Franklin, Wesly, and Naggiar, *Tally Ho*, Robert Emmett Dolan
Assistant Director: Gordon Hollingshead
Mr. Barrymore's Make-up: Johnny Wallis
Running Time: 83 minutes.

Cast: John Barrymore (Svengali), Marian Marsh (Trilby O'Farrell), Donald Crisp (The Laird), Bramwell Fletcher (Billee), Carmel Myers (Mme. Honori), Luis Alberni (Gecko), Lumsden Hare (Taffy), Paul Porcasi (Signor Bonelli), Ferike Boros (Marta), Adrienne D'Ambricourt (Madame Vinard), Yola D'Avril (Maid), Henry Otto (Man With Opera Glasses)

Synopsis: Svengali, an impoverished opportunist, survives in the artistic demimonde of Paris by teaching music. His aide, Gecko, is loyal but often finds it embarrassing that Svengali resorts to mooching and manipulation. Svengali also possesses a peculiar hypnotic ability; he employs it early on to drive a young matron to suicide after she tells him she has left her husband for him but refused a settlement.

While intruding on the hospitality of Taffy and the Laird, Scottish life painters, Svengali meets a lovely young model, Trilby O'Farrell. As she sings idly while disrobing to pose, Svengali is entranced by the power of her voice. Billee, a young painter from England who is boarding with Taffy and the Laird, finds himself fascinated by Trilby's gaminesque beauty.

Embittered by Trilby's engagement to Billee, Svengali catches her in a vulnerable

ALL PARIS DESIRED HER, BUT SVENGALI OWNED HER!

Weirdest romance ever pictured! With the screen's genius and his new find.

JOHN BARRYMORE *as* SVENGALI *with* MARIAN MARSH AS TRILBY

He hypnotizes! He thrills...! Any woman caught in his spell must obey.

Surpassing in scope of character even his portrayals of *Dr. Jekyll and Mr. Hyde* (1920), Ahab in two versions of *Moby Dick* (1925, 1930), and *Romeo and Juliet* (1936), *Svengali* represents John Barrymore's finest contribution to motion pictures. The role of the mesmerist sparkles with an enthusiasm Barrymore seldom applied to his more usual matinee-idol portrayals; his transformation as M. Svengali avoids the gross degeneration of an Edward Hyde or a Captain Ahab but rather plants nagging worry as an amusing rogue subtly changes into a brooding menace. In advance of production, Barrymore's message to Warner Studios was that Svengali must be laughable, almost likable at first so as to confront audiences with a moral question, whether or not to sympathize with him upon disclosure of his sinister side.

The picture opens with an amusing Svengali who eavesdrops from his piano studio as Honori arrives for her voice lesson. As Gecko tells Honori the Maestro is "composing," Svengali takes the cue and strolls out absently, quill and staff paper in hand. Awed, Honori laments "my days are so empty." Their talk makes it plain he is more to her than tutor—as does the lesson, for her shattered-glass voice carries his tolerance past its limits. Svengali is delighted, however, at a disclosure from her: "I've left my husband—for good!" He inquires, "And how much has he left you?" His warmth fades as she explains, "I've come to you just as I am." Suddenly, the other side of Svengali is revealed as he fixes his eyes upon the woman; she begs him to avert his gaze. With a moan of despair, she flees the apartment. Gecko later reports that Honori's body has been found in the River Seine. Svengali is philosophical: "She was very, very sweet—but a bad business woman."

Certainly Svengali seems a likable (if unsanitary) rogue when Gecko advises that the rent is due. Svengali has no time for such trivia. He suggests that they invite themselves to dine with "our English friends," who have not experienced "the fragrance of our society" in some time. Gecko protests but is easily manipulated. "In the bright lexicon of youth," the Maestro counsels him, "there is no such word as fail." He herds Gecko out, singing, "Avanti, signores"—"Forward, comrades!"

Toying with the Scots' patriotism, Svengali strikes up a stirring

state and mesmerizes her to respond to commands he will issue later. Under his influence, Trilby will grow to regard herself as unfit to accept Billee's innocent love for her. She vanishes at length after leaving a note suggesting her suicide. Svengali also has departed.

Five years later, Paris is soon to hear a concert by La Svengali, toast of the continent and wife of the long-absent maestro. Sighting La Svengali and recognizing her as Trilby, Billee comprehends that Svengali is running from "fear of the day when his spell . . . will be broken" and becomes intent on a confrontation. Svengali's failing health and his repeated refusals to honor concert com-

mitments finally reduce La Svengali to shabby bookings. Though bereft of will, she cannot return Svengali's affections except when under his commanding gaze.

Billee locates the company at a cheap cabaret in Cairo. Svengali promises Billee his chase is near its end. During Trilby's performance, Svengali clutches his chest and pitches forward. Trilby's voice wanders and she collapses. Billee rushes to her. Svengali, dying, utters a prayer: "O, God, grant me in death what you have denied me in life—the woman I love!" Trilby utters the name of Svengali and dies. Svengali's dying words are from the song that bespeaks his triumph: "Avanti, signores."

"God Save the Queen." Both men snap to attention, though it means The Laird must stand up from the bathtub in a draft. Svengali ridicules their God-

and-country pride and their habits of cleanliness. They ask when last he bathed, to which Svengali replies, "Not since I tripped and fell in the sewer!"

His sense of humor is tinged with hate when he learns that Billee and Trilby are engaged. He glares from a distance as Billee tells Trilby of his home-

Svengali - *The hypnotist watches jealously as Trilby (Marian Marsh) and Billee (Bramwell Fletcher) embrace.*

land in terms of "green fields and hedgerows," then he interrupts, adding: ". . . and fog, and pneumonia, and shopkeepers . . . Trilby in England would be like a butterfly in mutton soup!" As the tension abates, Trilby complains of a headache. Svengali realizes the time is right to hypnotize her. With Trilby under the spell of stars, he implants the suggestion that she "will think of nothing but Svengali . . . Svengali . . . Svengali." At his command, Trilby tilts her head so that he may inspect the structure of her mouth. It is as he expected: "a soundboard like the dome of the Panthèon!"

After he and La Svengali have achieved fame and fortune, Svengali appears to have traded his whimsical, Bohemian air for a dignity marred only by ill health, but he is still the manipulator. He accepts an aristocrat's gift, a bejeweled necklace for La Svengali, but discards the accompanying note and presents the bauble as though he is the giver. "Nothing is too beautiful for La Svengali," he tells the transformed Trilby. So great is the spell Barrymore weaves about the character that there are moments when he elicits pity for the scabrous creature. An especially poignant moment occurs in the bedchamber, as Svengali caresses Trilby longingly. His spell has yet to gain her love, but under his gaze she becomes a creature of passion. Appalled at his own power, Svengali snarls, "*Ach*! Close your eyes. You are beautiful, my manufactured love, but it is only Svengali, talking to himself again." Barrymore's body language here is indescribable; his back is to the audience during much of the scene.

Though Barrymore had his way with Svengali, and it is his presence which dominates throughout, the film is in no respect an *auteur* product. *Svengali* is instead the result of collaboration and compromise—faithful to the spirit of the novel which inspired it, and yet freehanded enough to accommodate the inventiveness of director Archie Mayo, designer Anton Grot, cameraman

Svengali - Svengali (John Barrymore) is no longer an amusing rogue when he uses his hypnotic powers.

Barney McGill, effects masters Fred Jackman and Hans Koenekamp, and the personally troubled but still magical Barrymore.

For the screenplay, J. Grubb Alexander modified a charming story of Paris student life in the nineteenth century (George du Maurier's *Trilby*, written in 1894 and subsequently adapted into a successful play) into a Gothic study heavily influenced by German cinema. The changes were realized fully on screen thanks to Barrymore's penchant for the bizarre, Mayo's pragmatic admiration for German art films, McGill's gift for artistic lighting and Grot's mastery of the expressionist setting. Some scenes

appear to be paintings come to life, with a richness of chiaroscuro an illustrator might envy; this blend of scene and motion is most striking in an amazing sequence engineered by Koenekamp.

In the dead of night Svengali's eyes glaze in a trance of concentration, his face a model for the Antichrist, as he projects his will from his attic across the jagged rooftops to the sleeping Trilby. To depict the hypnotist's mental voyage across the city, Koenekamp's wizardry pulls the camera away from Svengali's face, out the window, pulling back until he is a distant shape. The camera then turns right to fly over the rooftops, capturing shadowplay and gusts. Miles away, the camera turns again and races into Trilby's garret and to her bed as she awakens in terror. The effect gives the viewer the sensation of flight. The scene ends with a masterful flourish: Svengali laughs as he watches a black cat pawing at a mouse nest. This dazzling example of technical and artistic cinematography would be remarkable in a film of the present day; it is far more so for 1931, when camera mobility was the exception rather than the rule.

Koenekamp, in 1989, told us how it was done. The sets of the two apartments were built full scale at the opposite ends of the huge Stage 5. The city of rooftops was a large scale miniature which ran the length of the stage. The camera pulled back from Svengali's eyes, traveled over the miniature rooftops and into Trilby's bedroom. Mayo, strictly a big-timer among directors, addressed the 'Svengali motif' again in Warners' *The Man With Two Faces*, discussed later in this book (as is his naturalistic *Moontide*). *Svengali* was the first try at Germanic style for Mayo,

whose sixty-odd pictures include *The Petrified Forest* (1936; the film which made Humphrey Bogart famous), *Crash Dive* (1943), and *A Night in Casablanca* (1946) with the Marx Brothers.

For *Svengali*, Mayo was surrounded with players whose response to his tightly timed direction is as true as their physical similarities to du Maurier's written and sketched descriptions. Lumsden Hare and Donald Crisp are older and more mature than du Maurier envisioned the Scotsmen, but here their stability serves to anchor the impulsive young Englishman as played by Bramwell Fletcher. As Svengali's companion, Luis Alberni captures the novelist's description of small stature and spaniel-eyed loyalty—Gecko is assertive toward all but Svengali—but eliminates the youth and scarred countenance. Of Trilby, du Maurier wrote she "could hardly be called beautiful at first sight" but added that "you can never tell how beautiful—or how ugly—a face may be till you have tried to draw it." The film's Trilby, sixteen-

year-old Marian Marsh, is—need we say?—a knockout from the first glimpse, and yet her resemblance to the du Maurier drawings is remarkable. Though accounts vary as to the nature of her working relationship with Barrymore, he must receive some credit for the excellence of her portrayal. Warner publicists touted Miss Marsh as a Barrymore "discovery." It is said that Barrymore had asked Warners for the more seasoned actress, Evelyn Laye, and that, assigned instead to work with the relatively inexperienced Miss Marsh, he proved a patient tutor, seeing to it that she felt sufficiently comfortable around his satanic makeup that no unconscious reaction would register on film.

Music for Svengali is eclectic European, dominated by the sentimental traditional ballad, "Ben Bolt." Sinister underscoring is employed sparingly but effectively. There are classical selections from Chopin (*Fantasie Impromptu, Valse in A Flat*) and Donizetti (*Lucia di Lammermoor*) and

Svengali - *"You are beautiful, my manufactured love . . . But it's only old Svengali, talking to himself again."*

two French compositions, *Festa Napoletana* by Wesly and *Dieux Solaires* by Naggiar. An interesting bit of trivia is that for the sequence of La Svengali's performance, Warner borrowed Universal's Stage 28, where the Paris Opera House interior from the 1925 *Phantom of the Opera* stood, and stands to this day.

Svengali has been brought to the screen in other versions, including at least three silent adaptations and a 1954 retelling by an English company with Sir Donald Wolfit and Hildegarde Neff. These have met with varying degrees of success, but the 1931 production must be considered the most artistic and frightening version, in which full due is given to the gently romantic, the luridly melodramatic, the tragic, and the comic.

Guilty Hands

1931   Metro Goldwyn Mayer Film Corporation
Director: W.S. Van Dyke II
Producer: Hunt Stromberg
Dialogue: Bayard Vieller
Photography: Merritt Gerstad
Settings: Cedric Gibbons
Recording Supervisor: Douglas Shearer
Recording Engineer: Paul Neal
Film Editor: Anne Bauchens
Musical Director: Dr. William Axt
Music: L. Andrieu and Domenico Savin; *Kiddie Kareers*, Nathaniel Shilkret, Al Sherman and Lew Pollack
Running Time: 68 minutes

Cast: Lionel Barrymore (Richard Grant), Kay Francis (Marjorie West), Madge Evans (Barbara Grant), William Bakewell (Tommy Osgood), C. Aubrey Smith (The Reverend Mr. Hastings), Polly Moran (Aunt Maggie), Alan Mowbray (Gordon Rich), Forrester Harvey (Spencer Wilson), Charles Crockett (H. G. Smith), Henry Barrows (Harvey Scott), Blue Washington (Johnny)

Synopsis: In 10 years as District Attorney of New York, Richard Grant sent more than fifty men to the electric chair. "I didn't like it," asserts Grant. "Now that I've returned to private practice, I've kept a hundred of 'em out of it . . . A clever man in such a case could commit a murder so skillfully—you know what I mean?—so brilliantly, that he could get away with it."

Enlisted to draw up a will for a notorious womanizer named Gordon Rich, Grant learns to his horror that Rich is about to marry Grant's daughter, Barbara. Grant impulsively declares his intention to kill Rich.
There are failed attempts to sway Barbara from the marriage by her onetime sweetheart, Tommy Osgood, and by Grant, who characterizes Rich as a depraved lecher who recently drove a girl of sixteen to suicide. Grant pretends to resign himself to the situation and at an engagement party addresses Rich as "my son," toasting him with a concealed threat.

On the eve of the wedding, Rich leaves a confrontation with his longtime paramour, Marjorie West, and invades Barbara's room.

So striking was Lionel Barrymore's performance as a doomed alcoholic lawyer in MGM's *A Free Soul* (1931) that producer Hunt Stromberg was quick to cast him as another angst-ridden counselor in *Guilty Hands* filmed about two months later. The eldest member of the celebrated acting clan received an Academy Award for the earlier picture and widespread acclaim for the latter, which proved popular at the time but is little remembered today.

One of the better "perfect crime" yarns, *Guilty Hands* was written by the playwright Bayard Vieller to suit the Barrymore personality. More stable and dependable than his erratic brother John, Lionel Barrymore was an important figure at MGM, being a director, dramatic coach, and casting advisor as well as a leading player. He was also an accomplished etcher and a serious composer—in truth, a modern renaissance man.

The script permits the star to be almost entirely sympathetic despite his crime—a loving father who slays a sexual pervert who sorely wants killing. The audience instinctively roots for him, but he becomes progressively more demonic as he intimidates a devoted woman who is determined to reveal the truth. This shift of sympathy makes the ending more ironic than tragic.

Kay Francis, a fast-rising star of the day, brings an appropriate intensity to the difficult role of compatible perversion: the woman who has been tolerant until now of her lover's lustful indulgences. The victim, a thoroughgoing blackguard, is well performed—while he lasts—by Alan Mowbray, a hard-drinking *compadre* of John Barrymore's. His character is described by the elder Barrymore to his daughter as " . . . a beast about women . . . he's just like an animal, so that your wedding night, instead of being a thing of beauty . . . will be a horror and a shame . . . The memory of that time will stay

She locks him out and bursts into tears, recognizing that her father was right.

While the servants see Grant's pacing shadow on the drawn shade of his room, Grant appears in Rich's quarters and kills him. He arranges it to look like a suicide. The servants are still watching the moving shadow of Grant.

Marjorie discovers that Grant had rigged a paper silhouette to a slowed down phonograph turntable to create the illusion that he was pacing in his room. When she threatens to turn Grant over to the law, he counters with a threat to frame her for the murder.

The police examine Rich's body. The revolver Grant had used is still clutched in Rich's hand. As his muscles contract in rigor mortis the gun fires. Grant falls, mortally wounded.

Guilty Hands- *Rev. Hastings (C. Aubrey Smith), Marjorie (Kay Francis) and Grant (Lionel Barrymore).*

with you, spoil your life . . . a horror you'll never forget." Mowbray later became more keenly identified with comic-eccentric portrayals. The other players register strongly but have little to do, being upstaged throughout by Barrymore and Francis.

The best dramatic moment is Francis's confrontation with Barrymore, who enacts for her a courtroom scene in which she is convicted of his crime: "Have you ever seen a murder trial?" he begins. "Sit down, and I'll show you yours. . . Gentlemen of the jury, this woman . . . has been accused of the murder of her protector, Gordon Rich. You all know Mr. Rich was killed and the murder

Guilty Hands - Barbara (Madge Evans) finds solace in the arms of Tommy (William Bakewell).

Mowbray, the ominous engagement party with its veneer of cordiality, the murder during the obligatory thunderstorm, and the shock-value climax. Norbert Brodine's photography matches the impact of all these.

The ambiguity of the protagonists is matched by that of W. S. Van Dyke II, who was regarded as the studio's most dependable director. Well-loved by many, Van Dyke was considered sadistic by others. He was a rugged and adventurous outdoorsman, but also a writer of poetry. A former assistant to D. W. Griffith, Van Dyke began directing in 1917 as a specialist in outdoor action pictures. He joined MGM in 1926 and made one box-office

made to look like a suicide. Rich was tired of this woman. He was on the eve of his marriage to a beautiful, innocent girl who adored him. Life stretched out before him happily, but this woman couldn't bear the thought that another was to take her place, that her future was to be swept away. Look at her. There's no murder in her face, but there was murder in her heart when in the dark of night she crept from her room to his. The door was locked, but he opened it to her—he'd done it thousands of times before. Who else would have come to him at that hour? And so, with the pistol concealed in the folds of her wrap, she came to this man and he, poor, unsuspecting fool, let her come within striking distance, and before he could

move or cry out or give an alarm, she placed the pistol close against his breast and fired. And then, to hide this murder, she knelt beside the dead body and placed the pistol in his own hand and left him there, left him lying with the stigma of suicide on him. Who else could have killed him? Who else could have gained by his death? Who in all the world but this woman hated him? Look at her, the woman who was fired with jealousy, insane with rage! She killed her lover to gain the millions he'd left her in a will he didn't live long enough to destroy—and I can prove it. I swear, I'll put you in the electric chair."

But the tension is practically unrelieved; there are the tautly sarcastic exchanges between Barrymore and

hit after another, delivering only two or three "flops" out of forty-seven pictures. With few exceptions—1931's *Trader Horn* being the most conspicuous—he always brought in his films within budget and ahead of schedule.

Guilty Hands was Van Dyke's first venture into directing a pure mystery film, but it was far from the last. *Penthouse* (1933), *The Thin Man* (1934) and *Rage in Heaven* (1941), proved equally fine examples of the genre. Van Dyke's versatility may be gauged by these titles: *Tarzan, the Ape Man* (1932), *Naughty Marietta* (1935), *San Francisco* (1936), *Marie Antoinette* (1938), *Andy Hardy Gets Spring Fever* (1939), and *Journey for Margaret* (1942). The last named was his final job, completed shortly before his death.

The Unholy Garden

1931 Samuel Goldwyn Productions
Director: George Fitzmaurice
Producer: George Fitzmaurice
Screenplay: Ben Hecht and Charles MacArthur
Photography: George Barnes and Gregg Toland
Art Director: Willy Pogany
Musical Director: Alfred Newman
Supervising Editor: Stuart Heisler
Costumes: Bridgehouse
Make-up: Blagoe Stephanoff
Running Time: 75 minutes

Cast: Ronald Colman (Barrington Hunt), Fay Wray (Camille), Estelle Taylor (the Hon. Mrs. Elize Mowbry), Tully Marshall (Baron de Jonghe), Warren Hymer (Smiley Corbin), Ulric Haupt (Colonel von Axt), Mischa Auer (Prince Nicolai Poliakoff), Morgan Wallace (Captain Kruger), Lawrence Grant (Dr. Shayne), Henry Armetta (Nick-the-Goose), Kit Guard (Kid Twist), Lucille LaVerne (Mme. Lucie Villars), Henry Kolker—Arnold Korff in unreleased version—(Colonel Lautrac), Charles Hill Mailes (Alfred de Jonghe), Nadja (Native Dancer)

Synopsis: The Germans have placed a bounty on Barrington Hunt, a fugitive accused of murder. Believing Hunt bound for Palais Royal, a desert sanctuary for wanted men, the Algerian police arrange for the notorious Mrs. Mowbry to set a trap. But Hunt commandeers the woman's car and takes her to Palais Royal, a once-grand establishment now in decay. The guests include scholarly Dr. Shayne, who murdered three wives and uses the skull of the first as a tobacco jar; Prince Nicolai Poliakoff, a Hussar captain who killed his sweetheart for her pearls; Colonel von Axt of the Prussian Guards, who swindled his government out of millions; Kid Twist, a strangler; Nick-the-Goose, an international thief; and Smiley Corbin, an American hoodlum. The elderly Mme. Villars runs the establishment.

Aloof from the others are the aged Baron de Jonghe and his lovely granddaughter, Camille. The cutthroats plot to dispatch the Baron, who has been promised immunity if he will return a fortune in stolen securities.

It was an interesting kind of tension we felt, working on *The Unholy Garden,* " Fay Wray told us in 1989. "For all the importance that each had to the other, Ronnie Colman and Samuel Goldwyn were at odds on this particular project—not on speaking terms, for reasons that neither would explain—and Ronnie had this standing order that Mr. Goldwyn not intrude upon the set. I met with Mr. Goldwyn when I was hired, and then never heard from him again until after we had completed the principal photography."

As a team, Goldwyn and Colman had proved early in the game that talking pictures could be more than photographed stage plays. The proof they offered was *Bulldog Drummond* (1929), a droll high adventure thriller whose blending of words and pictures define the "talkie" concept. In silent-era Hollywood, Goldwyn had developed a reputation as a calculating businessman with discriminating middlebrow taste. He surrounded himself with creative people and inspired their best efforts. Ronald Colman was among this select group. Moderately significant as a silent player, Colman learned early on how to utilize the added dimension of sound and thus assured himself longevity as a star.

Bulldog Drummond established Colman as Goldwyn's chief player. Anxious to build upon this bonanza, Goldwyn cast Colman in *Condemned* (1929), a grim tale of Devil's Island; *Raffles* (1930), a comedy-melodrama about a suave crook; and *The Devil To Pay* (1930), another light melodrama. All were successful, but none as spectacularly so as *Drummond.* Goldwyn determined he must make a Colman vehicle that would exploit the same elements that had worked together so ideally in his first talkie: chilling horror, comedy, romance, and artistic appeal. Goldwyn hired the eccentric but efficient writing team of Ben Hecht and Charles MacArthur (authors of the hit play, *The Front Page*) to concoct an original script, *The Unholy Garden.* The great pictorial stylist, George Fitzmaurice, was signed to direct. The famed Hungarian illustrator-architect-muralist, Willy Pogany, made the production designs.

As work on *Garden* was beginning, Joseph M. Schenck decided he would step down as chief production executive of United Artists (of

Hunt is greeted meanwhile by Smiley, his accomplice. Asked about the loot from their last job, Smiley admits, "In Tunis, you see, I met a dame." It is decided that Hunt, as a stranger, may be able to pry the secret of the securities from de Jonghe. Toward that end, Hunt plans to woo Camille.

Gaining the old man's friendship, Hunt falls in love with Camille but feels unworthy of her. Mrs. Mowbry suspects a doublecross. Smiley seduces Mrs. Mowbry and learns the others mean to kill Hunt and the Baron, and to torture Camille to learn where the loot is hidden.

The Baron's brother, Alfred, arrives. Hunt plans an escape, then finds the concealed securities. The Baron is slain. Believing Hunt the killer, Camille starts to turn him over to the inmates but, swayed by love, hides him instead. Mme. Villars reveals that Nicolai killed the Baron. Hunt has tied up Mrs. Mowbry. Nicolai is shot to death.

Hunt hands Camille the loot and tells her to hurry away with Alfred. Over her objections that he come along, he bids her farewell: "And some day, when your eyes are shining and you meet an honest man, look at Paris for me and think of it as my wedding present." Hunt and Smiley, in Mrs. Mowbry's car, escape in a hail of bullets. Smiley asks if Hunt got as much loot as expected.

"Much more, Smiley, and here's your share," Hunt replies, handing over several petals from a rose Camille had given him. "I'm sorry, Smiley, but you see—I met a dame."

which Goldwyn was a member-owner) and asked Goldwyn to take over. Goldwyn accordingly increased his annual film schedule from four to eight productions, leading off with *Garden*. The picture was produced with the usual Goldwyn care, but the critics lambasted it so cruelly following its early previews that Goldwyn took it back for extensive retakes and editing, finally releasing it in October, 1931.

Fay Wray recalled: "I left for New York on a vacation after we had wrapped *The Unholy Garden*, and that was when I finally had direct contact again with Mr. Goldwyn. He caught up with me by telephone and demanded that I must come back immediately to

The Unholy Garden- *"Someday, when your eyes are shining and you meet an honest man, look at Paris . . . ".*

begin retakes. So I cut my vacation short, thanks to whatever problems Mr. Goldwyn was having with the early responses to our picture.

"The opportunity to work with Ronnie Colman was a pleasure, of course, whatever the tensions may have been at the time. He was a wonderfully skilled actor, and a man of genuine modesty. We became fast friends during the shooting, and we maintained that friendship over the years. A very *shielded* man, Ronnie was—didn't let out a great deal of information about himself— genial, but never garrulous. If he was outgoing toward you, that meant a great deal more than it would have meant from somebody else," added Miss Wray, "He was a figure of special quality."

History has distilled a critical consensus that *The Unholy Garden* must be the worst picture to feature a Colman performance. This oversimplified view takes into account some rather predictable elements of plotting and perhaps an overabundance of bizarre touches, but neglects to acknowledge that the production shimmers with high artistry. Not to mention that the cast, in support, serves up some of the most intriguing vamps and scamps any lover of melodrama could desire. *Garden* does sink deep into the *outré*, an excess that the viewer will find either charming or offensive. The skull-as-tobacco jar is one such example, but the most effectively disturbing touch is a Christmas party scene where the criminals sing carols in assort-

ed clashing keys and languages. The dialogue sparkles with romance and wit. Pogany's evocative sets are magnificently lighted and photographed to generously eerie effect by two of the great cinematographers, George Barnes and Gregg Toland. Colman's rakishly sophisticated demeanor is complemented beautifully by the innocence of Miss Wray; by the crudeness of his sidekick, Warren Hymer; and by the brashness of the femme fatale, Estelle Taylor. The villains are a grand crew of seriocomic fiends—Mischa Auer, Henry Armetta, Ulrich Haupt, and Kit Guard—under the menacing guidance of Lawrence Grant, who had provided a similarly depraved characterization for *Bulldog Drummond*.

The Unholy Garden - *The murderous Colonel von Axt (Ulrich Haupt) and Dr. Shayne (Lawrence Grant) watch as Camille (Fay Wray) is courted by Hunt.*

The Hatchet Man

1923   First National/Vitaphone/Warner Bros.
Director: William A. Wellman
In Charge of Production: Darryl F. Zanuck
From the Achmed Abdulla, David Belasco play
The Honorable Mr. Wong
Screenplay: J. Grubb Alexander
Photography: Sid Hickocks
Art Director: Anton Grot
Editor: Owen Marks
Gowns: Earl Luick
Music: Leo F. Forbstein and Otto Langey
Songs: *Poor Butterfly*, Raymond Hubbell;
When It's Sleepy Time Down South, Leon T.
Rene and Clarence Muse
Musical Performance: The Vitaphone
Orchestra
Conductor: Leo Forbstein
Make-up: Perc Westmore
Special Effects: Fred Jackman
Sound Recording: Robert Lee
Second Cameraman: Wesley Anderson
Stills: John Ellis
Running Time: 74 minutes

Cast: Edward G. Robinson (Wong Low Get),
Loretta Young (Toya San), Dudley Digges
(Nog Hong Fa), Leslie Fenton (Harry En Hai),
Edmond Breese (Yu Chang), Tully Marshall
(Long Sen Yat), Noel Madison (Charles Kee),
Blanche Friderici (Madame Si-Si), J. Carroll
Naish (Sun Yat Sen), Toschia Mori (Miss Ling),
Charles Middleton (Lip Hot Fat), Ralph Ince
(Malone), Otto Yamoka (Chung Ho), Evelyn
Selbie (Wah Lee), E. Allyn Warren (The
Cobbler), Edward Peil (Bing Foo), Wilie Fung
(The Notary and Fung Loo), Anna Chang
(Sing Girl), Doris Lloyd (Fan Yi), James B.
Leong

Synopsis: In San Francisco's Chinatown in
1916, the honorable hatchet man Wong Low
Get goes sadly under orders from Lam Sing
Tong to kill a member who has just been
judged guilty of murder. The doomed man,
Sun Yat Sen, is Wong's best friend. Sun Yat
Sen's last words are of forgiveness. Wong
swears before Buddha that his victim's daughter, six-year-old Toya San, will know only happiness.

Fifteen years later, Chinatown is a very different place. Wong has become an
Americanized merchant, and Toya San is a

The uncompromisingly tough directorial style of "Wild Bill" Wellman makes an unusual and exciting film of an outmoded play. The picture had a few playdates as *The Honorable Mr. Wong* before it went into general release under the more readily exploited title, *The Hatchet Man*. The adaptation by J. Grubb Alexander, somewhat more lurid than the source, boasts a shock ending that cannot help but elicit gasps.

Edward G. Robinson, who had replaced John Barrymore as First National's top character star, manages a compelling characterization of a sympathetic fellow who is nonetheless frightening. He handles with skill the change from Tong executioner to westernized businessman, a transition that makes his reversion to ancestral ways all the more remarkable. Loretta Young does fine work as the girl Robinson loves, as does Leslie Fenton as the dissolute young miscreant. Briefly seen, but memorable in his telling moments as a victim of tong vengeance, is J. Carroll Naish. A grand assortment of Western character actors proves entirely convincing in Asian-American roles, especially Dudley Digges, Charles Middleton, Edmond Breese and Tully Marshall. Even the consummate sinister housekeeper of numerous pictures, Blanche Friderici, is effective as the hardboiled madame of a Chinese brothel. These enactments are helped immeasurably by the young Perc Westmore's make-up artistry.

The production is handsomely designed by Anton Grot, who had proved himself with *Svengali* to be one of the more inventive of screen

The Hatchet Man - *Wong's adopted child, Toya San (Loretta Young), grown to womanhood, becomes Mrs. Wong.*

beautiful woman. Wong is deeply in love with his ward, and when she is of age, they marry. Though in many respects happy with Wong, Toya San longs for the company of people her own age. The Tong leaders, still more of East than West, are displeased that Wong is no longer active as their great hatchet man.

When American gangsters try to muscle in on Chinatown, the tong hires a young Chinese-American hoodlum, Harry En Hai, to guard Wong's wife and home. The Tong prevails upon Wong to halt the activities of Malone, a gang boss, in Sacramento's Chinatown. When his peaceful overtures fail, Wong disposes of Malone in traditional terms. Returning to San Francisco, he finds that Toya San and Harry have fallen in love. He allows her to leave but threatens Harry with death if she should come to grief. The Tong leaders, appalled that Wong has not killed his faithless wife and her lover, precipitate his downfall. Wong becomes a derelict wanderer.

Upon learning that Harry has sold Toya into slavery in China, Wong takes up his hatchet and searches relentlessly until he finds the pleasure house of Madame Si-Si. The madam bars his path. In the adjoining barroom, Harry sits against a wall in a stupor. Wong cautions Madame Si-Si that she cannot stand in the way of an honorable hatchet man; he produces from his sleeve the proof of his office and points to the eye of a dragon on the distant wall. Wong hurls the hatchet with breathtaking accuracy, splitting the glass eye of the dragon. The proprietress stands aside, and Wong goes to the contrite Toya San. No one molests him as he leaves with her.

Madame Si-Si storms into the bar and confronts the grinning Harry, who sits against the wall, shaking his head. On the other side, servants struggle to remove Wong's hatchet. They find its blade bloodied. Even the hardened madam is horrified to see Harry's body slide to the floor, his head leaving a trail of gore.

architects. Sid Hickox's photography artfully combines diffused, softly lit shots necessary for the atmosphere of old Chinatown with the stark lighted naturalism of the celebrated gangster pictures he filmed for the same company: the story belongs to two worlds, and the camera captures both.

The musical score is more elaborate than most others of this period. It encorporates venerable Tin Pan Alley tunes (including dramatic use of *Poor Butterfly* as a romantic theme), traditional Chinese music, and original works by Leo Forbstein, who was West Coast musical director for Warners. Forbstein also wrote two additional compositions for the elaborate preview trailer.

The Hatchet Man - *Wong discovers he has been betrayed.*

Behind The Mask

1949   Columbia Pictures Corporation
Director: John Francis Dillon
Producer: Harry Cohn
Story Adaptation and Dialogue: Jo Swerling
Continuity: Dorothy Howell
Assistant Director: Edward Sloman
Cinematography: Teddy Tetzlaff
Sound Engineer: Glenn Rominger
Film Editor: Otis Garrett
Musical Director: Louis Silvers
Music: Milan Roder and Dan Dougherty
Running Time: 68 minutes

Cast: Jack Holt (Jack Hart), Constance Cummings (Julie Arnold), Boris Karloff (Jim Henderson), Claude King (Arnold), Bertha Mann (Edwards), Edward Van Sloan (Dr. Munsell), Willard Robertson (Hawkes), Thomas Jackson (Agent), also Clarence Burton, John Ince and Charles Meacham

Synopsis: The Secret Service has failed to trace the identity of Mr. X, head of a narcotics ring. Not even his own gangsters are allowed to know who their boss is, for when one comes too near the truth, Mr. X arranges from him to die on the operating table of a private hospital run by Dr. August Steiner. Ostensibly legitimate, Steiner is aided by a sadistic nurse, Edwards. Steiner's knife also claims Secret Service agents who attempt to close in. Captain Hawkes, of the Secret Service, is under pressure from a civic-reform group led by Dr. Munsell.

Agent Jack Hart has himself imprisoned in order to meet a gang member, Henderson. When Hart escapes, Henderson refers him to an X henchman named Arnold, who expects to be purged for talking too much. Hart falls in love with Arnold's daughter, Julie. Discovering that Hart is a secret agent, the ringleader arranges for a fatal airplane accident at sea. Arnold and Julie are taken to Steiner's hospital, where Arnold succumbs to an "emergency appendectomy." Edwards guards Julie. Henderson has been freed and takes Arnold's place.

Hart outsmarts the gang. He has Arnold's body exhumed, and the casket is

Jack Holt in the early 1930s was Columbia's top star, having helped put the onetime Poverty Row company into the big time via his performances in the Frank Capra pictures *Submarine* (1928), *Flight*(1929), and *Dirigible* (1931). A typical Holt action vehicle, *In the Secret Service* was begun in November 1931, but in light of the success of Universal's *Frankenstein*, the story was amended with gruesome touches that justified its marketing as a horror film; the title became *Behind the Mask*. Advertising campaigns touted the presence of Boris Karloff, swept suddenly to fame for his performance in *Frankenstein*. The irony here is that Karloff, as a somewhat helpful heavy, has a role subordinate to that of Edward Van Sloan, the kindly professor of *Frankenstein*. In *Behind the Mask*, Van Sloan portrays one of the most fiendish villains in cinema. Especially memorable is his prelude to an "operation" on Holt: "Has it ever occurred to you . . . that you can commit almost any crime if you select the proper environment?" Van Sloan asks in his best lovable doctor manner.   "If I were to stick a knife into you in the street . . .I might have to answer embarrassing questions. But . . . here, on the operating table, nothing will happen," pause, "to me." He explains further, "It is only when I begin to cut on the inside that you will realize that you are having an experience. Wasn't it Nietzsche who said that unendurable pain merges into ecstasy? We shall find out whether that is an epigram or a fact. For my part, I know it will be ecstasy."

Behind the Mask - *The fiendish Dr. Steiner and Henderson spy on a secret service operative.*

found to be packed with drugs. Learning of Julie's danger, Hart goes to the hospital but is overpowered and strapped to an operating table. Steiner, a burly, bearded man with thick spectacles, looms over Hart, discussing the psychology of pain as he readies a scalpel. Hart comprehends that Steiner is not only Mr. X, but also has another identity. A shot is heard, and the surgeon falls dead. Julie has escaped Edwards to avenge her father and save her lover. Hart reveals that Steiner is in fact the reform-minded Dr. Munsell.

Jack Dillon, whose directing career had begun in 1917 with the Triangle company, worked the midcourse changes of *In the Secret Service/Behind the Mask* into a nicely coherent mingling of straightforward melodrama and horror. It was one of his last efforts: he made three more films including Clara Bow's comeback effort, *Call Her Savage* (1932), then died in 1934. Ted Tetzlaff, a lead-ing glamour photographer and later director of fourteen pictures including the suspense classic *The Window* (1949), sets the right tone throughout *Behind the Mask*, applying an almost documentary realism to the prison scenes and adding appropriate shadowplay at the cemetery and in the mad doctor's hospital.

Jack Holt is in his element as the hero, and Constance Cummings is excellent as the tragic heroine. Karloff (British accent notwithstanding) does well as the cigar-smoking gangster, although he is considerably less monstrous than the advertising campaign suggested. Bertha Mann is properly grim as Van Sloan's granite-faced assistant, and there are expert performances by Claude King, Willard Robertson, and Thomas Jackson.

Behind the Mask- *Hart (Jack Holt) shows evidence against the smuggling ring to Hawkes (Willard Robertson) and Dr. Munsell (Edward Van Sloan).*

Mystery Ranch

1932   Fox Film Corporation
Director: David Howard
In Charge of Production: Sol M. Wurtzel
From the Steward Edward White novel *The Killer*
Screenplay: Alfred A. Cohn
Sound Recording: Albert Protzman
Photography: Joseph August
Art Director: Joseph Wright
Film Editor: Paul Weatherwax
Wardrobe: David Cox
Assistant Director: Walter Mayo
Music: Hugo Friedhofer, Rex Bassett, Louis de Francesco, Arthur Kay, J. S. Zamecnik and William Kernell
Songs: *Cowboy Dan*, Cliff Friend; *Blue Bell*, T. Morse and Edward Madden; *Cheyenne*, Egbert Van Alstyne; *She Was Only a Bird in a Gilded Cage*, Harry von Tilzer; *On a Bicycle Built for Two*, Dacre; *Finlandia*, Jan Sibelius; *Why Are the Roses So Pale?*, P. I. Tschaikovsky; *Wedding March*, Felix Mendelssohn; *Concert Etude no. 3 in D Flat*, Franz Liszt
Additional Photography: John Schneiderman
Second Cameraman: C. Curt Fetters and Irving Rosenthal
Assistant Cameramen: Harry Webb, Jack Epstein, Lou Kunkel and James Gordon
Stills: Bert Lynch
Running Time: 57 minutes.

Cast: George O'Brien (Bob Sanborn), Cecilia Parker (Jane Emory), Charles Middleton (Henry Steele), Noble Johnson (Mudo), Charles Stevens (Tonto), Forrester Harvey (Artie Brower), Roy Stewart (Buck), Virginia Herdman (Homesteader's Wife), Betty Francisco (Mae), Russ Powell (Sheriff)

Synopsis: Arizona Rangers Chief Buck Johnson sends Bob Sanborn to Paraiso Valley to probe a reign of terror instigated by Henry Steele, owner of the Sierra Vista Ranch. Renegade Apaches prey on other ranchers but have a strange loyalty to Steele. Mudo, Steele's devoted Apache servant, is a giant, mute warrior as deadly as his master. Several men who have opposed Steele have been found hanged or garotted. Steele is known to have an obsession for killing not only men but also animals and even insects.

The 1920 novella, *The Killer*, tells of a rancher named Henry Hooper who is possessed by a mania to kill any creature that crosses his path. The author, Steward Edward White, said he based the character on a man who lived in Arizona during the late nineteenth century. Benjamin Hampton produced a good silent-film version in 1921 with Frank Campeau as the madman and Jack Conway as the man who brings him to bay. Fox used the property in 1932 for one of several high-grade Westerns, all of which starred George O'Brien and were adapted from novels by famous authors. A fine actor-athlete, O'Brien was a big name because of his roles in many John Ford productions and in F. W. Murnau's *Sunrise* (1927). Retitled *Mystery Ranch*, the White novel made for a fast-moving talkie which is probably the outstanding example of an unusual film genre, the Western horror story.

The free rein adaptation is by Al Cohn, whose thriller ventures include *The Cat and the Canary* (1927) and *The Last Warning* (1928). It is beautifully—and sparsely—dialogued, and its construction allows for rapid pacing and dramatic pictorial effects. These qualities are put to good use by director David Howard, who had done eight Spanish-language versions of Fox pictures, including *The Big Trail* and *Charlie Chan Carries On* (both 1931). Howard's first English-language film was a highly popular O'Brien version of Zane Grey's *The Rainbow Trail* (1932), which was followed by *Mystery Ranch*. Although he never acquired a place in the pantheon of celebrated directors, Howard was a master of the outdoor action film and, as *Mystery Ranch* indicates, could have done well with psychological drama.

Most of the picture was filmed on location in Arizona, with addi-

Mystery Ranch - Mudo (Noble Johnson, *left*), Tonto (Charles Stevens, *right*) and two Apaches overpower Bob.

Posing as an itinerant cowboy, Bob approaches Sierra Vista to find beautiful Jane Emory, who has been thrown from her horse. Bob brings Jane to Steele's hacienda, where the owner invites him to stay the night. Steele warns Bob not to leave the ranch lest he run afoul of Apache marauders. Jane conveys to Bob that she needs help. They meet in secret, and she reveals she is the daughter of Steele's former partner, who died mysteriously. Steele lured her to the ranch with a promise to give her a share of the estate. She believes Steele has some dire plan involving her.

Promising help, Bob leaves the ranch. Several of Steele's Indian henchmen waylay him, but Bob escapes and reaches Paraiso, where he telegraphs Ranger headquarters. Artie Brower, a little ex-jockey from England employed as a messenger, informs Bob that Steele is forcing Jane into marriage the following morning. Bob

and Artie ride back, reaching the ranch during the night. Too late, Bob learns that Steele had anticipated his move and is awaiting him in Jane's room with Mudo, Tonto, and other henchmen. Bob is imprisoned, but Artie rescues him; they in turn overpower Steele and rescue Jane. Steele recovers, sounds the alarm, and kills Artie while the Englishman is covering Bob and Jane's escape.

Bob and Jane climb into the Apache Stronghold, a towering formation of rocks, to make a stand. Bob sees Buck and the Rangers approaching. Steele and Mudo gain the summit, but after a struggle Bob topples the giant to his death. Bob shows Steele a warrant for his arrest. "If you want to serve that warrant, you will have to do it in hell," Steele says, and with a grim laugh he steps over the edge. Jane now owns Sierra Vista, and at the fadeout she suggests that Bob quit the Rangers and become manager of the ranch.

tional work near Los Angeles and at the old Fox Western lot, where many of the Tom Mix and Buck Jones silents were made. There was a comparatively leisurely shooting schedule of about five weeks, allowing for some stunning photography by Joseph August, who filmed *The Informer* (1934) and *Gunga Din* (1938), and John Schneiderman, Paramount's mystery specialist. Few other outdoor films have been so exquisitely photographed. Much of the picture has a pictorial style reminiscent of the German Expressionist films of the 1920s.

Nor can many action pictures of the period claim such elaborate and intelligent musical scoring. Dramatic passages were especially composed, for the most part, by the influential Hugo Friedhofer, Rex Bassett, Louis de Francesco, Arthur Kay, J. S. Zamecnik, and William Kernell. Ballads commonly associated with the West abound—but so do classical themes.

O'Brien's breezy acting style suits the heroics, and Cecilia Parker is a lovely ingénue. This is one of the few "star" Westerns, however, in which the villains take the palm. Charles Middleton, who never caught on with mainstream audiences as a top drawer heavy, is best remembered for his serial roles, especially as Emperor Ming in the three *Flash Gordon* serials. It is in

Mystery Ranch. though, that Middleton gives his most polished performance, creating a character both subtly and flamboyantly mad. There are no maniacal cackles as he trains his gun on O'Brien in the heroine's bedroom and says, "Well, this is indeed a pleasure. My dear, would you mind stepping aside a foot or so? I don't want to injure my bride-to-be." Middleton's chilling smile at the climactic moment, as he plunges to his doom, is unforgettable. His

depravity is ably abetted by the fascinating African-American actor, Noble Johnson, in a role similar to his Cossack torturer of *The Most Dangerous Game* (1932), and by Charles Stevens, the gaunt grandson of the famed Apache war chief, Geronimo. Forrester Harvey, better known as the pubkeeper in *The Invisible Man* (1933), contributes elements of Cockney humor which make his slaying at Middleton's hands all the more tragic.

Mystery Ranch - *Steele's (Charles Middleton) insanity threatens Jane (Cecilia Parker) and Bob (George O'Brien).*

The Old Dark House

1932   Universal Pictures Corporation
Presented by Carl Laemmle
Director: James Whale
Producer: Carl Laemmle, Jr.
From the J. B. Priestley novel *Benighted*
Adaptation and Screenplay: Benn W. Levy
Added Dialogue: R. C. Sheriff
Art Director: Charles D. Hall
Cinematography: Arthur Edeson
Film Editor: Clarence Kolster
Editorial Supervision: Maurice Pivar
Special Effects: John P. Fulton
Music: Bernhard Kaun
Make-up: Jack P. Pierce
Set Decorations: R. A. Gausman
Assistant Director: Joseph McDonough
Recording Supervisor: C. Roy Hunter
Recording: William Hedgcock
Cinematography: King Gray
Assistant Cameraman: Jack Eagan
Stills: Roman Freulich
Sound System: Western Electric
Running Time: 71 minutes

Cast: Boris Karloff (Morgan), Gloria Stuart (Margaret Waverton), Melvyn Douglas (Roger Penderel), Charles Laughton (Sir William Porterhouse), Raymond Massey (Phillie Waverton), Lilian Bond (Gladys DuCane), Ernest Thesiger (Horace Femm), Eva Moore (Rebecca Femm), John Dudgeon (Sir Roderick Femm), Brember Wills (Saul Femm)

Synopsis: A cloudburst maroons some English motorists in the mountains of Wales. The road ahead is flooded; a landslide makes retreat impossible. The driver, Phillip Waverton, and his wife, Margaret, are undecided whether to try to get through to Shrewsbury or to seek shelter. Their companion, Roger Penderel, a disillusioned and apathetic war veteran, opts to approach a stone mansion looming nearby because, "Something might happen here, but nothing ever happens in Shrewsbury."

A giant butler, scarred and bearded, answers their knock and mutters unintelligibly. The tall, thin Horace Femm descends from a precipitous staircase and explains that the butler, Morgan, is mute. Horace's sister, Rebecca, is next to appear. Squat, semi-deaf, and unfriendly, Rebecca agrees reluctantly to let the outsiders stay but shrieks, "No beds!" The

Following release of Universal's *Frankenstein* late in 1931, Boris Karloff handled several supporting roles until his Monster's great impact upon the public became evident to the company's president, Carl Laemmle, and his son, Carl, Jr., general manager of the studio. British director James Whale was promoted via the success of *Frankenstein*—his fourth film—into the top echelon at Universal. The Laemmles in 1932 considered Karloff one of their two most valuable properties (the other being Austrian actress Tara Birell) and sought stories that might be tailored to fit the "successor to Lon Chaney." Early that year the younger Laemmle acquired numerous properties: H. G. Wells' *Invisible Man*, J. B. Priestley's *Benighted*, Abner J. Geluka's *Automation*, Ted Fithian's *Wizard*, Robert Louis Stevenson's *The Suicide Club*, Tom Buckingham's *Destination Unknown*, Gordon Morris's *Bluebeard*, Nina Wilcox Putnam's *Cagliostro*, Gustav Meyerinck's *Golem*, and Philip Wylie's *Murderer Invisible*—all of which were announced as Karloff starring vehicles. Of the four of these that were eventually made at Universal, Karloff appeared in only two: *Benighted* became *The Old Dark House* and

The Old Dark House - Morgan, as he appeared in the picture, frightens Gladys.

woman accompanies Margaret to a bedroom and watches avidly as the pretty blonde removes her wet clothes.

"My sister died on this bed," Rebecca says. "She was a wicked one, handsome and wild. She fell off her horse and broke her spine. For months and months she lay here screaming in pain, praying for me to kill her, but I told her to turn to God. They were all Godless here. My father, Sir Roderick, is still alive. He's old—a hundred and two. He's upstairs, a wicked, blasphemous old man . . ." Margaret has put on a silken dress. "That's fine stuff," Rebecca snarls as she touches the material, "but it'll rot." Then she lays a clawlike hand upon Margaret's bosom, "That's fine stuff, too—but it'll rot, too, in time." The old woman leaves to see about Morgan, who she fears may have found a bottle of gin. "We wouldn't keep Morgan," she says, ". . . only on account of Saul." The lights go out suddenly and Margaret flees back to the sitting room.

Two other stranded motorists have arrived: Sir William Porterhouse, a rotund, good-natured businessman, and his companion, Gladys DuCane, a dancer. Supper is comprised of cold meat and potatoes. Morgan hovers, eyeing Margaret intently.

The lights flicker again as the generator fails. Rebecca orders Horace to get a lamp from the third floor landing. Noting Horace's reluctance, Phillip accompanies him. On the second landing, Horace flees to his room, leaving Phillip alone. On the third landing, Phillip encounters a bolted door. As he returns with the lamp, he hears a faint cry from one of the second-level rooms. The terrified Margaret appears, pursued by the drunken Morgan. As the giant lunges up the stairs, Phillip smashes the heavy lamp into Morgan's face, knocking him unconscious. Again the soft cry is heard, and the Wavertons investigate. They find the ancient, bedridden Sir Roderick.

"What was that noise? Was it Morgan?" the patriarch asks. His comments amplify Rebecca's earlier remark. "Morgan is a savage. Sorry. We wouldn't keep him if it weren't for Saul." Margaret asks about Saul. "You don't know Saul? Of course you don't. This is an unlucky house. Two of my children died, then madness came. We're all touched with it, a little that is, all except me. You shouldn't have come here . . . I must warn you . . . Saul is the worst. Poor Saul, he just wants to destroy, to kill. We have to watch him. He wants to set fire to this house. He tried to do it once before, to make a burnt offering . . . If Morgan gets very bad he will certainly let him out."

Penderel and Gladys, meantime, hide in the garage to steal some moments alone. Porterhouse is grumpily philosophical about Gladys's interest in Penderel. When Sir Roderick falls asleep, the Wavertons return to the stair landing. Morgan has gone, but Horace is there, frozen with terror. "Morgan has gone upstairs!" Horace cries. "He's gone to let Saul out! Wait for him downstairs and kill him!" Horace locks himself in his room as the Wavertons go downstairs. Rebecca and the guests are watching the stairs in dread. Morgan appears on the upper landing. A pallid hand emerges from the dark to rest on the banister behind Morgan. Rebecca begs Morgan to take Saul back, and the hand withdraws.

Morgan lurches downstairs and attacks Phillip. Rebecca flees to her room as Penderel and Sir William enter the fight. The men drag Morgan into another room, then Penderel returns to see to the safety of the women. An insane giggling is heard from the dark stair, and the hand reappears. Penderel locks the women in a closet. A pale, little old man comes down the steps. Saul, quaking with fright, pleads with Penderel "Don't let them shut me up again! I'm not mad! I swear to heaven I'm not mad. It's just that they locked me up. They're all wicked! I know a secret. They murdered Rachel. They're afraid that I'll tell. Morgan, he beats me." Penderel assures the man he will not let anybody harm him. Then Saul grabs a carving knife and orders Penderel to a seat. "I want to talk about flames," the madman says. "I know things about flames that nobody else in the world knows. Flames are really knives. They're cold, my friend, sharp and cold as snow. They burn like ice.

"Who is in the closet? Friends of yours, eh? Well, first I shall settle with you, then I will tell your friends about flames. It will be very amusing. Did you know my name was Saul? And yours is David. And it came to pass on the morrow that the evil spirit came upon Saul and he prophesied in the midst of the house and David played upon the harp and there was a javelin in Saul's hand and Saul cast the javelin" Saul throws the knife. Penderel dodges, but before he can regain his balance Saul fells him with a chair. Seizing a burning stick from the fireplace, Saul rushes to the balcony and sets fire to the draperies. Penderel recovers in time to snatch the torch and subdue the flames. Saul and Penderel fight savagely, crashing through the railing to the stone floor.

Morgan charges into the room, but his fury dissolves as he looks upon the pitiful corpse of Saul. He lifts the body of his friend and, moaning in despair, trudges upstairs. Penderel, thought dead at first, awakens in Gladys' loving embrace. Next morning the sun is shining and Horace Femm genially bids his guests farewell while Rebecca snarls at them from her window.

Cagliostro became The Mummy (1933).

Benn W. Levy and James Whale were assigned as writer and director of The Old Dark House. Levy, a successful British playwright who specialized in society dramas, had a recent fling at film directing in England in association with Alfred Hitchcock. R. C. Sheriff, a friend of Whale's and the author of the hit play Journey's End, also arrived from England in answer to a summons to write the adaptation for Whale's proposed film of Erich Maria Remarque's *The Road Back.* Instead, he was set to work writing dialogue for *The Old Dark House.* (Sheriff had just returned to Oxford to resume studies that had been interrupted by the war and his subsequent work.)

Shooting of *The Old Dark House* began in mid-April on the finest spooky house set of all, a cavernous crazy quilt designed by Charles Hall to include some of the most terrifying stairway angles imaginable. Top-billed now for the first time, Karloff headed a distinguished cast composed for the most part of English imports: Walter Byron, Lillian Bond, Charles Laughton, Ernest Thesiger, Eva Moore, Brember Wills, and one mysterious John Dudgeon, "102-year-old English actor," as a publicity handout stated. The last-named in actuality was Elspeth Dudgeon, an English *actress* several decades younger than the remarkable "John." Jack Pierce altered her appearance to suit the role of an ancient patriarch. Thesiger, a former artist and a longtime friend of Whale's, had come to the States to appear in Levy's *The Devil Passes on Broadway.* Laughton was also well known in the theater, but new to Hollywood.

The Americans in the cast were Gloria Stuart, a lovely blonde newcomer discovered at the Pasadena Playhouse, and Russell Hopton, a wry-faced Broadway actor with a penchant for playing world-weary types.

Jack Pierce had almost as much latitude in creating the makeup for Karloff's mute, crazed giant as he did with the Frankenstein monster, for Priestley had merely described the butler as "a lump." Karloff's guise at first included a mass of curly, greasy-looking hair, a bulging forehead, beetling eyebrows, and a matted beard. The early rushes displeased Junior Laemmle, who felt that the character could be more impressive.

The picture was shut down while further makeup tests were undertaken.

Walter Byron meantime was taken off the picture and replaced by a lanky Canadian-English stage actor, Raymond Massey. When shooting resumed, Karloff had been built up and padded out to appear about as massive as he had been in *Frankenstein.* Pierce also gave him straight, black hair and a beard, a built-out nose, and a variety of deep collodion scars. After a few days' shooting, Hopton was replaced by a young stage actor from Georgia, Melvyn Douglas. (Douglas had made his film debut the year before as Gloria Swanson's leading man in *Tonight or Never,* in which Karloff played a brief comic role.)

Sheriff and Levy had the good grace to follow the Priestley book closely. The only change of consequence is in the interest of a happy ending—a must in Laemmle-land—by allowing Penderel to survive the fall in which Saul is killed.

The Old Dark House, a prime example of Whale's work, is one of the most sophisticated of all horror films. As satisfying in its way as *Frankenstein.* It supersedes even *The Cat and the Canary* (1927) as the epitome of "old house" melodrama. Taste is impeccable with only one onscreen death and little gruesomeness (aside from the atmosphere and the Karloff makeup). Deft bits of dark humor artfully dispel a viewer's tendency to laugh nervously at the wrong places, and the romantic scenes, like the comic touches, are handled with somewhat more assurance than in *Frankenstein.*

Most of the story is disclosed through the experiences of the ingénue, Gloria Stuart, although there are brief changes of point of view. It is she who is menaced first, and it is through her that most of the secrets of Femm House are revealed—or rather, what few secrets we are allowed to learn; there remains at the close a residuum of mystery. We never know what crime has made Horace a fugitive or whether Rebecca murdered her sister. With Margaret we gain an appreciation of the

The Old Dark House - *An uneasy gathering by the fire: Gladys (Lilian Bond), Penderel (Melvyn Douglas), Margaret (Gloria Stuart), Horace Femm (Ernest Thesiger), Philip (Raymond Massey) and Sir William (Charles Laughton).*

heroic qualities of her outwardly common place husband and the annoyingly jaded Penderel, and we learn that the flashy Gladys is in fact a nice country girl named Perkins.

Terror builds with particular cunning toward the introduction of the mad Saul. This suspense commences early on and grows until at last the hand of Saul is perceived on the stair railing. Inasmuch as the Femms are more fearful of Saul than of the brutish Morgan, the audience is led to believe the locked-away member of the household must be a monster of the most horrendous sort. On seeing Saul as a frail and frightened old man, we chuckle, relax, and half accept his plea for protection. Then, while the hero's attention is directed elsewhere, Saul's bland face contorts for an instant into a mask of cunning hatred. This is not unlike the unmasking of Erik in *The Phantom of the Opera* (1925), but is more subtle. Saul spouts Biblical love and talks softly about his study of flames, but when he attacks, biting and giggling, he is a wild beast.

Arthur Edeson's camera pokes about the angular sets, peering anxiously into the shadows and gazing up at the towering figures of Thesiger and Karloff. The same interiors were used often in later films, both by Universal and by independent companies that rented facilities at the studio, but never again were they lit and photographed with such high artistry. (Prominent examples of subsequent use of these sets are *Secret of the Blue Room, Secret of the Chateau, The Great Impersonation,* Chesterfield's *Strange People* and Majestic's *The Vampire Bat.*

Karloff is a marvel in pantomime, a horrendous brute who manages to command sympathy in a single touching scene. A foreword (signed by Carl Laemmle) explains that the man who plays Morgan is the same actor who was

The Old Dark House - *"That's nice stuff . . . "Miss Femm (Eva Moore) terrorizes Margaret.*

the *Monster of Frankenstein.* Massey and Douglas are engaging as unlikely heroes. Laughton, in his first American film (he took the supporting part while awaiting the start of production on his starring role in MGM's *Payment Deferred*), is quite winning as comedy relief. Lillian Bond and Gloria Stuart are opposites physically but equally attractive and capable.

The show really belongs, though, to the horrible Femms. Thesiger, who possessed the most expressively sinister nose imaginable, is a superb Horace, a thin, effeminate, and thoroughly frightened scoundrel, his shabby gentility masking some horrid past indiscretion—one of the more winning grotesque characterizations extant. In his opening scene he picks up a bundle of flowers, snuffling "My sister was on the point of arranging these" before throwing them into the fireplace. No other actor could have done as much with the dinner scene in which Thesiger forcibly urges his guests to "have a potato" every time

the conversation veers toward forbidden areas. In his long career he topped this performance but once—in a later Whale film, *The Bride of Frankenstein* (1935).

Eva Moore, the shapeless, shrieking Rebecca, conveys to perfection the character of a guiltridden lesbian and possible murderess driven by conscience into a morass of religious fanaticism and insanity. In one memorable shot she pauses to admire her distorted reflection in a warped mirror after carping at Margaret for being interested only in "your long white legs and how to please your man." To Brember Wills falls the most terrifying moment, when the innocent-appearing Saul suddenly reveals his fixation with knives and flames.

The Old Dark House went to the cutting rooms in the second week of June 1932 and saw release the following October. Although it never captured the public fancy to the extent *Frankenstein* had, it gained a devoted following.

The Mask of Fu Manchu

1932 Metro Goldwyn Mayer Distributing Corp. Metro Goldwyn Mayer Presents a Cosmopolitan Production
Director: Charles Brabin
Screenplay: Irene Kuhn, Edgar Allan Woolf and John Willard
From the story by Sax Rohmer
Sound Director: Douglas Shearer
Art Director: Cedric Gibbons
Film Editor: Ben Lewis
Photography: Tony Gaudio
Gowns: Adrian
Special Effects: Warren Newcombe
Musical Score: Dr. William Axt
Make-up: Cecil Holland
Electrical Properties: Kenneth Strickfaden
Recording: Andrew MacDonald
Assistant Director: John Waters
Set Decorations: Edwin B. Willis
Animal Supervision: Jack Allman
Running Time: 72 minutes

Cast: Boris Karloff (Dr. Fu Manchu), Lewis Stone (Nayland Smith), Karen Morley (Sheila), Charles Starrett (Terrence Granville), Myrna Loy (Fah Lo See), Jean Hersholt (Von Berg), Lawrence Grant (Sir Lionel Barton), David Torrence (McLeod), E. Allyn Warren (Goy Lo Sung), Ferdinand Gottschalk (Dr. Nicholson), C. Montague Shaw (Dr. Fairgyle), Steve Clemente (Knife Thrower), Edward Peil, Sr. (Coolie Spy), Lal Chand Mehra (Indian Prince), Tetsu Komai (Swordsman), Everett Brown (Slave), Willie Fung (Steward), Chris-Pin Martin (Potentate), James B. Leong (Guest), Allen Jung (Coolie), Clinton Rosemond (Slave), Victor Wong (Opium Attendant), Ray Benard (Corrigan) (Stuntman), (deleted scenes, Director: Charles Vidor, Gertrude Michael (Sheila), Herbert Bunston (Dr. Fairgyle)

Synopsis: Sir Nayland Smith, of the British Secret Service, is aware that archeologist Sir Lionel Barton has secretly learned the location of the tomb of Genghis Khan. He enlists the archeologist's aid to excavate the tomb before the master crime lord, Dr. Fu Manchu finds it. Should Dr. Fu obtain the mask and sword of Genghis Khan he can declare himself the Khan returned to life and lead all Asia against the rest of the world. They meet

MGM, the largest and richest of movie companies, generally shied away from horror films. They preferred to put their "more stars than there are in Heaven" into the more acceptable formats of drama, romance and comedy. Whenever they did veer into the macabre, however, they usually did it with a vengeance, piling on the horror more thickly than the less powerful studios ever did. Thus we have such harrowing fare as *Kongo, Freaks, Mad Love* and a handful of others that were widely condemned in their day.

Such a curiosity is *The Mask of Fu Manchu* which seems on the surface to be a glossy action piece about the mysterious "Yellow Peril" that was for so long an object of popular hysteria. A deeper look reveals its decadent layers: racial hatred, religious frenzy, opium addiction, sadomasochism, incest, torture, mutilation and dismemberment. It's almost as if a Rover Boys novel became interleaved among the pages of a Krafft-Ebbing report. It can also be seen as one of the influences evident in George Lucas's delightful *Indiana Jones* trilogy.

The picture appalled the critics but delighted a large segment of the public and brought in respectable grosses. However, it caused the studio a great deal of trouble and the costs were considerably greater than had been anticipated.

The basis was a novel of the same name by British author Sax Rohmer (Arthur Sarsfield Ward), which was serialized weekly in *Collier's* magazine from May 7 through July 23, 1932, and published in book form by Doubleday Doran in October. MGM at the time had a production and distribution agreement with Cosmopolitan Productions, motion picture branch of the Hearst publishing empire. Intrigued by Boris Karloff's success in *Frankenstein,* Cosmopolitan-MGM bought rights to the novel early in August and borrowed Universal's new horror star as he was finishing *The Old Dark House,* and was on hold for *The Mummy* and *The Invisible Man.*

Dr. Fu Manchu, a

Thrill piled upon thrill, shudder on shudder! The destroyer without pity, the beautiful temptress without a soul, in a new Fu Manchu masterpiece from the pen of Sax Rohmer.

THE MASK OF FU MANCHU

The Wall of Knives!

Closer—to the Jaws of the Crocodiles!

The Bell That Never Stops!

The Serum That Enslaves!

with BORIS KARLOFF
LEWIS STONE, KAREN MORLEY, CHAS. STARRETT, MYRNA LOY, JEAN HERSHOLT. *Directed by* CHARLES BRABIN.
A Cosmopolitan Production
From the story by Sax Rohmer
A Metro-Goldwyn-Mayer PICTURE

secretly at the British Museum to recruit Von Borg and McLeod for the expedition. Fu's agents, hidden in mummy cases, seize Sir Lionel.

Days later, Sir Lionel's daughter, Sheila, and her fiancé, Terrence Granville, learn of the kidnapping from Smith. They join the expedition to the edge of the Gobi Desert. Nearby, in an underground palace, Sir Lionel is brought before Fu Manchu, who promises him great wealth and possession of Dr. Fu's beautiful daughter, Fah Lo See, if he will tell the location of the tomb. Sir Lionel refuses and is put to the torture of the bell, which rings incessantly until the victim is driven insane. Dr. Fu brings tribal leaders to his palace and has his daughter tell them of the coming return of the Khan.

Smith's expedition finds the tomb, which bears a 700-year-old inscription: "May the curse of the gods descend on him and his forever who dares enter herein." MacLeod, standing guard that night, is murdered. Later, Sir Lionel's severed hand drops from the darkness. Goy Lo Sung arrives with a message that Dr. Fu demands the mask and sword or other "evidence" will be forthcoming. Sheila and Terrence decide secretly to deliver the relics to the House of 10,000 Joys in the Street of the Dragon, Nankow, as instructed.

Taken before Fu Manchu, they are graciously received and assured that Sir Lionel is an honored guest. But when Dr. Fu tests the sword in an electric arc, it melts— Smith has substituted a replica. Fah Lo See has Terrence lashed unmercifully, then makes love to the unconscious youth. Meantime, Sir Lionel's corpse is delivered to expedition headquarters.

Smith, on the trail of his friends, finds the tunnel to Dr. Fu's headquarters and is captured. Dr. Fu injects Terrence with a serum that, he explains, will make his body a mere extension of Fu Manchu's will. Terrence returns to camp during a raging storm and leads the others into a trap. Now Dr. Fu has the genuine sword and mask. Under Sheila's influence Terrence regains his mind and spurns Fah Lo See.

Smith is placed on a slowly tilting board at the mercy of crocodiles. Von Borg is put in "the room of the slim silver fingers," in which spiked walls close toward him. Terrence is again placed in the custody of Fah Lo See, Dr. Fu explains, "To await further injections of that interesting serum which, as you may have noticed, will make him her more than willing slave until, of course, she tires." Sheila is brought before the horde of chieftains Dr. Fu has gathered and they are told that her maiden blood will baptize the sacred sword.

Smith escapes and frees Von Borg and Terry. From the laboratory above the banquet hall, Smith turns a death ray invented by Dr. Fu onto the celebrants. Terrence seizes the sword, chops down Fu Manchu, and carries Sheila to safety. Later, on a ship bound for England, Smith flings the sword into the sea, saying, "Genghis Khan, wherever you are, I give you back your sword."

genius of crime featured in a long string of novels, had a pre-sold name. He had been portrayed on film by Harry Agar Lyons in twenty-three silent two-reelers made in England in 1923-24, and was played by Warner Oland in three good Paramount talking features, *The Mysterious Dr. Fu Manchu (1929)*, *The Return of Fu Manchu (1930)* and *Daughter of the Dragon (1931)*.

By the beginning of September, principal photography of *Mask* had already begun with Charles Vidor directing—a gifted but sometimes difficult Hungarian emigré. Gaetano "Tony" Gaudio, one of the top men in his field, was the cinematographer. Supporting Karloff was a wonderful cast: Myrna Loy as Fu Manchu's daughter, Fah Lo See; Lewis Stone as his archenemy, Sir Nayland Smith; Gertrude Michael and Charles Starrett as the juvenile leads;

Lawrence Grant, Jean Hersholt and David Torrence as Smith's archeologist allies. Almost simultaneously, *Rasputin and the Empress* began shooting at MGM with John, Lionel and Ethel Barrymore and a huge cast under the direction of the British-born veteran, Charles Brabin.

Both pictures had begun prematurely, with shaky screenplays and other unresolved problems. The usual *modus operandi* at MGM was to have shooting scripts thoroughly polished before production began and to demand that directors "stick to the script." Before the end of August the studio halted production on the troubled pictures and both Vidor and Brabin were fired. Richard Boleslavski took over *Rasputin*—the insider title of which was now Disputin. Vidor was put at liberty and Brabin was transferred to *Mask*. All available staff writers were assigned to work on the two pictures.

After two weeks a new story plan for *Mask* was agreed upon and a new script went into preparation. Indecision reigned all through September and there were numerous rewrites and retakes. Karen Morley replaced Michaels and some minor roles were recast. On October 9, the trade papers reported that both *Rasputin* and *Mask* were "still in the throes of story trouble, with no satisfactory ending yet written for either." *Mask* finally wrapped late in October. Only Irene Kuhn, Edgar Allan Woolf and John Willard (playwright of *The Cat and the Canary* and *Fog*) received screen credit.

Karloff comes closer to being the definitive Fu Manchu than his predecessors, although the MGM concept of the character omits the better side of his nature (in the stories he was wholly admirable before being driven mad by the destruction of his family during the Boxer Rebellion and he was adamantly opposed to war). Oland captured both aspects of the insidious one perfectly in his well-shaded performances, but the portly Swedish actor bore no physical resemblance to the tall, thin mandarin of Rohmer's imagination. Physically, Karloff is perfectly cast, looking much taller than he really was and depicting the evil side of Dr. Fu to the king's taste, but the script permits nothing of pathos or understanding for him—a pity, for Karloff's greatest talent was in the sympathetic portrayal of menacing characters.

He is matched all the way by Myrna Loy's beguiling performance as a sadistic nymphomaniac, equally bereft of pity. Her unusual beauty lent itself well to Asian characterizations, of which *Mask* was the last of many. Afterwards she became an important star because of her delightful performances in sophisticated comedies and romantic dramas.

Make-up artist Cecil Holland, in an article in *American Cinematographer* ("Orientals Made to Order," December 1932) said that in making up Karloff he filled in the area between eyelid and brow because Chinese eyes are set in the head differently than those of Europeans. This was done with thin layers of cotton saturated with collodion and shaped to fit, then surfaced with nose putty and blended into the natural contours. He drew the eyebrows up and shaved off the ends to give "the Mephisto effect necessary for so malign a characterization." He distended Karloff's nose with plugs in the nostrils and built up the outside with nose putty. The ears were built up with putty and

pointed slightly. Thin teeth caps, a coarse black wig with forelock, an unusual moustache, long fingernails and some specially formulated greasepaint completed the illusion. It took three hours of hard work each day to get Karloff camera-ready over a long schedule.

Myrna Loy was much easier, Holland said, because her round face and high cheekbones made her look more Asian to begin with. Tapes under her wig drew her eyes and brows up into a slant and her lips were painted to appear fuller. "Such character makeup is certainly no game for amateurs," Holland remarked.

Stern-visaged, authoritative Stone is the best of the screen's many Nayland Smiths and the usually villainous Grant is the stoic Briton incarnate as the tragic Sir Lionel. Karen Morley, one of the more interesting young actresses of the time, lends grace to the ingénue role. The classically handsome Starrett, later to become a popular Western star at Columbia, does well as the romantic adventurer and delivers a chilling performance in a scene in which, under the influence of a satanic drug, he laughs maniacally at having delivered his colleagues into Fu Manchu's hands. Hersholt, Torrence and E. Allyn Warren (as a minion of Dr. Fu) give sturdy support.

Visually eloquent, the big sets (augmented in some instances by Warren Newcombe's fine matte paintings) are filled with gigantic gold idols. The museum is replete with dinosaur skeletons, mummies, a pterodactyl and other impressive props, including a crocodile and the giant gorilla from *Tarzan: the Ape Man*. The sought-after tomb features two sets of ornately carved golden doors and the enthroned, jewel bedecked skeleton of the great Khan. Fantastic pseudo-scientific electrical equipment was supplied by Kenneth Strickfaden, who created the machin-

Mask of Fu Manchu - *Nayland Smith (Lewis Stone) is horrified at the treatment of Terrence at the hands of Dr. Fu and his evil daughter.*

ery for Universal's *Frankenstein* and *Flash Gordon* productions. Strickfaden stood in for Karloff in some of the scenes in which Dr. Fu melts the fake scimitar in a huge electrical arc; he was almost killed in the process. The substitution is obvious because Strickfaden was a much shorter man.

The costuming of the Manchus is spectacular. The biggest scenes are those of Dr. Fu's banquet for his hundreds of chieftains, for which MGM made some 200 brocaded garments in addition to many rented from sources in the Chinatowns of Los Angeles and San Francisco. A museum loaned the costumes of the six Samurai warriors who escort Loy to the feast.

Among the pre-code delights is one of the most perversely erotic sequences in films of this period, wherein the gorgeous, innocent-looking Fah Lo See orders Terrence flogged by two muscular African Americans. Myrna Loy's heretofore placid features become contorted with lust as she cries, "Aiee! Faster! Faster! Faster! Faster! Faster! Faster!" She has the unconscious youth placed on her bed and sends the slaves away. Panting heavily, she kisses his lips and runs her hands over his half-naked, bleeding torso. When her father walks in on this charming scene, she is quite composed and says coyly, "He is not entirely unhandsome, is he, my father?" "For a white man, no," is the reply.

Racial slurs are hurled back and forth by the Britishers and Dr. Fu without restraint. The insults begin when Fu and Sir Lionel meet: "You're Fu Manchu, aren't you?" "I'm a Doctor of Philosophy from Edinburgh, I'm a Doctor of law from Christ's College, I'm a Doctor of Medicine from Harvard. My friends, out of courtesy, call me Doctor." "Oh, I beg your pardon! Well, three times doctor, what do you want from me?" When the offer of a million pounds to reveal the location of the tomb fails to sway Sir Lionel, Dr. Fu turns to Fah Lo See. "My daughter, explain to this gentleman the rewards that might be his. Point out to him the delights of our lovely country, the promise of our beautiful women. Even my daughter, even that, for you!" "Fu Manchu, I'm not for sale." Later, Sir Lionel's daughter seizes an opportunity to regale Dr. Fu with "You hideous yellow monster!" Sir Nayland also gets in a nasty dig: "Is this a friend of your family?" he asks Dr. Fu as a snake goes slithering past.

The aristocratic Dr. Fu matches such insults with dignity. He calls Terrence a "cursed son of a white dog" and warns Smith that "The slightest move will send a bullet crashing through your stiff British spine." When Smith demands the release of Terrence in the name of the British Government, Dr. Fu loses his composure: "British Government! I'll wipe them and the whole accursed white race off the face of the earth when I get the sword and mask that will call the teeming millions of Asia to the uprising. . ." He also promises Smith "[I'll] dispatch you to your cold, saintly Christian paradise," and tells his other guests "You . . . will have the pleasure of entering your Christian heaven together."

Introducing the blonde, diaphanously gowned Sheila to his hordes, Dr. Fu exults, "Would you all have maidens like this for your wives? Then conquer and breed! Kill the white man and take his women!"

The joy Fu Manchu derives from torturing his guests is exquisite. His description to Sir Lionel of what lies in

Mask of Fu Manchu - *Fah Lo See finds Terrence "not unhandsome."*

store as the latter is strapped down under a huge bell is delivered with gloating pleasure. "You've read about this, Barton: the torture of the bell. It never stops. Minute after minute, hour after hour, day after day. Seems harmless, doesn't it? Just a bell ringing. But the percussion and repercussion of sound against your eardrums will soften and destroy them until the sound is magnified a thousand times. You can't move, you can't sleep, you will be frantic with thirst, you will be unspeakably foul, but here you will lie, day after day, until you tell." Later Dr. Fu brings a bowl of food and drags a bunch of grapes across his stubborn guest's lips. "Aren't you hungry? Just nod your

head and I'll feed you." Still later he has the bell stopped temporarily. "Rest and quiet! Now for a nice, long drink." He puts a goblet to Barton's lips, Barton chokes, Dr. Fu laughs. "Oh, I forgot to tell you it was salt. . . Fresh water, fresh food, a bath, sleep. Sleep, man, sleep! Day in, day out, sleep!"

The mandarin describes to Sir Nayland the serum via which he will enslave Terrence: "The injection . . . will make his brain mine. In other words, he becomes a reflection of my will. He will do as I command exactly as though I were doing it. So much better than hypnotism!" Later, with Terrence stripped to a loincloth and strapped down in an arty surgical room, Dr. Fu orders a

struggling slave brought in and has him bitten by a snake. While the man dies, Dr. Fu draws some of his blood and adds it to a mixture which he prepares to inject into Terrence's carotid artery. Pausing, he gently assures the youth that he will not be poisoned. "This serum, distilled from dragon blood, my own blood, the organs of different reptiles, and mixed with the magic brew of the secret seven herbs will only change you into the living instrument of my will. You will do as I command. You will think as I think, see as I see." The same serum is also used to make Terrence a suitable lover for Fah Lo See, an interesting touch heightening the depravity of the proceedings.

Mask of Fu Manchu - *Terrence, enslaved by Fu Manchu, receives his prize for bringing the real sword of the Khan.*

Secrets of the French Police

1932   RKO Radio Pictures, Inc.
Director: A. Edward Sutherland
Executive Producer: David O. Selznick
Screenplay: Samuel Ornitz, Robert Tasker and Edward Sutherland
Based on the *American Weekly* series by H. Ashton Wolfe *Secrets of the Sureté: the French Police Detectives*, and on Samuel Ornitz's *Lost Empress*
Musical Director: Max Steiner
Art Director: Carroll Clark
Photography: Alfred L. Gilks
Sound Recording: George D. Ellis
Assistant Directors: Jo von Ronkel and Dewey Starkey
Technical Advisor: L. E. Anselme
Film Editor: Arthur Roberts
Added Dialogue: Robert Benchley
Adaptations: Rufus King, Aubrey Wisberg and Frank Moss
Associate Producer: Willis Goldbeck
Unit Manager: Fred Fleck
Dialogue Director: Gene Lewis
Special Effects: Vernon L. Walker, Linwood Dunn and Donald Jahrous
Set Decorations: Thomas Little and D. Burke
Make-up: Sam Kaufman
Hairdresser: Gwen Holden
Script Clerk: Adele Cannon
Second Cameramen: Harry Wild and Joseph Biroc
Assistant Cameramen: Harold Wellman and Jimmy Daley
Chorus Master: Dudley Chambers
Songs: *Beau Idéal*, *Chi Chi*, *Valse Lente*, *Ninette*, *Sérénade*, Max Steiner, *Berceuse*, Rudolph Friml
Orchestrations: Joseph Mueller and Leonid Raab
Sound Recording: Murray Spivack
Marionettes: Dorothy Goldner
Stills: Edward Cronenweth and P. MacKenzie
Running Time: 59 minutes.

Cast: Gwili André (Eugénie Dorain), Gregory Ratoff (General Han Moloff), Frank Morgan (St. Cyr), John Warburton (Léon Renault), Murray Kinnell (Bertillon), Lucièn Prival (Baron Feodor Lomzoi), Julia Swayne Gordon (Madame Amienes), Kendall Lee (Réna), Christian Rub (Anton Dorain), Arnold Korff (Grand Duke Maxim), Guido Trento (Count

Probably the most popular series ever published in the Hearst newspapers' Sunday supplement, *The American Weekly* was "Secrets of the Sureté, the French Police Detectives," by H. Ashton-Wolfe, an operative associated with the celebrated Bertillon. Running in double-truck format and superbly illustrated, the long series was so popular as to merit reprinting several years after its initial appearance. The film script, which included parts of *The Lost Empress* by the influential leftist author, Sam Ornitz, was the product of a large number of writers including Ornitz, mystery novelist Rufus King, director Edward Sutherland, Robert Tasker, Robert Benchley, Frank Moss and Aubrey Wisberg. L. E. Anselme, former Sureté operative who sent six murderers to the guillotine, was found working as a watchmaker in Los Angeles and hired as technical director.

David O. Selznick, then RKO production chief, saw the picture as a showcase for his glamorous Danish import, Gwili André, who he hoped to fashion into a rival to Garbo and Marlene Dietrich. Like most European actresses at that time she failed to catch on with American audiences. Frank Morgan was cast as Ashton-Wolfe and proved himself a capable dramatic actor in this respite from whimsical roles. Even more uncharacteristic is the chilling performance of Russian actor Gregory Ratoff, usually cast as a dialect comedian but fascinating here as a reptilian plotter and murderer. After 1936, Ratoff devoted most of his life to directing and producing, piloting thirty movies before his death in 1960. Some were memorable: *Intermezzo* (1939), *Adam Had Four Sons* (1941), *The Corsican Brothers* (1941), *Moss Rose* (1947) and *Black Magic* (1949). Production coincided with a near-epidemic of influenza. Rod LaRoque was set for the romantic lead and Nils Asther was borrowed from Walter Wanger Productions as a last moment substitute. When Asther had to be replaced due to illness, a likable

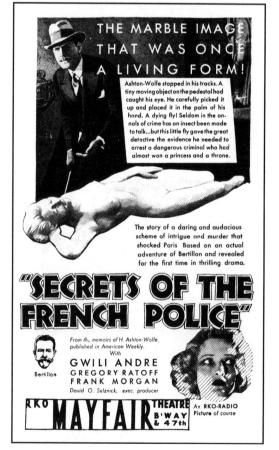

THE MARBLE IMAGE THAT WAS ONCE A LIVING FORM!

Ashton-Wolfe stopped in his tracks. A tiny moving object on the pedestal had caught his eye. He carefully picked it up and placed it in the palm of his hand. A dying fly! Seldom in the annals of crime has an insect been made to talk...but this little fly gave the great detective the evidence he needed to arrest a dangerous criminal who had almost won a princess and a throne.

The story of a daring and audacious scheme of intrigue and murder that shocked Paris Based on an actual adventure of Bertillon and revealed for the first time in thrilling drama.

"SECRETS OF THE FRENCH POLICE"

From the memoirs of H. Ashton-Wolfe, published in American Weekly.
With
GWILI ANDRE
GREGORY RATOFF
FRANK MORGAN
David O. Selznick, exec. producer

Bertillon

RKO MAYFAIR THEATRE B'WAY & 47th
An RKO-RADIO Picture of course

de Marsay), Rochelle Hudson (Agent K-31), Evelyn Carter Carrington (Madame La Prop), Michael Visaroff (German), Kate Lawson (Concierge), Dina Smirnova (Russian), Reginald Barlow (Préfect), Harry Cording, Arthur Thalasso, Sam Appel, Malcolm Waite (Detectives), Gertrude Pilar, Eleanor Vandevier (Ladies in Waiting), Cyril Ring (Gendarme), Virginia Thomas (Model), Wong Chung, Ming Woy, Wong Haye, Chester Gan (Tartar Servants), Capt. Girardo Garcia, Al Garcia, Gilbert Sanchez, Octavio Gerard (Policemen), Chic Collins, Wesley Hopper, Helen Lambert (Stunts), also H. Koontz, Wells Blanton, Mark McFee, Jean Girard, Betty Rome, Eugene Beday, Jimmy Coleman, Ray Cooper, Major Nichols, H. A. Perline, Fay Holderness, Nick Shaid, William Lally, Gino Corrado, Harry Cornbleth

Synopsis: Léon Renault, a handsome rogue who makes his living as a pickpocket in Paris, is bethrothed to Eugénie Dorain, a lovely flower vendor; her foster father, Anton, is bitterly opposed to the marriage. General Han Moloff, late of the White Russian Army, schemes to obtain a fortune; he seeks a girl who can pass for the missing Princess Anastasia, of the Russian royal family, and through her claim the banked millions from the estate of the murdered Czar. Accomplices are his mistress, Réna, and another fallen nobleman, Baron Feodor Lomzoi. The latter discovers Eugénie selling flowers on the streets of a tenement district and decides she is suited to Moloff's purposes. Eugénie is abducted and her father is stabbed to death by Moloff.

Lomzoi, who knows too much, is fished out of the Seine.

Clearing himself of suspicion, Léon becomes allied with François St. Cyr, assistant to the great Bertillon, the most celebrated detective of the Sureté Français. St. Cyr sends the nimble thief to Moloff's mansion in the mountains. To his horror, Léon peers through a skylight and sees Moloff spreading plaster over the dead body of Réna. He learns that Eugénie is in the house, but he is discovered before he has a chance to see her. He escapes Moloff's henchmen and reports to St. Cyr.

Moloff informs the Russian Grand Duke, in exile in London, that he has found the Princess. If the Duke accepts Eugénie as genuine the fortune will be given her. The night the Duke arrives at Moloff's retreat, Léon creeps through the upstairs rooms. He listens as the Duke questions Eugénie, who recites words Moloff has coached her to say under a hypnotic spell. The Duke announces that he has misgivings after the sight of some flowers causes Eugénie to become confused. The sentiment is echoed by Count de Marsay, the French diplomatic escort. Léon sees Eugénie, then rushes back to the city to inform St. Cyr. Meantime, the Duke and the Count leave the house in a limousine. As they round a curve they are almost blinded by automobile lights. The limo plunges over a cliff. The other car was, in fact, a rear-projected motion picture image placed at a curve in the road by Moloff's minions.

St. Cyr discovers the diabolical trap and, using the car "accident" as an excuse, calls upon Moloff next day. While Moloff is out of the room he sees a fly drop dead from a statue of a reclining nude girl. He has seen flies die of formaldehyde poisoning in the morgue. Cutting a small hole in the underside of the statue, he reaches inside and blanches in horror; he has found the missing Réna. Returning with Léon and the police, St. Cyr breaks into the house. Eugénie is rescued from Moloff's embalming room. Handcuffed, Moloff breaks free and slams his wrists into a power control panel, electrocuting himself. Eugénie is restored to Léon, who promises to go straight.

Secrets of the French Police- *Anton Dorain (Christian Rub) and Eugénie (Gwili André).*

British actor, John Warburton, made his American debut in the role. Gwili André also became ill and production had to be rescheduled to shoot around her for a full week. Ratoff was also ill for several days.

Secrets of the French Police was photographed during August and September 1932. Sets included a Paris street, tenements and a sidewalk café, all constructed at the RKO ranch in Encino, café and tenement interiors and a standing castle set at the Pathé Culver City lot— the same one used for *The Most Dangerous Game* a short time before. Selznick rode herd on the picture, bringing in New Yorker humorist

Robert Benchley to add more sparkle to the dialogue, and demanding retakes of many scenes, particularly those of Miss André (to accentuate her glamorous image), and at the same time taking the company to task because by September 9 it had gone $15,000 over its $172,646 budget. Part of the overage was attributable to the wrecking of a Rolls Royce limousine, which was driven over a 30-foot embankment. The full scale crash was deemed unacceptable and it was remade with one of Don Jahrous' flawless miniatures. About the only thing Selznick didn't growl about in his famous memos was the photography: "I approve highly of Al Gilks' work."

After principal photography wrapped on September 14, Selznick ordered further changes. Among other things, Ashton-Wolfe was renamed François St. Cyr, villainess Zenia Harka was redubbed as Réna, and a different setting was demanded for a sequence in which White Russian exiles sang their traditional anthem. The picture reached the scoring stage in October. Max Steiner conducted a full orchestra for the titles and dramatic passages, Dudley Chambers directed an eleven voice Russian choir, and Steiner led an eight piece musette group for café scenes. Final negative cost was

$195,805. Editing left a running time of 59 minutes, a slick and fast-moving picture whose neglect is undeserved.

Ratoff's excellence in a role that ordinarily would have been filled by, say, Bela Lugosi, is a pleasant surprise. Moloff's depravities include a passion for surrounding himself with many species of dead cats, which he preserves in a secret chamber. He also embalms his mistress there, then makes her into a statue. Utterly selfish, he kills his own cohorts to minimize the possibility that his plot to produce a fake Princess Anastasia might be found out. In one neatly underplayed scene, his mistress opines that too many people know about his scheme; he replies casually, "Several have died."

The picture would have been considered highly censorable within two years; the Motion Picture Producers

and Distributors code would have eliminated a nude shot of Kendall Lee, a scene in which Morgan pokes a finger into a statue containing a female corpse, a close up of Ratoff's hands turning black as he is electrocuted, and the denouement in which the romantic thief escapes having to pay for his crimes.

The light touch that keeps the grimness of the plot from becoming oppressive can be traced largely to Sutherland, whose specialty was comedy. His direction and the performances of the cast wear especially well for a 1932 movie. The realism of the sets and the cinematographer's artistic use of diffusion add to the French ambience. In a lengthy career, Sutherland walked the fine line beetween humor and horror only one other time, in the following year's *Murders in the Zoo*.

Secrets of the French Police - *Frank Morgan as the ace Sureté detective, St. Cyr.*

Murders in the Zoo

1933   Paramount Productions, Inc.
Director: A. Edward Sutherland
Screenplay: Philip Wylie and Seton I. Miller
Photography: Ernest Haller
Art Director: Hans Dreier
Musical Director: Nat W. Finston
Music: Rudolph G. Kopp, Karl Hajos, John M. Leipold and Sigmund Krumgold
Incidental Music: *Please*, Leo Robin and Ralph Rainger; *Look Who's Here*, Harold Adamson and Burton Lane; *At the Bow Wow Ball*, Edward Heyman and Boyd Bunch; *Roses from the South*, Johann Strauss
Stills: Sherman Clark
Running Time: 66 minutes

Cast: Charlie Ruggles (Peter Yates), Lionel Atwill (Eric Gorman), Gail Patrick (Jerry Evans), Randolph Scott (Dr. Woodford), John Lodge (Roger Hewitt), Kathleen Burke (Evelyn Gorman), Harry Beresford (Professor Evans), Edward McWade (Dan), Walter Walker and Edwin Stanley (Doctors), Syd Saylor, Lee Phelps, Stanley Blystone, Syd D'Albrook and Eddie Boland (Reporters), Ethan Laidlaw (Reardon), Duke Green (Stevedore), John Rogers (Steward), Jane Darwell, Samuel Hinds and Cyril Ring (Zoo Patrons)

Synopsis: In a remote Indian jungle, zoologist Eric Gorman gloats over the helpless visitor who had kissed Gorman's wife during a drinking party. Trussed and with his lips sewn together, the young man is left to predators. "A Mongolian prince taught me this, Taylor," Gorman says. "Now you'll never lie to a friend again and you'll never again kiss another man's wife." Evelyn Gorman asks Gorman on his return what Taylor said. "He didn't say anything," is the flippant reply. Returning to America with a cargo of animals for a municipal zoo, Gorman senses an affair budding between Evelyn and a handsome passenger, Roger Hewitt.

The zoo, run by Professor Evans and Dr. Woodford, faces financial ruin. Evans hires Peter Yates, a press agent, to publicize the zoo. When Gorman delivers the animals, Woodford is particularly interested in a rare

Unusual optical titles get *Murders in the Zoo* off to an appropriate start. The main title and credits are superimposed over scenes of animals in the zoo. Then an applauding seal dissolves into comical Charlie Ruggles, a bear to crusty old Harry Beresford, a dove and an owl become romantic scientists Gail Patrick and Randolph Scott, a pair of sleek pumas dissolve to the handsome but hungry Kathleen Burke and John Lodge, while a snarling tiger introduces Lionel Atwill.

As a portrayer of mad scientists, Atwill was without peer. No other actor could convey with comparable eloquence a man so monomaniacal as to regard human life as worthless compared with his often diabolical plans. Atwill is at his best in *Murders in the Zoo* wherein he not only removes anybody who displeases him but also takes unholy glee in doing so by the most gruesome and agonizing means at hand. It's also made explicit that he becomes sexually aroused whenever he has committed murder. Top-billed Charlie Ruggles adds comedy, and romance is supplied by an unusually handsome couple, Randolph Scott and Gail Patrick. There is fine support from sultry, sloe-eyed Kathleen Burke as Atwill's faithless wife, Lodge (later Governor of Connecticut) as one of her unfortunate lovers, Beresford as the befuddled zoo director, and Edward McWade as a cranky keeper. Not even all their capable work can keep Atwill from stealing the show throughout; darkly witty dialogue aids his theft.

Murders in the Zoo - Yates (Charlie Ruggles) learns about animals from Jerry (Gail Patrick).

green mamba snake, inasmuch as he wants to develop an antitoxin for its deadly poison. Yates arranges a banquet at the zoo as part of a fund-raising campaign.

Evelyn is surprised to find Roger Hewitt seated next to her at the banquet. Gorman sits across from them. Suddenly Hewitt cries out and falls, his face contorted in agony. He dies in five minutes. The fang marks of a mamba are found on his swollen leg, and it is discovered that the snake has escaped. The guests flee in panic.

Later that evening, Evelyn sees Gorman working in secrecy on some strange device. Investigating, she finds it to be an artificial snake-head with poison-laden fangs. Taking the instrument she hurries to the zoo, but Gorman sees her and gives chase. He overtakes her on the bridge spanning a pit of crocodiles. Failing in his attempts to reason with her, he throws her into the pit, where she dies horribly.

Notoriety of the recent deaths causes a withdrawal of public support. So many layoffs are necessary that Yates must double as a workman to keep his job. Yates captures the mamba, collapses, and afterwards asks if there's a good laundry in town. Woodford and his fiancée, Jerry Evans, take the reptile to his laboratory in order to extract venom. Woodford discovers that the fangs are not spaced as widely as those which left their mark on Hewitt. Suspecting that Gorman has another mamba, Woodford sum-

mons him to the zoo and confronts him with the discovery. Gorman sinks the fangs into Woodford's hand and shoulder, then kills the mamba as Woodford writhes on the floor.

Jerry arrives and finds Woodford unconscious. She rushes to get the new serum, but Gorman pursues and tries to inject her with the poison. Eluding Gorman, Jerry gives the serum to Woodford while Yates summons help.

As guards search for Gorman, the madman releases some of the dangerous animals to create a diversion while he hides in a supposedly empty cage. A giant python seizes his leg in its jaws and quickly enfolds him in its deadly coils. Gorman tries to cry out but is silenced as the snake coils about his face. Woodford recovers, saved by his own serum.

Early on he speaks of animals: "I love them! Their honesty, their simplicity, their primitive emotions. They love, they hate, and they kill." Of his wife's "secret" lover, he says "Just a veddy good friend" and "like one of the family." Later, in the lover's apartment in a Paris hotel, well aware that his wife is hiding in the bedroom, he notes that "On the boat you and I seemed to have a mutual interest. I was referring to my animals." When his wife accuses him of being responsible for causing her friend to be fatally bitten by a mamba at a banquet, he snorts, "You don't think I sat there all evening with an eight-foot mamba in my pocket, do you? It would be an injustice to my tailor!" Then he berates her for not being more concerned for her husband's safety.

Atwill's passion for his wife is heightened enormously by the fact that he has killed for her. "I know—you're going to make love to me," she cries in disgust. "I've never wanted you more," he pants. "I'm not going to kiss you—you're going to kiss me!" Later, trying to reason with her on the bridge, he argues, "If I lacked the courage to kill for you I couldn't expect you to go on loving me."

The crocodile feast is a shocker. The saurians converge on the struggling woman, seizing her in their jaws and spinning in the water to tear their prey apart, pausing only to lift their heads as they gulp down their meal.

English-born Edward Sutherland, usually a specialist in light comedy, made two notable contributions to the horror film in 1932–33—(*Murders in the Zoo* was preceded by his equally neglected *Secrets of the French Police*).

The setting of the zoo, especially in the night scenes where it is suggestive of the jungle, is as frightening as any gothic castle. Ernest Haller's distinctive photographic style makes each shadow a potential menace. There is effective dramatic scoring for the Indian scenes and for a tour of the zoo in which a separate motif is introduced for each animal, plus incidental music and comic passages for Ruggles. The relative sparseness of orchestral music during later action passes unnoticed; varied animal cries keep the soundtrack sufficiently occupied with disturbing noises.

Murders in the Zoo - *Jerry finds Woodford near death from mamba venom as Gonnan plays at being helpful.*

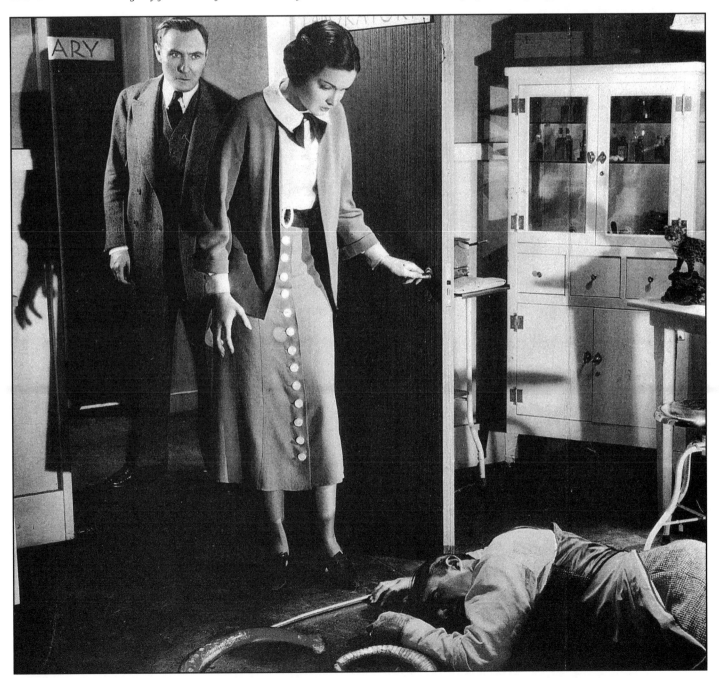

I Cover the Waterfront

1933   Reliance Pictures, Incorporated
A United Artists Release
Joseph M. Schenck Presentation
Produced at United Artists Studios
Director: James Cruze
Executive Producers: Harry M. Goetz and Edward Small
Producer: Edward Small
Based on a book by Max Miller.
Screenplay: Wells Root
Additional Dialogue: Jack Jevne
Music Orchestration and Composition: Alfred Newman
Theme: *Weiner Maederlin,* Ziehrer; *Love Song,* Minnie Wright
Assistant Director: Vernon Keays
Art Director: Albert S. D'Agostino
Photography: Ray June
Sound Technician: Oscar Lagerstrom
Film Editor: Grant Whytock
Operative Cameraman: Stuart Thompson
Assistant Cameramen: Hal Carney and Ellis Carter
Second Unit Photography: Harry Perry
Assistant: Jimmy Hackett
Running Time: 70 minutes

Cast: Claudette Colbert (Julie), Ben Lyon (Joseph Miller), Ernest Torrence (Eli Kirk), Hobart Cavanaugh (McCoy), Maurice Black (Ortegus), Harry Beresford (Old Chris), Purnell Pratt (John Phelps), George Humbert (Silva), Rosita Marstini (Mrs. Silva), Claudia Coleman (Mother Morgan), Wilfred Lucas (Randall), Florence Dudley (The Blonde), Al Hill (Thug), Burr McIntosh (Old Man)

Synopsis: Julie Kirk knows her father, Eli, is troubled, but she cannot exact an explanation. The fact is, the Coast Guard has come too close for comfort to Kirk's Chinese-smuggling operations. Kirk has resorted to murder to evade discovery, and a reporter, Joseph Miller, has vowed to expose Kirk. Miller is marginally acquainted with Julie.

Old Chris, a harbor salvage bum, sinks his dragline and dredges up the corpse of a Chinese bound in a chain from Kirk's fishing smack.

Kirk goes on a binge at Mother Morgan's establishment. Miller and a bibulous colleague, McCoy, arrive somewhat later. Julie

James Cruze—like such other successful silent-era directors as D. W. Griffith, William Nigh, Fred Newmeyer, and Erich von Stroheim—found his talking pictures career a succession of peaks and valleys. The collapse of his production company in 1932 and a dizzying plunge into alcoholism blighted a decade in which his great talents were only occasionally displayed. Cruze was hired by the newly

organized Reliance early in 1933 to direct its first picture, *I Cover the Waterfront.* Reliance was established by Edward Small and Harry Goetz, with the partial backing of Joseph M. Schenck of United Artists. *Waterfront,* based loosely on a successful book by reporter

I Cover the Waterfront - Eli Kirk (Ernest Torrence) and his daughter, Julie (Claudette Colbert).

comes to seek her father, and Miller helps her cart him home. Julie and Miller have a rendezvous the next day on the waterfront.

Miller and federal agents meet the next arrival of Kirk's boat, which appears to contain only giant sharks. Miller slashes open one of the sharks—and a Chinese is found inside. Kirk strikes Miller down, is wounded by the agents' leader, and escapes after a struggle. Julie turns

against Miller on learning he tipped the authorities. Miller traces Kirk to a partially sunken barge, where the wounded smuggler shoots Miller. As he is about to do away with the reporter, Julie appears. Sensing his daughter's affection for Miller, Kirk helps her take him aboard a speedboat. Kirk dies before he can make a getaway. Miller survives the wound, and he and Julie are reunited.

Max Miller of the San Diego *Union,* is a bright spot in Cruze's career, for here he mixed lurid fact with lurid fiction in a virile mixture of near-documentary realism and chilling drama.

In addition to United Artists Studios work, the production involved use of locations at San Pedro and in the Pacific off San Pedro, San Diego, and Monterey. A harpooning expedition brought in several sharks in the twenty-foot class for scenes in which illegal aliens are hidden in shark carcasses. Special breathing masks attached to snorkels enabled the hardy Chinese-American extras to survive the scenes in which they are placed, bound in chains, inside the sharks.

The harbor at San Pedro provides a colorful backdrop. The U. S. S. Constitution, the Pacific Fleet, and the Carma (the yacht on which Captain Walter Wanderwell had recently been murdered) appear in some scenes. The company was at work in the United Artists facilities when the Southern California Earthquake hit, dumping Ben Lyon out of the bed in which he was emoting, and killing the lights and power on the lot.

The nominal stars, Lyon and Claudette Colbert, do fine work as a waterfront waif and her boyfriend. The real star, however, is Ernest Torrence, a former con-cert pianist and baritone from Edinburgh who became famous as an actor after portraying the degenerate Luke Hatburn in *Tol'able David* (1921). Six-foot-four, lantern-jawed, and muscular, Torrence created in Eli Kirk what must be his finest characterization. It is difficult to imagine a more cruel, more fearsome villain than this tobacco-spitting smuggler and killer, and yet Torrence invests the man with enough sympathy to make an audience feel regret at his passing. His bumbling affection for his daughter, his loyalty to his murderous colleagues, and even his drunken revel in a bordello are curiously humanizing. Few actors have accomplished this feat (Karloff in the *Frankenstein* films comes to mind, as do Brian Donlevy in the 1939 *Beau Geste* and James Cagney in *Public Enemy*). This was Torrence's last performance; he died shortly after completion of *Waterfront.* Others who give notable accounts of themselves in the cast include Harry Beresford as a harbor scavenger and Hobart Cavanaugh as a happily inebriated reporter.

Ray June, a real master of the camera, managed to overcome somewhat Cruze's usual reluctance to vary angles; the result is an eerie mood that suffuses both location and studio shots. This is a somber picture, yet it avoids being depressing, and even includes a discreet pre-Code swimming scene for Claudette Colbert.

I Cover the Waterfront - *Kirk tries to kill Mille (Ben Lyon).*

The Mystery of Mr. X

1934   Metro Goldwyn Mayer Film Corporation
Director: Edgar Selwyn
Producer: Lawrence Weingarten
Based on the Doubleday-Doran Crime Club novel *The Mystery of the Dead Police* by Philip MacDonald
Screenplay: Howard Emmett Rogers
Adaptation: Philip MacDonald
Additional Dialogue: Monckton Hoffe
Art Direction: Merrill Pye
Interior Decoration: Edwin B. Willis
Gowns: Adrian
Photographer: Oliver T. Marsh
Music: Dr. William Axt
Songs: *This Is the Night, We'll Make Hay While the Sun Shines*, Nacio Herb Brown and Arthur Freed
Film Editor: Hugh Wynn
Sound Supervision: Douglas Shearer
Special Effects: James Basevi and Robert T. Layton
Running Time: 84 minutes

Cast: Robert Montgomery (Nicholas Revel), Elizabeth Allan (Jane Frensham), Lewis Stone (Inspector Conor), Henry Stephenson (Sir Herbert Frensham), Ralph Forbes (Sir Christopher Marche), Forrester Harvey (Palmer), Ivan Simpson (Hutchinson), Leonard Mudie (Mr. X), Alec B. Francis (Judge Malpas), Charles Irwin (Willis), Lumsden Hare (Officer), Claude King (Crown Prosecutor), Olaf Hytten (Reporter), Barlowe Borland (Waiter), Ted Billings (Drinker)

Synopsis: Five London policemen are stabbed to death on five successive nights by the mysterious X. Each murder follows a warning note to the Metropolitan Police. Commissioner Sir Herbert Frensham hurries back from a rest cure with his daughter, Jane. They are met at the depot by Sir Christopher Marche, Jane's fiancé, a pleasant but rather lackadaisical young playboy. Sir Herbert finds another warning that a sixth policeman will die tonight. X is true to his word.

The sixth victim dies outside the house where Nicholas Revel, a gentleman burglar, is removing the fabulous Drayton Diamond from a safe. Sir Christopher, on a drunken

The Mystery of Mr. X started a trend: the murder mystery in which urbane, romantic comedy replaced heavy-handed attempts at humor, such as the rather vulgar witticisms of *The Thirteenth Guest* (1932). With the release of the even more popular *Thin Man* by the same company about two months later, the genre became so well established as to inspire many imitations. The mixture was a difficult balance to strike, as it required unusual directorial finesse and leading players possessed of great charm.

Mr. X easily matches *The Thin Man* for wit and surpasses it in atmosphere and suspense. Scripting and dialogue are as sophisticated as a British drawing-room comedy, but the romance and cleverness yield at the right moments to the mood of gathering horror. The

ROBERT MONTGOMERY

... thrills you!
... charms you!

MYSTERY OF MR. X

with Elizabeth ALLAN
Lewis STONE

He Was Dangerous As a Crook . . .
but more so as a lover! He wasn't the culprit . . . but he was forced to find him to solve the mystery of a dozen murders and save a city from an unknown terror!

Montgomery . . . dashing —devil-may-care—at his best!

a Metro-Goldwyn-Mayer Picture

wager, knocks a bobby unconscious and takes his helmet as a loving cup. X finds the fallen policeman, draws a sword from his cane, and kills him. The police theorize that whoever took the diamond killed the bobby. A scarf clutched in the victim's hand is traced to Sir Christopher, and he is charged with murder. Revel steps forward to clear Sir Christopher, who is let off with ten days for striking an officer. Revel has several comically suspenseful experiences as he tries to keep the jewel out of sight.

Jane invites the charming Revel to dinner. Sir Herbert is impressed with Revel's theories about how to capture X, but Inspector Connor is mistrustful. When Sir Christopher is released from jail he finds Jane making tea in Revel's apartment and, in a misunderstanding, breaks off their engagement. Jane and Revel realize they are in love.

The X murders continue, and Sir Herbert comes under fire from both the press and the public. The press concludes that the police are wrong in their theory regarding the missing diamond. To help Sir Herbert, Revel forges a letter in the style of X by pasting together letters snipped from various publications. This he mails with the diamond to Scotland Yard. "Here's your diamond," the message states, "Now try to catch me." A complication arises, though; Revel's

accomplice, a hack-driver named Palmer, reports that another cohort, Hutchinson, is being questioned by the police. Revel realizes Hutchinson may talk when confronted with the diamond—and Revel would be established as Mr. X.

Jane, aware of Revel's imminent arrest, begs that he clear himself with her. She is stunned at his revelation that he is a diamond thief. He sets out to prove that he is not X by capturing the madman. By studying a map, Revel discerns that the pattern of the murders forms an X-shape in the heart of London. Disguised as a bobby, Revel walks the beat he has determined to be X's next target.

Revel almost becomes victim number nine. After a desperate chase, Revel corners X in an abandoned warehouse. They fight on an upper story, and X falls just as Connor and the police arrive. The dying X laughs and says, "Squared it, Connor, with your blasted p'lice. Fifteen years before I escaped. Swore I'd get one for every year. Got eight. Nearly nine. I hate you. Hate you."

Sir Herbert decides that the man who ended X's reign of terror should be allied with Scotland Yard. With Jane and Connor to keep him on the straight-and-narrow, Revel decides it can be arranged.

straight-mystery novel on which the film was based was a Crime Club selection in July 1933. Its author, the exceptionally gifted Philip MacDonald, wrote the screen adaptation.

One camp of mystery fans feels the film betrays the rules of the game by cheating armchair detectives of the opportunity to identify the culprit from among the suspects; Mr. X proves to be

a character not introduced until the end. Director Edgar Selwyn, untroubled by this consideration, gave this view on the effective exposition of mystery and horror:

"The most mysterious of all mysteries is the one which tells the least. This is not a conundrum but a tenet of all mystery-story creation. The most dire feeling of dread is instilled by keeping the menace a secret. Its effect is felt, but it must not be seen. This is an iron-clad formula in the creation of eeriness.

". . . The horror is known only as 'X,' whose shadow is seen passing over the inert bodies of his victims. The snatch of song he whistles is heard. His living quarters are seen, even part of his shoulder. But not until the final exciting sequence does he appear. The underlying psychology is based on the world-old recognition that fear

The Mystery of Mr. X - *Scotland Yard detectives Connor (Lewis Stone) and Willis (Charles Irwin) question a suspect, Hutchinson (Ivan Simpson).*

of an unknown assailant is more terrible than fear of a tangible object, no matter how imposing. Strong men have been known to break down as a result of imagined adversaries.

"Fear is instinctive. It is strongly allied with superstition and lurks in even the most sophisticated human mind. Thus mystery stories are always popular."

The director lives up to his words in

The Mystery of Mr. X - *Mr. X commits another murder.*

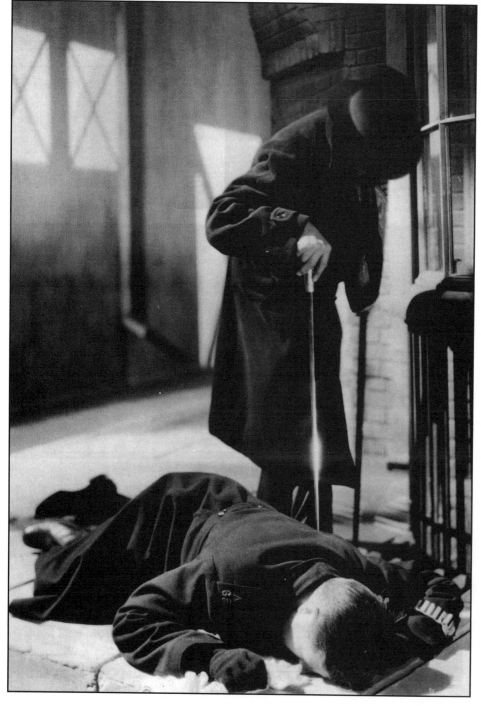

Mr. X. Selwyn, in addition to being a film pioneer, was a successful writer, actor, director, and producer on Broadway. His production of *Within the Law* in 1912 was one of the first plays to net $1,000,000. He and his younger brother, Arch, founded the All Star Feature Films Corporation in 1912. The names of Selwyn and Samuel Goldfish were combined with the founding of the Goldwyn Pictures

Corporation in 1917. (Goldfish liked the coined name so well that he changed his own to match.) From 1929 until shortly before his death at sixty-eight in 1944, Edgar Selwyn worked for MGM, first as a writer-director—(his *Sin of Madelon Claudet* won an Academy Award for Helen Hayes in 1932)—and later as a producer and executive.

Selwyn had the right partners on *X* to achieve the desired results. Merrill Pye's settings, superbly lighted and photographed by Oliver Marsh and draped in studio fog, provide the ideal milieu for the intrusion of the menacing shadow. The killer's whistling—an idea which may have been purloined from Fritz Lang's *M* (Germany, 1930) but which was not yet a cliché—adds to the eeriness. The atmosphere of terror is all the more pronounced because of the contrast provided by the cheerful romantic scenes and the activities of a gang of likeable crooks. The role of thief-detective-lover seems tailor-made for Robert Montgomery, who as a romantic rogue was the closest rival to Ronald Colman (see *The Unholy Garden* above). English actress Elizabeth Allan projects an innocence that makes her the ideal reformer for such a scoundrel.

Montgomery's chicanery finds fitting foils in Lewis Stone's taciturn and suspicious inspector and Henry Stephenson's cranky but gullible commissioner. Forrester Harvey as an unscrupulous Cockney hack driver and Ivan Simpson as a grouchy insurance agent make the partners-in-crime cleverly convincing. As the killer, veteran English character actor Leonard Mudie provides a chilling glimpse of implacable hatred in his brief scenes at the climax.

The story was remade with very few changes in 1952 by MGM British Studios as *The Hour of 13* with Peter Lawford and Dawn Addams.

The Black Cat

1934   Universal Pictures Corporation
Presented by Carl Laemmle
Director: Edgar G. Ulmer
Producer: Carl Laemmle, Jr.
Associate Producer: E. M. Asher
Suggested by the Edgar Allan Poe story
Screenplay: Peter Ruric
Story: Edgar Ulmer and Peter Ruric
Additional Dialogue: Shirley Kassel
Continuity: Tom Kilpatrick
Art Director: Charles D. Hall
Musical Director: Heinz Roemheld
Camera: John Mescall
Film Editor: Ray Curtiss
Special Effects: John P. Fulton
Camera Effects: David S. Horsley
Make-up: Jack P. Pierce
Matte Paintings: Jack Cosgrove and Russell Lawson
Set Decorations: R. A. Gausman
Assistant Directors: William Reiger and Sam Rosenthal
Sound Supervision: Gilbert Kurland
Music Recording: Lawrence Aicholtz
Costumes: Edgar Ulmer, Vera West and Ed Ware
Art Titles: Max Cohen
Script Clerk: Moree Herring
Running Time: 64 minutes

Cast: Boris Karloff (Hjalamar Poelzig), Bela Lugosi (Vitus Werdegast), David Manners (Peter Alison), Jacqueline Wells (Joan Alison), Lucille Lund (Karen), Egon Brecher (Majordomo), Harry Cording (Thamal), Henry Armetta (Gendarme), Albert Conti (Lieutenant), Anna Duncan (Maid), André Cheron (Conductor), George Davis (Bus Driver), Tony Marlow (Border Patrolman), Paul Weigel (Station Master), Rodney Hildebrand (Brakeman), John Carradine (Organist), Michael Mark, Paul Panzer, Symonia Boniface, Frazer Acosta, King Baggot, Louis January, Peggy Terry, Virginia Ainsworth, Duskal Blaine and Harry Walker (Cultists), Cut from release version: Andy Devine, Lenore Kingston, Herman Bing, Alphonse Martel, Luis Alberni and Albert Poulet.

Synopsis: On honeymoon in Europe are

arl Laemmle, Sr., a family man who took pride in providing wholesome entertainment, was a founder and backer of the Motion Pictures Producers & Distributors Association, which industry leaders set up in 1922 as a self-regulator to help stem state and local censorship problems. The 1930 Production Code which members observed militated against material that might be construed as profane or salacious or would tend to glorify criminal or licentious behavior. The Code was lenient enough to pose few problems, and there was little worry over occasional nudity or profanity.

The honeymoon ended in the spring of 1934, when a committee of Catholic bishops formed the National Legion of Decency, a pressure group that urged all Catholics to boycott theatres showing films deemed immoral. An alarming tightening of the Production Code resulted. For reasons that defy understanding, horror films were a prime target; the Legion automatically classed them as "objectionable." A corresponding attitude surfaced among the British censors, who barred children from seeing horror films even after the pictures had been scissored beyond recognition. Some such films were refused permits to enter the country on the basis that they were "against nature." Several Continental European countries were equally intolerant.

The pressure hurt most at the box office. It is hardly surprising, then, that Universal released only one genuine horror film during 1934. This was *The Black Cat*, which as the first film to co-star Karloff

The Black Cat - Lugosi as Vitus Werdegast. " . . . An intense and all-consuming horror of cats."

Peter Alison—author of *The Triple Murder, The Sixty-Ninth Crime* and *The Purple Spot*—and his bride, Joan. A mixup in train reservations at Budapest obliges the couple to share a compartment with the debonair but vaguely sinister Dr. Vitus Werdegast, who is bound for Vizhegrad "to visit . . . an old friend." Peter is disturbed by the stranger's piercing scrutiny of Joan. Werdegast explains she reminds him of his wife, whom he has not seen since he went to the battlefront— "Kaiser and country, you know"—eighteen years ago. He had been imprisoned three years later at the infamous Kurgaal in Siberia. "Many men went to Kurgaal, and few have returned," Werdegast says bitterly. "I have returned."

The train reaches Vizhegrad during a rainstorm. As the Alisons board a bus bound for the resort of Gombos, they are joined by Werdegast and a giant, mute servant, Thamal. En route along the muddy mountain road, the driver explains they are traversing one of the great battlefields of the war.

"Tens of thousands of men died here . . . That ravine was piled twelve deep with dead and wounded. The little river was red, a torrent of blood . . . There is the site of Fort Marmaros. The house of Engineer Poelzig now stands there. He built his home on the very foundations of the fort. Marmaros, the greatest graveyard in the world!"

The bus skids and crashes into a ravine, killing the driver and leaving Joan unconscious. Reaching the Poelzig home, the survivors are confronted by the evil-faced Andreas, the majordomo. Werdegast orders the man to wake his master, then takes Joan to a bedroom where he dresses her wounds. He explains to Peter she is not seriously hurt as he gives her a sedative. When Poelzig enters, Alison leaves. Poelzig regards Werdegast silently as the latter accuses him of having stolen Werdegast's wife and daughter and of betraying Marmaros to the enemy.

Peter enters the room, and the old "friends" become smilingly polite. Werdegast extols Poelzig as a brilliant architect while Poelzig reveals that the other was, before the war, a celebrated psychiatrist. Peter remarks that the house has an atmosphere difficuit to describe. "It may be an atmosphere of death," replies Werdegast. Poelzig agrees, saying the fort still is undermined with dynamite.

Poelzig's black cat wanders in. Werdegast cries out in horror, hurls a knife that kills the cat, and collapses into sobbing. As the cat dies, Joan enters, and Peter observes that a strange change seems to have possessed her. As Werdegast recovers, Poelzig apologizes for him: "You must be indulgent with Dr. Werdegast. He is the victim of one of the commonest phobias, but in an extreme form. He has an intense and all-consuming horror of cats."

Removing Joan to her room, Werdegast explains to Peter that the change in her is only a momentary one caused by her head injury and that she may have become "in a sense mediumistic, a vehicle for all the intangible forces in operation around us."

After the guests have retired, Poelzig, carrying a living black cat —"the black cat does not die," he has said—descends to the subterranean corridors of the old fort. He pauses before each of several glass cases containing the suspended bodies of young women. Later he returns and resumes his conversation with Werdegast, who demands to be taken to his wife. Poelzig conducts him to the underground area and shows him one of the dead women. Werdegast is horrified.

"You see, Vitus? I have cared for her tenderly and well. She died . . . of pneumonia . . . Is she not beautiful? I wanted to keep her beauty for all time. I loved her too." Poelzig adds that Werdegast's daughter, named Karen after her mother, also died. Werdegast accuses Poelzig of killing them both and draws a revolver. The shadow of the black cat appears on a wall, so demoralizing Werdegast that he drops the weapon. Poelzig escorts him back to his room, insisting that if they are to play a "game of death" they must wait until the others are gone.

In his bedroom, Poelzig lies down beside his sleeping wife, who exactly resembles the dead Karen. She is Werdegast's daughter. "You are the very core and meaning of my life," he says. "No one shall take you from me . . ." From a book, *The Rites of Lucifer*, he reads: "In the night, in the dark of the moon, the High Priest assembles his followers for the sacrifice. The chosen maiden . . ."

Next morning Werdegast notes Poelzig's lustful glances at Joan. He accuses Poelzig of planning to keep the girl. "Tonight is the dark of the moon," Poelzig says. "Perhaps you'd better join us. The ceremony will interest you." Werdegast says he intends to let Joan escape. "Do you dare play chess for her?" asks Poelzig. The game begins. Peter and Joan, luggage readied, ask to be driven to the village.

Andreas reports the car is out of commission. Peter tries to telephone. "Did you hear that, Vitus?" Poelzig asks with an evil smile. "Even the phone is dead." He redirects his attention to the chessboard and a moment later adds, "Checkmate." As the Alisons seek to leave, Thamal, now under Poelzig's command, strikes Peter down. Joan is locked in her room, and Peter is imprisoned in a gun turret below. Werdegast comes to see Joan.

"We're all in danger," he tells her. "Poelzig is a mad beast . . . He took Karen, my wife, and murdered her, and murdered my child. Did you ever hear of Satanism . . .? Herr Poelzig is the great modern priest of that ancient cult . . . If I am not mistaken, he plans for you to play a part in that ritual. A very important part."

After Werdegast leaves, Karen enters from an adjoining room. Joan realizes who the girl must be and tells her her father is alive and has come for her. Poelzig enters and forces Karen into the other room.

The worshippers gather. Joan is arrayed in sacrificial robes and taken to an altar surmounted by a leaning, double cross. Werdegast and Thamal hide and watch as Poelzig performs the Latin invocation to Satan. A woman in the congregation faints. Werdegast and Thamal take advantage of the diversion and carry Joan down the long, spiral staircase to the turret rooms. They encounter Andreas, who shoots Thamal. Thamal kills the man with his bare hands. Meantime, Werdegast finds the body of his daughter on a table in Poelzig's embalming room. His mind snaps.

Poelzig arrives and struggles with Werdegast. Thamal, with his dying strength, helps his master chain Poelzig to a rack. "Did you ever see an animal skinned, Hjalamar?" Werdegast asks. "That's what I'm going to do to you: flail the skin from your body, slowly, bit by bit." He sets to work with a scalpel.

Peter escapes, takes Andreas' pistol, and is drawn to the embalming room by the screams of Joan and Poelzig. Misunderstanding the situation, he shoots Werdegast. "You poor fool! I only wanted to help," says- Werdegast. "Now go—please go!" As the couple flees, Werdegast reminds Poelzig of the undermining explosives. "It's the red switch, isn't it? In five minutes, Marmaros, you and I, and your rotten cult will be no more." He slams the lever into place and waits, triumphant. An instant before the explosion he says, smiling, "It has been a good game."

Later, on the train to Budapest, Peter finds a newspaper review of his latest mystery novel. It chides him for writing about things so fantastic they couldn't possibly happen.

and Lugosi—if one ignores a cornball meeting staged for the Universal Newsreel—was publicized heavily. It went before the cameras late in February after a long evolution.

Plans began germinating in December 1932, when stories were being bought for Karloff. Scenario editor Richard Schrayer made a tentative adaptation. A treatment, "The Brain Never Dies" by Jack Cunningham and Stanley Bergerman, utilized ideas from two Edgar Allan Poe stores, *The Black Cat* and *The Fall of the House of Usher*, and created for Karloff the role of Dr. Metta, a mad scientist. When this was rejected, Cunningham wrote an expansion of Schayer's version, Karloff's role being that of Edgar Doe, who seals up his wife behind a basement wall. This version also failed, and another treatment was developed by Tom Kilpatrick and Dale Van Every. E. A. Dupont, director of the German classic *Variety*, was slated to direct, but the project was abandoned when Universal suspended operations temporarily.

Edgar G. Ulmer, who was assigned to direct the property in late 1933, decided to write his own scenario. He concocted an entirely different plot suggested by the headlined escapades of an English Satanist leader, Alastair Crowley. (Crowley had inspired W.

Somerset Maugham's novel, *The Magician*, which Rex Ingram filmed as a silent.) The Ulmer script, completed by a young detective story writer, Peter Ruric—known in the pulp magazines as Paul Cain—with input from Tom Kilpatrick and Ulmer's future wife, Shirley Kassel, was approved in February 1934—on condition that a black cat be worked into the script. One was, but only just. Script revisions continued long after filming was under way. Principal photography began on February 28, 1934 and finished nineteen days later at a cost of only $95,745. This includes two days and nights of retakes, which were done mostly to make Lugosi's role less villainous.

No sooner had shooting been completed than the Legion of Decency made its influence felt. While *The Black Cat* was being readied for an early-summer release, it was bombarded by Code demands that led to the worst mauling of any Universal film since 1923, when Erich von Stroheim's *Foolish Wives* ran afoul of the New York State censors. Among the casualties were key scenes making it explicit that the young bride had been possessed by the soul of a demonic cat, an idea only hinted at in the finished product. Also cut were details of the Black Mass, including a dance called "The Appassionata" as

performed by Anna Duncan, cousin of the famed Isadora. The well-advertised dancer was left with only a few brief scenes as a maid-servant.

Even this shadow of the original was denounced. It remains today a focus of controversy. Some present-day observers echo what many contemporary critics called it: a confusing hodgepodge of morbidity and bad taste. Others consider it a genuine classic of horror as well as the masterwork of the erratic but highly individualistic and artistic Ulmer. The director, more than thirty years later, said *The Black Cat* was his own favorite. It is easy to see why; seldom in commercial cinema has a film so reflected the personal vision of its principal creator. Ulmer took a hand in set and costume design and encouraged his brilliant but alcoholic cameraman, John Mescall, to provide photography markedly different from most work of the period.

There was tension on the set because Karloff had the juicier role and a much larger salary than Lugosi, who carried the bitterness to his grave. Certainly Ulmer pampered Karloff, who had wanted a respite from horrors, by designing for him a magnificently sybaritic wardrobe. Arrayed in robes, black silk pajamas, and a smoking jacket fashion designers were quick to copy, and made up by Jack Pierce with a plunging widow's peak that made him appear sinister but fascinating, Karloff reveled in the experience of being a suave and dignified monster. This is one of Karloff's few hundred percent villains, one in which even he could find little humanity, but it also is his most glamorous characterization.

For Lugosi, Ulmer provided no less interesting a change of pace—a tailor-made role that is one of the best of a checkered career. He is mysterious, balanced precariously upon the brink of madness and with something dangerous lurking just beneath the surface, yet wholly sympathetic in the final picture. It has been suggested that the roles should have been reversed, but Lugosi ultimately admitted he was pleased to be permitted to play a tragic hero. Wholly himself, Lugosi plays it straight, even when the script indulges in some rich self-kidding. When the juvenile lead suggests that Lugosi's talk of Satanism is "a lot of supernatural baloney," Lugosi replies with pompous *misterioso*, "Supernatural, perhaps. Baloney, perhaps not. There are many things under the sun." After Karloff has had the hero beaten unconscious and ordered the fainting girl imprisoned, Lugosi sternly tells him, "I hope you won't carry this too far, Hjalamar!"

Some of the dialogue is almost poetic, such as Lugosi's accusation of Karloff: "Fifteen years ago you sold Marmaros to the Russians. You left the rest of us to die. It is not to be wondered at, that you chose this place to build your home. A masterpiece of construction built upon the ruins of the masterpiece of destruction—the masterpiece of murder. The murderer of ten thousand men returns to the scene of his crime. Those who died were fortunate. I was taken to Kurgaal . . . where the soul is killed slowly. Fifteen years I've rotted in darkness . . . Now I've come back, not to kill you, but to kill your soul."

Sets are far removed from the Medieval gloom of most other

The Black Cat - *Karloff as Hjalmar Poelzig.*

Universal chillers. Action is concentrated in luxurious, futuristic surroundings. Some of the super-house's appointments—a digital clock, for example—seem quite familiar today, having been assimilated by designers during the intervening decades, but the overall effect is one of ultra-modernity.

Stunning visuals justify fully the languorous unfolding of the story. This gradual building process terminates abruptly in a savage climax that is the

more dramatic for its unexpectedness. The dominant tone is one of hovering, impatient evil. Early on we learn that the house is mined and wired for destruction. This oppressive aura is made more grim by Karloff's necrophilia and his prurient interest in the young bride, and intensified by Lugosi's smoldering hatred.

The camera performs with a virtuosity difficult to describe. There are deep-focus shots in the best James Wong Howe manner, yet focus shifts artfully from background to foreground and back again when Karloff's hand tightens upon a statuette of a nude woman as the possessed bride passionately kisses her bewildered husband. Carefully composed stationary shots are juxtaposed with scenes in which the camera "walks," as when Karloff and Lugosi are traversing the underground domain. Here the camera becomes subjective, roaming the shadowy corridors as Karloff's voice comes over softly and almost free of emotion:

"Come, Vitus, are we men, or are we children? Of what use are all these melodramatic gestures? Are we not both as much victims of the war as those whose bodies were torn asunder? You say your soul was killed, that you have been dead all these years. And what of me? Did we not both die here in Marmaros 15 years ago? Are we not both the living dead? And now you come, playing at being an avenging angel, childishly thirsting for my blood. We understand each other. We know too much of life. We shall play a little game, a game of death if you like."

An earlier dream-like passage is handled much differently. In a sequence of seven curiously angled shots linked by slow dissolves, Karloff walks the same corridors, absently stroking the black cat cradled in his arms. Five times he halts before the showcased corpses of sheer-gowned young women, gazing inscrutably at these sacrifices to Satan. This fascinating sequence anticipates by a dozen years the celebrated journey of Josette Day through the chateau in Cocteau's *La Belle et la Bête* (France, 1946), but without resort to the artifice of slow-motion. Such curious but poetic scenes, needless to say, annoyed many critics and patrons.

Music is as important to the mood of *The Black Cat* as are dialogue, settings and camerawork. Heinz Roemheld's score is one of the most elaborate to be composed during the 1930s, a far cry from the "loud silences" of 1931's *Dracula* and *Frankenstein* and more sophisticated than the effective music for *The Mummy* and *The Invisible Man* of

The Black Cat - *Poelzig's interest in Joan (Jacqueline Wells) isn't entirely spiritual.*

1933. In recent years, Roemheld has termed it the most difficult of his works.

The main title is accompanied by a free orchestral adaptation of the opening to Liszt's "Piano Sonata in B Minor," followed by a sensuously beautiful original theme, "Cat Love," which was inspired by Roemheld's idolization of Tschaikowski. Early in the film Karloff turns a dial and the house is flooded with the strains of Schubert's *Symphony No. 8* which underscores the scene in which Lugosi betrays his fear of cats. Excerpts from other classical works are similarly woven into the fabric, but the score is not at all like the pastiches used by cue-sheet arrangers as accompaniment for silent pictures; rather, it is a superbly unified fantasia upon classical and original themes.

The appropriately melodramatic music of Liszt predominates, with portions of the *Sonata in B Minor, Les Preludes, Rakoczy March, Tasso,* and the *Hungarian Rhapsody No. 3.* The second movement of Beethoven's *Seventh Symphony* forms an ominous accompaniment to a speech by Karloff. Dramatic use is made of a Chopin prelude, Brahms' *Sapphic Ode,* and Schumann's *Piano Quintet.* Bach's *Doric Toccata* and *Adagio in A Minor* are played on-screen by "organists" Karloff and John Carradine as celebrants gather for the Black Mass. Interwoven with the music of the old masters are seven variations on *Cat Love* ("Scream," "Neutral," "Foreboding," "Suspense," "Crawl," "Interlude," and "Threat") as well as fourteen other compositions bearing such manuscript titles as "Hungarian Train," "Fantasy," "Introduction and Religioso," "Karloff," and "Hungarian Burlesque." Much of this music gained popularity in the *Flash Gordon* serials in later years; "Cat Love" is particularly remembered as Queen Azura's theme in *Flash Gordon's Trip to Mars* (1938) and continually is confused with Tschaikowski's overture to "Romeo and Juliet."

Grim as it is, the picture has some leavening of humor. The best such bit is provided by two comical gendarmes played by Albert Conti and Henry Armetta. Manners and Wells, at another point, play upon the pronunciation of Karloff's character's name to good, light effect.

Viennese-born Edgar George Ulmer was educated at the Academy of Arts & Sciences of that city, then went to Berlin to study for his M. Ph. degree. By the time he was eighteen, he had sufficient experience as an actor and set designer for stage productions to be given an art director's berth at Decla-Bioscop. He was production assistant to two of Germany's most celebrated directors, Paul Wegener and F. W. Murnau. He also worked on several of Max Reinhardt's stage spectacles, coming to America with Reinhardt in 1923. During the next ten years he designed sets for Universal, Fox, MGM, Ufa in Berlin, and the Philadelphia Grand Opera Company. Again he worked with Murnau, this time at Fox.

Like von Stroheim, Ulmer was often at loggerheads with studio bosses, and consequently most of his pictures were made cheaply for independent companies. He even made a sex hygiene film, Polish and Yiddish dialogue films, and "all-Negro" pictures for very limited markets during the 1930s, but occasionally he was able to tinker with respectable budgets on such visually rich projects as *The Strange Woman* (1946), *Carnegie Hall* (1947), and *Ruthless* (1948). Some of his most intriguing work occurred late in life (Ulmer died September 30, 1972), including a color remake of *L'Atlantide* (1961) and—his last production—the unusual italian film, *The Cavern.*

Quite a cult following has developed around Ulmer, largely on the basis of the uneven but often artistic pictures he made cheaply for PRC during the middle 1940s such as *Bluebeard* (1944) and *Detour* (1946). As a result, the maligned *Black Cat* has received belated recognition as the remarkable work it is.

The Black Cat - *Poelzig and Karen (Lucille Lund).*

The Love Captive

1934 Universal Pictures Corporation
Presented by Carl Laemmle
Director: Max Marcin
Producer: Carl Laemmle, Jr.
Associate Producer: E. M. Asher
Associate Director: Edward Dan Venturini
Based on the Max Marcin play *The Humbug*
Dialogue and Continuity: Karen DeWolf
Photography: Gilbert Warrenton
Director: Charles D. Hall
Film Editor: Ted Kent
Special Effects: John P. Fulton
Musical Score: Bernhard Kaun, Howard Jackson, Sam A. Perry, and Cecil Arnold
Set Decorations: R. A. Gausman
Make-up: Jack P. Pierce
Running Time: 65 minutes

Cast: Nils Asther (Dr. Alexis Collender), Gloria Stuart (Alice Trask), Paul Kelly (Dr. Norman Ware), Alan Dinehart (Roger Loft), Renée Gadd (Valerie Loft), Virginia Kami (Mary Williams), Russ Brown (Larry Chapman), Addison Richards (Dr. Collins), John Wray (Jules Glass), Robert Grieg (Butler), Jane Meredith (Mrs. Fordyce), Ellalee Ruby (Annie Nolan), Franklyn Ardell (Peter Nolan), Sam Godfrey (Dr. Blake), Demetrius Alexis (Dr. Freund)

Synopsis: Dr. Alexis Collender, a smooth but unscrupulous hypnotist, maintains a shabby office in a large American city. Through his strange powers, Collender influences his office nurse, Alice Trask, to break her engagement to Dr. Norman Ware and move in with Collender. When a reporter, Larry Chapman, publicizes Collender's work in treating ailments through hypnosis, Collender becomes sufficiently well known to move into luxurious quarters. Ware wants to kill the charlatan but is dissuaded by his lawyer, Roger Loft. Ware does, however, prompt charges against Collender by the County Medical Society, alleging unethical practices. Ware finds Mary Williams, a former victim of the hypnotist, who promises to testify. Collender is able to bring the girl once more under his power, though, and she retracts her statements against him.

Alice tells Collender the Medical Society is meeting at Loft's mansion. Collender

Virtually forgotten, even by aficionados of the Universal chillers, is an oddity entitled *The Love Captive*. This variation on *Svengali* deals effectively in weirdness without making use of any of the expected dark shadings. Even as a new release, the picture failed to attract much attention—the moviegoers' loss, for it is a creditable "perfect crime" yarn with a satisfying surprise ending.

Max Marcin, onetime New York newspaperman and magazine writer, came to Hollywood during the early talkie craze after creating a string of successful Broadway plays including *House of Glass, Cheating Cheaters, See My Lawyer, Three Live Ghosts, The Woman in Room 13, Silence,* and *The Humbug,*

all of which were purchased by various movie firms. In the course of adapting some of his own works to the screen, Marcin ventured into directing, making several features for Paramount. Early in 1934, he was brought to Universal to direct an adaptation of *The Humbug*.

Marcin avoided Gothic trappings and frightful make-ups in this well-mounted production, which was filmed during April and May

The Love Captive - Loft (Alan Dinehart) obeys Collender's command to aim the revolver. Renee Gadd is in the foreground. Among the witnesses are Glass (John Wray, standing, left), Dr. Colllns (Addison Richards) and E. Allyn Warren.

demands that he be allowed to demonstrate his power via an experiment in which a person under his influence cannot fire a hair-trigger pistol. Barred from the meeting, Collender wanders into the garden, where he meets Loft's beautiful young wife, Valerie. He places her in a hypnotized state in which she is willing to give herself to him. When she returns to the house, both Loft and Ware discern that Valerie has fallen under a strange influence.

Ware forces Collender to release Alice. The hypnotist already has determined to rid himself of Alice and secure Valerie instead. Valerie becomes increasingly restless when kept away from Collender. Loft decides the hypnotist must be destroyed. At last Collender is granted a hearing to display his power. In the hospital amphitheatre, Loft volunteers himself as a subject for the revolver experiment. Collender stares into Loft's eyes and makes the gestures that have placed others under his sway. "You will try to shoot me but will be unable to do so," he says. Loft aims at Collender's heart and squeezes the trigger. The hypnotist is killed, and the lawyer is exonerated of any crime.

with the assistance of movie veteran Edward Venturini. Marcin meant to give the picture a sophisticated, up-to-date look with a glamorous villain, lavish settings, clever dialogue, and characters from the upper crust of big-city society. Much of the action takes place in a palatial mansion; the climactic scenes are enacted in a hospital amphitheatre where hundreds of scientists have gathered. Gil Warrenton, former cinematographer to the German master Paul Leni, lighted most of the scenes in a sparkling style usually reserved for the best romantic dramas.

Nils Asther, a darkly handsome Swede who specialized in portrayals of Valentino-like romantic heroes, was chosen to be the sinister mesmerist. Marcin even had Asther shave off his well-known moustache so he would have none of the trademarks of the typical movie villain. The actor's almost Asiatic eyes, shown in closeup during the scenes involving hypnosis, are Marcin's only concession to "horror" atmosphere. Alan Dinehart and Paul Kelly are dynamic enough to bring more than the usual color to the "straight" roles. Gloria Stuart, the near-perfect ingénue, and Renée Gadd, an English musical-comedy star, are charming and sympathetic as innocent victims. Marcin, needless to say, was horrified when the New York office, at the last moment, changed the release title to *The Love Captive*.

The Love Captive - *Nils Asther as the charming but dangerous Dr. Alexis Collender.*

The Man with Two Faces

1934   Warner Bros. Pictures, Incorporated
A First National and Vitaphone Production
As Produced by Sam H. Harris Theatrical
Enterprises, Incorporated
Director: Archie Mayo
Based on the play *Dark Tower*, by George S.
Kaufman and Alexander Woolcott
Screenplay: Tom Reed and Niven Busch
Photography: Tony Guadio
Film Editor: William Holmes
Art Director: John Hughes
Music: The Vitaphone Orchestra
Conductor: Leo F. Forbstein
Musical Score: Leo F. Forbstein
Songs: *Stormy Weather*, Ted Koehler and
Harold Arlen; *Am I Blue*, Harry Akst
Make-up: Perc Westmore
Special Effects: Fred Jackman
Sound Effects: Hal R. Shaw
Running Time: 72 minutes.

Cast: Edward G. Robinson (Damon Wells),
Mary Astor (Jessica Vance), Ricardo Cortez
(Weston), Mae Clarke (Daphne), Louis
Calhern (Stanley Vance), Arthur Byron (Dr.
Kendall), John Eldredge (Barry), David
Landau (Curtis), Emily Fitzroy (Hattie), Henry
O'Neill (Inspector), Arthur Aylesworth
(Morgue Keeper), Margaret Dale (Martha),
Virginia Sale (Peabody), Wade Boteler
(Detective), Guy Usher (Weeks), Joseph
Crehan (Editor), Dorothy Tree (Patsy), Mary
Russell (Debutante), Milton Kibbee (Rewrite
Man), Howard Hickman (Jones), Maude
Turner Gordon (Mrs. Jones), Frank Darien
(Doorman), Douglas Cosgrove (Lieutenant),
Ray Cooke (Bellhop), Dick Winslow (Call
Boy), Bert Moorhouse (Driver), Mrs. Wilfred
North (Society Matron), also Leni Stengel,
Harry Tyler and Barbara Blair

Synopsis: Scion of a celebrated theatrical
family, Damon Wells is the most brilliant
director-actor of the Broadway stage and his
beautiful sister, Jessica Vance, is one of the
theater's brightest stars. Having recovered
from a mental and physical breakdown,
Jessica is about to return to Broadway in a
new play, *Dark Tower*, which is being directed by Damon and produced by her lover,
Weston. Questioning Jessica's Aunt Martha,
Weston receives confirmation of his suspi-

A faithful adaptation of *Dark Tower*, a recent play by two of Broadway's favorite "characters," Alexander Woolcott and George S. Kaufman, was filmed during April and May 1934. Before release the title was changed to *The Man With Two Faces* which, along with advertisements and ballyhoo about Edward G. Robinson's dual role, tipped off the audience to a mystery angle which the play and the film's script saved until last. The picture sur-mounts such gaucherie, though, and it remains one of the better—although lesser known—examples of the *Svengali* theme. Dialogue, most of it retained from the play, sparkles with wit despite the grim-ness, and the theatrical background is well realized. It was an open secret that the authors based the characters upon certain real per-sonalities of the New York theatre scene, although no attempt is made in the film to retain the physical characteristics of the life-models.

Robinson dominates with forceful performances as the actor and his French-accented alter ego (done on Broadway by Basil Sidney). Make-up artist Perc Westmore transformed the star into M. Chautard by utilizing a false nose, blond hair, moustache and goatee,

cions that Jessica's illness was caused by her husband, Stanley Vance, who maintained a mesmeric influence over her.

And now Vance returns, cheerfully admitting that he has been in San Quentin for a crime committed under another name. Jessica lapses into decline under his baleful influence, going about in a trance and seemingly without emotion. Weston bests Vance in a fight but is unable to persuade Jessica to leave. The family doctor, Kendall, is no less frustrated.

M. Chautard, purportedly a wealthy theatrical producer from France, calls Vance to say he is interested in purchasing Jessica's interest in foreign motion picture rights for her current play. Chautard also makes it plain that he is enchanted personally with Jessica. Vance takes Jessica to Chautard's hotel suite. Chautard leaves no question that he wants something more than Jessica's theatrical interests. For the right price, Vance is willing to sell both her rights and her honor. Chautard suggests that the deal can best be consummated "between gentlemen" and that Jessica might prefer to return home. After they are alone, Chautard kills Vance—poisons him, then watches the man's death agonies with great pleasure. Jessica arrives home in an incoherent state. Later, the body of Vance is discovered in the closet of Chautard's suite.

Chautard has disappeared. The killer seems to have left no clues. All the police except the Inspector give up in bafflement. The Inspector makes a thorough investigation of Vance's past, learning that under other names he had been involved in numerous criminal endeavors includ-

ing the murder of a previous wife for her money. The Inspector also is intrigued by the memory of having seen a character in a play some years earlier—a character who fits the description of the vanished Chautard. The Inspector haunts the theatre where Damon Wells is appearing.

One night in Wells' dressing room, the Inspector hands the actor a blond moustache. He found it, he explains, in the Gideon Bible in the room where Vance was murdered. The crime is reenacted: Wells created and posed as Chautard, lured Vance to the suite, and killed him to save Jessica; only Weston knows the truth. Wells asks if he can have his moustache back, and the Inspector tells him he cannot because it is evidence. After tonight's performance, Wells is advised, it will be necessary for him to accompany the Inspector to headquarters. His friend, the district attorney, the Inspector says, is a very understanding man. Jessica again rises to new success and finds personal happiness with Weston.

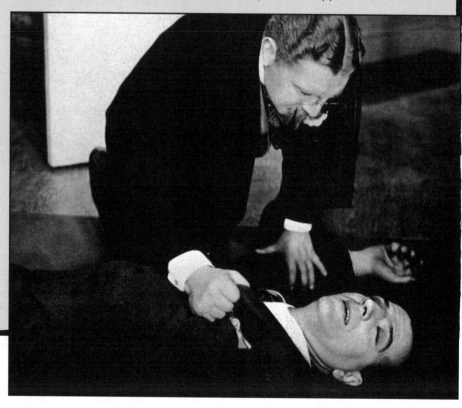

The Man With Two Faces - *Vance receives a well-deserved reward.*

teeth caps, and pince-nez glasses. Somehow he made Robinson's eliptical eyes appear round and the sharply arched eyebrows seem bland. Mary Astor is equally adept as the Trilby of the piece. The tall, high-nosed Louis Calhern makes Vance a rat-like and completely despicable character, deserving of a description given by one of the other characters, "the lowest form of animal life." As if to illustrate the point, Calhern is shown as being fond of a pair of mice he befriended in prison and now keeps in a cage but as regarding his fellow humans with an arrogance that inspires dislike at once.

(A servant takes scornful notice of the mice and remarks to Calhern, "I'd like to know when the three of you are leaving." Calhern replies with mincing malevolence, "If you hurt these mice, I shall have the extreme pleasure of knocking you down and kicking your brains out.")

In numerous other scenes we are given ample reason to agree that

Calhern should be exterminated. "Did you ever see a snake with a bird, Mr. Weston?" Martha asks Jessica's fiancée. "That was Jessica and Stanley Vance. Horrible! Of course you know the night she collapsed was the night he left. But this is something you might not know: the day she learned he had been shot dead in San Francisco was the day her mind began to heal." "The doctors who really understood these cases are all dead," the family doctor explains. "They died in the Middle Ages. They would have said that she was possessed, and they would have been right, perhaps. Whoever would rid the earth of Stanley Vance would be doing a public service."

Henry O'Neil is convincing as the theatre-loving detective. The other players—such notables as Mae Clarke, Ricardo Cortez, and Arthur Byron—perform lesser roles with skill. Archie Mayo, director of the superbly Gothic *Svengali* does an equally good job here of presenting a similar idea in a modern, glamorous setting. The scenes of

theatrical life, both on and off stage, have realism and depth, in marked contrast to the depictions seen in the many backstage musicals filmed on the same Warners sets. Tony Guadio's manipulation of lights and camera angles is vital to the tone of sophistication combined with the sinister.

The picture originally ended differently from the released version. It had to be reshot to meet the restrictions of the newly strengthened Production Code. In the original version, after the Inspector confronts Wells with the telltale moustache, Wells is certain he will be jailed for murder, but the Inspector

merely advises him to be more careful henceforth about where he leaves things. The world is better off without Vance, the Inspector muses, and as far as he is concerned the case is unsolved.

In 1939, the same studio scheduled a new version from a script by Anthony Coldewey, projecting Claude Rains and Boris Karloff for the Robinson and Calhern roles. It was aborted because of Production Code objections. Later it was passed on to Warners' British company, which produced it in 1943 as *Dark Tower* with Ben Lyon and Herbert Lom, this time in a circus setting.

The Man With Two Faces - *The sympathetic characters of* The Man With Two Faces: *Ben Weston (Ricardo Cortez), Martha Temple (Margaret Dale), Dr. Kendall (Arthur Byron), Daphne Martin (Mae Clarke), Damon Wells (Edward G. Robinson), Barry Jones (John Eldredge), Jessica Wells (Mary Astor) and Hattie (Emily Fitzroy).*

Smoking Guns

1934   Ken Maynard Productions, Inc.
Universal Pictures Corp.
Director: Alan James
Producer: Ken Maynard
Supervisor: Henry Henigson
Original Story: Ken Maynard
Screenplay and Dialogue: Nate Gatzert
Photography: Ted McCord
Art Director: Ralph Berger
Sound Supervisor: Earl Crane
Editor: Charles Harris
Properties: Tom Summerville
Musical Score: Louis de Francesco, Sam A. Perry, Heinz Roemheld and David Broekman
Titles: Max Cohen
Second Unit Photographer: Ken Maynard
Sound System: RCA Photophone
Running Time: 65 minutes

Cast: Ken Maynard (Ken Masters), Gloria Shea (Alice Adams), Walter Miller (Dick Logan), Harold Goodwin (Hank Stone), William Gould (Silas Stone), Bob Kortman (Bill), Jack Rockwell (Captain Adams), Ed Coxen (Bob Masters), Charles "Slim" Whitaker (Slim), Martin Turner (Cinders), Etta McDaniel (Clementine), Wally Wales, Frank S. Hagney, Ben Corbett, Edmund Cobb, Cliff Lyons, Cliff Smith, Fred McKaye, Bill Stone, Charles Murphy, Ted Billings, Jim Corey, Hank Bell, Bob Reeves, Blackjack Ward, Cliff Lyons, Dick Dickenson, Musicians: Ken Maynard's Buckaroos

Synopsis: Ken Masters secretly returns to the home town he left as a youth to accuse Silas Stone of framing Ken's father into prison on a murder charge. A fight ensues and Silas's son, Hank, in attempting to hit Ken with a chunk of ore, kills Silas. Texas Rangers arrive and arrest Ken for the murder, but Ken escapes.

Three years later, in Yucatan, Ranger Dick Logan tracks Ken down in the swamp where he has hidden. Ken surrenders willingly, for he has decided to go back to try to clear his name and that of his father. Logan collapses with malaria. Ken carries the ranger to his boat and they begin the trip upriver. The boat is capsized by alligators, one of which mangles Logan's leg. Ken rescues his captor and takes him to an abandoned cabin.

Imagine a Western in which most of the action occurs on Halloween night in a haunted house replete with hidden panels and portraits with peep-hole eyes. Add a spooky graveyard, a lost mine, a jungle manhunt, malaria, alligators, murder, suicide, insanity, amnesia, mistaken identity and black superstition. Mix in some standard Western ingredients—brawls, chases, gunfights and Texas Rangers—and you'll have some idea what *Smoking Guns* is like.

This weirdest horse opera of 1934—or, perhaps, any other year—stars Ken Maynard in a story by Maynard produced by Ken Maynard Productions, Inc. The credit titles don't mention that Maynard also did the second unit photography (in Yucatan, whence he flew in his own airplane), and arranged the music performed for a dance sequence by a band he organized, The Buckaroos. Had the situation demanded it, he also could have composed the theme music and done the singing and fiddle playing, as he had in some of his earlier films. He didn't direct—his associate, Alan James, did—but *Smoking Guns* is as intensely personal a film as anything by Chaplin or Von Stroheim—and just as eccentric.

Remarkably, this venture into Texas Gothic manages to supply the traditional slam-bang action demanded by Western fans. The fights and chases resulted in a broken foot and lacerations for Harold Goodwin, two missing teeth for Eddie Cobb, a black eye for Cliff Lyons, a lost thumb-tip for Tom Summerville and multiple injuries for Benny Corbett. Maynard displays some of his brilliant stunt riding and rope climbing. It's probable, however, that the youngsters who made up a large portion of Maynard's audience were puzzled by the gag in which black comedian Martin Turner recovers his lost

Gangrene sets in and Ken, explaining that "In the three years I was on the dodge I learned a lot of things—I lived among strange people," prepares to perform an emergency amputation. Logan commits suicide, leaving a note to be delivered to Alice Adams, daughter of Logan's boss, Captain Adams.

On Halloween, Ken returns to town clean-shaven and with his blond hair dyed black. He passes himself off as Logan, to whom he bears a marked resemblance. He manages to fool everybody except Alice and Hank Stone. Ken gives to Alice a note from Logan in which the ranger declares his belief in Ken's innocence. Hank, who is in love with Alice, orders his benchmen to kill Ken on the night of the Halloween barn dance. During the party Adams's servant, Cinders, takes his girl friend, Clementine, to the graveyard to spoon. Nearby, on the balcony of the reputedly haunted Masters house, appears the "ghost" of Ken's father, who supposedly died in prison years ago.

Ken and Cinders hurry back to the old house. They have a harrowing time eluding "ghosts" (Stone's men). Meantime, Alice overhears Stone arranging for his men to ambush Ken. She tells her father, who rounds up his rangers. Actually, the "ghost" of Bob Masters is the man himself, his mind a blank because of his experiences at the hands of Stone and his men. One of the heavies beats the old man; when Masters awakens, his mind has cleared. He is found by Ken and Cinders, who now learn the reason for Stone's actions: a rich gold mine lies under the house. Stone and his men surround the place and begin shooting. Adams and the rangers arrive in time to save the trapped men and round up the heavies. Stone, seizing Alice as hostage, escapes in a buckboard. Ken pursues on Tarzan, snatching Alice to safety before resuming the chase. Leaping into the wagon, he fights Stone until the vehicle breaks free and plunges over a cliff. The fight continues until the rangers arrive and take charge of the badly beaten Stone. His name cleared, Ken asks Alice to be his wife.

rabbit's foot from inside his buxom girlfriend's dress, as well as the ending wherein Ken makes love to *his* bosomy sweetheart in a wagon bed instead of riding away on his famed palomino, Tarzan. Also not for the kids are the ravings of the crazed ranger when he realizes he has gangrene (". . . rotting like carrion in the sun! Eating its way up, up, up! . . . To lay here and die by inches, to rot away like something unclean . . .")

Smoking Guns - *Ken rescues his captor from a giant alligator.*

Smoking Guns - *Ken fights one "ghost" (Slim Whitaker) while another (Ed Coxen) menaces from a secret panel.*

Maynard's productions invariably cost more than the studio wanted to spend. This sixteenth and last of his pictures for Universal, which was made under the title *Doomed To Die,* went well past the three-week shooting schedule and costs soared beyond the $125,000 maximum budget. Carl Laemmle, Jr., studio chief and son of the president, considered the script outlandish—an opinion not entirely unjustified—and ordered parts of the film to be remade to conform to more conventional lines, thus triggering Maynard's infamous temper. Already seething because he suspected the Laemmles were planning to replace him with Buck Jones, Maynard gave Junior a tongue-lashing and left for Europe without altering the picture. Junior wanted to shelve the film but couldn't because it had been pre-sold. It was previewed in April, 1934, as *Doomed To Die* but was recalled and finally released two months later under its final title. Maynard was through at Universal and the most popular Western series of the early thirties came to an end. His later films for Columbia and other companies were not produced by him and are but pale shadows of his Universals.

Maynard was a unique star with a fanatical following. At Universal he received from $40,000 to $60,000 per picture plus a hefty percentage. Whatever his shortcomings as an actor and however illogical his story sense, his films were so non-formula and so permeated with his zest for living as to stand apart.

This delightfully outrageous show, which is sometimes castigated by modern writers, was very popular. It has beautiful photography by Ted McCord, good settings by Ralph Berger and some spirited, authentic Western (not Country-Western) music. The dramatic scoring is that of a weird mystery film rather than that of the usual Western.

Maynard's scenes of real gators in Yucatan are interspersed with backlot action involving some scary but definitely bogus saurians left over from *East of Borneo* (1931). Interiors and outdoor scenes in the swamp, the town, the graveyard and the old house were made at the studio. The climactic chase and fight were photographed on Dark Canyon Road, in the mountains just southeast of the backlot.

Gloria Shea is a lovely heroine and there are colorful performances from Walter Miller (Pathé's former serial star), Harold Goodwin, Bob Kortman, Jack Rockwell, Martin Turner, Etta MacDaniels and the stock company of horse opera heavies. Tarzan, as always, is magnificent.

The Man Who Reclaimed His Head

1934   Universal Pictures Corporation
Director: Edward Ludwig
Prouder: Carl Laemmle, Jr.
Associate Producer: Henry Henigson
Screenplay: Jean Bart and Samuel Ornitz
Based on the play by Jean Bart
Director of Photography: Merritt Gerstad
Musical Director: Heinz Roemheld
Art Director: Albert S. D'Agostino
Film Editor: Murray Seldeen
Supervising Film Editor: Maurice Pivar
Special Effects: John P. Fulton
Assistant Directors: W. J. Reiter and Fred Frank
Set Decorations: R. A. Gausman
Matte Art: Jack Cosgrove and Russell Lawson
Music Recording: Lawrence Aicholtz
Sound System: Western Electric
Running Time: 82 minutes

Cast: Claude Rains (Paul Verin), Joan Bennett (Adele Verin), Lionel Atwill (Henri Dumont), Baby Jane Quigley (Linette Verin), Henry O'Neill (de Marnay), Wallace Ford (Curly), Lawrence Grant (Marchand), William B. Davidson (Charlus), Henry Armetta (Laurent), Gilbert Emery (Excellency), Hugh O'Connell (Danglas), Rollo Lloyd (Jean), Bessie Barriscale (Louise), Ferdinand Gottschalk (Baron), Lloyd Hughes (André), Noel Francis (Chon-Chon), Valerie Hobson (Mimi), Lois January (Girl), Carol Coombe (Clerk), Doris Lloyd (Baroness), Edward Van Sloan, Walter Walker, Crawford Kent (Magnates), Emerson Treacy (Peace Speaker), Ted Billings (Newsboy), Boyd Irwin (Steward), George Davis (Private), Russ Powell (Railway Conductor), Harry Cording (Burly Man), G. P. Huntley, Jr. (Pierre), William Ruhl (Angry Man), Charles Meacham (Older Man), Phyllis Brooks, C. Montague Shaw, Purnell Pratt, Crauford Kent, Jameson Thomas, Judith Wood, John Ince, James Donlan, Anderson Lawler, Bryant Washburn, Will Stanton, Lionel Belmore, Wilfred North, Margaret Mann, John Rutherford, Grace Cunard, Nell Craig, William Worthington, Rudy Cameron, Hyram Hoover, Lee Phelps, Norman Ainslee, Harry Cording, Lilyan Irene, Rolfe Sedan, Ben F. Hendricks, Maurice Murphy, William Gould,

Having completed his first film, *The Invisible Man* (1933), Claude Rains returned to New York for the filming of *Crime Without Passion*. He was summoned back to Universal in September of 1934 and contracted to do two pictures, *The Man Who Reclaimed His Head* and *The Return of Frankenstein*. Rains and Jean Arthur had starred on Broadway in the first, an antiwar play by Jean Bart (Marie Antoinette Sarlabous), produced in 1932. Lowell Sherman was supposed to direct the film version, but a respiratory ailment necessitated his replacement. Sherman died of pneumonia in December while working on the first three-color Technicolor feature, *Becky Sharp* (1934).

The Man Who Reclaimed His Head was filmed in September and October under the direction of Russian-born Edward Ludwig. Substantial production values were applied to the film, which the Laemmles hoped would match the appeal of their previous pacifist epic, *All Quiet on the Western Front* (1930). Miss Bart and Sam Ornitz wrote the screenplay. This sobering drama was quite a change for Ludwig, whose specialty had been comedy with such high points as *They Just Had To Get Married* (1932) and *Friends of Mr. Sweeney* (1934). Throughout a long career Ludwig handled many comedies, but he also was associated with mysteries (*Fatal Lady*, 1935), musicals (*Old Man Rhythm*, 1935), John Wayne vehicles (*Wake of the Red Witch*, 1948), and science fiction (*The Black Scorpion*, 1957)

Direction and photography of *The Man Who . . .* are unusual for their avoidance of the clichés of both horror and war cinema. Even such grand-manner performers as Rains and Lionel Atwill give restrained, subtle portrayals. The night scenes of Paris blanketed in

Carl Stockdale, Ted Billings, Tom Ricketts, Josef Swickard, William West, Colin Kenney and Russ Clark

Synopsis: Air raid sirens herald German bombers over Paris on a snowy night in 1915. As bombs rain and the populace seeks shelter, a single light gleams from the upper window of an isolated villa. There is a sound of breaking glass followed by a woman's scream. A moment later, French Corporal Paul Verin emerges from the house carrying his child, Linette, and a bulky valise. He hurries through the empty streets to the home of Fernande de Marnay, a lawyer, who perceives that his old school friend is highly agitated. As Verin stammers out his story, de Marnay notes he clutches the valise protectively. "I was shy; it's been my curse," Verin says. "You were the only one who was kind to me, respected me."

"Come, come, you had a brilliant mind," de Marnay tells him. "What have you done with it?"

"What have I done with it?" Verin cries. He opens the valise. De Marnay blanches in horror. Verin babbles meaninglessly, then calms himself and tells his story.

A flashback takes us to the year preceding war. In a poor suburb of Paris, Verin and his young wife, Adele, are celebrating their fifth wedding anniversary. An idealistic writer, Verin hopes to prove the futility of war by educating children in the ways of peace. "Give me a child's mind for the first twelve years of its life," he says, "and I'll sweep war from the earth." Adele longs only for wealth and excitement.

Henry Dumont, a charismatic author and publisher, urges Verin to work for him. "I lack the one thing you have: your mind. Give me that, Verin. I'll pay you for it!" Failing to convince Verin, he charms Adele. At his wife's urging, Verin agrees to "ghost" Dumont's articles.

Verin's writing makes Dumont the hero of the hour, admired the world over for his work for peace. On the street someone tells Verin he should be more like Dumont, who "has a real head on his shoulders." Verin finds a measure of contentment in Adele's happiness, in his new financial security, and in the fact that at last he is being read—even though Dumont takes the credit.

Munitions magnates, through threats and promises of wealth to Dumont, coerce a revision of his policy. When Archduke Ferdinand is assassinated, Verin writes a pacifist plea which Dumont rewrites as a pro-war tract. Verin quits his job and writes an exposé of the munitions trust's guilt in fomenting war, but Dumont has it suppressed.

In order to pursue Adele, Dumont has Verin drafted into the Army and sent to the front. The frustration unhinges Verin's mind; he deserts and boards a train to Paris. He finds Adele, who has had a reversal of feeling, fighting off Dumont's advances.

"My wife was not included in our bargain, Dumont," the crazed Verin snarls, drawing his bayonet as he approaches. The blade flashes, the window is shattered, and Verin works grimly in the darkness. Adele screams and faints. The flashback has come full-circle.

"I felt that I was Dumont," Verin tells de Marnay. "I wanted back what was me, what was mine, that was all." He gestures meaningfully to the valise. The police arrive, summoned by a servant. So does Adele, who begs her husband's forgiveness.

"You are not the accused, you're the accuser," de Marnay tells Verin after assuring him he will do everything possible to help the reunited family.

The Man Who Reclaimed His Head - *A smirking secondary villain, Marchand (Lawrence Grant).*

snow are more beautiful than ominous. The framing sequence is strange but not gruesome; the lawyer's home is lighted by candles—that is, cameraman Merritt Gerstad made it appear so—which cast giant, flickering shadows. Rains's closeups in the climactic murder scenes are not handled in a violent style but in the manner of glamour portraits, with diffusion and soft lighting. The effect is stunning.

Heinz Roemheld's very European-styled music is similarly restrained, with none of the expected "stings" or crescendoes usual in highly dramatic subjects.

There are several large-scale crowd scenes, including a Bastille Day celebration in which hordes of costumed extras appear. A sequence in which Atwill and Joan Bennett watch a performance of *Tristan und Isolde*, filmed

on the set built in 1924 for *The Phantom of the Opera*, also employs a large number of dress extras on stage and in the audience. The unusual handling of the film suggests that the director, whom historians have ignored, should be given a closer look.

The pacifist message, although laid on too thickly, is more subtle by far than in the Broadway version. The propaganda includes an interesting prophecy. When Lawrence Grant twists logic to sway Atwill, he says: "Sometimes I think I'm a better pacifist than you. If we could release the energy in one atom, two armies could destroy each other in an instant. Then we would have seen our last war."

The use of the ominous valise containing the severed head looks ahead to a celebrated play and film, Emyln Williams' *Night Must Fall*— the M G M version of which appeared two years later. Universal tried two advertising angles, one emphasizing the antiwar aspect, the other touting a horror picture. Exhibitors, aware that Depression-era audiences would reject anything as solemn as a pacifist tract, opted for the latter. The horror fans, expecting a sequel to *The Invisible Man* were disappointed. When Realart Pictures brought out the reissue in 1949, an all-out horror campaign was used, alienating a new generation. Now, on television, the picture fares somewhat better because audiences are more tolerant of "problem plays," but it has never been popular.

The property was remade in 1945 as *Strange Confession* with Lon Chaney, Jr. wielding a machete to reclaim his head from J. Carroll Naish. This, too, was reissued by Realart with a blood-and-horror campaign and a new title: *The Missing Head!*

The Man Who Reclaimed His Head - *A corporal (George Davis) challenges Verin, who has deserted to seek vengeance.*

The Mystery of Edwin Drood

1935 Universal Pictures Corporation
Presented by Carl Laemmle
An Edmund Grainger Production
Director: Stuart Walker
Producer: Carl Laemmle, Jr.
Based on the Charles Dickens novel
Screenplay: John L. Balderston and Gladys Unger
Adaptation: Leopold Atlas and Bradley King
Art Director: Albert S. D'Agostino
Photographer: George Robinson
Music: Edward Ward
Technical Advisor: Madame Hilda Grenier
Special Effects: John P. Fulton
Film Editor: Edward Curtiss
Make-up: Jack P. Pierce
Second Unit Director: David Bader
Matte Effects: Jack Cosgrove and Russell A. Lawson
Effects Cameraman: David S. Horsley
Piano Music: James Dietrich
Set Decorations: R. A. Gausman
Music Recorded by Lawrence Aicholtz
Assistant Directors: Phil Karlstein and Harry Mancke
Running Time: 86 minutes

Cast: Claude Rains (John Jasper), Douglass Montgomery (Neville Landless), Heather Angel (Rosa Bud), David Manners (Edwin Drood), Valerie Hobson (Helèna Landless), Francis L. Sullivan (Mr. Crisparkle), Walter Kingsford (Hiram Grewgious), E. E. Clive (Thomas Sapsea), Forrester Harvey (Durdles), Louise Carter (Mrs. Crisparkle), Ethel Griffies (Miss Twinkleton), Zeffie Tilbury (Opium Den Hag), Vera Buckland (Mrs. Tope),   Elsa Buchanan (Tisher), Georgie Ernest (Deputy), J. M. Kerrigan (Chief Verger Tope), Adele St. Maur (Cook), Anne O'Neal (Maid), Walter Brennan (Talkative Villager), Will Geer (Lamplighter), John Rogers, D'Arcy Corrigan and Harry Cording (Opium Smokers)

Synopsis: England, 1864. A handsome young couple is being married in the ancient cathedral at Cloisterham Village. The church spire dissolves into a bedpost, and it becomes evident that the wedding occurred only in the mind of John Jasper, who now awakens in a London opium den. On Sunday Jasper returns to work as choirmaster at Cloisterham. When

VANISHED into NOWHERE!

THE **MYSTERY** of EDWIN DROOD

Into thin air, before their very eyes, on the eve of his wedding! How could he have disappeared so magically? What strange power swished him away so strangely? For what mysterious reason?

CARL LAEMMLE PRESENTS
A UNIVERSAL PICTURE WITH
CLAUDE RAINS
DOUGLASS
MONTGOMERY
HEATHER ANGEL · DAVID MANNERS
FRANCIS L. SULLIVAN · VALERIE HOBSON
DIRECTED BY STUART WALKER
PRODUCED BY CARL LAEMMLE, JR.

2A

Early in 1934 Stuart Walker directed for Universal a commendable version of Dickens' *Great Expectations* with Henry Hull as Magwitch, a role first planned for Karloff. While the picture did poorly at the boxoffice—insiders joked that the elder Laemmle had decided not to pick up Dickens' option—Walker was given the go-ahead and a substantial budget to film Dickens' *Mystery of Edwin Drood*. A script by Leopold Atlas and Bradley King was completed in August 1934, but this was recalled for revision by John L. Balderston and later given further doctoring by Walker's sometime stage collaborator, Gladys Unger.

Because the original novel was left uncompleted by Dickens, it was necessary to devise an ending. More than 120 authors had published their opinions as to how Dickens would have resolved the mystery. Karloff had been slated to portray the opium-crazed Jasper and another English actor, Frank Lawton, was supposed to follow his role in James Whale's *One More River* with that of Jasper's rival, Landless. Script problems caused several postponements of the starting date, necessitating cast changes between early September, when production was scheduled to begin, and November 14, when shooting actually started. By then background scenes had been filmed in Rochester, England, by a second unit organized by David Bader of Universal's London office. Art director Albert S. D'Agostino had reshaped Universal's permanent European town to resemble Dickens's Cloisterham. He designed impressive sets for the old cathedral, using some elements of the cathedral built for the 1923 *Hunchback of Notre Dame*, and the underground crypt, which contained some details built for *The Phantom of the Opera* and *Dracula*.

Claude Rains, upon completing *The Man Who Reclaimed His Head*, was scheduled to portray Dr. Pretorius in *The Return of Frankenstein* (which became *Bride of . . .*). More juggling of schedules put Rains, not Karloff, in the role of Jasper. Douglass Montgomery replaced Lawton, who, curiously enough, had gone to MGM to act the title role in another adaptation from Dickens, *David Copperfield*. There were more delays as dozens of children were tested for the role of the tattered youngster, Deputy, who aids in solving the mystery. Georgie Ernest, later to become a perennial member of Twentieth Century-Fox's Jones Family series, was the eventual choice.

Madame Hilda Grenier, an authority on Victorian England and a close friend of the royal family, was engaged to assure authenticity of settings and performances. Under her supervision the strictness of Victorian manners is scrupulously observed throughout the picture.

Extra personnel were hired for the task of providing mid-Victorian wardrobes and character makeups for 488 cast members. Jack Pierce claimed that he and his staff used 2,200 pounds of crepe hair and greasepaint during the course of production. In making up young Montgomery as the ancient Datchery, Pierce made a white wig and beard of natural hair and transformed the actor's nose into an aquiline beak shaped of bone and collodion. For Rains he devised a subtle makeup to differentiate between the good and evil sides of Jasper's personality. For the evil side he made barely perceptible changes in the eyes, ears, nose and mouth. Sideburns were tapered to sharp points and false wisps were added to the hair over the inside edges of the ears. This, plus some of the Frankenstein Monster's gray-green paint, made the ears seem thinner and pointed. The eyebrows were brought closer together with an eyebrow pencil and the lips were painted down so that the mouth seems a thin slit.

Such aids from Pierce and

The Mystery of Edwin Drood - *A charming Dickensian gathering: Rosa Bud (Heather Angel), Neville Landless (Douglass Montgomery), Edwin Drood (David Manners), Mrs. Tope (Vera Buckland), John Jasper (Claude Rains), Crisparkle (Francis L. Sullivan), Maid (Anne O'Neal), Helena Landless (Valerie Hobson) and Mrs. Twinkleton (Ethel Gritfies).*

Grewgious, Rosa's guardian, gives Edwin a ring that belonged to Rosa's mother, who asked that it be "given from the grave" at Rosa's wedding. Edwin shows the ring to Rosa and tells her he will step aside because he is aware of her love for Neville and that he will give it to Neville at the proper time. Jasper, watching from a distance, is enraged to see Rosa's kiss of gratitude. That night, Jasper visits Durdles, the sexton and stonemason, and asks to be shown through the ancient Norman crypt under the cathedral. In the workshop Jasper notes a quantity of quicklime. He gives Durdles some liquor and, when Durdles falls asleep, makes a wax cast of the key to the crypt.

Jasper arranges a Christmas dinner for Edwin and Neville, ostensibly to help them patch up their differences. On his way to Jasper's home Edwin meets an old hag who has come from London to warn him that one Horridge, a customer at her opium den, has raved of his desire to strangle a "Ned." At Jasper's home Edwin and Landless shake hands in a vow of friendship. A great storm strikes, uprooting trees, breaking down streetlamps and flooding the river. Next morning Jasper reports that Edwin and Neville fought and went out into the storm together. Now Edwin has disappeared. Seen walking toward London, Neville is dragged back by a mob. He is accused of doing away with Edwin, but there is no evidence to prove it. Neville volunteers to lead a search of the river. That night, Edwin's watch is found in the water.

Driven near madness by drugs and conscience, Jasper collapses when he learns from Grewgious that Edwin and Rosa had decided not to marry. Rosa has quit her musical studies and Jasper pleads with her to return. When he tries to make love to her, Rosa flees to Neville. She explains that Edwin had freed her: "Edwin was going to give you the ring, my mother's ring. He took it with him to his death." Neville declares he must go away and not return until he can clear his name. Jasper insists that Neville's disappear-

ance is proof of his guilt and Mayor Sapsea orders that a search begin.

A bearded old man called Datchery comes to the village. Only Grewgious knows he is the disguised Neville. Grewgious has learned that Jasper is a drug addict and that he has made a key to the crypt. Jasper, meantime, returns to London.

"Over and over again, always in the same way, hundreds of thousands of times I've done it," Jasper cries as he dreams of killing and the hag listens. "It was pleasant to do. When it was finally done it seemed not worth the doing, it was done so soon . . . Rosa!" He grasps the crone's throat and almost strangles her before he wakens. The hag returns to Cloisterham and, seeing Jasper, identifies him to Datchery as the murderous Horridge. Leaving the woman in his rooms Datchery hurries to fetch Sapsea. They return to find the woman dead; Jasper, having seen her, had sneaked into the house during Datchery's absence. Sapsea decides the woman had fallen and struck her head, but Datchery discovers that she was bludgeoned with a poker.

Datchery that night gets Deputy, a ragamuffin who works at the churchyard, to take him to Durdles. They find that the quicklime has been stolen and that an ancient sarcophagus has been opened and resealed. Durdles hurries to summon Sapsea while Datchery attepts to pry the lid from the vault. Jasper, who has been watching from the shadows, attacks Datchery. In the ensuing fight Neville is unmasked. Sapsea and his men separate the two. The sarcophagus is opened to reveal the outlines of a body and a few bones in a bed of quicklime. The wedding ring carried by Edwin lies encrusted among the bones.

"Ned! What have I done?" Jasper cries as he flees to the church tower. The great bells toll. Shattered by remorse, Jasper says, "Rosa, the journey is made!" and leaps to his death. Later, the bells ring again—for the marriage of Rosa and Neville.

the costumers couple with the acting to provide all that could be desired from the principals, with Rains giving a superb account of the conscience-striken murderer, a very human but nonetheless frightening monster. He is properly evil when skulking among the shadows of the crypt or raving about his crime while in an opium stupor, yet entirely pitiable during his less murderous moments. Montgomery's passionate young man and bent old one are well conceived characters, the latter being unrecognizable in voice and appearance. David Manners is a bright and sympathetic Ned, Heather Angel a primly attractive Rosa, and Valerie Hobson an enchanting

Helèna.

The lesser characters are true to Dickens in every respect, particularly Francis L. Sullivan (who appeared in many movie versions of Dickens novels) as the lovable Septimus Crisparkle, Walter Kingsford as the gruff but kindly Grewgious, Forrester Harvey as a happily intoxicated Durdles, Georgie Ernest as the sharp Deputy, E. E. Clive as the pompous mayor, and Zeffie Tilbury (a most remarkable character woman, herself possessed of a Dickensian name) as the old harridan who runs the opium den and tries with tragic results to see justice done.

Walker and cinematographer

George Robinson managed the changing moods of the tale so well that one never is conscious of the confines of the studio. There are clever transitions—the cathedral spire of Rains's Freudian dream becomes a bedpost in the opium den as he wakens; a shot of Rains's legs as he leaves the den dissolves into a similar view of his legs as he enters a choir loft. The fateful gathering of characters on the night of the murder is shown outside the house, through a window. The storm itself is a marvelous piece of special effects work. There is atmosphere of a superior kind in the gloomy-night river search for the body of the missing man—torches flickering in the rain and vapors of

The Mystery of Edwin Drood - *Neville and Edwin eye each other balefully as Jasper schemes.*

breath puffing from the mouths of the searchers. Throughout, the eerieness is enhanced by Edward Ward's imposing score, consisting of no fewer than eighty-nine cues. It is highly effective during the storm sequence and the climactic moments in the cathedral. The score also utilizes selections from Handel, Haydn and Bossetti.

Stuart Walker was a curious, scholarly man in his mid-fifties who had long before earned fame for contributions to stage drama. Kentucky-born, he left his job with a creosoting company to attend the American Academy of Dramatic Arts in New York City. He soon found employment with David Belasco as an actor, reader, stage manager and director. In 1915 he went out on his own as playwright, actor and producer, designing and patenting a portable stage complete with lighting equipment which could be set up in

The Mystery of Edwin Drood -
In a vicious fight, Jasper unmasks Datchery as the missing Neville.

an hour. His company, Stuart Walker's Portmanteau Theatre, played in some seventy cities, performing plays written by Walker. One of these, *Six Who Pass While the Lentils Boil*. written in 1915, is one of the most often performed American one-act plays.

Walkers "X-Ray System" of stage lighting, utilizing special mirrors and a primary color process, was widely imitated. In 1918 he introduced the spotlight system, which became the most popular system of stage lighting. He operated a repertory company in Indianapolis for about ten years and another company in Cincinnati for eight years. His dramatizations of *Seventeen* and The Book of Job toured the country for years under his direction, and he gained widespread recognition for his productions of Lord Dunsany's fantastic and satirical plays

In 1930 he wrote several scripts for Columbia and then joined Paramount Publix as a producer-director. During the next three years he made several pictures, among them the war drama, *The Eagle and the Hawk* with Fredric March, Cary Grant, and Carole Lombard. He came to Universal in 1934 to direct the two Dickens films, which were followed by his celebrated *Werewolf of London*.

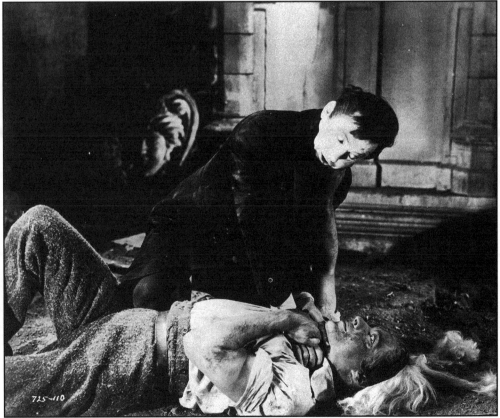

Mark of the Vampire

1935   Metro Goldwyn Mayer Film Corporation

Director: Tod Browning
Producer: Edward J. Mannix
Screenplay: Guy Endore and Bernard Schubert
From Tod Browning's *The Vampires of Prague*, reworked from his silent picture of 1927 *London After Midnight*, and his story *The Hypnotist* .
Recording Director: Douglas Shearer
Art Director: Cedric Gibbons
Associates: Harry Oliver and Edwin B. Willis
Gowns: Adrian
Director of Photography: James Wong Howe
Film Editor: Ben Lewis
Music: Edward Ward, Domenico Savino and Dr. William Axt
Organ Music: Price Dunlavy, Gypsy Songs arranged by Frank J. Virgil
Assistant Director: Harry Sharrock
Second Cameraman: Charles Salerno, Jr.
Photographic Effects: Warren Newcombe
Sound: G. A. Burns, S. J. Lambert, Ralph Pender, R. L. Stirling, Don Whitmer, James Graham, T. B. Hoffman, Mike Steinore and M. J. McLaughlin
Running Time: 80 minutes (at preview) 60 minutes (in release)

Cast: Lionel Barrymore (Zelen), Elizabeth Allan (Irena), Bela Lugosi (Count Mora), Lionel Atwill (Newmann), Jean Hersholt (Otto), Henry Wadsworth (Fedor), Donald Meek (Dr. Doskil), Jessie Ralph (Midwife), Ivan Simpson (Jan), Franklyn Ardell (Chauffeur), Leila Bennett (Maria), June Gittleson (Annie), Carol Borland (Luna), Holmes Herbert (Karell), Michael Visaroff (Innkeeper), James Bradbury, Jr. (Vampire), Egon Brecher (Coroner), Rosemary Goltz (Village Woman)

Synopsis: Fear grips the Czechoslovakian village of Visoka; the long-dead Count Mora and his daughter, Luna, are said to have risen from the depths of Borotyn Castle. The beloved Sir Karell Borotyn is found dead in his study at the castle—two punctures in his throat, his body drained of blood. Dr. Doskil,

This delightful sham showcases such production genius and bravado acting as to compensate somewhat for viewer outrage at being cheated of any supernatural horrors. This plot twist notwithstanding, *Mark of the Vampire* still delivers a proper (if caricatured) abundance of fearful atmosphere, particularly in a sequence where a village hag snags her clothing while fleeing from a bat in a graveyard, and in another where the vampire girl soars through the castle. Bela Lugosi's scowling countenance (seen here much as he appeared in *Dracula* [1931] with the addition of a bullet wound to one temple), views of the cavernous castle interiors, and a precipitous low-angle shot of a rushing carriage are genuinely unnerving. In the inevitable comparison with *Dracula*, *Mark of the Vampire* fares well; where the earlier film veered drastically from its opening aura of ancient evil, *Mark* holds throughout to a feeling of Old World rural superstition.

The premise of the killer's *modus operandi* requires more suspension of disbelief than any other element. The question of what Jean Hersholt did with all that blood catches one offguard, as does the abrupt realization that "the play's the thing"—that Lionel Atwill and Barrymore have resorted to an elaborate masquerade to confuse a murderer with his own smokescreen. The screenplay credited to Guy Endore and Bernard Schubert stems in fact from a scenario by director Tod Browning called *The Vampires of Prague*. This, in turn, is a reworking of Browning's Lon Chaney film, *London After Midnight* (1927), which was based upon Browning's story, "The Hypnotist"—an early example of the plot-to-unveil-a-plot theme popularized many years later in *Diabolique* (1955). (Endore, author of *The*

the local physician, blames vampires, but the official version is that some human fiend is responsible. Inspector Neumann of Prague holds to this account despite superstitious testimony from the locals, but a lack of clues stymies his investigation.

Sir Karell's daughter, Irena, becomes a house guest of the family confidant, Baron Otto. Her fiancé, Fedor, survives an attack near the now-deserted castle; Irena finds wounds about his throat. Apparitions of Mora and Luna are seen. When Irena is attacked, Professor Zelen is summoned; he insists vampires are responsible. Zelen declares Sir Karell has joined the undead—the body has disappeared from its tomb.

Zelen leads a search of the castle, proposing to behead the vampires before nightfall. Otto finds what he believes to be Sir Karell and starts to sever the head when Zelen stops him lest the others attack.

Irena seems to have succumbed to the vampires' will. She returns to the castle. Zelen hypnotizes Otto into reenacting the events of a year before—the night Sir Karell died. In the study, Irena sobs that she cannot carry on; the man Otto nearly beheaded, she says, resembles her father too closely. She rallies at the insistence of Neumann and Zelen.

Otto is shown in. The murder night is re-created, with Otto almost betraying his desire to marry Irena. Karell's medicine is dispensed; Otto secretly mixes a potion into it, then takes his leave. The proxy Sir Karell pretends to collapse. Otto steals back in, making ready to puncture his host's throat and "cup" the wounds—vacuum the blood with a heated glass. Neumann and company seize Otto, and Zelen breaks the hypnotic spell.

"Count Mora" and his colleagues are seen removing their make-up and packing to leave. The "Count" is waxing eloquent about his inspiration for a new stage routine: "This vampire business—it has given me a great idea . . . I will be greater than any *real* vampire!" His partners advise him to get to work with the loading.

Werewolf of Paris and *Babouk*. was an eccentric who startled the studio folk by going about even on the coldest days without shoes, only sandals.)

Browning, who had been called "the Edgar Allan Poe of the screen" since his silent pictures with Chaney, said in a press release that he relied upon vast settings to provide an unsettling framework because "dialogue and description could not produce such an effect. Attempts to describe the gnawing fear of a vampire cult would only weaken the idea"—Barrymore is allowed only one speech in his style of direction—"but a weird, desolate sky, fantastic cloud-images, and the right lighting impress the effect on the brain through the eye. The sky was used with different effects throughout the picture. We built our sets before it, tore them down and built more, so that the weird sky was always the shadow behind the action."

Such a commitment to visuals had worked for Browning in *Dracula*, and it proved still more effective in *Mark of the Vampire* which, with the remarkable James Wong Howe in charge of cameras, is above all a treat to the eye. Howe, who years later related to us his fascination with "big skies" achieved in indoor settings through projection of forms, made striking use of the planetarium-styled sky of *Mark*. This was a huge cyclorama built the length of a sound stage and given its effects by the use of stereopticon and sciopticon projection to cast clouds onto it. Howe said Browning was "very oldfashioned" in his handling of actors and staging but permitted great freedom in innovative cinematography—a godsend to Howe, whose bent for photographing a setting "just as the eye would see it" is shown here to good advantage.

Great pains were taken in production and writing to advance and embellish cinematic vampire legendry. A byword in the dialogue is "bat-thorn," as opposed to the more conventional

Mark of the Vampire - *A gathering of vampires: Luna, Karell (Holmes Herbert), Vampire (James Bradbury Jr.), Mora.*

garlic and wolf-bane. Creatures presented to flavor the doings include assorted dogs, two timber wolves (borrowed from a Los Angeles zoo), a rat, and a great horned owl. The prop department provided mechanical bats and spiders. *Mark of the Vampire* was the proving ground for a fog-producing machine which used a chemical mist slightly denser than air. Compressed into forms and then released, the mist theoretically would expand, retaining a semblance of the original shape—but only on days of low atmospheric pressure. The crew was obliged to watch a barometer to know when the effect could be employed. In the staging of the scene where the vampire girl flies through the cobwebbed castle, mechanical problems were encountered. "It took us days to get that one scene," Howe told us.

MGM touted "modern psychological orchestration" for *Mark* and the picture does have a uniquely maudlin score—but not of the type that was first commissioned. A leading composer-conductor at the studio, Herbert Stothart, delivered music which purported to represent the lead players with individual instruments (bassoon for Lionel Barrymore's grouchy hypnotist, muted trumpet to echo Lionel Atwill's clipped voice, French horn for the Lugosi character, and so forth). Stothart's work was publicized in connection with the film but is not heard in the released version, having been set aside for more understated music dominated by low-register and often dissonant organ chords.

The players work well together, with the assertive Atwill and Barrymore contrasting nicely with the befuddled Hersholt, seen here as a more suave villain than usual. The scene where Hersholt almost beheads one of the mock-vampires cues one of Barrymore's best-ever chidingly pompous lines: "Why, their fury would follow us to the ends of the earth!" The teen-aged Carol Borland is chilling in her silence, broken once by a reptilian

hiss. Howe said Rita Cansino (Hayworth) came close to landing the part; Miss Borland was selected for her unusual eyes, which lent themselves to good photographic effects, and by virtue of her stage experience with (and a recommendation from) Lugosi. As a Czech Dracula, Lugosi conveys menace without a line of dialogue, then steps out of character to end the show on a comic note. (Lugosi, Howe recalled, "was a very funny guy—he seemed to think he really was a vam-

pire.") The appropriately named Donald Meek has some amusing moments as a scared-silly doctor intimidated by the pragmatic Atwill. The other players of consequence are innocuous but competent.

The rapid-fire action of *Mark of the Vampire* seems not so much the result of preplanning as of last-minute scissoring. MGM, which was literally painstaking about its horror efforts, cut twenty minutes of it between preview and release.

Mark of the Vampire - *Principals of* Mark of the Vampire. *Left row from top: Otto (Jean Hersholt), Irena (Elizabeth Allan), Fedor (Henry Wadsworth); center row: Zelen (Lionel Barrymore), Count Mora (Bela Lugosi), Luna (Carol Borland); right: Jan (Ivan Simpson), Maria (Leila Bennett), Inspector Newman (Lionel Atwill).*

Let 'Em Have It

1935   Reliance Pictures Corporation
Presented by Harry M. Goetz and Edward Small
Released through United Artists
Director: Sam Wood
Producer: Edward Small
Writers: Joseph Moncure March and Elmer Harris
Photography: J. Peverell Marley and Robert Planck
Music: composed and conducted by Hugo Riesenfeld
Additional Music: Edward Powell, Alfred Newman, Charles Rosoff and Constantin Bakaleinikoff
Songs: *My Sweet Jeanette,* Wayne Allen; *Moon of Monte Cristo,* Richard Whiting and Sidney Clare; *Song of Surrender,* Harry Warren and Al Dubin
Art Director: John Ducasse Schulze
Technical Director: Captain Don Wilkie
Film Editor: Grant Whytock
Montage: Slavko Vorkapich
Assistant Director: Nate Watt
Photographic Effects: Paul Eagler
Matte Paintings: Jack Robeson
Cameramen: Harry David and William Snyder
Sound Recording: Frank Maher, Roger Heman and Vinton Vernon
Stunt Supervisor: Cliff Bergere
Produced at RKO-Pathé Studio
Running Time: 92 minutes

Cast: Richard Arlen (Mal Stevens), Virginia Bruce (Eleanor Spencer), Alice Brady (Aunt Ethel), Bruce Cabot (Joe Keefer), Harvey Stephens (Van Rensseler), Eric Linden (Buddy Spencer), Joyce Compton (Barbara), Gordon Jones (Tex), J. Farrell MacDonald (Mr. Keefer), Bodil Rosing (Mrs. Keefer), Paul Stanton (Department Chief), Robert Emmett O'Connor (Police Captain), Jonathan Hale (Scientist), Hale Hamilton (Ex-Senator Reilly), Dorothy Appleby (Lola), Barbara Pepper (Milly), Mathew Betz (Thompson), Harry L. Woods (Big Bill), Clyde Dilson (Pete), Matty Fain (Brooklyn), Paul Fix (Sam), Donald Kirke (Curley), Eugene Strong (Dude), Christian Rub (Henkel), Eleanor Wesselhoeft (Mrs. Henkel), Wesley Barry (Walton), Ian MacLaren (Reconstructionist), George

*L*et 'Em Have It seems the legitimate ancestor of the cycle of highly realistic crime dramas made more than a decade later. Subject and handling put it well ahead of its time, although its impact was blunted by the release about two weeks earlier of Warners' celebrated *G-Men,* a similar film which created a sensation by using the viewpoint of the authorities rather than the outlaws. Edward Small did likewise in *Let 'Em Have It* which evidently was filmed earlier, but the Warners got their entry to the boxoffice first. *Let 'Em Have It* is the more realistic film, for while both employ a semi-documentary approach, Warners tailored theirs as a star vehicle for James Cagney; Small opted for a strong featured cast with reduced emphasis on "star quality." Sam Wood, whose direction is noted for subtlety and lack of theatrics, held to low-key portrayals that are convincing throughout. The Grand Guignol touches—the

Pauncefort (Dr. Hoffman), Joseph King (Instructor), Clarence Wilson (Reynolds), Katherine Clare Ward (Ma Harrison), Jonathan Hale (Technician), Landers Stevens (Parole Chairman), Sidney Bracy (Butler), Dave O'Brien (Agent), Tom London (Guard)

Synopsis: The Federal Bureau of Investigation, about to mount an unprecedented assault on organized crime, accepts three recruits: attorney Mal Stevens, sportsman Van Rensseler, and cowboy Tex Logan. The new friends foil the kidnapping of Eleanor Spencer, a debutante. Her chauffeur, Joe Keefer, suspected of engineering the plot, draws a three-year sentence for illegally carrying a gun. Eleanor considers Keefer innocent and, over Stevens' objections, secures a parole. Keefer masterminds a prison break for some pals and soon a reign of terror begins in the Midwest.

Eleanor's young brother, Buddy, so admires the three agents that he gains a Justice Department appointment. Undercover for Stevens, Buddy traces the Keefer gang's hideout. Keefer recognizes Buddy and kills him. Eleanor blames Stevens, who has fallen in love with her.

Keefer, now considered Public Enemy Number One, kidnaps Dr. Hoffman, a plastic surgeon, forces him to alter his features, and then kills him. Keefer's girlfriend, Lola, is rounded up along with other consorts of the gangsters. Angered by Keefer's infidelity, Lola gives information that leads to the hideout. Keefer eludes the law and later, at an old farmhouse, he removes the bandages from his face in the presence of his henchmen and his new moll, Milly. To everyone's horror, Keefer's features have been mutilated and his initials carved into his face. Dr. Hoffman has avenged himself from beyond the grave!

Stevens falls into the hands of the gang. FBI men attack the house. Stevens and Keefer fight atop a high staircase. Stevens is stunned but Keefer is killed in a fall through the decaying balustrade, his body impaled on the broken railing. Stevens and Eleanor are reunited.

Let 'Em Have It! - *Van, Mal and Tex are friendly rivals for Virginia Bruce.*

mutilation of the villain and the grotesque ending—are all the more effective for the contrast they strike with the overall tone.

Bruce Cabot plays the gang boss so perfectly as to steal the show from everyone else. Late in the film he appears in an elaborate horror makeup that would have done justice to Karloff. "That makeup was very painful," Cabot told the present writers in 1967. "I had to check in before daylight every morning, and it took three men about six hours to make me up. Then I couldn't take it off until after work each night. This happened every day for ten days."

Richard Arlen, Harvey Stephens and Gordon Jones are splendid as the FBI musketeers, and Virginia Bruce is a charming heroine. Barbara Pepper does well as a gang moll, and Harry Woods, Donald Kirke, Mathew Betz, and Paul Fix stand out among a fine group of heavies.

Crime lab operations are depicted in fascinating detail. It is shown, for example, how one's features are reconstructed from studying the bite in an apple, how a strand of hair and a footprint can yield a description of a suspect, and how it is determined how long ago a bullet was fired.

Direction and script are straightforward, with more emphasis on characterization and significant detail than on movement. The photography follows suit with a minimum of Hollywood glamour effects, achieving the hardbitten quality of a newsreel. This sense of authenticity is advanced by a sparseness of background music—opening and closing patriotic strains, action passages for a "war on crime" montage, and incidental popular tunes. The picture was filmed at the RKO-Pathé studio.

Let 'Em Have It! - *Keefer realizes the ransom money is marked. Because Treasury Department regulations forbade photographing domestic currency, Mexican pesos were used as U. S. greenbacks in the movies.*

Show Them No Mercy

1935   Twentieth Century Pictures, Inc.
A Darryl F. Zanuck/Twentieth Century
Picture
Presented by Joseph N. Schenck
Released by Fox Film Corporation
Director: George Marshall
Associate Producer: Raymond L. Griffith
Story: Kubec Glasmon
Screenplay: Henry Lehrman
Director of Photography: Bert Glennon
Art Direction: Jack Otterson
Film Editor: Jack Murray
Sound Direction: W. D. Flick and Roger
Heman
Musical Director: David Buttolph
Special Effects: Fred Sersen, Louis J. Witte
and J. O. Taylor
Second Cameraman: Irving Rosenberg
Music Recording: Vinton Vernon
Western Electric Sound System
Produced at Metropolitan Studio
Running Time: 75 minutes

Cast: Rochelle Hudson (Loretta Martin),
Cesar Romero (Tobey), Bruce Cabot (Pitch),
Edward Norris (Joe Martin), Edward Brophy
(Buzz), Warren Hymer (Gimp), Herbert
Rawlinson (Kurt Hansen), Robert Gleckler
(Gus Hansen), Charles C. Wilson (Clifford),
William B. Davidson (Chief Haggerty), Frank
Conroy (Reed), Edythe Elliott (Mrs. Hansen),
William Benedict (Willie), Orrin Burke (Judge
Fry), Boothe Howard (Lester Mills), Paul
McVey (Dr. Peterson), Edward LeSaint

Synopsis: Joe and Loretta Martin, driving to
California with their baby son and a pet terrier,
are caught in a Midwestern rainstorm. Their
auto becomes mired, and they seek shelter in
a desolate farmhouse. The place proves to be
occupied. The inhabitants—Tobey, Pitch, Buzz,
and Gimp—are in hiding with a satchel of ransom money, having engineered the kidnapping
of a wealthy family. Pitch wants to kill the
interlopers, but Tobey, the gangleader, orders
them locked in a room. Examination of the
money shows the bills are unmarked.

The Justice Department, meantime, has
organized a manhunt. The criminals have
made a clean getaway, but the serial numbers of the ransom bills are known.

angland is the setting of the first all-talking feature, *The Lights
of New York* (1928), not a particularly good film, but one
which proved to the fledgling talkie industry that spoken
slang and sounds of violence added a great deal of charm to such a
story. The next dozen years saw a large number of gangster thrillers,
much to the horror of censors and many critics. Despite efforts to
stem the flow, the genre flourishes as a vital, hard-hitting kind of
melodrama. Among the many actors who achieved renown in these
films were Edward G. Robinson of *Little Caesar* (1931), James Cagney
of *The Public Enemy* (1931), Paul Muni and George Raft of *Scarface*
(1932), Humphrey Bogart of *The Petrified Forest* (1936), and Richard
Widmark of *Kiss of Death* (1948). From the gangster films came inno-
vations in styles of acting, writing of dialogue, and editing of film—
fundamental developments in the evolving art of the talking picture.

The high priest of the genre was Darryl F. Zanuck, who, as executive in charge of production at Warner Bros. First National, launched
such trend-setters as *Little Caesar* and *The Public Enemy*. Zanuck left the
Warners in 1933 to establish Twentieth Century Pictures, an aggres-

Show Them No Mercy - *Another load of pesos stands in for a ransom pay-
off, but hoods Tobey (Cesar Romero), Gimp (Warren Hymer) and Pitch
(Bruce Cabot) don't mind.*

The kidnappers grow edgy. Pitch, drinking heavily, becomes surly except when exercising his macabre sense of humor on Buzz. His hatred of Pitch and of the hammering of a woodpecker drives Buzz to the breaking point. Pitch continues to threaten Joe and his family, alienating Tobey.

Tobey sends Joe to town to pass off some of the ransom money. Loretta and the baby are held hostage. The money leads the authorities to the area. Buzz and Gimp decide to leave with part of the money for another part of the country. Cornered by federal agents, Buzz is killed. Gimp becomes a churchgoer, placing large bills in collection plates and taking change. He, too, is killed by government agents.

Pitch leaves after an argument outside the house with Tobey. Later, he returns and convinces Tobey they should continue as partners. As soon as Tobey turns his back, Pitch guns him down, then goes after the Martins, who have contrived to escape. Pitch beats Joe to the ground and draws aim on the helpless youth. Before he can squeeze the trigger, Pitch is riddled with bullets from his own machine gun, wielded by Loretta.

sive independent company allied with the United Artists group. So successful was the venture that a merger with an ailing major studio, Fox Film Corporation, was effected in 1935 with Zanuck elected vice-president for production. The first group of Twentieth Century-Fox releases included *Snatched!*, one of Zanuck's indepen-

dent productions and his first gangster film since his days at Warners. Written by Kubec Glasmon, co-author of *The Public Enemy*, it was suggested by the Weyerhauser kidnap case which had been solved by the Federal Bureau of Investigation.

The Production Code Administration refused to sanction a

film in which details of a kidnapping would be shown. A canny rewrite had the story begin *after* the crooks have collected a ransom. The man and wife and baby held by the kidnappers became a family which blunders into the gang's hideout. The title also had to be changed before the Code's "purity seal" would be granted, hence the clumsy

Show Them No Mercy - *Tension mounts among the kidnappers. At left is Buzz (Edward Brophy).*

release title, *Show Them No Mercy*. After some controversy, Zanuck was permitted to retain a startling special effects scene in which machine-gun bullets (superimposed) stitch a row across the bare chest of Bruce Cabot; still, some local censors excised the scene. Wailing also was heard from some quarters because one of the gangsters is shown using church collection plates to pass "hot" money.

By 1935, producers had so knuckled under to censorship that, generally, the emphasis no longer was upon criminals but upon the law-enforcement personnel, as in *G-Men*, *Let 'Em Have It* and *Public Hero Number One*. This shift at first created a sensation but soon became the rule—to which *Show Them No Mercy* is a refreshing exception. It shows the federal men in a heroic light but keeps them very much in the background. The mainstream is devoted to the horrifying plight of the trapped family as well as the mental deterioration of the fugitives as a consequence

of their own fear and greed.

The director is George Marshall, who started in 1914 with Universal and gained his greatest renown as a master of comedy (*You Can't Cheat an Honest Man*, 1939, and *The Ghost Breakers*, 1940) and large-scale Westerns (*Destry Rides Again*, 1939 and *Tap Roots*, 1948). With his handling of the fast-moving and hard-bitten *Show Them No Mercy*, Marshall forcefully invaded William Wellman-Archie Mayo-Howard Hawks territory. The cold and snappy photography by Bert Glennon suits to perfection the compact relentlessness of the script and direction.

Rochelle Hudson and Edward Norris portray the menaced couple, typifying the courageous young adults of the Depression era. The kidnappers are an ensemble, each actor contributing definitive portrayals of widely differing criminal personalities. Cesar Romero, in what he often called his favorite role, creates a character he called "cruel, ruthless, cowardly, . . . slim slits in his

shell which allowed a little kindness to show through, simply made his general character darker by contrast." Romero's flashy gangleader is ironically sympathetic at times, as when he sings "Oh, You Nasty Man" while contemplating the pile of money his villainy has brought him, or when he refuses to permit the slaughter of the prisoners (albeit for at least partially selfish reasons). Warren Hymer, the perennial "dumb lug," adds dimension to his usual characterization by revealing glimpses of the brute lurking behind the simple-minded outlaw. The small, squeaky-voiced, balding Eddie Brophy provides a remarkable study of a semi-comical mobster driven by nerves and the vicious jibes of his companions to a state of dangerous near-hysteria.

Bruce Cabot's terrifying performance bests even his psychopathic hoodlum in the preceding *Let 'Em Have It*. Initially perceived as merely a rather primitive henchman who seems on good terms with his accomplices, Cabot gradually is revealed as a sadist whose idea of a joke is to set fire to a newspaper under which Brophy is sleeping. Under the influence of alcohol he becomes increasingly vicious, degenerating at length into a savage with no regard for human life. Cabot told us, "I based my interpretation in part upon the personality of Vincent ('Mad Dog') Coll," a New York racketeer whose demise was welcomed even by his confederates.

It is unfortunate that *Show Them No Mercy* dosen't enjoy the reputation of some of the earlier gang melodramas, for it is the equal of the best in the field. The plot of *Show Them No Mercy* was recycled by Twentieth Century Fox as a western—a very good one—called *Rawhide* (1951), with Tyrone Power and Susan Hayward.

Show Them No Mercy - *Pitch, apparently contrite, tries to befriend Tobey again.*

The Walking Dead

1936 Warner Bros. Productions Corporation
Director: Michael Curtiz
Screenplay: Ewart Adamson, Peter Milne, Robert Andrews and Lillie Hayward
Story: Ewart Adamson and Joseph Fields
Photography: Hal Mohr
Film Editor: Thomas Pratt
Dialogue Director: Irving Rapper
Art Director: Hugh Reticker
Gowns: Orry-Kelly
Musical Director: Leo F. Forbstein
Music: Bernhard Kaun
Special Effects: Fred Jackman, Edwin A. DuPar, Paul Detlefsen and James Gibbons
Sound: Stanley L. Jones, Gerald Alexander and Harold Shaw
Make-up: Perc Westmore
Operative Cameraman: Robert Surtees
Mechanical Heart: Stanley Fox
Stills: Mac Julian
Running Time: 66 minutes

Cast: Boris Karloff (John Ellman), Ricardo Cortez (Nelson), Edmund Gwenn (Dr. Beaumont), Margurite Churchill (Nancy), Warren Hull (Jimmy), Barton MacLane (Loder), Henry O'Neill (Werner), Joseph King (Judge Shaw), Addison Richards (Warden), Paul Harvey (Blackstone), Robert Strange (Merritt), Joseph Sauers (Trigger), Eddie Acuff (Betcha), Kenneth Harlan (Stephen Martin), Miki Morita (Saka), Ruth Robinson (Mrs. Shaw), James Burtis and John Kelly (Bodyguards), Adrian Rosley (Florist), Frank Darien (Caretaker), Wade Boteler, Edward Gargan (Guards), Gordon Elliott (American Announcer), Crauford Kent (English Announcer), Earl Hodgins , Eddie Shubert, Larry Kent, Milt Kibbee, Charles Marsh, Isabelle LaMal, Lucille Collins, Charles Sherlock and Paul Panzer (Reporters), James Pierce (Gunman), Lee Phelps, Tom Brower, Harry Hollingsworth and Lee Prather (Bailiffs), George André Beranger (Servant), Nick Moro (Cellist Convict), William Wayne (Trusty), Edgar Sherrod (Priest), Chris Corporal, Tom Schamp, Ed Carli and Jim Pierce (Prisoners), Boyd Irwin (British Doctor), Jean Perry (French Doctor), Nicholas Kobliansky (Russian Doctor), Paul Irving, Malcolm Beach, Malcolm Graham (Guests), Sarah Edwards (Physician), Harrington Reynolds (Doctor),

Each studio that produced horror movies had distinctive ideas. Warners' early efforts during the silent and early sound periods were generally heavy on gothic atmosphere and comedy. Two 1931 pictures starring John Barrymore, *Svengali* and *The Mad Genius* were pure gothic dramas, beautifully produced and performed but not great audience favorites. *Dr. X* and *The Mystery of the Wax Museum*, Warner's Technicolor chillers of 1932-3, both directed by Michael Curtiz, set the unique Warner style for future horror pictures. Here the gothic look of the Barrymore pictures was combined with elements of the typical gangster pictures for which Warners was famous, and a considerable leavening of comedy was added. Traditional horror motifs and characters were intermingled with bootleggers, dope peddlers, snappy newspaper people, hard-boiled cops and slumming socialites. Here, too, the fast editing technique (aptly called "visual shorthand") integral to Warner gangster yarns was applied, a drastic break from the rather stately pacing of most horror films. This approach was adhered to in *The Walking Dead* as well as some later Warners' efforts such as *The Return of Dr. X* (1939) and *The Smiling Ghost* (1941).

The Walking Dead was the first of Boris Karloff's four starring roles for Warner Bros. and it was handsomely produced. Michael Curtiz

Edward Peil, Sr. (Train Engineer) Alphonse Martel (Florist), Michael Curtiz (Interne)

Synopsis: Stephen Martin, a crooked politician, is on trial in Judge Shaw's court. His defender is Nelson, a slick society lawyer who is the secret leader of Martin's political machine. Other members of the ring are Loder, Merritt and Blackstone. The jury finds Martin guilty. Shaw, in defiance of death threats from the gang, sentences him to a long term. Nelson instructs Loder to call in Trigger, an assassin.

John Ellman, a former concert pianist who was sentenced to ten years by Shaw after Ellman killed his wife's lover in a fight, is selected as a "patsy." Trigger, claiming to be a detective hired by Mrs. Shaw to obtain evidence for a divorce case, offers the destitute Ellman a job watching Shaw's house at night. The judge is murdered and dumped in Ellman's rented car. Leaving the scene, the killers are seen by Nancy and Jim, a young engaged couple. The killers return and warn the couple to keep their secret or die.

Indicted for murder, Ellman is defended by the highest priced lawyer in town, Nelson, who volunteered for the job. Nelson plays into the hands of District Attorney Werner. Ellman's only chance is blasted by the refusal of the terrified witnesses to come forward.

In his death cell, Ellman waits hopelessly for word of a commutation. The day of execution arrives. As per Ellman's last wish a fellow convict plays his favorite melody (the cloister music from Rubinstein's *Kamenoi Oistrow*) during the "last walk." Meanwhile, Jimmy and Nancy ask the advice of their employer, Dr. Beaumont, a research scientist. Beaumont phones Nelson, who casually finishes a sumptuous meal and delays getting the information to the governor. At last he calls Werner and goes with him to Beaumont's laboratory. Werner calls the Governor, who tries to halt the execution. The Warden calls the death house just as Ellman is being strapped into the electric chair. Even with Nelson's calculated procrastination Ellman could be saved, but the guards are too busy discussing baseball to answer the phone in time.

Beaumont, who has worked for years trying to find a way to revive the dead, has the body rushed to his laboratory. His great experiment is successful: Ellman lives again. In the ensuing days Ellman seems a crippled shell of a man who only sits and stares, having no apparent memory of his former life. Nancy, conscience stricken, cares for him tenderly. One day she plays the Rubinstein music on the piano. Ellman rises, walks to the piano, and plays. Nelson and Werner enter, the former having asked to be made Ellman's guardian (and guardian of the $500,000 awarded Ellman by the court). Ellman glares at Nelson and orders him to leave.

Werner confides to Beaumont his suspicion that Nelson framed Ellman. Both men agree that Elman somehow gained in death a strange insight that could be useful in apprehending the killers of Shaw. They arrange a piano recital for Ellman, making certain that Nelson, Loder, Blackstone and Merritt attend. During his performance Ellman fixes each of the four with a glare, singling them out of the audience even though he had never before seen Merritt or Blackstone. So unnerved are the suspects that Werner is convinced of their guilt.

Blackstone hires Trigger to kill Ellman. Before Trigger can leave his room, Ellman appears and asks, "Why did you kill Judge Shaw?" Drawing his pistol, Trigger backs away in sudden fear. He stumbles and falls, the gun explodes, and Trigger is killed. Blackstone finds the body and tries to leave town. He is met at a rural train station by Ellman, who asks, "Why did you have me killed?" Fleeing in terror, Blackstone falls in the path of a speeding locomotive.

Barricading himself in his penthouse, Merritt is abandoned by his guards. When Ellman arrives, Merritt's fear brings on a heart seizure and a fatal fall from a high window.

Ellman's friends find him wandering in a cemetery. Beaumont determines that although an operation on Ellman could kill him, if he lives it will enable him to remember matters of vital interest to the police as well as to science. That night, before Beaumont can enact his plan, Ellman again disappears. Nancy hurries out into a blinding rainstorm. Nelson and Loder trail her to the cemetery, where she finds Ellman seeking shelter in the caretaker's cabin.

When Nelson and Loder arrive, Ellman goes out to confront them. Loder empties his gun into Ellman. Beaumont and Jimmy arrive as the killers flee. Beaumont questions Ellman desperately, hoping to learn from his fading mind the truth about death. Elman tells him, "Leave the dead to their maker. The Lord, our God, is a jealous God." Meantime, the car bearing Nelson and Loder swerves off the road and crashes into a power station. High tension wires fall upon the overturned car, electrocuting both men. At this instant, Ellman rallies. "Now I think I can remember," he says. "After the first shock there was a great feeling of peace. And then—" Death halts his statement. Beaumont, ever the cold scientist, murmers sadly: "It will never be known. The Lord, our God, is indeed a jealous God!"

was in the first echelon of Warners contract directors and the supporting cast was top drawer. Certainly it is among Karloff's better pictures, one that actually seems to improve with age. In large measure this can be credited to the intelligent script by Ewart Adamson, Peter Milne, Robert Andrews and Lillie Hayward from a story by Andrews and Joseph Fields. These writers were more interested in developing a believable narrative than in trying to scare the

The Walking Dead - *Nancy (Marguerite Churchill) helps Ellman prepare for his piano recital.*

wits out of the viewers.

Then, too, there is the sure-handed direction of Curtiz, that much maligned tyrant of the Warners lot who had the know-how to make any type of picture better than almost anyone else. Amazingly versatile, he is best remembered for his large scale historical epics—*Moon of Israel* (1924), *Noah's Ark* (1928), *Captain Blood* (1935), *The Charge of the Light Brigade* (1936), *The Adventures of Robin Hood* (1938), *The Private Lives of Elizabeth and Essex* (1939), *The Sea Hawk* (1940), etc. It is hard to imagine the volatile, Hungarian-born director teamed with the gentle Karloff, but the results are splendid.

The photography of Hal Mohr meshes well with Curtiz's liking for angular compositions and significant shadow patterns. A daring expression-istic touch occurs during the piano recital as Karloff glares at each of the men who betrayed him: the lighting of each closeup of both accuser and accused changes on camera. Hugh Reticker's settings are realistic, yet contain some expressionistic touches that mesh well with the photographic style.

The scenes in which Karloff is brought back to life are detailed and surprisingly convincing, based on experiments conducted by contemporary scientists. Shown in operation is a replica of the Lindberg Heart, or Perfusion Pump, which was developed by famed pilot Charles A. Lindberg under the supervision of Nobel Prize winner Dr. Alexis Carrel, of the Rockefeller Institute. The intricate device, made of glass and tubing, was designed to function in place of the human heart to maintain life in the tissues and organs of a dead person. The "heart" in the movie was built by Stanley Fox, a pathologist and vice president of Western Scientific Research Laboratories.

During the operation Karloff lies on a replica of the tilting table, a see-saw device used by Dr. Robert Cornish, a Berkeley scientist who claimed to have revivified a dead dog. Other electrical devices jazz up the set. The long sequence is a superbly edited montage made up of wildly angled, swiftly changing views and accompanied by wildly pulsing music.

In many of his portrayals of villains and monsters, Karloff evoked sympathy and menace in almost equal measure. Karloff creates in John Ellman a monster that is not only viewed with sympathy but is actually the only *wholly* sympathetic character among the principals.

This despite a subtle but forbidding post-electrocution make-up created by Perc Westmore. Karloff was built up four inches taller than he was before going to the chair. The left side of his body appears shrunken and partly paralyzed and his face is shaded and highlighted accordingly. His eye sockets were darkened to make the eyes appear deeply sunken and the left eye seems smaller than normal, an effect achieved by creating false eyelids. The other eye, by way of contrast, was stretched larger by hidden clips. A streak of white hair was added to Karloff's prison haircut.

There is a large and formidable gang of villains of the darkest hue arrayed against him, consisting of a corrupt political ring, a professional assassin and a gang of hired thugs. The saturninely handsome Ricardo Cortez, the movies' first Sam Spade (in the 1931 *The Maltese Falcon*) exudes crafty menace as the crooked lawyer and gang leader. Robert Strange and Paul Harvey are realistic political crooks. Barton MacLane, the loudest and meanest of the Warner Bros. gangsters, sets forth with chilling conviction a figure of brute instincts. Joseph Sauers (later known as Joe Sawyer) gives an unusual portrayal of a coldly efficient killer, particularly in a scene in which he coolly defeats his employers at billiards while telling them his plans for the doomed judge.

Even the seeming good guys let Ellman down, although most of them are contrite and try to make amends. The honest judge he is accused of murdering had condemned him to a long term in the penitentiary on a manslaughter charge in a case with obvious mitigating circumstances. The juvenile leads could come forth and save him from being executed for a

The Walking Dead - *Ellman in his "home"—the graveyard.*

crime he didn't commit, but are so fearful of underworld reprisals that they withhold their information until it is too late. District Attorney Werner rightly suspects that the defense attorney is railroading the accused man to the electric chair, but doesn't let that stand in the way of his desire to obtain a conviction. The scientist who brings Ellman back from the dead, perceived initially as a kindly and even lovable man (who could be more lovable than Edmund Gwenn?), becomes so cold-hearted in his scientific zeal that he is willing, for the sake of knowledge, to sacrifice the patient who has brought him fame.

Beaumont reveals his gnawing curiosity to Werner: "What effect did the experience of death have on his subconscious mind? . . . He seems to be driven by strange impulses, as though he were the instrument of some supernatural power." Beaumont's worshipful assistant tells his fiancée that Dr. Beaumont has

changed. "He's forgotten everything we set out to do. All he thinks of now is trying to find out what Ellman experienced while he was dead—putting his soul under a microscope."

Eventually Beaumont tells Werner that he wants to try to "unlock" Ellman's mind with a brain operation, but that Ellman then would have only one chance in a thousand of living more than a few minutes. To Werner's objection, he replies, "But it's *worth* that chance! Why not? The evidence that Ellman will be able to give to you will be nothing compared to the information he'll be able to give *me.* Secrets from beyond! Things that no man has ever dreamt of will be in my reach—think of it!" The D. A. does think of it (and of the crooks he'll be able to prosecute) and nods in agreement. And when Ellman dies again Beaumont has no remorse for the loss of a good man, only regret that now "it will never be known."

Trouble For Two

1936 Metro-Goldwyn-Mayer Corporation
Director: J. Walter Ruben
Producer: Louis D. Lighton
Screenplay: Manuel Seff and Edward E. Paramore, Jr.
Based on *The Suicide Club* by Robert Louis Stevenson
Musical Score: Franz Waxman
Art Director: Cedric Gibbons
Associates: Joseph C. Wright and Edwin B. Willis
Director of Photography: Charles G. Clarke
Film Editor: Robert J. Kern
Sound Supervision: Douglas Shearer
Special Effects: A. Arnold Gillespie, Warren Newcombe and Tom Tutwiler
Costumes: Dolly Tree
Assistant Director: Dolph Zimmer
Make-up: Jack Dawn
Contributing Authors: A. E. Thomas, A. W. Hannemann, Keene Thompson, Jack Murray, Allen Boretz and Vincent Lawrence
Running Time: 83 minutes

Cast: Robert Montgomery (Prince Florizel), Rosalind Russell (Miss Vandeleur), Frank Morgan (Colonel Geraldine), Reginald Owen (President), Louis Hayward (Young Man with Cream Tarts), E. E. Clive (The King), Walter Kingsford (Matheus), Ivan Simpson (Collins), Tom Moore (Major O'Rook), Robert Greig (Fat Man), Guy Bates Post (Ambassador), Pedro de Cordoba (Sergei), Leyland Hodgson (Captain Rich), Pat O'Malley (Ship's Captain), Forrester Harvey, Edgar Norton, Sidney Bracy, Paul Porcasi, Philo McCullough and Leonard Carey

Synopsis: In 1880 the King of Karovia resumes arrangements begun fifteen years before with the King of Irania to wed Karovian Crown Prince Florizal with Iranian Princess Brenda. Florizel remembers Brenda as "Mushmouth," a scrawny youngster. The Princess is equally appalled. His father allows Florizel a month for one last adventure before the event. As "Theopholus Godall," Florizel boards a channel steamer for England. He is accompanied by "Major Hammersmith"—actually his guardian, Colonel "Gerry" Geraldine, and a dog, Sultan.

Florizel accepts an invitation to come to

The filmgoer who insists upon categorizing pictures according to genre might do well to avoid *Trouble for Two*, MGM's adaptation of Robert Louis Stevenson's *The Suicide Club*, a story from *The New Arabian Nights*. A Ruritanian romance, a comedy, a swashbuckler and a mystery thriller all in one, this handsomely staged entertainment met an end typical of what became of most "costume pictures" during the mid-1930s: failure at the box office. Chances are it would have fared better four years earlier when Universal came within days of putting it into production as a Karloff vehicle scripted by John L. Balderston, scenarist of several of the studio's most effective chillers. At MGM, the most star-conscious of studios during the heyday of the star system, the story was regarded primarily as a showcase for a romantic escapade between two glamorous and sophisticated personalities, with a bit less emphasis on action and mystery than Stevenson or Balderston would have wished. Both stars are at their sparkling best, well served by witty dialogue, elaborate costuming, impeccable makeup, glistening photography and a top-drawer supporting cast.

It is well that J. Walter Ruben, one of the more versatile directors at the time, chose to lavish similar care on the weird and eccentric aspects of the tale. Reginald Owen—whose own versatility may be gauged by the fact that in different films he portrayed both Sherlock Holmes and Dr. Watson—is a wonderful menace. Looming from the darkness, his acquiline features accented by sinister looking makeup that includes a domed forehead and shaggy eyebrows, Owen suggests Conan Doyle's written description of Holmes's archenemy, Professor Moriarty. An eerie musical theme by Franz Waxman, one of the best composers then working in pictures, adds an extra chill to Owen's presence. Backup vil-

Trouble For Two - Prince Florizel (Robert Montgomery) and Col. Geraldine (Frank Morgan) meet the President (Reginald Owen) of the Suicide Club.

stateroom 9 to "aid . . . a lady in distress." He finds the lady to be beautiful and mysterious. She gives him an envelope that certain persons, she says, will stop at nothing to possess. He is to carry it ashore and return it to her at the foot of the gangplank. A husky man demands the envelope; Gerry's arrival averts a fight. The lady does not appear after the ship docks. Gerry opens the envelope, which contains blank sheets of paper.

A hotel waiter suggests that Florizel and Gerry dine at a dive in Soho. There they meet a young man accompanied by liveried servants bearing trays of cream tarts, which he offers to sell to the patrons. Florizel buys the tarts and invites the young man to dine. The youth is John Cecil Northmore, age twenty-eight and penniless, having spent the last scrap of his squandered fortune on the tarts. His life has been useless and the tarts are symbols of his determination to do away with himself. "And now, gentlemen, I go to keep my tryst with death," he says, noting that he has found a way to achieve death without disgrace. Florizel tells him that "We too are ruined, hopeless men, eager to seek an exit that will not be vulgar." Northmore offers to take them to the Suicide Club but they must hurry before the "door of death" is locked for the night. The mystery woman from the ship watches as they hurry away.

Entering through a dark courtyard, they find themselves in an antechamber. The tall and saturnine president enters, at last accepting their initiation fees and inviting them into the main room. It resembles any well-ordered gentlemen's club but fear and tension show through the false hilarity displayed by the affluent members. The elderly Matheus has been waiting two years for his time to come. Northmore explains the rules:

The President each night deals fifty-two cards to the members. The ace of spades is the card of death and its recipient is the next to die. The recipient of the ace of clubs becomes "death's high priest," the executioner. The President gives secret orders to the executioner as to how, when and where the sentence will be carried out. Death is made to appear the consequence of murder or accident. A door opens and the mysterious beauty from the ship enters, showing no sign of recognition. The President deals out the cards; on the third deal the lady receives the ace of clubs and Northmore the ace of spades. The principals are led away by the President and sent through a hidden exit. Northmore's obituary appears the following day.

That evening, Florizel and Gerry attend another meeting where again the lady receives the ace of clubs. The death card falls to Florizel. In the President's office Florizel is introduced to Miss Vandeleur, who is given her secret instructions. Executioner and victim are sent in a cab to honor the decree. Florizel is taken to a zoo on an island in the middle of a lake, where he is to be torn apart by a lion. At the door to the cage the girl breaks down and says she cannot continue. She explains that she sent Northmore to Paris with a pocket full of money and placed his death notice in the newspaper.

A bullet narrowly misses Florizel. Pursued by the gun-wielding President, he and the girl seek refuge at an inn. The girl explains that she is "Mushmouth" and that she ran away rather than marry someone she had hated as a child. Recognizing Florizel on the ship, she decided to learn more about him. Gerry arrives, having followed the President; but he has lost him in the woods. They decide to return to Karovia next morning.

At breakfast Collins, a waiter, tearfully tells Florizel that his dog is about to be put to death by the Bramley District Court for having killed a bird. Florizel agrees to intercede, going with Gerry and Collins to the courthouse. The President of the Suicide Club sits at the bench wearing the wig and robes of a magistrate. Florizel is accused of treason. The accuser is Dr. Franz Noel, who had been exiled from Karovia for treason and is now President of the Suicide Club. As Florizel tries to fight his way free, Gerry lifts a round object and threatens to blow up the entire gathering unless he and Florizel are permitted to leave. Freedom is almost attained when the "bomb"—actually a plum pudding—springs a leak. In a fight, Florizel escapes but Gerry is trapped. Returning with the police, Florizel finds the courthouse vacated.

At the hotel Collins informs Florizel that Gerry is a prisoner of war and hands over a map designating a place outside London where Dr. Noel will be open for negotiations at 2 A.M. Florizel is led through woods and hills to a deserted house. Two men are digging a grave. Noel tells him there will be no duel, only a double hanging. Florizel stalls until help arrives—men the Princess has recruited from the Army and Navy CLub. Sultan has led them there by following the scent of cinnamon oil from the tip of Florizel's cane.

Florizel insists upon the duel, which proceeds to the edge of the open grave. Run through, the dying Noel falls into the pit. The royal wedding takes place as planned.

lainy is capably provided by sculptor-actor Ivan Simpson in a role reminiscent of the sniveling manservant he portrayed on the stage and in two screen versions of *The Green Goddess* and by an assortment of skulking ruffians.

The beloved Frank Morgan is the courageous but comically flustered bodyguard of the hero. Some effectively eccentric touches are added by Louis Hayward (destined soon to achieve stardom) and Walter Kingsford as the youngest and eldest of the eccentrics who joined the Suicide Club. E. E. Clive is, as always, a delight as the kindly king.

The dialogue has a nice "period" ring to it; at the end of the climactic swordfight Florizel tells Dr. Noel "Well, sir, here we are," as he backs him to the edge of a yawning grave. "I must not detain you." Charles Clarke's photography limns the glamorous, the humorous and the bizarre aspects of the adventure with equal force.

Sweeney Todd, the Demon Barber of Fleet Street

1936 George King Productions/MGM-British
Director: George King
From the George Dibdin Pitt play *A String of Pearls*
Screenplay: Frederick Hayward
Dialogue: H. F. Maltby
Assistant Director: Ronnie Kinnoch
Production Manager: Billy Phelps
Photography: Jack Parker
Art Director: Percy Bell
Editor: John Seabourne
Recordist: J. Byers
Continuity: Olga Brook
Cameraman: Ronald Neame
Produced at Sound City
Recorded on Visatone
Running Time: 68 minutes

Cast: Tod Slaughter (Sweeney Todd), Stella Rho (Mrs. Lovatt), Johnny Singer (Tobias), Eve Lister (Johanna), Bruce Seton (Mark), D. J. Williams (Stephen Oakley), Davina Craig (Nan), Jerry Verno (Pearly), Ben Souten (Beadle), Billy Holland (Mr. Parsons), Herman Pierce (Mr. Findley), Aubrey Mallallieu (Trader Peterson)

Synopsis: London, 1936. A grouchy customer visits a barber shop on Fleet Street. He inquires about an old framed cartoon labeled "Sweeney Todd ready to give a general polishing up." The barber tells him that Todd, an ancestor of his, was the greatest exponent of the razor in history. He tells the story:

At the waterfront at Fleet Street a century earlier, Sweeney Todd watches the Golden Hope unload its cargo. The ship's mate, Mark, and Seaman Pearly are greeted by their sweethearts, Johanna Oakley and her maid, Nan. Johanna's father, owner of the ship, doesn't approve, nor does his silent partner, Todd, who has designs on the girl. Todd gives Oakley a large amount of money— "The fruits of my razor—so many I've polished off."

The Beadle brings Tobias, an orphan boy, to Todd's barber shop. Todd has in the recent past had seven other assistants from the orphanage, which pays him seven guineas each to take them in. All have "run away." A Mr. Findlay, returning from a trading voyage with a bag of jewels, is met

Tod Slaughter is, definitely, an acquired taste. In a free-for-all contest of extravagant acting he could, while bound and gagged, have out-hammed Charles Laughton, Robert Newton and Bela Lugosi combined. Slaughter portraying a sneaky, lecherous scoundrel (his customary role) makes W. C. Fields seem akin to Freddie Bartholomew. When offered a motive and the opportunity to commit murder, Slaughter did so with a chuckle and, often, a witticism. Those of us who love him have little luck at winning him many converts; for most movie-lovers he is an enigma, an anomaly, a perennial square peg.

N. Carter "Tod" Slaughter (1885-1956) was a lifelong producer-actor in the provincial theaters of England. His specialty was presenting Victorian melodramas (which he termed "new-old melodramas") in the style in which they originally were performed. The results were both comical and horrifying, the humor arising from the florid acting and dialogue of the period rather than any attempt at parody. His portly but lean-legged figure was undeniably frog-like. Large, heavy-lidded eyes, a generous, wedge-shaped nose, a crocodilian smile and an oily voice all contributed to an impression of unbridled lust and evil.

George King, a movie producer-director who delivered both "quota quickies" and prestige pictures (although his lucrative specialty was the former), decided in 1935 to produce one of Slaughter's most popular road shows, *Maria Marten* or *The Murder in the Red Barn*. It was almost a literal screening of the stage version but it was enacted in good studio sets and in the countryside. Sold to MGM-British for their quota program, it enjoyed a certain success in the U. K. and received some bookings in the U. S. Slaughter eventually appeared in about fifteen films, most of them based on his stage shows and produced by King.

The second King-Slaughter picture, *Sweeney Todd, the Demon Barber of Fleet Street*, is their most famous, partly because of the more recent

at the dock by Todd, who invites him in for "a general polish up." Todd gives Tobias a penny to buy a meat pie "big enough to last while you walk to Charing Cross and back" from Mrs. Lovatt's shop next door. After Mr. Findlay has been properly lathered and made comfortable in the "special chair," Todd pulls a concealed lever which causes the chair to flip over, dumping its occupant into the basement. Todd goes downstairs to "polish off" the victim, who is then taken in charge by Mrs. Lovatt, whose meat pies are famed for their unique flavor.

On the African coast, Mark and the captain go ashore to the jungle headquarters of Trader Peterson, which is under seige. During the fight the Captain is killed and Peterson is mortally wounded. The dying man gives Mark a bag of pearls. Mark returns to England a wealthy man and master of the ship. Alighting at Fleet Street, he is invited to Todd's shop. After he is plunged into the basement, the unconscious Mark is hidden in a cupboard by Mrs. Lovatt, who is jealous of Todd's attentions to Johanna. Mark escapes.

Mr. Parsons, who has been acting as a "fence" for Todd, tries blackmail to get possession of the pearls.

Todd clubs him with a stool, puts him in the chair and drops him into the basement. Later, Mark, disguised as a wealthy farmer, goes to the barber shop to get the goods on Todd while Pearly sneaks into the basement. When the chair flips, Mark hangs onto the arms and is helped down by Pearly.

Todd, realizing Mrs. Lovatt has betrayed him, murders her in the basement. He builds a woodpile, planning arson to destroy evidence. Disguised in Tobias' clothes, Johanna goes to Todd's shop to look for evidence. Todd knocks her unconscious and puts her in a closet. Going downstairs, he sets the fire and flees with his hoard of valuables. He returns when he sees Mark enter the burning building looking for Johanna. The men fight. A blow sends Todd falling into the "special chair." As Mark and Johanna escape, flames burn through the mechanism of the chair and Todd, awaking too late, is plunged into the flames.

So ends the story told by the barber. His customer remarks the odor of cooking meat from the pie shop next door. The barber strops his razor—and looks up to see his toweled and draped customer running down Fleet Street.

Sweeney Todd - Mrs. Lovatt (Stella Rho) listens as Sweeney Todd (Tod Slaughter) tells Tobias (Johnny Singer) what happens to little boys who talk too much.

Sweeney Todd - Mr. Findley (Hubert Pierce) makes a fatal mistake.

popularity of a musical play of that name. The original play, "The String of Pearls," was written in 1847 by George Dibdin Pitt and Slaughter had performed it often. His film version was made at the new Sound City at Shepperton, an elegant seven-stage studio on a sixty acre country estate complete with mansion. Without spending an unusual amount of money King was able to pull together some fairly impressive sets of Fleet Street as it appeared in the early 1800s and a good lot of extras in Dickensian costumes. The cellar where Todd dumps his victims and Mrs. Lovatt bakes those infamous meat pies is an appropriately grim, rat infested place. There are good period interiors, a trading ship with rear projected seas, and a jungle stage.

The ripe dialogue is delivered with chop-licking sincerity by Slaughter. Looking over the passengers and crew alighting from a ship, he tells an acquaintance: "A lovely lot of throats, the lot of them . . . Rich and mellow to the razor." Greeting a gentleman carrying a bag of valuables, he asks, "What could be more pleasant than a haircut, shave, a shampoo and a general polish up?" Cozening the well-heeled customer into a certain chair, he explains:

"My special chair, sir, for men like you, sir, from abroad, sir." The gentleman, seeing him give his assistant a penny for a pie, observes that Todd has a kind heart. "Tender as a chicken, sir; my one weakness," Todd responds, just moments before he flops the special chair over and sends his customer hurtling headlong to the cellar floor. Another patron is informed that

"When I've finished with you, you won't know yourself . . . You have a beautiful throat for the razor, sir."

Lechery is an important part of any Slaughter portrayal. "Pearls for your teeth, rubies for your lips and sapphires for your eyes," he tells the young woman of his choice as he presents her with jewelry inherited that very day from his latest customer. He speaks less kindly to his jealous mistress, the old and ugly Mrs. Lovatt: "Oh, I should like to polish you off!" We also see him applying dye to his hair before he goes calling on the lovely Johanna, who is set forth with proper innocence by Eve Lister. Bruce (later Sir Bruce) Seton is the stalwart hero.

There is some comedy supplied by Jerry Verno as Seton's shipmate, and Davina Craig as a slightly dotty maid. At one point the action slows long enough to reveal Verno in the basement enjoying one of the notorious meat pies.

Some of the later Slaughter melodramas were slicker and better, especially the 1939 *The Face at the Window* and *The Crimes at the Dark House* but for many the quintessential Tod Slaughter is the reptilian tonsorial artist chuckling happily as he creeps down the cellar stairs, open razor in hand.

Sweeney Todd - Nan (Davina Craig) tells Mark and his shipmates that Johanna is in danger.

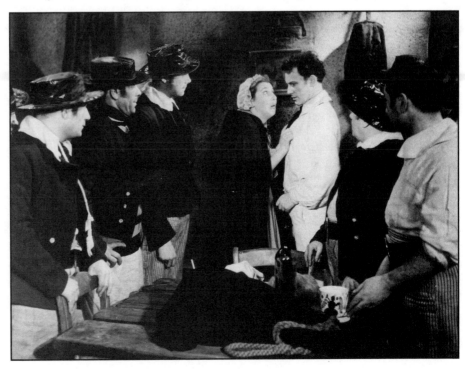

Broken Blossoms

1936 Twickenham Film Corporation
U.S. release via Imperial Pictures Corporation
Director: Hans (John) Brahm
Producer: Julius Hagen
From the Thomas Burke story "The Chink & the Child," and from D. W. Griffith's motion picture of 1919
Screenplay: Emlyn Williams
Lighting Cameraman: Curt Courant
Operative Cameraman: Hal Young
Film Editors: Jack Harris and Ralph Kemplen
Production Supervisor: Bernard Vorhaus
Art Director: James Carter
Special Settings: Paul Minine
Sound Recording: Baynham Honri and Carlisle Mounteney
Musical Director: W. L. Trytel
Music: Karol Rathaus
Running Time: 87 minutes

Cast: Dolly Haas (Lucy Burrows), Emlyn Williams (Chen), Arthur Margetson (Burrows), Ernest Sefton (Manager), C. V. France (High Priest), Basil Radford (Mr. Reed), Edith Sharpe (Mrs. Reed), Ernest Jay (Alf), Bertha Belmore (Daisy), Gibb McLaughlin (Evil Eye), Donald Calthrop (Old Chinaman), Kathleen Harrison (Mrs. Lossy), Kenneth Villiers (Missionary), Jerry Verno (Bert), also Dorothy Minto and Sam Wilkinson

Synopsis: Chen, a young Buddhist missionary, leaves China and opens a small antiques shop in London's Limehouse district. He meets Lucy Burrows, a fragile beauty in her teens whose father is Battling Burrows, an East End prizefighter. It is Burrows' custom to beat Lucy; she resembles her dead mother, whom Burrows hated.

One night, Lucy staggers out and collapses in the snow. Chen carries her to his house. As he nurses her back to health, Chen falls in love with Lucy. Robing her in silk and lodging her in a shrine of a room, he worships the girl as he would a princess of Cathay.

On the eve of his East Side title bout, Burrows learns from the half-caste Evil Eye that Lucy is living with a Chinaman. Burrows wants to search for her, but his manager demands that he fight. Burrows wins and soon is swaggering down the street, fol-

D.W. Griffith's *Broken Blossoms* (1919) is one of the most exquisite productions of the silent screen. Based upon one of the lurid short stories from Thomas Burke's "Limehouse Nights," the film is a directorial tour de force which utilizes harsh naturalism to convey spiritual beauty through a tale of shabbiness and violence. Its cast is superb: Richard Barthelmess as the missionary, Lillian Gish as the tragic waif, and Donald Crisp as the sadist. Elaborate tinting and toning of the release prints lent some gentleness to the cruelly grim film.

In July 1935, D. W. Griffith was in London, where he signed a contract with Julius Hagen, head of the tiny but very busy Twickenham Studio, to remake *Broken Blossoms* as a talkie. Inactive in pictures since the failure of *The Struggle* (1931), Griffith went to work with enthusiasm but was soon quarreling with the studio chiefs over script preparation. When actual filming was beginning, in September, further disagreements erupted over the casting of the female lead. Griffith withdrew, selling his rights in the production for "a gratifying sum." He was replaced by the studio's production supervisor, the German director, Hans Brahm, who as John Brahm achieved American renown for such films as *The Lodger* (1944), *Hangover Square* (1944), *Guest in the House* (1944) and *The Locket* (1946).

The screenplay is by Emlyn Williams, author of a number of successful plays including *Night Must Fall* and *The Corn is Green*. He also plays the Barthelmess role. Curt Courant, one of the best of the continental cinematographers, was brought in by Brahm.

Several critics censured the company for making a "gruesome" and "horrifying" version of a classic film they remembered as "spiritual" and "poetic." Actually, the remake is almost a literal translation of the original, and the horrors provided descend from Burke and Griffith—although certainly the addition of sound makes

IMPERIAL PICTURES Presents DOLLY HAAS in BROKEN BLOSSOMS
A JULIUS HAGEN PRODUCTION

lowed by admirers. He proceeds to Chen's house. Chen has gone to buy flowers for Lucy, and Burrows finds her alone. Lucy tries to hide in a closet, but Burrows beats her unmercifully. Chen returns to find the wreckage and, hurrying to Burrows' place, finds the battered corpse of Lucy. His vows to Buddha cast aside, Chen kills Burrows and carries Lucy back to her shrine, where he takes his own life.

Broken Blossoms - *Emlyn Williams as Chen greets English visitors (Basil Radford, Edith Sharpe) in the stylized monastery set.*

them more harrowing. The direction is firm, the photography is artistic, and the performance by Brahms' wife, the Austrian star Dolly Haas, is as astonishing as the Gish original. In these particulars, the picture is fully the equal of the original. However, Emlyn Williams—his own excellence as an actor notwithstanding—is far less convincing than Barthelmess, and Arthur Margetson comes out a poor second to Crisp.

Much of the picture was filmed in Limehouse in the actual places described by Thomas Burke, and the baleful atmosphere of the area near the West India Docks is palpable. This realism contrasts with a dream-like depiction of Chen's monastary in China, a deliberate rendering of the unreality of the young priest's cloistered life. These were designed by a well-known artist, Paul Minine.

Broken Blossoms - *Lucy and the vicious Battling Burrows (Arthur Margetson).*

Uncivilized

1936 Expeditionary Films, Ltd., Sydney, Australia
Boxoffice Attractions, Inc., U.S. Release
Also released in U. S. under title *Pituri*
Director: Charles Chauvel
Producer: Charles Chauvel
From a scenario by Charles Chauvel
Original Story: E. V. Timms
Photographer: Tasman Higgins
Music Composer and Conductor: Lindley Evans
Choreographer: Richard White
Special Effects: George D. Malcolm
Running Time: (in U. S.): 77 Minutes

Cast: Dennis Hoey (Mara), Margot Rhys (Beatrice Lynn), Ashton Jarry (Akhbar Jahn), Marcelle Marnay (Sondra), Kenneth Brampton (Trask), Victor Fitzherbert (Hemmingway), E. Gilbert Howell (Vitchi), Edward Silveni (Salter), P. Dwyer (Blum), Rita Aslim (Nardin), John Fernside (Captain), Jessica Malone (Secretary), Richard Mazar (Tong), Z. Gee (Tiki), D. McNiven, P. Rutledge and C. Francis (Troopers), also a cast of aboriginal tribesmen

Synopsis: Australian novelist Beatrice Lynn learns from her publisher that the public has tired of her drawing room stories—she should write something controversial. He suggests she search the Northeastern wilds for the fabled Mara, half-wild white king of a remote tribe. En route, Beatrice is captured by Akbar Jahn, an Afghan camel trader, who sells her to Mara for permission to traffic in pituri, a narcotic made from the leaves of a wild shrub. Mara seems as savage as his subjects.

Mara wants Beatrice as his mate, but so does the tribal witch doctor, Tiki, a terrifying gnome who uses pituri to enslave the tribesmen. Trask a smuggler, haunts the area planning to steal the tribe's treasure. Sondra, a beautiful half-caste, loves Mara and tries to poison Beatrice with an overdose of pituri. Beatrice is saved by Mara's medicine, but the effects of the drug fill her with sexual desire. Angered that the woman who has spurned him should want him only when under the influence of the narcotic, Mara bans pituri.

The witch doctor organizes his devotees

Here is a little-known film without which Paul Hogan's extraordinarily popular *"Crocodile" Dundee* adventure comedies of recent years might not exist. Hogan, a born-and-bred Australian whose brief screen career hangs on his portrayal of the rugged outback adventurer Mick "Crocodile" Dundee, volunteered as much in 1986 when we brought up the name of Charles Chauvel.

"Chauvel!" Hogan told us. "The Aussie Griffith! Did you ever hear of a picture of his called *Uncivilized?* You must've or you wouldn't have mentioned him.

"You might say this first *'Crocodile'* picture is my way of paying notice to Chauvel, to *Uncivilized* which I've loved since I saw it as a boy. Of course, there's a little of *Tarzan's New York Adventure* in *Crocodile* as well, but yes, my big influence here is *Uncivilized* and its 'white savage' hero."

Geographic isolation has long kept Australia from competing fully in the film business with the East and the West. There has been an active, highly independent film industry in Australia from the earliest days of the medium, however, and for several decades one of its most aggressive and productive practitioners was Charles Chauvel, president of Expeditionary Films, Ltd., with headquarters in Sydney. Adventure was Chauvel's specialty and his approach was very much in the manner that characterized the making of Flaherty's *Nanook of*

to make war on Mara. Mara and Beatrice narrowly escape. With aid from the arrival of government agents, Mara's forces are victorious. The witch doctor is killed and Trask is taken into custody by Inspector Peter Radcliffe, the supposed Afghan. Mara has won Beatrice's love without the aid of drugs. She decides to remain with him in the jungle.

the North (1921) and the Cooper-Schoedsack *Grass* (1925) and *Chang* (1927). For his on-location story films, Chauvel shipped over much of the South Pacific, worked under great difficulty in the jungles of Cape York, and staged an Anzac Army spectacle in the Great Australian Desert.

Most of *Uncivilized* was filmed in the jungles of North and Northeastern Australia, in the Kimberly Mountains, and in the central desert, with night scenes and interiors completed in Sydney. The company faced less than ideal conditions on location, being plagued by mosquitoes and an astonishing variety of deadly snakes. One of the crew was snake bitten and, far removed from the nearest Western doctor, was treated by natives who lanced the wound, sucked the venom, and applied a poultice of clay. (He survived).

In December 1935 Chauvel returned to Sydney with some of the tribesmen from Palm Island along with a number of gigantic pythons which he had to purchase from them for eight shillings per foot. (Yes, they do have pythons in Australia.) A celebration at the new Pagewood Studio, complete with tribal dances and spear throwing, was followed by the turning on of lights for the interior sets by New South Wales Premier Bertram Stevens. *Uncivilized* was the first feature made at Pagewood.

Uncivilized is an elemental melodrama somewhat along the lines of *Trader Horn* (1930), except that here a white

Uncivilized - *Composite showing the principals of* Uncivilized: *Trask (Kenneth Brampton), Beatrice (Margot Rhys), Mara (Dennis Hoey), Akhbar Jahn (Ashton Jarry) and Sondra (Marcelle Marnay).*

girl searches out a white man who rules a savage tribe instead of vice versa. There are magnificent, unique backgrounds, some of the best being shown in a river trip through mangroves and jungles into the mist-shrouded mountains. There are numerous scenes depicting rituals of tribes then untouched by civilization (it's a different story today). Especially memorable is a corroboree—a spectacular night celebration with dances and singing—which is photographed with documentary attention to detail.

The story, for all its basic simplicity, develops some twists and turns that are at times difficult to follow. In some ways the picture differs little from American-made jungle films; there's even a renegade named Trask, without which no jungle adventure is truly complete. There are occasional instances of crude production methods, but for the most part it is well done, with imaginative photography by the top-ranked Tasman Higgins and a fresh musical score worthy of the concert hall. The spidery witch doctor, Z. Gee, is a scary character worthy of any who's who of film fiends.

Because of scenes involving narcotics, the liberal use of swear words, some heated love scenes, and a tasteful nude swimming scene with Margot Rhys, *Uncivilized* was shown as an "adults only" attraction in the United States. Lacking the Production Code seal it could not be played in most legitimate movie theaters, so it was seen only in burlesque theaters and "specialty houses." Later, the title was changed to *Pituri* (with the subtitle, *It Makes Them Uncivilized*). Such was the fate of one of Australia's best-loved films in this country.

The rugged Mara is Dennis Hoey, an opera singer who later came to Hollywood and is best remembered as Inspector Lestrade in the Basil Rathbone-Nigel Bruce *Sherlock Holmes* pictures of the 1940s. Hoey is very much the Victor McLaglen type here, not handsome in a matinee idol sense but looking every bit a man of strength. He also sings a bit in his jungle and gives a good account of himself as a character initially menacing but at length proving to be sympathetic. Margot Rhys is a beautiful and accomplished leading lady, and Ashton Jarry is effective as a Secret Service agent in disguise. It is the aborigines to whom the show rightfully belongs, however.

Uncivilized - *Sondra's attempt to poison Beatrice with pituri backfires.*

Blake of Scotland Yard

1937   Victory Pictures Corporation   A serial in fifteen chapters, thirty reels
Also released in a Six-Reel Feature Version through Ace Pictures Corporation
Director: Robert S. Hill
Producer: Sam Katzman
Story: Rock Hawkey
Screenplay: Basil Dickey and William Buchanan
Supervisor: Robert Stillman
Production Manager: Ed W. Rote
Photography: Bill Hyer
Film Editors: Holbrook N. Todd and Fred Bain
Sound: Hans Weeren
Settings: Fred Preble
Electrical Effects: Kenneth Strickfaden

Cast: Ralph Byrd (Jerry Sheehan), Herbert Rawlinson (Sir James Blake), Joan Barclay (Hope Mason), Lloyd Hughes (Dr. Marshall), Dickie Jones (Bobby), Nick Stuart (Julot), Lucille Lund (Duchess), Gail Newbury (Mimi), Sam Flint (Henderson), Jimmy Aubrey (Baron Polinka), George de Normand (Pedro), Ted Lorch (Daggett), John Elliott (Father), William Ferrell (Count Basil Zegaloff), Frank Wayne (Charles), Robert Terry (Peyton), Dick Curtis (Nicky), Henry Hall (Official), Herman Brix (Adolph)

Chapter Titles: 1) Mystery of the Blooming Gardenia 2) Death in the Laboratory 3) Cleared Mysteries 4) Mystery of the Silver Fox 5) Death in the River 6) The Criminal Shadow 7) Face to Face 8) The Fatal Trap 9) Parisian House Tops 10) Battle Royal 11) The Burning Fuse 12) The Roofs of Limehouse 13) The Sting of the Scorpion 14) The Scorpion Unmasked 15) The Trap Is Sprung

Synopsis: Sir James Blake, retired C.I.D. inspector with Scotland Yard, finances a death ray invented by Jerry Sheehan and Blake's niece, Hope Mason. Munitions magnate Count Basil Zegelloff offers a fortune to the mysterious Scorpion to get the machine. After an unsuccessful attempt, the Scorpion locks Blake, Jerry, Hope, and Hope's young brother, Bobby, in a vault. Before stealing the ray, the mystery man plants a bomb, but

Last of the independent Poverty Row serials, *Blake of Scotland Yard* excited much interest among chapter-play enthusiasts because of its colorful masked villain. The skulker is fascinating, although such an active master criminal as the Scorpion must have found the disguise—with hunched back, cape, and a claw apparatus over the right hand—more a liability than an asset. Inspiration for this release came from a successful Universal silent serial of the same title made in 1927 under direction of Robert S. Hill, who also directed this talkie version. An important writer-director during the silent era, Hill, plagued with ill health, spent most of the thirties with the small independent companies. At Victory, Sam Katzman's Culver City Studio, he made seven features and two serials during 1937-38. He also wrote the originals under

Blake of Scotland Yard *- A fight in the catacombs with the Scorpion lurking in the background. Participants are Nicky (Dick Curtis), Bobby, Hope, Peyton (Robert Terry), Adolph (Herman Brix) and Jerry (Ralph Byrd).*

the explosion frees the prisoners. Jerry is kidnapped.

Disguised as Basil, Blake traces the Scorpion gang to a Paris café. He secures Jerry's release, but when the real Count appears, the gang overcomes them, and Jerry is thrown into a sewer. Then Jerry rescues Blake. Hope and Bobby, lured to Paris by a forged note, fall into the Scorpion's clutches. When Jerry and Blake go to her rescue, Hope is struck in the back by a knife thrown by Julot, an Apache. She falls downstairs but escapes death. Mimi, Julot's jealous lover, helps the three to freedom. Blake's friend, Dr. Marshall, lends assistance.

Back in London, Blake and company face a renewed assault. The police save them from one attack. Hope and Bobby are abducted, and Blake is thrown into the Thames. He survives to find Bobby's prison. The Scorpion makes another unsuccessful bombing attempt but gets away. From Pedro, Hope's captor, Jerry extracts information that leads Blake to the Scorpion's lair. The Scorpion disappears.

The chase leads again to Paris, where Blake fights with Scorpion henchmen and is knocked through a skylight into the room where the ray is hidden. Jerry and Hope save Blake from death by hanging. Mimi helps them recover the ray, which they take back to London.

Overcoming Hope and Bobby with tear gas, Scorpion agents recapture the ray. Blake and Jerry chase them but fall into the hands of a giant half-wit who throws them off a building into the Thames. They swim to safety. The Scorpion attacks them with the death ray. Retrieving the ray, Blake charges it with electricity and sets a trap. When the Scorpion—exposed as the "helpful" Dr. Marshall—tries again to steal the machine, he is held by the electrical field. Marshall is turned over to Scotland Yard, and the invention is presented to the British government.

the pseudonym of Rock Hawkey, and filled in as a bit actor.

Blake is strapped with too slight a plotline to sustain fifteen episodes and suffers from the necessity of repetitious situations. Hill rescued the picture to some extent with a good pace to which the London and Paris settings add atmosphere and interest. Fights are well staged, with George de Normand performing many of the stunts. The secret of the Scorpion's identity is not as well kept as that of the usual serial villain because there is a scarcity of suspects.

There is some welcome comedy here and there, including a wild sequence in which Byrd and Barclay escape from an unfriendly café after routing the enemy with service trays and dishes as missiles.

Ralph Byrd, newly established as a serial favorite with Republic's just-released *Dick Tracy,* is impressive as the young hero. Silent serial star Herbert Rawlinson portrays Blake with energetic dignity. There is a good assortment of players representing thugs, international agents, streetwalkers, crippled beggars, Cockneys, French Apaches, a giant homicidal idiot, and a terrifying old hag who blows her nose on her shawl. Extensive use of fog-filtered photography helps mask the penurious budget

typical of producer Katzman, adds to the sense of danger, and gives some Culver City streets a foreign look. The sound recording is tinny compared to major-studio work of the period.

An example of the facts of life on Poverty Row may be observed in the uncredited appearance of a heavily disguised Herman Brix (later Bruce Bennett) as a moustached, patch-eyed heavy. Brix was officially Katzman's principal feature star at the time. Victory Pictures' studio was wiped out by a fire, but Katzman rose from the ashes with later deals with Monogram and Columbia. His pictures weren't award winners, but they were almost invariably profitable.

Blake of Scotland Yard - Hope in the hands of French apaches Julot (Nick Stuart) and Mimi (Gail Newbury).

Island of Doomed Men

1930   Columbia Pictures Corporation
Director: Charles Barton
Associate Producer: Wallace MacDonald
Executive Producer: Irving Briskin
Original Story and Screenplay: Robert D. Andrews
Director of Photography: Benjamin Kline
Film Editor: James Sweeney
Art Director: Lionel Banks
Gowns: Kalloch
Musical Director: M. W. Stoloff
Music: Gerard Carbonara
Assistant Director: Thomas Flood
Running Time: 67 Minutes

Cast: Peter Lorre (Stephen Danel), Rochelle Hudson (Lorraine Danel), Robert Wilcox (Mark Sheldon), Don Beddoe (Brand), George E. Stone (Siggy), Kenneth MacDonald (Doctor), Charles Middleton (Cort), Stanley Brown (Eddie), Earl Gunn (Mitchell), Bruce Bennett (Hazen), Addison Richards (Agent 46), Forbes Murray (Chairman of Parole Board), Howard Hickman (Judge), Donald Douglas (Secret Service Officer), Walter Miller (Detective), Trevor Bardette (District Attorney), Richard Fiske (Convict), George McKay (Bookkeeper), Sam Ash (Ames), Eddie Laughton (Borgo), Al Hill (Clinton), John Tyrrell (Durkin), Ray Bailey (Mystery Man), Lee Prather (Warden), Bernie Breakston (Townsend), Harry Strang and Charles Hamilton (Policemen), William Gould (Parole Board Member)

Synopsis: Mark Sheldon, new undercover agent meeting in secret with Federal Bureau of Investigation Agent 46, learns of Dead Man's Island and its satanic master, Stephen Danel, who uses paroled convicts as slaves in his diamond mines. Brand, a henchman of Danel, murders Agent 46 and plants clues so that Sheldon is blamed. Convicted, Mark is sentenced to 20 years. Danel arranges for Mark's parole to Dead Man's Isle.

At first treating Mark and the other new arrivals cordially, Danel soon proves a menace. Mark is fascinated with the beauty of Danel's wife, Lorraine, who is magnificently gowned and showered with diamonds but is

Peter Lorre, the screen's greatest master of soft-spoken villainy, made several pictures during the early 1940s for Wallace MacDonald's "B" unit at Columbia, producers of Boris Karloff's popular series of mad scientist films. The first, and least remembered, of the Lorre Columbias is *Island of Doomed Men* which was filmed and advertised initially as *Dead Man's Isle.* It was made in twelve shooting days for under $90,000.

The story differs little from a number of other penal-institution melodramas, but the short, sadeyed Lorre adds dimension. He is at his best here as a cultured, soft-spoken sadist who dotes on Chopin nocturnes (performed by his tormented wife) and who with seeming gentleness expresses his regrets to convicts he has ordered to be

Island of Doomed Men *- The Danels at home (Rochelle Hudson and Peter Lorre).*

as much a prisoner and victim of Danel's cruelty as the workers. Danel torments Mark, certain that Mark is there to investigate the racket. Lorraine tries to meet with Mark but is thwarted by an electric fence around Danel's mansion. Mark gets a chance to escape when he is sent to the drunken doctor after a brutal lashing. Overpowering the doctor, Mark flees into the jungle. He is apprehended by Cort, the head guard. Cort agrees to leave Mark's manacles unlocked so that the two can steal Danel's diamonds. Brand spies on the pair and reports to Danel.

That night Mark meets Lorraine at the fence. He urges her to steal the keys to the gate. She obtains the keys while Danel pretends to be asleep. As she and Mark attempt an escape, they are recaptured. Mark and

Cort are imprisoned, but they escape, killing Brand and a guard. Cort frees the other prisoners and announces that he is the leader of the rebellion and that Lorraine is his property.

Mark renders the electric fence useless by prying the wires apart with a forked limb. He enters the house, but Danel gets the drop on him. When Lorraine rushes to Mark's side, Danel decides to kill them both. Cort and the convicts intervene, but Danel manages to kill Cort and regain the upper hand. Siggie, Danel's abused houseboy, steals into the room and stabs Danel in the back with a butcherknife. Before he dies, Danel kills Siggie.

With ample evidence of his innocence in hand, Mark looks forward to a new life with Lorraine.

Island of Doomed Men - *Mark has overcome the guard (Bruce Bennett).*

flogged ("I sincerely hope you will be more careful next time.") Although he pretends to detest violence, occasionally he erupts savagely, as when he kills his servant's pet monkey. Beautifully gowned in a series of seven Kalloch creations, Rochelle Hudson is Lorre's beautiful bird in a gilded cage. Robert Wilcox, a fine, sensitive actor whose promising career was drowned in alcohol and an early death, makes a memorably moody romantic lead. The picture benefits from the contributions of other notable character players, including Charles Middleton and Don Beddoe as secondary villains, George E. Stone, Addison Richards, Bruce Bennett and Earl Gunn.

Much of the exterior photography was done at Bronson Canyon, a granite quarry seen in hundreds of adventure pictures and located only a few miles north of Columbia's Hollywood studio. The plush exterior of the jungle home and adjacent jungle, as well as all interiors, were set up in sound stages at the Columbia Ranch in Burbank. The diminuitive director, Charles Barton, best known for some of Paramount's Zane Grey pictures of the 1930s and several of the best Abbott and Costello films of the 1940s, gets a great deal of atmosphere out of the sunbaked canyon and the shadowy jungle.

Expert photography and an unobtrusively eerie musical score help to maintain a sinister mood. Both are at their best in a scene in which the lovers sneak past the supposedly sleeping Lorre and the camera moves in to show his heavy eyelids opening. First and foremost, the picture gives Lorre control in a leading role instead of having him play second fiddle to more romantic stars as was so often the case.

Island of Doomed Men - *Eddie (Stanley Brown) is lashed by Cort (Charles Middleton) as Danel expresses his regrets.*

Stranger on the Third Floor

1940   RKO-Radio Pictures, Incorporated
Director: Boris Ingster
Producer: Lee Marcus
Story and Screenplay: Frank Partos
Music: Roy Webb
Director of Photography: Nicholas Musuraca
Special Effects: Vernon L. Walker
Optical Effects: Linwood Dunn
Art Director: Van Nest Polglase
Associate: Albert S. D'Agostino
Wardrobe: Renie
Recording: Bailey Fesler
Film Editor: Harry Marker
Running Time: 62 minutes

Cast: Peter Lorre (The Stranger), John McGuire (Michael Ward), Margaret Tallichet (Jane), Charles Waldron (District Attorney), Elisha Cook, Jr. (Joe Briggs), Charles Halton (Meng), Ethel Griffie (Mrs. Kane), Cliff Clark (Martin), Oscar O'Shea (Judge), Alec Craig (Defense Attorney), Otto Hoffman (Police Surgeon), Charles Judels (Nick), Frank Yaconelli (Jack), Paul McVey (Lieutenant Jones), Robert Dudley (Postman), Frank O'Connor (Officer), Herbert Vigran, Robert Weldon, Terry Belmont and Gladden James (Reporters), Harry C. Bradley (Court Clerk), Greta Grandstedt (Chambermaid), Katherine Wallace (Woman), Bud Osborne (Bartender), Lynton Brent (Taxi Driver), Broderick O'Farrell (Minister), Emory Parnell, Jack Cheatham and Del Henderson (Detectives), Don Kelly (Cop), Henry Rocquemore (Boss McLean), Jane Keckley (Landlady), Bess Wade (Charwoman), Ralph Sanford (Truck Driver), James Farley (Policeman), Betty Farrington (Stout Woman), Ray Cooke (Drugstore Attendant), Donald Kerr (Man), William Edmunds (Janitor), Lee Phelps (First Taxi Driver), Max Hoffman (Second Taxi Driver), Bobby Barber (Italian), Frank Hammond (Second Janitor)

Synopsis: Newspaper reporter Michael Ward is in a lunch stand near his boarding house when the proprietor has an altercation with Joe Briggs, a young taxi driver. Several nights later, Michael sees Briggs run out the back door of the eatery. Michael finds the owner

Two years before Val Lewton proved (with *Cat People*, 1942) that a so-called "B" picture, given tasteful development with skill and inventiveness, can outclass the high-budget product, another film from the same studio achieved a comparable degree of excellence. RKO's *Stranger on the Third Floor* unfortunately drew little critical attention and did nothing to advance the careers of the persons responsible. *Stranger* was something more than the usual B-for-budget picture; it was given a full month's schedule, starting June 3, 1940, and finishing July 3, with a negative cost of $171,192.

Producer Lee Marcus, a former RKO executive, became impressed with the possibilities of Frank Partos's story in 1936 but was in no position to do anything about it. Four years later he was able to induce the studio to buy the story and hire Partos to write a script. A successful scenarist, Boris Ingster, was given the opportunity to debut as a director. (He did not have another directing job until *The Judge Steps Out* [1949] and *Southside 1-1000* [1950], both successful but hardly "arty" films. These three titles represent the entire feature directorial credits of Boris Ingster.)

Peter Lorre is virtually alone here as a "name" performer. (Admirers of the venerable character actor, Elisha Cook, Jr., might justifiably take exception to a categorical statement regarding Lorre's "aloneness.") Lorre received $7,000 for his rather brief participation; the other cast members found remuneration substantially less—more in line with their standing as "house" players. Marcus selected unknowns for the youth leads after studying screen tests of hopefuls. A former secretary at Paramount, Margaret Tallichet was "discovered" by Carole Lombard and came within shouting distance of the Scarlett

HE DREAMED A CRIME . . . AND THE CRIME CAME TRUE!

Solve the baffling mystery of the—

STRANGER ON THE THIRD FLOOR

with PETER LORRE

John McGuire
Margaret Tallichet
Charles Waldron

Haunting nightmare turns grim reality . . . as murder witness almost dreams himself into the electric chair.

RKO RADIO
Picture

dead with his throat cut. Briggs is arrested, and Michael gains notoriety as the principal witness. He gets a raise and a byline as a consequence. When Briggs is sentenced to death, Jane, Michael's fiancée, is horrified. Jane feels that Briggs is innocent.

Michael begins to worry as the execution date nears. Michael and Jane are caught in a rainstorm one night and retreat to his quarters. Mr. Meng, a crochety old neighbor, breaks in on them with the landlady in tow, screaming, "Look at 'er legs!" and demanding that the couple be evicted. Michael threatens to kill Meng as he throws him out of the room.

Coming home alone at night, Michael encounters an odd-looking stranger who tries to enter the boarding house but leaves after Michael shuts the door in his face. In his dingy room, Michael is assailed by doubts about Briggs. As he surveys his surroundings and listens to the snoring of Meng, Michael hopes desperately that he and Jane can marry soon and have their own home. He starts toward the third-floor community bath; in the hall he encounters the stranger. Michael accosts the man, who runs away; Michael chases but loses the stranger in the darkness. As he returns to his room, Michael notes that Meng's snoring has ceased. He almost knocks at Meng's door but hesitates, realizing that if Meng is dead, nobody will believe his story about the odd little man—and the landlady and other tenants would testify that he and Meng had quarreled.

In a fitful sleep, Michael dreams of his arrest for Meng's murder. In the fantasy, he can convince no one of his innocence. His story of the stranger is discredited, and he goes on trial before a ghostly, half-human jury. As the stranger prowls the courtroom, Michael is sentenced to die. He sees himself dragged toward the electric chair and Joe Briggs jeers at him from another death cell.

Michael wakes with a start. There is still no sound from Meng's room. Michael finds the door unlocked and enters to be confronted by the corpse of Meng, killed in the same way as the lunch stand owner. He packs and steals away, later telephoning Jane to bring him all the money she can get.

Jane pleads with him to call the police and put them on the trail of the real killer. Michael is convinced that both the diner man and Meng were slain by the stranger. He and Jane go to the police. His unsubstantiated story interests the police and the District Attorney. The latter has suspicions, however, and points out that Michael's discovery of both victims may be more than coincidence. Michael is jailed pending investigation.

Jane haunts the neighborhood in hopes of finding the stranger. Late one evening she encounters her suspect. The man tells her he is an escapee from a mental institution, and he admits to both murders. Jane arouses the stranger's suspicions when she tries to phone the police. She attempts to enter a boarding house, but the landlady locks the door. The stranger tries to strangle Jane, but she breaks free and dashes across the street. Pursuing, the stranger is struck down by a street-cleaning vehicle. As he dies, he confesses before witnesses, clearing both Michael and Briggs.

Stranger on the Third Floor - *Mike encounters the Stranger (Peter Lorre) on the apartment stairs.*

O'Hara role in *Gone With the Wind* (1939). Marcus thought *Stranger* would make her a star, but it didn't. She married director William Wyler and retired from the screen. John McGuire had been a bit player before *Stranger;* he returned to mostly small roles.

Whatever its lack of success, *Stranger* is a prime example of intelligent filmmaking. Careful pre-production included the making of 243 scene sketches and the reproduction in miniature of sets and characters. Lighting effects and camera angles were photographed in miniature before actual shooting began, enabling high polish within the time limit. To find a more handsomely photographed picture of the same year, one must resort to *Citizen Kane* or *The Long Voyage Home*. The cinematographer, Nicholas Musuraca, ASC, later worked with Val Lewton, which may

Stranger on the Third Floor - *An image from the dream montage: Mike is being readied for the electric chair. Broderick O'Farrell is the Priest.*

account for the similarity of visual style evident in the Lewton films.

The *pièce de résistance* of the show is a long dream sequence, most of it set in a fanciful courtroom—inspired, perhaps, by James Cruze's *Beggar on Horseback* (1925), but more fantastic in execution. Furnishings were built on mobile platforms so they could be rearranged, raised, or lowered to permit bizarre camera angles and the casting of gigantic shadows on a grey cyclorama. Floors were brightly painted and lighted to give the impression that the players were walking in empty space. Among the remarkable props for this sequence are a newspaper front page with the word MURDER printed from specially made wooden type nineteen inches high, an outsized judge's bench,

and a grotesque Justice figure—a skeleton with a scythe in one hand and the symbolic scales in the other. Dazzling opticals include a dissolve of the judge into the Justice image. The most harrowing moments are those in which the court refuses to believe the existence of the stranger even though the hero can see him climbing over the gallery chairs, and in which McGuire is being readied for execution, a barber working on him while a chaplain recites a prayer. There also is an impressive montage depicting Miss Tallichet's frustrating search.

Acting of the principals—from Lorre's beautifully underplayed man of mystery, to the realistic portrayals of McGuire and Miss Tallichet, to the waspish nastiness of Charles Halton—

could scarcely be bettered. Many scenes are enacted on the RKO New York street (the same gloomy setting where Robert Armstrong chanced upon Fay Wray in *King Kong*, 1933). The ramshackle boarding house with its perilous stairways provides a perfect setting for murder and mystery. A psychologically effective musical score by Roy Webb adds a great deal to this brilliant, underrated film.

Just *how* underrated *Stranger* was— and by its own company—is evident in an RKO memorandum of 1949. A proposed remake was quashed with the words: "Must have been an effective 'B' and could be again, but see no real reason to remake it." Very belatedly the picture has received recognition from film historians as the first *film noir.*

Dark Eyes of London

1939 U.S. Title *The Human Monster*
Argyle British Productions, Ltd.
Produced at Welwyn Studios, Garden City, Herts.
World distribution by Pathé Pictures, Ltd.
U.S. distribution, Monogram Pictures Corp.
Director: Walter Summers
Producer: John Argyle
Screenplay: Patrick Kirwan, Walter Summers and J. F. Argyle
Additional Dialogue: Jay Van Lusil
From the Edgar Wallace novel
Director of Photography: Bryan Langley
Musical Composition and Arrangement: Guy Jones
Organ Music: C. King Palmer
Production Manager: H. G. Inglis
Production Assistant: George Collins
Recording Supervisor: H. Benson
Sound Recording: A. E. Rudolph
Film Editor: E. G. Richards
Art Director: Duncan Sutherland
Assistant Director: Jack Martin
Camera: Ronald Anscombe
Running time: 76 minutes (U.S. 73 minutes)
Credits include this note: "The producers gratefully acknowledge the cooperation of the National Institute of the Blind."

Cast: Bela Lugosi (Dr. Orloff and Mr. Dearborn: voiced by Oliver B. Clarence), Hugh Williams (Inspector Holt), Greta Gynt (Diana Stuart), Wilfrid Walter (Jake), Edmon Ryan (Lieut. O'Reilly), Julie Suedo (Secretary), Alexander Field (Grogan), Arthur E. Owen (Lew), Gerald Pring (Henry Stuart), Bryan Herbert (Walsh), May Halliatt (Policewoman), Charles Penrose (Drunkard)

Synopsis: Scotland Yard is on the spot to connect the Thames drownings of five generously insured people into a formal investigation. "An extraordinary coincidence," declares Dr. Freder Orloff, a small-time lender and insurance broker, when Inspector Larry Holt notices that Orloff's Greenwich Insurance Co. has paid off to absentee beneficiaries in such drownings.

It is Orloff's practice to draw up policies as guarantees against money lent to desperate individuals. His latest customer is a struggling inventor named Henry Stuart, whose admiring remarks about Orloff's charitable nature

ela Lugosi, an abler talent than his industry or even Lugosi himself came prepared to acknowledge, had become in 1931 the first actor for whom horror films would both define and frustrate a career. Within months of that year's release of *Dracula*, the watershed starring vehicle for Lugosi, Boris Karloff had followed suit with his career-cinching portrayal of the Monster in *Frankenstein*. But where Karloff's greater degree of social confidence (not to mention a more thorough Americanization, for both artists were immigrants) helped him to deal constructively with the perils of casting to type, Lugosi found himself virtually enslaved to his bogeyman celebrity. The crunch came toward the close of the 1930s: A ban on such pictures in Hollywood's lucrative U.K. and European markets caused almost two years' abandonment of the genre. Karloff retrenched into character assignments, a holding pattern that demonstrated his versatility and kept his name in view pending a reassertion of the film-going public's appetite for unabashed chillers. Lugosi lapsed into impoverished obscurity, gracing only one high-adventure serial (1937's *S.O.S. Coast Guard*) and losing title to his imposing residence

prompt the broker to counsel Stuart to become a supporter of a haven known as Dearborn's Home for the Destitute Blind.

Proprietor Dearborn is a saintly, sightless oldster who dispenses meals and sermons with a missionary passion. Orloff, who admits to being a frustrated physician, frequents the shelter whose clinic houses a huge cast-iron tank and an array of electronic equipment. Dearborn's helper, a blind and disfigured hulk called Jake, accepts braille messages from Orloff via Lew, a blind and mute street musician. Complicating Holt's progress is the arrival of Fred Grogan, a forger being extradited from America to face justice in London. Grogan's escort, Lieut. O'Reilly of the Chicago police, extends his stay to study Scotland Yard procedures. Also newly arrived is Diana Stuart, daughter of Henry Stuart.

Orloff, while showing Henry about the Dearborn Home, has expressed surprise to learn that his borrower has a daughter. Henry turns up soon as the latest drowning victim in the Thames' mud flats. Grogan, freed on bail, is coerced by Orloff to imitate Stuart's signature on an insurance document. For Diana's peace of mind, Holt hopes an autopsy will show Stuart's death to have occurred by accident. Evidence suggests suicide until the coroner's office determines that the victim drowned in tap water; this disclosure lends significance to a waterlogged scrap of paper, found with Stuart's body and bearing the letters M-U-R in braille.

Orloff shows the police a convincingly signed Stuart document, but Holt and O'Reilly decide to confront Grogan. They reach his flat too late: Jake has broken in and drowned the forger in his bathtub. "Don't they ever shoot anybody in this country?"

O'Reilly asks Holt.

Orloff gains Diana's confidence and secures for her a job with "a very dear friend who runs a home for the blind." Holt intercepts Diana and, taking advantage of her eagerness to expose her father's killer, enlists her help. Diana is convinced that Orloff means well, but she accepts Holt's argument that "somewhere between" Orloff's office and the Dearborn place is the answer.

Lew, Orloff's messenger, has been placed in restraints in the Dearborn Home's clinic. "You're blind, and you can't speak. But you can hear," Orloff snarls accusingly then deafens the man with an electrical jolt.

Though charmed by Dearborn's manner, Diana scouts about and finds documentation of her father's visit to the shelter. While telephoning this information to Holt, she is attacked in her rooms by Jake, whom she disables with a bedside lamp. Jake escapes through a window just as Holt and O'Reilly arrive.

Holt has sufficient evidence to order a manhunt for Orloff. Returning to the shelter at Holt's behest, Diana reads to a saddened Dearborn a news story about the search. In Dearborn's absence, she finds a piece of jewelry bearing her father's initials. Confronted with the item, Dearborn unthinkingly *looks* at it. Diana berates Dearborn as a phony, accusing him of shielding Orloff. Dearborn reveals himself to be Orloff.

It appears Diana will become the next drowning victim, but she manipulates Jake into turning on Orloff by revealing that Orloff has murdered Jakes friend, Lew. By the time the law arrives, Jake, although mortally wounded, has hurled Orloff to his death in the Thames' mud flats.

in the Hollywood Hills. He was living in a leased house only a short distance from Universal Studios, the focal point of his heyday, when 1939 saw a renewed demand for his distinctive gifts. A showman named Emil Umann had launched the revival almost offhandedly in 1938, tapping a pent-up popular demand by booking a lineup that included *Dracula* and *Frankenstein* into the Regina Theatre in Beverly Hills. This provocation of a comeback for the genre translated into a triumphant reversal of personal fortunes for Lugosi, who at age fifty-seven soon found himself toplining Universal's horror serial *The Phantom Creeps*; rejoin-

Dark Eyes of London - *The gentle Mr. Dearborn.*

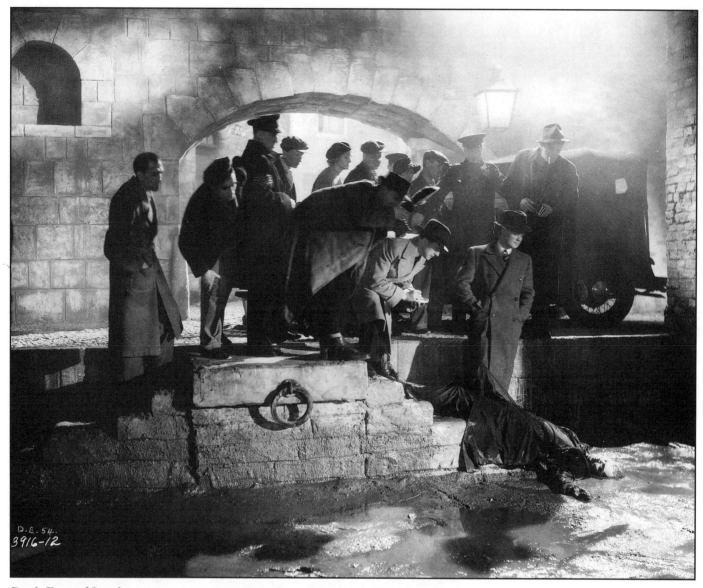

Dark Eyes of London - *Another body is found in the mud flats of the Thames.*

ing Karloff at Universal for *Son of Frankenstein,* their first teaming since 1936's *The Invisible Ray* and their only shared outing to allow Lugosi the meatier role; taking a high-comedy supporting turn at MGM in *Ninotchka;* and journeying to England to star in *Dark Eyes of London.*

Challenged by *Dark Eyes of London* to deliver two pivotal impersonations far removed from his own age range (the wicked Dr. Orloff is said to be forty-eight; the mild Mr. Dearborn appears a generation older), Lugosi responded with a thoroughgoing immersion in character that gives the climactic unmasking of Dearborn a keen edge of surprise. He was helped along, of course, in the Dearborn part by the dubbed voice of an uncredited Oliver B. Clarence, a busy English character man who is best remembered today as the Aged Parent in David Lean's *Great Expectations* (1946) for no amount of vocal coaching could have subdued Lugosi's thick Hungarian accent. But Dearborn's physical presence is vastly more than a white wig and moustache and dark eyeglasses: Lugosi's oily arrogance as Orloff vanishes during the bad man's masquerade as the kindly missionary (his enactment benefitted from technical advice supplied by England's National Institute of the Blind), and his hesitant motions bespeak superb timing. Lugosi cautiously lets slip clues that the blind do-gooder might know more than he lets on, and in one delicious moment when the plucky leading lady Greta Gynt remarks admiringly on the ease with which he moves about, Lugosi hesitates guiltily before managing a disarming reply about how "every sorrow . . . has its compensation."

Granted a modest reprieve from typecasting by the Dearborn part, Lugosi uses the Orloff role to embody all his admirers had expected of him since *Dracula.* Orloff's history as a disgraced physician is never adequately explained, but tantalizing hints of it validate the queasy "mad doctor" sequences in the Dearborn Home's infirmary and allow for a classic Lugosi speech:

"I wanted to devote my life to the healing of mankind," Orloff snarls. "I wanted to be a doctor. But they got together, these narrow-minded, prejudiced medical men, to see how they could ruin me. 'Brilliant but unbalanced,' that was the verdict." Then, relaxing, he adds: "And so, I serve the blind."

The screenplay keeps sufficient faith with Edgar Wallace's source novel, retaining the not-quite-who-dunit narrative structure as well as the interest in procedural detective work but concentrating throughout on the atrocities. The British Board of Film Censors inaugurated its *H* certificate ("horrific; persons under 16 not admitted") on *Dark Eyes of London*, and with abundant reason: the portrayal of handicapped paupers as pawns of a murderer is disturbing enough, but specific moments—a body afloat in the muddy Thames, the hulking Wilfrid Walter's Old Dark House-like rampage through Greta Gynt's darkened apartment, the bathtub drowning of a likable felon, the torture of a helpless blind man, and Lugosi's agonized drowning in river mud—convey a terror that transcends shock value. The asylum where Lugosi holds forth is a claustrophobic wonder, its nightmarish qualities compounded by Bryan Langley and Ronald Anscombe's precipitous camera placements and use of light-and-shadow effects. Most of the settings, both location and studio, seem designed to create a deliberately ugly and oppressive atmosphere.

As the chief detective who must crack the insurance scam while playing host to a visiting American colleague, Hugh Williams offsets his overly boyish appearance with an intrepid relentlessness that borders on cruelty. The American cop is played by Edmon Ryan with an extroverted boorishness that belies an efficient determination, and his wisecracks supply a helpful leavening of unobtrusive comedy. As the heroic young woman who willingly plays along with Williams's dangerous game of entrapment, Greta Gynt sup-

Dark Eyes of London - *Wilfrid Walter as the blind Jake.*

plies so much more than a decorative presence that her romantic attraction to Williams at the fade-out seems artificial. Shakespearean actor Wilfrid Walter's turn as the hideous blind killer is surprisingly understated rather than emphasized to the point of absurdity and his relationship with the Lugosi character(s) suggests that director and co-author Walter Summers had studied the teaming of a monstrous Boris-Karloff with a manipulative Lugosi in *The Raven* (1935) as well as *Son of Frankenstein*, which had been issued early in 1939. Whatever its influences, *Dark Eyes of London* in short order

proved influential in its own right, defining the Lugosi characters of *The Devil Bat* (1940) and *Black Dragons* (1942) and serving as a virtual template for the story of another Lugosi vehicle, *Bowery at Midnight* (1942).

A noted realist among British directors, Walter Summers had entered the film industry from a childhood stage career while still in his teens, landing his first directing assignment at age twenty-seven in 1923. *Dark Eyes of London* was his next-to-last picture. His son, Jeremy Summers, became a director in England some twenty years later, specializing in modestly budgeted thrillers.

The Ape

1940 Monogram Pictures Corporation
Director: William Nigh
Production Supervisor: Scott R. Dunlap
Associate Producer: W.T. Lackey
Screenplay: Kurt Siodmak and Richard Carroll
Adaptation: Kurt Siodmak
Suggested by the Adam Hull Shirk play
Director of Photography: Harry Neumann
Film Editor: Russell Schoengarth
Musical Director: Edward J. Kay
Technical Director: E.R. Hickson
Assistant Director: Al Wood
Sound: Karl Zint
Production Manager: Charles J. Bigelow
Makeup: Gordon Bau
Operative Cameraman: Fleet Southcott
Assistant Cameraman: Roy Ivey
Stills: Warner Crosby
Running Time: 63 minutes

Cast: Boris Karloff (Dr. Bernard Adrian), Maris Wrixon (Frances Clifford), Gertrude W. Hoffman (Housekeeper), Gene O'Donnell (Danny Foster), Henry Hall (Sheriff Jeff Holiday), Jack Kennedy (Tomlin), Dorothy Vaughan (Mrs. Clifford), Philo McCullough (Mason), Selmer Jackson (Dr. McNulty), George Cleveland (Head Trainer), Jessie Arnold (Mrs. Briil), Stanford Jolley (Trainer I), Pauline Drake (Girl), Buddy Swan (Child) Donald Kerr (Townsman), Mary Field (Mrs. Mason), Harry T. Bradley (Druggist), Gibson Gowland (Posse Member), Ray Corrigan (Ape)

Synopsis: Shunned by his neighbors and under vague suspicion of conducting dangerous experiments, the kindly Dr. Bernard Adrian lives as a virtual recluse outside a rural community. His home is a favored target of schoolboy vandals. Adrian's career has become an obsessive search to find a cure for infantile paralysis, which claimed the lives of his wife and their daughter. His only companions are an aged housekeeper, Jane, and two friendly locals, the widow Clifford and her daughter, Frances, who has been confined to a wheelchair since childhood. Adrian concludes that an effective serum must contain human spinal fluid, taken from a living or newly deceased donor.

While a circus has stopped in town, a trainer is mauled by a gorilla he has torment-

In 1938—more than a year after an English and European horror ban had caused severe repercussions in Hollywood—the preeminent horror star Boris Karloff dealt with the drying-up of his genre by signing with Monogram. His strategy was to star in a series of films based on Hugh Wiley's novels about an Oxford-educated Chinese detective named James Lee Wong. These low-budget productions were made to compete with Twentieth Century-Fox's popular *Charlie Chan* titles. Of the other great horror stars, Peter Lorre found refuge in the *Mr. Moto* detective series at Fox; the less adaptable Bela Lugosi found himself reduced to poverty during this time.

Karloff marked time impressively through five *Wong* pictures. By 1940, the horror genre had regained some measure of prestige, and in a move that proved financially sound, Monogram had Karloff fulfill his contract for a sixth film with an old-fashioned chiller, *The Ape*. Keye Luke, who had become best known as Number One Son to Warner Oland's Charlie Chan, replaced Karloff in the last of the *Wong* pictures, *Phantom of Chinatown*. William Nigh, who had directed the Karloff films, was assigned to *The Ape*.

Although *The Ape* cannot be counted among the better Karloff vehicles, it is a cut above most of his others at Monogram. (*Mr. Wong, Detective,* that series' opener, is a jewel.) But then, Monogram seldom made remarkably fine pictures; it was a Poverty Row company, having neither the money nor the top-shelf talent of the major studios.

Exteriors for *The Ape* were made at the old Western town set at Newhall. Interiors were shot at

Monogram's own studio in East Hollywood. A surprisingly big-league contributing talent is Curtis (Kurt) Siodmak, one of the genre's leading writers. The German author wrote the popular novel *Donovan's Brain*, from which three films have been made, and contributed numerous stories and screenplays to the Universal horror pictures of the 1940s, including *The Wolf Man* and *Frankenstein Meets the Wolf Man*. The basis of the screenplay is an unspecified play by Adam Hull Shirk, likely *The House of Mystery*, which was filmed at Monogram in

ed. The beast escapes. Called upon to treat the trainer, Adrian fails to save the victim's life but seizes the opportunity to extract a vial of spinal fluid. He quickly prepares a serum and administers it to Frances, whose legs begin to register feeling. Although given cause for hope, Adrian knows a cure will require a series of such treatments.

Drawn by the scent of the hated trainer's clothing, the gorilla breaks into Adrian's laboratory. Adrian blinds the attacking monster with acid, then stabs it to death. And yet an ape remains on the prowl, killing one of the town's least-loved citizens. Next day, Adrian gives Frances another treatment. Sheriff Jeff Holliday leads a posse on a vain search for the killer ape. Another man is found mangled. A searcher observes that the victims were "ornery cusses" whose demises can hardly be considered losses. Sheriff Holliday finds it intriguing that the beast strikes only at night and invariably vanishes near Adrian's house.

Adrian's progress with Frances is interrupted by the arrival of a onetime colleague, Dr. McNulty, who represents the foundation that had banished Adrian for unorthodox methods. Skeptical at first, McNulty is awed to see Frances take her first painful steps. "May I notify the foundation that you'll come back to us?" asks McNulty. Adrian's reply: "Too late."

The searchers sight the ape in an attack on Tomlin, an alcoholic member of the posse. The monster escapes but not before Tomlin has stabbed it. Frances, sitting on her porch in the wheelchair, screams out a warning as the ape staggers toward Dr. Adrian's door. Sheriff Holliday comes running and fires on the ape.

Holliday finds the dying creature to be a man clothed in the skin of an ape. Removing the headpiece, the sheriff reveals the face of Dr. Adrian, who lives just long enough to see Frances rise from her wheelchair and walk toward him.

1934. *The Ape* resembles *The House of Mystery* only in that a man masquerades as an ape while committing murders. Shirk was rather a good spinner of tall tales: The continuity of the notorious gorilla picture *Ingagi* (1930) is his, and among his noteworthy short fiction, "The Mandrake" appeared twice in the celebrated *Weird Tales* magazine. For all its faulted modesty, *The Ape* is a genuine star vehicle, showcasing at every turn one of Karloff's more driven impersonations. He gives the gentle monster, Dr.

Adrian, a sensitive reading in a setting of hostility radiating from a supporting ensemble of cracker-barrel reactionaries. Even through his unconscionable actions, Karloff holds the viewer's sympathy. The film takes especial pains to locate greater evils in other characters: the (genuine) ape's first victim is an impulsively sadistic carney type, played with slimy zeal by Stanford Jolley; later along, the counterfeit ape does away with a hated loan shark and wife beater, played to the repulsive hilt by Philo

McCullough. Karloff's obsessive nature is never at issue—his captive-audience patient, Maris Wrixon, tells him, "You're so intense, you frighten me sometimes"—but a nagging fault with the story is its failure to explain why the narrow-minded locals should fear him as though he were the very devil. He is shown only to be a gloomy but kindly gent who rides about town on a bicycle, heals an injured dog ("What I've done for you, I could do for men if they'd let me"), and ministers without charge to the hurt knee of a youngster who likes to chuck rocks at Adrian's house. (The boy, incidentally, is Buddy Swan, who that same year portrayed Charles Foster Kane as a child with a sled called Rosebud in *Citizen Kane*.)

There are other story elements that fail under scrutiny: how does the elderly doctor manage to mangle his victims with seemingly superhuman strength? And even accepting the ease with which he must have gutted and flayed the gorilla—off camera—how did he fashion the pelt so promptly into a suit approximating the ape's proportions and heft? Karloff's convincing show of desperation and loneliness (recalling de Maupassant's warning that "solitude

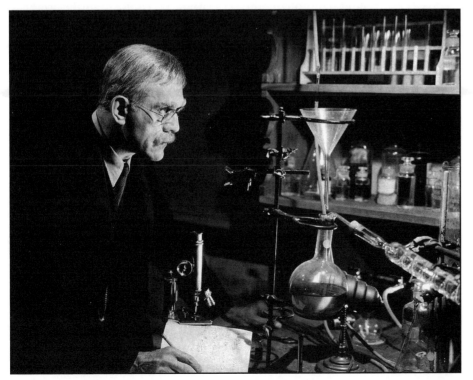

The Ape - Adrian realizes that his serum is getting results.

The Ape - *Inside the ape suit is famed Western star Ray Corrigan. Tomlin (Jack Kennedy) is his intended victim.*

is dangerous for active minds") is a big help in getting over the rockier patches.

It helps, too, that intervening history has lent *The Ape*—as with Karloff's better-respected "mad doctor" films of the same period at Columbia—an importance validated by real-world scientific breakthroughs. *The Ape*'s anticipation of the Salk vaccine against polio more than a decade later is of a piece with the prophecies of cryogenics and artificial-organ technology in which Karloff participated during his run of Columbia starrers.

The Ape's title creature is Ray Corrigan, who at the time was a Western star at Republic. His Republic contract permitted Corrigan to carry on a lucrative sideline as a gorilla performer provided it did not interfere with his other work and he did not

receive cast billing. Although the Corrigan gorillas—he had several ape suits—cannot be called authentic, they remain among the most imposing in the movies, and certainly the scariest.

The Ape boasts good support work from Maris Wrixon, a slender blonde beauty who had done some nice work at Warners. In 1984 the actress told us that, unlike most performers who were sidetracked into a Poverty Row sojourn, she had fond recollections of *The Ape.* "I liked it," she said. "It wasn't so much a horror picture as a tragic drama about a man obsessed with the desire to benefit mankind. Boris Karloff was wonderful to work with."

Philo McCullough has a rousing prelude to his demise at the ape's hands, in a cruel scene with his abused wife, touchingly played by Mary Field.

Gertrude W. Hoffman, in her youth a pioneer in modern dance, is effective as Karloff's aged housekeeper, whose silent comings and goings are punctuated strikingly by one whispered line. Gene O'Donnell is a stock small-town juvenile lead, serving chiefly to embody the townsfolks' intolerance of Karloff. Highly polished small performances are contributed by Henry Hall, Jack Kennedy, Dorothy Vaughan, George Cleveland, Donald Kerr, Selmer Jackson, and Harry T. Bradley. The cinematography, which includes many night shots, is effectively atmospheric; it is by Harry Neumann, who usually made Westerns. Edward Kay's musical score is elaborate and well conceived, ranging from blaring circus marches to sentimental traditional melodies to a variety of evocative "menace" passages.

The Mad Doctor

1941 Paramount Pictures, Inc.
Director: Tim Whelan
Producer: George Arthur
Screenplay: Howard J. Green
Based on a screenplay by Ben Hecht and
Charles MacArthur
Director of Photography: P. Ted Tetzlaff
Musical Score: Victor Young
Art Directors: Hans Dreier and Robert Usher
Film Editor: Archie S. Marshek
Costumes: Edith Head
Sound: Harry Mills and John Cope
Special Photographic Effects: Gordon
Jennings
Process Photography: Farciot Edouart
Interior Decoration: A.E. Freudeman
Assistant Director: Joe Youngerman
Running Time: 90 minutes

Cast: Basil Rathbone (Dr. George Sebastien),
Ellen Drew (Linda Boothe), John Howard
(Gil Sawyer), Barbara Allen (Louise Watkin,
"Vera Vague"), Ralph Morgan (Dr. Charles
Downer), Martin Kosleck (Maurice Gretz),
Kitty Kelly (Winnie - Housekeeper), Hugh
O'Connell (Lawrence Watkins), Hugh
Sothern (Hatch), Howard Mitchell (Station
Master), Charles McAvoy (Conductor), Billy
Benedict (Mickey), Henry Victor (Dr.
Thurber), Douglas Kennedy (Hotel Clerk),
Frances Raymond (Librarian), Harry Hayden
(Ticket Seller), Harry Bailey (Man with
Newspaper), James Seay, John Laird
(Interns), Ben Taggart (Motorman), Ned
Norton (Passenger), Max Wagner (Taxi
Driver), Edward Earle (Attendant),Jean
Phillips, Kay Stewart, Wanda McKay (Girls),
Betty McLaughlin, Dorothy Dayton
(Cigarette Girls),George Chandler (Elevator
Operator), Norma Varden (Susan), Jacques
Vanaire (Waiter), Laura Treadwell (Woman),
William J. Kline (Butler), Larry McGrath
(Photographer), William Wayne (Taxi
Driver), Johnnie Morris (Newsboy), George
Walcott (Chauffeur), Charles Hamilton
(Cop), Dick Rich.

Synopsis: Dr. Charles Downer, the only prac-
ticing physician in a New England town called
Midbury, learns from Dr. George Sebastien
that the latter's wife, Downer's patient, has
died. Downer suspects that Sebastien, a psy-

'Twas ever thus. A hefty body of film criticism tells the reader more about the critics' prejudices than about the topic. There is an abiding tendency to judge a picture by its title, a refusal to divorce lurid subject matter from expectations of shoddy or sensational execution, and a contemptuous overuse and misuse of the industry term, *B movie*, as though the letter represented some schoolmarmish scale of grading for quality. Such failings helped to scuttle prospects of popular acceptance for *The Mad Doctor* in its day—and have figured in the inaccuracy of its reputation these many years later. "Not a horror film," Leonard Maltin's influential *TV Movies and Video Guide* explains today, "but a polished B . . ."

No more a B-for-budget picture than its contributing talents can be dismissed as second stringers, *The Mad Doctor* is a lavishly mounted, elegantly played psychological chiller, of prestigious origin and elaborate development. The film supplied director Tim Whelan with a fittingly classy return to Hollywood (he had ended a long stay in England as co-director on 1939's *The Thief of Baghdad*); it allowed Basil Rathbone a showy, cerebral role that should weight any argu-

chiatrist from Vienna, has murdered his wealthy wife.

Downer's suspicion is well founded. Sebastien is in fact Dr. Frederick Langamann, a fugitive from an Austrian death sentence. Unhinged by his first wife's infidelity, he had slain her and her lover, then decided he must marry one monied woman after another and do away with them by scientific means. The obsession has brought him to the United States and his latest victim. Sebastien's charm, good looks, and knowledge of the mind serve him well in his sinister campaign.

Moving to New York, Sebastien and his friend and aide, Maurice Gretz, find a ready clientele of neurotic rich women. The lovely Linda Boothe, an orphaned heiress who suffers a suicidal complex, seems an ideal victim.

Linda's former fiance, Gil Sawyer, is a sharp journalist who sets out bitterly to expose Sebastien as a charlatan. But Sebastien falls in love with Linda and chooses to bury his past and pursue a normal life. Finding his plan endangered by Gil's investigation, Sebastien hastily marries Linda.

Gil seeks out Dr. Downer and compares observations. An autopsy is ordered in the death of Sebastien's Midbury wife. Gretz goes to steal and dispose of the body before the official exhumation can take place, killing a cemetery watchman in the process.

Gil arranges to bring Dr. Downer to New York. Downer telephones Linda and tells her of the mystery surrounding the death of the prior Mrs. Sebastien. Linda hurries to meet Downer at a subway station. Sebastien, learning of the rendezvous, dispatches Gretz. Linda arrives just as Downer is pushed from a platform to his death under the wheels of a train.

Returning home, Linda accuses her husband. Sebastien, resigned, calmly admits the truth and tells her that, with their chance for happiness together destroyed, he will have to kill her. The madman carries his fainting wife to a window. Gil arrives with the police in time to save Linda from a fatal drop. Sebastien flees onto a ledge, hundreds of feet above the street. As the law closes in, Sebastien looks toward the sky and dives headfirst into space. "You should have seen his face," Linda tells Gil. "His eyes so cruel, and yet so sad."

ment for his supremacy among screen villains; it inspired a memorably brooding orchestral score from the great composer Victor Young; it showcased superb cinematography by future director Ted Tetzlaff; and it established—however belatedly and secretively—a brilliant working relationship that had existed between Paramount Pictures and the independent company of Ben Hecht and Charles MacArthur. And yet the *New York Times'* Bosley Crowther, upon considering *The Mad Doctor* as a new release, pronounced it best not to wonder what misfortunes had placed so high a calibre of artistry at the service of such a motion picture.

In fairness, *The Mad Doctor* proves to have suffered as much from its own poor timing of production and distribution as from its generally unkind notices. The film reached the screen only after a long period of false starts, neglect, hurried and indecisive final preparation, and postponed distribution.

Those madcap neo-renaissance men, Hecht and MacArthur, had conceived the screenplay as a star vehicle for John Barrymore, naming it *The Monster* in a sly reference to a nickname bestowed by the wanton actor's comrades. Later, Hecht and MacArthur rewrote the piece as *Destiny* for Noel Coward, who had just starred in *The Scoundrel* (1935) for their outfit at Astoria, Queens. The Hecht-MacArthur films had proved unprofitable for Paramount, which provided financing and distribution, and the partners' company was dissolved. From the collapse, Paramount inherited *Destiny*—for which the big studio had already paid $50,000. Basil Rathbone had turned down the picture, but with a title change and a new opening scene

The Mad Doctor - *Sebastien feigns grief at his wife's funeral. Dr. Downer (Ralph Morgan), at right, is devastated by the unexpected death.*

The Mad Doctor - *Sebastien (Basil Rathbone), Linda (Ellen Drew) and Gil (John Howard) in* The Mad Doctor.

ordered by producer George Arthur, Rathbone took the job.

Retitled *A Date with Destiny*, the property was put into production on January 22, 1940. It was given preview showings more than a year later as *Destiny*, then finally was rechristened *The Mad Doctor* for its March 4 release. The names of Hecht and MacArthur were dropped from the credits.

Time lost between completion and playdates cost *The Mad Doctor* dearly in acceptance among fashion conscious audiences of the day, who found the reappearance of 1940 hemlines, heels, and hairstyles jarring in a "new" picture. The horror audience, drawn by the title and lulled into readiness by an ominous first reel, must have found the subsequent leisurely pacing and sparse deployment of shock value to be tedious and could not have been much help in the word-of-mouth department. The critical brethren—who had reached a consensus of praise for the commercially unsuccessful Hecht-MacArthur Paramounts—had no knowledge of the source-authorship of this film, which would otherwise have signaled them to trot out the superlatives.

But if *The Mad Doctor* appeared superficially behind the times in fashion sense or ill-matched to its exciting title, it was more cripplingly ahead of its time in terms of subject matter and manner of portrayal. Such painstakingly characterized psychological horrors would become quite the rage all during and following the Second World War—as this book demonstrates by example—but *The Mad Doctor* emerged in first run as an anomaly.

Taken today without prejudice or false expectations, the film succeeds on practically all counts. What *The Hollywood Reporter* singled out as a "wildly hypnotic" title sequence—a

The Mad Doctor - Gretz (Martin Kosleck) on a mission of body snatching and murder.

stairwell.

Whelan, who worked again with Rathbone on 1941's *International Lady*, directs across the board to suggest in Rathbone the combination of cruelty and sadness that leading lady Ellen Drew finally puts into words for the fade-out. Even the bustling Manhattan social whirl, once Rathbone has arrived, seems cold and dark. A faint leavening of comic relief is desultory and forced, especially where a scatterbrained young matron pronounces Rathbone's character to be one of history's great minds. "What about Socrates?" asks the impressively grumpy John Howard, as the news reporter who will bring Rathbone's Dr. Sebastien to bay on selfish accounts and with an incomplete understanding of the beast. Replies the matron, a trademark bubblehead portrayal by Barbara "Vera Vague" Allen: ". . . Well, if Dr. Sebastien doesn't work out, we'll try him."

Such attempts at humor at least demonstrate efficiently what easy marks Rathbone has selected. More convincing is the California-for-New York location work, especially a Coney Island montage comprising shots made at the now-extinct Ocean Park Amusement Pier. Elsewhere, the body of water where Kosleck disposes of a cemetery truck containing a snatched body is Lake Sherwood, site of the MGM *Tarzan* pictures (1932-1942) and a portion of *Frankenstein* (1931). There are some convincing large-scale process background shots by Farciot Edouart and some nifty day and night matte shots by Gordon Jennings which blend a roof garden nightclub into the rest of the city.

rainstorm is integral to the lettering's illusion of three dimensions, with water dripping from the words—gives way to creepy Martin Kosleck's dead-of-night summoning of the town physician, Ralph Morgan. Basil Rathbone is a study in forced dignity and restrained rage from his entrance until, after a show of mock tenderness at his New England wife's graveside, he begins letting the controls slip almost imperceptibly.

Railing in privacy about the newly buried wife's suffocating affections, Rathbone provokes this from his fellow miscreant, Kosleck: "She's dead. Isn't that enough?" Rathbone snaps back: "No! I can never forgive her the eight months spent in this cave of romance!" (The "cave" is a mansion.) Throughout, there surface suggestions of a homosexual bond between the Rathbone and Kosleck characters, culminating in some pointedly bitchy

harshness as Rathbone dares to acknowledge his genuinely tender feelings toward intended victim Ellen Drew. "Has it ever crept into that aboriginal skull of yours," he rants to Kosleck, "a slight wonder as to why anyone so brilliant, so superior, as I should have gone through life like some, some medieval monster?" This element appears a vestige of the script's having been tailored at one point to the flamboyantly gay Noel Coward.

Kosleck, as the subordinate monster, accounts for the welcome occasional jolt of terrifying violence. Recalling by turns the polished menace that Peter Lorre could radiate and the feral presence of Dwight Frye, Kosleck tallies a small but impressive body count in the service of Rathbone until an unsavory past literally catches up with him—in a rather clumsily contrived chance encounter—and he meets his doom in a subway station's

Among the Living

1941 Paramount Pictures, Incorporated
Director: Stuart Heisler
Producer: Sol C. Siegel
Associate Producer: Colbert Clark
Screenplay: Lester Cole and Garrett Fort
Story: Brian Marlow and Lester Cole
Director of Photography: Theodor Sparkuhl
Art Directors: Hans Dreier and Haldane Douglas
Set Decorations: A. E. Freudeman
Film Editor: Everett Douglas
Music Score: Gerard Carbonara
Sound Superviser: Hugo Grenzbach
Assistant Director: Arthur Black
Running Time: 68 minutes

Cast: Albert Dekker (Paul Raden/John Raden), Susan Hayward (Millie Pickens), Harry Carey (Dr. Ben Saunders), Frances Farmer (Elaine Raden), Gordon Jones (Bill Oakley), Jean Phillips (Peggy Nolan), Ernest Whitman (Pompei), Maude Eburne (Mrs. Pickens), Frank M. Thomas (Sheriff), Harlan Briggs (Judge), Clarence Muse (Waiter), Patti Lacey, Roy Lester, Ray Hirsch and Jane Allen (Jitterbug Dancers), also Dorothy Sebastian, Rod Cameron, Archie Twitchell, Ella Neal, William Stack, Lane Chandler, Catherine Craig, Eddy Chandler, Abe Dinovitch, Jack Curtis, Christian Frank, Bessie Wade, Delmar Watson, Richard Webb, Mimi Doyle, John Kellogg, Blanche Payson, George Turner, Harry Tenbrook, Ethan Laidlaw, Charles Hamilton, Frank S. Hagney, Lee Shumway, James Millican, Len Hendry

Synopsis: Maxim Raden, hated owner of the lately closed Radentown Mills, is lowered into his grave while millworkers crowd outside the private cemetery, wondering what their future holds. At the grave is Maxim's son, John, who has been away for twenty-five years; John's wife, Elaine; and Dr. Ben Saunders, family confidant. Watching from a distance is Pompey, an aged black man who has guarded the family secret for a quarter of a century. Strapped in a straitjacket in a secret room at Radenhouse, the gigantic and forbidding mansion at the edge of town, is John's twin brother, Paul, reputedly dead after a childhood "accident."

Later, Saunders explains to John that Paul

tuart Heisler had been a film editor for twenty-four years when he made a tentative stab at directing *Straight From the Shoulder* (1936) for Paramount and handled the second-unit work for John Ford's *The Hurricane* (1937). He returned to the Moviola for another three years before Paramount entrusted him with direction of a low budget film about a boy and his dog, *The Biscuit Eater* (1940), which to the studio's surprise proved to be a notable "sleeper," widely praised for its deft touches and atmosphere. He followed in 1941 with two horror films, *The Monster and the Girl* and *Among the Living*. Critical praise for the latter catapulted him into the "A" director class. Although Heisler's bigger pictures include such interesting items as *The Glass Key* (1942), *Along Came Jones* (1945), *Tulsa* (1949), and *The Star* (1953), it is in *Among the Living* that his mastery of the medium is best exemplified. It ranks high among the handful of outstanding psychological thrillers that preceded and followed it, matching any of them for suspense, dramatic construction, and sustained terror.

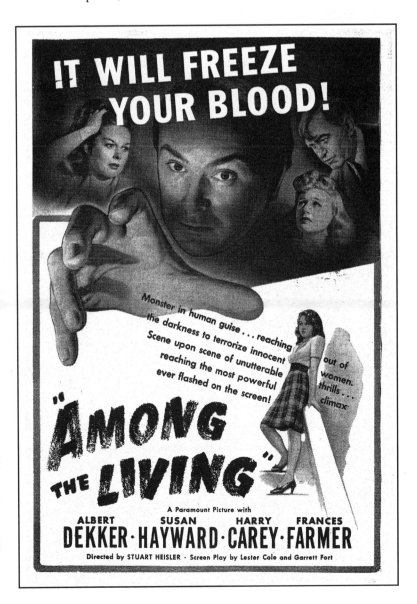

is alive, a hopeless lunatic. Twenty-five years ago Paul had sought to defend his mother from the brutal Maxim and was hurled headlong against a wall. Paul's only lasting memory is that of his mother's agonized scream. Maxim refused to commit Paul to an institution, instead bribing Saunders to sign a false death certificate and bury another child's body as Paul. Pompey has looked after Paul in a secret part of the house.

That night at Radenhouse, during an electrical storm, Paul becomes excited and demands to be allowed to visit the grave. Next day, John and Saunders find Pompey strangled, his hands frozen in rigor mortis over his ears as if to shut out some horrible sound. Paul has also dug up his father's grave, unwilling to let the body lie next to that of his mother. Afraid to inform the Sheriff, they search frantically.

Paul exults in his freedom. He falls in love with the first girl he meets, an unemployed mill worker named Millie Pickens. He wanders into a honky-tonk frequented by mill hands. Pretty, blonde Peggy Nolan flirts with Paul, who stares at her legs as she dances to a black swing band. A fight erupts among the mill hands. The excited Paul chases Peggy into an alley. Next morning, Peggy's strangled body is found in an alley near the mills.

Terror grips the town. A frenzy of greed follows when Saunders tricks John into offering a $5,000 reward for the killer's capture. Millie obtains a revolver and recruits Paul, who remembers neither murder, to go with her to Radenhouse. Bill Oakley, Millie's jealous sweetheart, follows. A mob also heads toward Radenhouse. Catching Paul in the act of strangling Millie, Oakley shoots Paul, who escapes into the great hall where he encounters John. The twins struggle, and Paul exits through a window, leaving John unconscious. The mob arrives, and Millie identifies John as her attacker. The mob cries for a lynching. Elaine, who has learned the truth, pleads with Saunders to save John's life. The crowd accuses Saunders of having been bribed to concoct the story of the insane brother. John, about to be hanged, dives through a window into the garden. He runs to the family cemetery, where he finds the body of Paul lying across his mother's grave. Dr. Saunders surrenders to the Sheriff.

Albert Dekker's acting as Paul is a study in understatement, avoiding the leering cliches and gimmicks so often utilized in portraying madness. He builds sympathy for the beast, whose adventures bear more than a passing resemblance to those of the Monster in Universal's *Frankenstein* (1931), another innocent but dangerous creature who kills his keeper, escapes from his chambers, kills one girl, terrorizes another, and is pursued by a howling mob. That the script was written in part by Garrett Fort, co-author of *Frankenstein*, may account in part for the similarity. There are many nice details to his characterization, such as a scene in a café where Paul listens to the angry villagers raving that the unknown killer must be caught and killed, tries to concentrate on the problem, becomes concerned and finally nods his head in innocent agreement. The massively built Dekker also does well by the normal brother, an unusual characterization for an actor who had just become famous as the monstrous *Dr. Cyclops* (1939).

Susan Hayward, poised on the threshold of stardom, is splendid as a small-town tart, prototype for many similar roles in her later films. She's cheap, flashy and vulgar, avaricious and gutsy enough to try to capture a maniac killer for the reward money. "For $5,000 I'm not afraid of anything, not even death," she tells the unsuspected killer. "What're you scared of? He only chokes people. We've got a gun!" Needless to say, she turns against Paul just as easily as she had taken up with him.

Harry Carey, Ernest Whitman, and Gordon Jones do good trouping in important roles, and Jean Phillips has

Among the Living - Principals in Among the Living: *Jean Phillips as Peggy Nolan, Frances Farmer as Elaine Raden, Susan Hayward as Millie Pickens and Albert Dekker as Paul Raden.*

a brief but telling sequence as a victim. The tragic Frances Farmer registers well in the "straight" part as Dekker's wife, although she said later that her mental state was such at the time that she hardly knew what she was doing. Maude Eburne, as Hayward's slovenly mother, steals scenes with some low-brow comedy. "Us Pickenses has always had a weakness for refinement," she says as she picks at her backside.

The photography by Theodor Sparkhul—a German cameraman who had found a niche in Hollywood after the rise of Hitler—creates menace without trickery. Sharply etched shadows, dramatic tonal patterns and hard-lighted close-in shots give the film a consistent visual style. The separate worlds of the mansion and the blue-collar town are delineated throughout, the fence that separates them being kept to the fore from the first scene. Well executed matte paintings of the mills and smokestacks are well composited with live action in the town.

The most remarkable sequence has Jean Phillips (who bore a strong resemblance to Ginger Rogers) dancing wildly to a jitterbug tune in a sweaty, smoky, blue-collar nightclub, the River Bottom Café. The camera angles and cutting become increasingly bizarre until an almost orgiastic frenzy is reached. The child-like murderer watches her flashing legs, mesmerized. Inevitably, there is a confrontation outside and the woman flees into an alley, pursued by the madman. The camera sees the actual murder scene from a far distance in a carefully framed composition that emphasizes deep perspective and black, angular shapes.

The kangaroo court scenes are also highly dramatic and worthy to rank with the celebrated similar sequences in Fritz Lang's German masterwork, *M* (1930) and Cecil B. DeMille's *This Day and Age* (1933). The sequence is imaginatively edited and includes striking swish-pans from one agitated mob member to another. The detail and atmosphere in the depiction of the small mill town and its people are an unusual counterpoint of cinematic realism. A somewhat impressionistic score by Gerard Carbonara adds to the burden of fear and unease that permeates this remarkable thriller.

Among the Living - *John Raden (Albert Dekker), Elaine, Dr. Ben Saunders (Harry Carey) and Pompey (Ernest Whitman) in the opening sequence of Among the Living.*

Who is Hope Schuyler?

1942 Twentieth Century-Fox Film
Corporation
Director: Thomas Z. Loring
Executive Producer: Sol M. Wurtzel
Screenplay: Arnaud D'Usseau
From a Stephen Ransome novel
Director of Photography: Virgil Miller
Art Directors: Richard Day and Chester
Gore
Set Decorations: Thomas Little
Film Editor: Louis Loeffler
Costumes: Herschel
Sound: Oscar Lagerstrom and Harry M.
Leonard
Technical Advisor: Detective Lieutenant
Frank L. James
Musical Director: Emil Newman
Music: David Raksin
Running Time: 57 minutes

Cast: Tom Mason, Joseph Allen Jr. (Tom
Mason), Mary Howard (Dianne
Rossiter), Sheila Ryan (Lee   ), Ricardo
Cortez (Anthony Pearce), Janis Carter
(Vesta Hadden), Joan Valerie (Phyllis
Guerney), Robert Lowery (Robert Scott),
Rose Hobart (Alma Pearce), Paul Guilfoyle
(Carl Spence), William Newell (Perley
Seymour), Pat Flaherty (Nash), Charles
Trowbridge (Rossiter), Frank Puglia
(Baggott), Edwin Stanley (Stafford), Edward
Keane (Judge), Cliff Clark (Lieutenant
Palmer), Jeff Corey (Coroner), Eddie Acuff
(Guerney), Bud Geary (Policeman)

Synopsis: Special Prosecutor Tom Mason
finds his case collapsing against District
Attorney Anthony Pearce. He cannot find
or even identify Hope Schuyler, Pearce's
mistress and the go-between connecting
Pearce with a vicious fortune-telling and
extortion racket. The court grants Mason
forty-eight hours to produce the vital witness; otherwise the case will be dismissed.
Mason rejects advice that he drop the case
from Rossiter, the politically prominent
father of Mason's attractive assistant,
Dianne.

Courthouse reporter Lee Dale learns
Pearce has been paying large sums to Bill
Guerney, operator of a small airport. Mason
learns Guerney has been renting an airplane

Short, slick, and suspenseful, *Who Is Hope Schuyler?* is a delightful example of the high-quality product from the Twentieth
Century-Fox "B" unit of the early 1940s. Photography, sets, and
sound are equal—if not superior—to the work in the general run of
top of the line pictures. The effective musical scoring is the work of
David Raksin (whose

later output includes
the celebrated scores
for *Laura*, 1944, and
Forever Amber, 1947) and
Emil Newman, later
head of Samuel
Goldwyn's music
department. Direction,
by the little-known
Thomas Loring, has
snap and style, building
upon the mystery and
suspense called for by the script.

Virgil Miller was a versatile cinematographer best known as a master of mystery lighting. He was Lon Chaney's favorite at Universal in
the silent days, Fox used him in some of the best of their Charlie
Chan and Mr. Moto talkies and he photographed several of

Who Is Hope Schuyler? - *Winning lawyer Stafford (Edwin Stanley),
Alma Pierce (Rose Hobart) and Anthony Pierce (Ricardo Cortez) smile for the
news cameras while defeated prosecutor Torn Mason (Joseph Allen Jr.) glares.*

to Hope Schuyler but is ignorant of her true identity. While Guerney is fueling a plane, he receives a visit; the mystery woman pitches a lighted cigarette into a gasoline spill. Guerney is burned to death.

Investigator Carl Spence trails Pearce's secretary, Vesta Hadden. He is murdered by Hope Schuyler. Mason now believes that Hope Schuyler must be Vesta, Lee, Guerney's widow, Phyllis, or Pearce's wife, Alma. Three more prospective witnesses are murdered by Hope Schuyler.

Mason, Dianne, and Lee go to Cedarville, where Pearce maintains a lodge. They find Vesta Hadden and Phyllis Guerney at the lodge. Pearce arrives moments later. By identifying a melted cigarette lighter found at the airport, Mason reveals that Hope Schuyler is Dianne Rossiter. Dianne produces a hidden pistol. Alma Pearce arrives and fires three bullets into the body of Hope Schuyler. Mason now is assured of Pearce's conviction.

Universal's Sherlock Holmes series in the 1940s. His work in *Who is Hope Schuyler?* emphasizes rim lighting and dense shadows to great effect.

The cast, while hardly an assemblage of big box office "names," is an unusually dependable ensemble in which Ricardo Cortez stands out as a smooth villain (almost a repeat of his role in *The Walking Dead* of six years earlier) and Mary Howard earns praise as the mystery woman. Rose Hobart shines briefly in the crucial role as Cortez' crazed wife. Joseph Allen Jr. and Sheila Ryan are a good romantic team. Janis Carter and Joan Valerie add both beauty and mystery to the show. The strong supporting cast of character actors is as good as can be found any big budget movie.

Who Is Hope Schuyler - *Dianne, Lee (Sheila Ryan) and Mason catch Phyllis (joan Valerie) snooping around the mysterious hunting lodge.*

The Man Who Wouldn't Die

1942 Twentieth Century-Fox Film Corporation
Director: Herbert I. Leeds
Executive Producer: Sol M. Wurtzel
Screenplay: Arnaud D'Usseau
Based on a Clayton Rawson novel and the character "Michael Shayne" created by Brett Halliday
Director of Photography: Joseph P. MacDonald
Art Direction: Richard Day and Lewis Creber
Set Decorations: Thomas Little
Film Editor: Fred Allen
Costumes: Herschel
Sound Directors: Harry M. Leonard and Joseph E. Aiken
Technical Advisor: Detective Lieutenant Frank L. James
Musical Director: Emil Newman
Music: David Raksin
Running Time: 73 minutes

Cast: Lloyd Nolan (Michael Shayne), Marjorie Weaver (Katherine Wolff), Helene Reynolds (Ann Wolff), Henry Wilcoxon (Dr. Haggard), Richard Derr (Rodger Blake), Paul Harvey (Dudley Wolff), Billy Bevan (Phillips), Olin Howland (Chief Meek), Robert Emmett Keane (Alfred Dunning), Leroy Mason (Zorah Bey), Jeff Corey (Coroner Larson), Francis Ford (Caretaker), Charles Irwin (Merlini) also Ruth Warren, Mary Field, Harry Carter

Synopsis: In the dark of a stormy night at Dudley Wolff's country estate, three men carry a body to the nearby cemetery and bury it. Meantime, daughter Catherine Wolff arrives unexpectedly and is met by her young stepmother, Ann. Catherine relates that she has just married Roger Blake, who will arrive in a few days. The three men who have staged the burial—Wolff; his secretary, Dunning; and a family friend, Dr. Haggard—are flustered to find Catherine.

Catherine retires, only to be awakened when an intruder with glowing eyes fires a shot at her. Her cries bring the rest of the household. She is told she only dreamed the incident. Unnerved by Catherine's description of the assailant, Wolff returns to the cemetery; the grave is empty.

Michael Shayne, Brett Halliday's genial private eye, made his film debut in the person of Lloyd Nolan in January of 1941. The picture, *Michael Shayne, Private Detective* proved profitable for Twentieth Century-Fox, which had come to rely upon handsomely produced and moderately priced melodramas made by Sol Wurtzel to compensate for losses incurred by some of the bigger releases. Over a two year period, Wurtzel produced six more Shayne-Nolan mysteries. While the initial entry was based upon a Halliday story, the others utilized adaptations of novels about other detectives by Raymond Chandler, Frederick Nebel, Richard Burke, Borden Chase, Jo Eisinger, and Clayton Rawson. The fifth—and, arguably, best—of the generally excellent series is *The Man Who Wouldn't Die* based on a yarn by Rawson, whose detective hero was a magician called Merlini. In the adaptation, the detective work is done by Shayne, with Merlini making only a token appearance.

The screenplay gets under way quickly and is developed with

The Man Who Wouldn't Die - *Private eye Michael Shayne (Lloyd Nolan) meets spoiled heiress Ann Wolff (Helene Reynolds).*

Catherine calls in the fast-talking Michael Shayne, a private detective, who poses as the new husband. That night, Shayne hears a shot and gives chase. Losing sight of the fleeing man, Shayne returns to find that Haggard has been murdered. The police join the search. The killer escapes in an automobile, which crashes into a ravine. At the morgue, his body is identified as that of Zorah Bey, an East Indian magician.

The real Roger Blake arrives. Shayne, exposed as an imposter, is ordered from the house. Wolff changes his mind when he learns that Zorah Bey's body has vanished from the morgue. Shayne demands to know the story behind the secret burial. Wolff explains that Zorah Bey is an old enemy. Secretly, he asks Shayne to stay. When Zorah Bey returns, Shayne sets a trap. The killer and the detective fight it out, and Shayne puts a bullet through Bey's heart. This time the Indian is decidedly dead. It is revealed that Zorah Bey had learned to feign death through self-hypnosis, an art he used in a theatrical act in which he was supposed to be buried alive.

admirable suspense punctuated by rapid action and well timed comedy. Herbert I. Leeds' smooth direction should have earned him a "kick upstairs" to the high-budget shows, but it didn't.

The amazingly versatile Lloyd Nolan plays the wisecracking detective with an easygoing, realistic manner. Marjorie Weaver, a gifted light comedienne, brings a welcome sprightliness to the ingénue role. Hélène Reynolds is convincing as a "rich bitch" while the excellent Henry Wilcoxon is wasted in an undemanding role. In addition to the detective's banter, neat comic touches are contributed by Billy Bevan as a Cockney servant, Olin Howland as a small-town police chief, Jeff Corey as a coroner, and Francis Ford as a crochety caretaker. Paul Harvey is appropriately nervous as a threatened millionaire, and Richard Derr is a satisfactory juvenile lead. The swarthy but handsome Leroy Mason is an impressive presence in his silent portrayal of the title character.

Joseph MacDonald's photography is beautifully composed, and lighting effects are highly dramatic. MacDonald was one of the studio's top contractees whose work includes *My Darling Clementine* (1946), *Yellow Sky* (1948), *Panic in the Streets* (1950) and *The Young Lions* (1958). Effects worth singling out for their contributions to the suspense include a well staged car crash and the low key scenes in which Mason's eyes appear to glow. The score by David Raksin derives largely from the composer's work on *Dr. Renault's Secret* (1942).

The Man Who Wouldn't Die - *Dunning (Robert Emmett Keane), Ann and Shayne hear Dudley Wolff (Paul Harvey) tell of the mysterious happenings at his country estate.*

Moontide

1942 Twentieth Century-Fox Film Corporation
Director: Archie Mayo
Producer: Mark Hellinger
Executive Producer: Darryl F. Zanuck
Screenplay: John O'Hara
From the Willard Robertson novel
Director of Photography: Charles G. Clarke
Art Directors: Richard Day and James Basevi
Set Decorations: Thomas Little
Film editor: William Reynolds
Costumes: Gwen Wakeling
Makeup: Guy Pearce
Sound: Eugene Grossman and Roger Heman
Music: Cyril J. Mockridge and David Buttolph
Special Effects: Fred Sersen
Songs: *Moontide,* Alfred Newman and Charles Henderson; *Remember the Night,* Irving Berlin
Script Revisions: Nunnally Johnson
Western Electric Sound System
Running Time: 94 minutes

Cast: Jean Gabin (Bobo), Ida Lupino (Anna), Thomas Mitchell (Tiny), Claude Rains (Nutsy), Jerome Cowan (Dr. Brothers), Helene Reynolds (Woman on a Boat), Ralph Byrd (The Reverend Mr. Price), William Halligan (Bartender), Sen Yung (Takeo), Chester Gan (Hirota/Henry the Chinaman), Robin Raymond (Mildred), Arthur Aylesworth (Pop Kelly), Arthur Hohl (Hotel Clerk), John Kelly (Mac), Ralph Dunn (Policeman), Tully Marshall (Mr. Simpson), Tom Dugan (First Waiter), also William Forrest, Blackie Whiteford, Pat McKee, Constantine Romanoff, Vera Lewis, Julian Rivero, Paul J. Burns, Thomas Mack, Forrest Dillon, Bruce Edwards, Max Wagner, William Forrest, Gertrude Astor, Marian Rosamond, Roseanne Murphy

Synopsis: Among the coarse seafarers crowded into the Red Dot Saloon—toughest dive in San Pedro—are seated an affable philosopher, Nutsy, and the surly Tiny. Bobo, a big, fun-loving dockworker, arrives carrying a duffle bag and accompanied by his mastiff. Tiny tries to get Bobo to come with him, but Bobo wants to get drunk. At length, Bobo passes out. Awakened by the glare of the sun, Bobo finds himself lying on a bait barge, unable to remember what has happened and how he

Seventh Heaven, a Fox picture made in 1927 by Frank Borzage, caused a sensation with its successful combination of Germanic pictorialism and sentimental story of love and beauty amidst squalor. For decades the studios strived to emulate this success; some magnificently designed and photographed films followed, including *Street Angel* (1928), *Heaven on Earth* (1931), *Zoo in Budapest* (1933), *A Man's Castle* (1933), and another *Seventh Heaven* (1937). Twentieth Century-Fox revived the theme with a vengeance in Moontide, an adaptation of a sordid but beautifully written novel by actor Willard Robertson. Novelist John O'Hara wrote the script, lightening the downbeat tone of the book by making the lovers less tawdry and the ending less tragic, but not sacrificing the somber atmosphere. Veteran screenwriter Nunnally Johnson polished the script without screen credit.

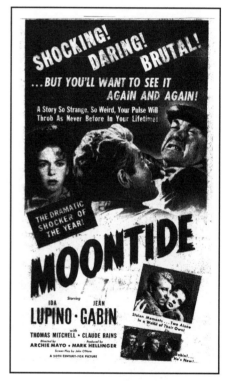

Such a project was a "natural" for the great German director, Fritz Lang, who originally was assigned to the film. Lang, who had been suffering from a gall bladder infection, withdrew after the fourth day of shooting. The same thing had happened with his previous assignment at the same studio, *Confirm or Deny* (1941); in both instances Lang was replaced by the versatile Archie Mayo. Like Lang, Mayo was a hard taskmaster.

Moontide was the American debut of Jean Gabin, who had come to the United States the previous year. Gabin, a leading French star, was a brilliant actor of the naturalistic school—not handsome in the matinée idol sense but in a rugged, tight-lipped, he-man way. The American stars most like him were Richard Dix and, especially, Spencer Tracy, a pioneer of un-prettified acting. Gabin was completely unlike previous Continental stars brought to America; they tended to be "boudoir lover" types such as Charles Boyer and Raoul Roulien.

Darryl Zanuck, studio production chief, did not set Gabin afloat alone. Assigned to the picture were Ida Lupino, principal contender for Bette Davis's throne as the screen's leading dramatic actress, and two great character stars, Claude Rains and Thomas Mitchell. The picture abounds with topnotch acting, with Gabin (in a role reminiscent of his performance in the 1938 classic, *La Bête Humaine*) cannily underplaying in contrast to Lupino's more volatile histrionics

came to be wearing a nautical cap. Hirota, owner of the barge, arrives and reveals that he has hired Bobo. Bobo is about to resign when Hirota mentions that Pop Kelly was strangled during the night. Bobo wracks his mind trying to remember if he might have killed Kelly during an alcoholic stupor. Bobo spends the day trying to reconstruct the events of the previous night. Tiny thinks they should leave town. Nutsy learns the cap belonged to Pop Kelly. Without revealing this fact, Nutsy destroys the cap.

That night, Bobo rescues a destitute girl trying to drown herself and takes her to the barge. The girl, Anna, at first rails at Bobo for saving her. Later she straightens up the living quarters and sells bait while Bobo sleeps. As the days pass, Bobo falls in love and asks Anna to marry him. Tiny, infuriated, intimates to Anna that Bobo strangled Pop Kelly. Anna is as frightened of Tiny as she is of the possibility that Bobo is a murderer. The wedding day is happy for everybody but Tiny. After the ceremony, Bobo goes to help his benefactor, Dr. Brothers, with his boat. Tiny comes to the barge, drunk and vengeful. He tries to make love to Anna, who accuses Tiny of being the murderer. Tiny beats Anna horribly. Bobo returns to find Anna near death. Dr. Brothers ministers to her as Bobo sets out to find Tiny. After a harrowing search he finds the terrified man, who tries to hide on the breakwater. Bobo stalks Tiny until the latter falls to his death on the breakers. Anna recovers after weeks of care.

while Rains quietly upstages both. Thomas Mitchell brings off the cleverest coup of all, moderating his role until near the climax, when he reveals himself as a murderer and sex pervert. The supporting cast is uniformly competent, and the colorful bit players score as waterfront grotesques.

Strong production values are evident in the elaborate studio settings designed by Twentieth Century-Fox's two most celebrated art directors, Richard Day and James Basevi. Charles Clarke's photography, featuring some memorable night lighting and fog effects, is marvelous in its evocation of the changing moods of the story. Clarke said the entire film—even including the ocean scenes—was shot in the studio. The score used for the opening was the ominous title music from *Swamp Water* (1941) by David Buttolph. Popular songs are utilized as romantic themes, and some honkytonk tunes provide background for a fine montage depicting Gabin's orgy of drunkenness.

The Chinese actor Chester Gan played a sympathetic barge owner named Hirota and is so listed in the cast; by the time the picture was completed, World War II had erupted, and by an adroit bit of soundtrack dubbing, Gan became "Henry the Chinaman" in the release prints.

The studio advertisements emphasized Gabin with such catch-lines as: "S-a-a-a-y Girls—come and meet Jean Gabin—He's different!" and, "Be ready when he comes! Jean Gabin, who can do more with one glance than others with ten pages of script! See him rise to American stardom in Moontide ... the strangest romance ever lived!"

Critics liked the picture and were ecstatic about Gabin, several of them comparing him favorably to Spencer Tracy. The public, though, was as hostile as ever to foreign stars (most of the writing about the tremendous popularity of Greta Garbo, Rudolph Valentino, Marlene Dietrich, et al. is exaggerated) and gave his debut little attention. A second advertising campaign lessened the emphasis on "star quality" and concentrated on scaring the customers into the boxoffice: "A Story So Strange, So Weird, Your Pulse Will Throb As Never Before In Your Lifetime!"; or, "A gentle vagabond turned into a savage beast you'll shudder!"

A 1943 American film, Universal's *Imposter*, generated virtually no popular enthusiasm for Gabin, who soon returned to France and resumed his reign. He was still an important star when he died in 1976.

Moontide - Bobo (Jean Gabin) and Anna (Ida Lupino) *learn to love one another.*

The Night Has Eyes

1942 U.S. Title *Terror House*
Pathé Films, Limited
An Associated British Production
Director: Leslie Arliss
Producer: John Argyle
Screenplay: Alan Kennington
From the Alan Kennington novel
Director of Photography: Gunther Kramph
Art Director: Duncan Sutherland
Music: Charles Williams
Sound: Harris Benson and Albert Ross
Production Manager: Mannon G. Inglis
Film Editor: Flora Newton
Camera: Ronald Anscombe
Make-up: Bob Clark
U.K. Release by Pathe Films, Running Time:
79 minutes
American Release by Producers Releasing
Corporation,
Running Time: 74 minutes

Cast: James Mason (Stephen Deremid), Wilfrid Lawson (Sturrock), Mary Clare (Mrs. Ranger), Joyce Howard (Marian Ives), Ann Tucker McGuire (Doris), John Fernald (Barry Randall), Dorothy Black (Mrs. Fenwick), Amy Dalby (Miss Miggs)

Synopsis: The serious-minded Marian, intent on learning more about the disappearance two years ago of her best friend, Evelyn, sets out onto the Yorkshire moors with a fellow schoolteacher, Doris. They lose their bearings in a downpour and find shelter in a gloomy mansion occupied by Stephen, a morose young composer. A flood has isolated the house by morning, but at last Stephen's lovably bucolic servants, Sturrock and Mrs. Ranger, arrive to take the girls to the village.

Marian feels a compulsion to return. The strange recluse, she learns, is a wounded survivor of the Spanish Civil War and is subject to lapses believed to be fits of homicidal mania. Mrs. Ranger, who was his nurse in Spain, has cared for Stephen since his injury. Stephen discloses that he has been known to slaughter domesticated animals. More significantly, he reveals he had carried on an affair with Evelyn—the missing schoolteacher—and he believes he must have killed her during a spell. Marian insists upon staying, overcoming Stephen's objections and soon proving so good an influence as to enable him to resume

But for some weaknesses in supporting performances, *The Night Has Eyes* might easily be mistaken for vintage Alfred Hitchcock. An old-fashioned Gothic tale in the vein of *Jane Eyre* and *Rebecca*, it spotlights the best Byronic hero of the period, James Mason, as a man who may or may not be a mad killer. His polished performance admirably achieves the proper counterpoint between the sinister and the romantic. Wilfrid Lawson and Mary Clare strike the right notes as an initially appealing pair whose monstrous natures become apparent only at the climax. This is one of the earliest directorial efforts of Leslie Arliss, a scriptwriter of the 1930s who specialized in comedy. Following his success with *The Night Has Eyes*, Arliss directed Mason in two much more popular romantic mystery works, *The Man in Grey* (1943) and *The Wicked Lady* (1945), but remained in England after Mason moved to the United States. Arliss directed other novelettish period pieces into the early Fifties and thereafter specialized in television direction.

There is striking photography of rain and fog on the moors (built in a stage for better fog control) and of a rather spectacular old

The Night Has Eyes - *Reclusive composer Stephen Deremid (James Mason) finds something to live for in Marian Ives (Joyce Howard).*

work as a composer.

One day while Stephen is out, Marian finds a skeleton in a hidden room. A doctor she had befriended comes to take her away, but she rejoins Stephen upon learning the skeleton is that of a monk who died three centuries ago. Her return is timely; she catches Mrs. Ranger in the act of strangling a pet rabbit—a long-standing ruse to dupe Stephen into considering himself a psychopath. Mrs. Ranger and Sturrock drag Marian into the bogs, intent upon killing her as they had Evelyn. The servants have plotted for years to keep Stephen in doubt of his sanity so that he will leave his estate to the "devoted" Mrs. Ranger.

Stephen arrives and rescues Marian. The villains are forced at gunpoint into the swamp; only one of three paths will lead safely across. They choose a path, and Stephen explains they have taken the safe one, otherwise he would have stopped them. Sturrock and Mrs. Ranger stop to argue, however, and fall into the quicksand. Before Stephen can reach them, they are beyond help.

stone house by the German master, Gunther Kramph. Kramph cleverly used midgets on the long shots to give the moors sets a greater illusion of depth. Charles Williams' score, a pocket-concerto for piano and orchestra, is ideal for the mood of the piece and possesses the same charm as his "Dream of Olwyn" from *While I Live* (1947). The shock scene in which the servants are revealed in their true colors is heightened greatly by the lighting and a well timed musical sting.

The picture was saddled with an H-Certificate rating in England because of its horror content. In the United States, it ran into criticism because of the frank portrayal of the relationship between hero and schoolteacher, the earthiness of Lawson's portrayal, and the soundtrack's liberal peppering of hells and damns.

The Night Has Eyes - *Sturrock convinces Stephen that he is a murderer.*

The Leopard Man

1943 RKO Radio Pictures, Inc.
Director: Jacques Tourneur
Producer: Val Lewton
Screenplay: Ardel Wray
Based on the Cornell Woolrich novel *Black Alibi*
Additional Dialogue: Edward Dein
Director of Photography: Robert de Grasse
Film Editor: Mark Robson
Art Directors: Albert S. D'Agostino and Walter E. Keller
Set Decorations: Darrell Silvera and Al Fields
Music: Roy Webb
Musical Director: C. Bakaleinikoff
Sound Recording: John C. Grubb
Assistant Director: William Dorfman
Optical Effects: Linwood Dunn
Running Time: 66 minutes

Cast: Dennis O'Keefe (Jerry Manning), Margo (Clo-Clo), Jean Brooks (Kiki Walker), Isabel Jewell (Maria), James Bell (Dr. Galbraith), Margaret Landry (Teresa Delgado), Abner Biberman (Charlie How-Come), Richard Martin (Raoul Belmonte), Tula Parma (Consuela Contreras), Ben Bard (Chief Robles), Ariel Heath (Eloise), Fely Franquelli (Rosita), Robert Anderson (Dwight), Jacqueline DeWit (Helene), Bobby Spindola (Pedro), William Halligan (Brunton), Kate Drain Lawson (Sra. Delgado), Russell Wade (Man in black car), Ottola Nesmith (Sra. Contreras), Jacques Lory (Phillipe), Margaret Sylva (Marta), John Dilson (Coroner), Charles Lung (Manuel), Brandon Hurst (Cemetary Keeper), George Sherwood (Police Officer), Eliso Gamboa (Sr. Delgado), Mary McLaren (Nun), Betty Roadman (Clo-Clo's Mother), Rosarita Varella (Clo-Clo's Sister), Rene Pedrina (Injured Waiter), Tom Orosco (Window CLeaner), Joe Dominguez (Policeman), John Tettemer (Minister), John Piffle (Flower Vendor), Rose Higgins (Indian Woman), Dynamite (Leopard)

Synopsis: To gain attention for nightclub singer Kiki Walker, publicist Jerry Manning hires a black leopard from an Indian trainer, Charlie How-Come. Making a spectacular entrance at the club with the beast on a leash, Kiki upstages a temperamental dancer, Clo-Clo. The dancer lunges at the leopard, rattling her castanets, and the startled beast breaks

C ornell Woolrich's *Black Alibi* is an episodic, rather sadistic novel with marvelous characterizations and a brilliantly sustained aura of dread and melancholy. The Val Lewton-Ardel Wray adaptation of 1943, which the studio titled *The Leopard Man* to tie in with Lewton's highly successful *Cat People* of the previous year, captures well the unique vision of the author. This is so despite a number of changes, the two most conspicuous being the shift of setting from South America to New Mexico and the shift of blame for the crimes from the chief of police to a mild-mannered museum curator.

The Leopard Man is third in a series of 11 moderately budgeted films made at RKO during 1942 and 1946. These were the work of a special unit headed by Lewton, a Russian-born novelist previously employed in various capacities by MGM and Selznick-International. Each entry was budgeted at about $150,000—somewhat higher than the average "B" but well below what the studio allotted to its prestige product. An artistic, literary producer, Lewton was given considerable freedom in his handling of the films, all but two of which were horror pictures saddled, by the head office, with lurid, exploitable titles.

The first title handed him was *Cat People*. In March 1942, while searching for stories to fit this inflexible title, Lewton encountered "Black Alibi" and urged his boss, Lou Ostrow, to purchase it. "To my mind, this is still the best horror story I have been able to uncover," Lewton wrote in a memo of April 9, 1942. "It seems particularly good to me because it has the cat element which Mr. Koerner {studio chief} desires; we could use the title *The Cat People* for it with some reasonability and, if it is horror that is wanted, the two murders, first the killing of Teresa Delgado then that of Conchita Contreras are, to my mind, the most chilling sequences I have read in recent fiction."

RKO bought the rights for $5,175, but Lewton decided to use an

free, disappearing into the night after clawing the hand of a waiter. Police Chief Robles berates Manning and Kiki for endangering citizens. The cat eludes capture.

On the outskirts of the New Mexico town, Sra. Delgado sends her teen-aged daughter, Teresa, to buy flour. The leopard stalks the girl, killing her as she arrives home. Chief Robles' opinion that the leopard killed Teresa is bolstered by Dr. Galbraith, curator of the local museum. Jerry, consciencestricken, joins in attempts to capture the cat.

Pretty Consuela Contreras is awakened as her mother and the servants bring flowers for her birthday. She decides to take some of the flowers to her father's grave, where she plans to meet Raoul Belmonte, her secret lover. She is delayed. Raoul waits until long past the appointed time and finally leaves. Consuela arrives moments later and remains, hoping Raoul will return. As night gathers, the old keeper, not knowing Consuela is inside, locks the cemetery gates. A short time later the girl is killed and mutilated.

Robles and Galbraith attribute the death of Consuela to the leopard. Jerry disagrees because "It doesn't eat what it kills." Charlie How-Come says the leopard may have killed once out of fear but now must be in hiding in terror. Charlie, fearing he may have killed the girl himself during a binge, asks to be jailed.

Clo-Clo learns from Maria, a fortune teller, that her fate is to meet a rich man who will give her money, after which she will die; she is warned to beware of something black. She meets the middle-aged Mr. Brunton, who, on learning she supports her mother and sisters, gives her a $100 dollar bill. Clo-Clo walks home through the dark streets, fearful because of the prophecy. A young man in a black car tries to pick her up, but she flees home. Discovering that she has lost the money, Clo-Clo goes back to search. Something watches from the shadows.

Next day, Clo-Clo is named the third victim. Jerry, Kiki and Raoul work on the theory that the killer is a man. Dr. Galbraith, who is working late in the dark museum, hears disturbing noises accentuated by the clacking of Clo-Clo's castanets. He thinks he sees her; actually, the apparition is Kiki impersonating the slain dancer. Galbraith dashes outside, followed by Jerry and Raoul, who have become convinced he is the guilty man. They apprehend Galbraith in the hills, where he has joined a religious procession of hooded monks.

Galbraith admits his guilt, saying that something within him was unleashed when he saw the torn body of Teresa, who was in fact killed by the leopard. Galbraith tracked and killed the leopard and made weapons of its claws. He was passing the cemetery when he heard Consuela's call. He climbed up, planning to help her, but he saw "something in her face" which drove him to a frenzy. "I didn't want to kill them, but I had to," Galbraith says before he is shot to death by the crazed Raoul.

original story for *Cat People* and save *Black Alibi* as a basis for a third management-mandated title that loomed on the horizon: *The Leopard Man.*

Lewton, whose distinctive and detail-conscious touch is evident in the writing and direction of each of his films, utilized the power of suggestion and implied menace conveyed through frightening atmosphere rather than horrific make-ups or (with certain rare exceptions) gruesome scenes. His use of sound to intensify dread and to provide startling punctuation was most imaginative and has been much imitated.

The first two Lewtons, *Cat People* (1942) and *I Walked With a Zombie* (1943) are prime examples of the poetry that can be found in an intelligently made horror film, however slim the cost and horrendous the title. The director of these, Jacques Tourneur (son of the great French director, Maurice Tourneur), also did *The*

Leopard Man as his last collaboration with Lewton before being promoted to high-budget pictures. It was filmed entirely at the RKO Radio and Pathe Studios in just under a month during February and March of 1943. The New Mexico location was suggested through sets and props based upon photographs made by Wray during a quick visit to Santa Fe. (On-the-spot research paid off for Lewton, as will be demonstrated again in the following chapter on *The Seventh Victim*). Although he does not receive a writing credit, Lewton wrote the adaptation in story form and prepared the final shooting script, which retains the curious episodic structure of the book. One segment, the stalking of a girl on holiday, was dropped. So, unfortunately, was a terrific ending in which the killer is trapped in his lair, an underground torture chamber beneath an ancient church.

Unlike his first two pictures, *The*

Leopard Man contains several explicitly gruesome scenes which Lewton repudiated later as being at variance with his generally subtle approach. Only once did he return to the ambivalent style of *The Leopard Man* in the extremely popular *The Body Snatcher* (1945), tenth of the RKO series. Tourneur's direction is superb; it's easy to see why the studio was anxious to put him in charge of more "important" projects. Oddly, none of the big pictures he directed—and some of them are excellent—has a reputation comparable to his films for Lewton. There are numerous scenes with what Lewton called "black patches"—shadows to be filled in with whatever menace the spectator's mind will conjure. Typical of the fine cinematographers who worked with the Lewton unit, Robert de Grasse achieves throughout the suggestion of unseen menace.

Augmenting the disturbing images of light and shadow are equally unnerv-

The Leopard Man - Galbraith (James Bell) suspects that Kiki knows his secret.

ing sounds: castanets clattering on deserted streets and in darkened rooms, leaves rustling in a graveyard, a train rumbling overhead, the sudden hiss of the big cat. The castanet sounds, representative of the tragic dancer, form almost a leitmotiv. They are heard during the title music, continue through the opening scenes and recur in other key sequences. After Clo-Clo's death the castanets are used to unnerve the murderer.

There is one sequence that cannot be forgotten. Mrs. Delgado sends the frightened teenaged Teresa to the grocers after nightfall. The girl, frightened by news of the escaped leopard, hurries to a nearby store, but it has just closed for the night. The proprietress yells that "It means putting the lock on again . . . too much trouble." To get to another store she must go down an

arroyo and under a railroad trestle. The terrors of the journey are amplified by the sounds of wind and a distant train whistle. As she timidly approaches the trestle a tumbleweed comes rustling out, scaring the girl (and the audience). She passes through the dark tunnel, which echoes with dripping water and seems to writhe because of distorted reflections on the ceiling. She reaches the store, purchases the flour, and now must return. This time she imagines she sees the cat's eyes glowing among the reflections. As she waits for it to attack there is a horrendous sound—a train roaring overhead. Teresa hurries through and turns to look back. The black leopard is looking down at her. She runs to her house to find that the door has been locked to teach her a lesson. She screams to be let in but her mother doesn't believe

she's in danger until she hears, "It's coming! It's coming closer! I can see it!" Her mother and little brother try to get the door open but the rusty lock won't budge. There is a heavy thud outside. Then a rivulet of blood flows under the door.

The atmosphere of the scenes in the arroyo and tunnel were achieved by photographing them on a stage, where lighting could be controlled fully. A matte composite was used to expand the set to include a night sky and other details.

The killing of Consuela in the cemetery is almost as chilling. Preoccupied, she becomes aware of the watchman's warning whistle the second time it's sounded. When she realizes she is locked in, the sounds of wind and rustling leaves become increasingly disturbing while each shrub seems menacing and the faces of the statues seem to

The Leopard Man *- Raoul (Richard Martin) and Jerry drag Galbraith from a religious procession.*

leer at her. Running through the shrubbery, Consuela almost falls into a yawning grave. Hearing the sound of a car starting on the other side of the wall, she screams. Brakes screech, the car backs up and a man's voice answers. When she explains, the voice says he'll borrow a ladder and be back. No sooner has he left than Consuela hears a rustling atop the wall. A tree branch bends, then springs back—and the scene fades. The music in this sequence is handled with subtlety and poignance.

Characterizations, fine though they are, are secondary to atmosphere. Dennis O'Keefe, adept at both comedy and heroics, is ideal as a flashy promoter with a soft heart, and Jean Brooks is equally so as a nice girl trying to be a success in a hard racket. Margo is by turns brittle and touching in her portrayal of a brassy but vulnerable entertainer trying to overcome her peasant origins. The refugee Finnish actress,

Tula Parma, is fine as the victim in the cemetery, and lovely young Margaret Landry is memorable as the girl who falls prey to the leopard. The fatalistic theme is emphasized by the observations of the sad-eyed fortune teller, played with her usual skill by Isabel Jewell. Some of the character parts are quite fine, such as the philosophical cemetery gatekeeper, played by the venerable old stage actor, Brandon Hurst. "Time is strange," he tells us. "A moment can be as short as a breath or as long as eternity."

James Bell, a low-key actor somewhat reminiscent of Harry Carey, renders the murderer deliberately sympathetic, a seemingly gentle, scholarly, pipe smoking dreamer. He even establishes the philosophy of the picture when he indicates a ball dancing in the jet of a fountain and says, "We know as little of the forces that move us and move the world around us as that empty ball."

Later he gives his opinion of what the murderer is like: "He'd go about his business calmly except when the fit to kill was on him." When trapped at the climax he tells his captors, "You don't know what you're doing, you don't understand . . . I couldn't rest, I couldn't sleep. All I could see was Teresa Delgado's body . . . I didn't want to kill, but I had to! . . . I was going to help {Consuela} over the wall, and then I saw her white face . . . There was something . . . Fear, that was it!"

Roy Webb's music, while less arresting than his celebrated score for *Cat People*, adds materially to the artistry and effectiveness of this weirdly beautiful production. Columbia's *The Devil's Mask* (1946) also utilized the theme of a leopard man killer. The *Leopard Man* was virtually remade in Mexico as *Han Matado a Tongele (They've Killed Tongele)*, a musical mystery thriller, in 1948.

The Seventh Victim

1943 RKO-Radio Pictures, Incorporated
Director: Mark Robson
Producer: Val Lewton
Screenplay: Charles O'Neal and DeWitt Bodeen
Director of Photography: Nicholas Musuraca
Film Editor: John Lockert
Art Directors: Albert S. D'Agostino and Walter E. Keller
Optical Effects: Linwood Dunn
Effects Cameraman: Harry Underwood
Set Decorations: Darrell Silvera and Harley Miller
Music: Roy Webb
Musical Director: C. Bakaleinikoff
Costumes: Renie
Sound: John C. Grubb
Assistant Director: William Dorfman
Orchestrations: Maurice De Packh
Dialogue Director: Jacqueline DeWit
Running Time: 71 minutes

Cast: Tom Conway (Dr. Louis Judd), Jean Brooks (Jacqueline Gibson), Isabel Jewell (Frances Fallon), Kim Hunter (Mary Gibson), Evelyn Brent (Natalie Cortez), Erford Gage (Jason Hoag), Ben Bard (Bruins), Hugh Beaumont (Gregory Ward), Chef Milani (Mr. Romari), Marguerita Silva (Mrs. Romari), Mary Newton (Mrs. Redi), Wally Brown (Durk), Feodor Chaliapin (Leo), Eve March (Miss Gilchrist), Ottola Nesmith (Mrs. Lowood), Edythe Elliott (Mrs. Swift), Milton Kibbee (Joseph), Marianne Mosner (Miss Rowan), Elizabeth Russell (Mimi), Joan Barclay (Gladys), William Halligan (Radeau), Lou Lubin (August), Dewey Robinson (Conductor), Lloyd Ingraham (Watchman), Kernan Cripps (Policeman), Sara Selby (Miss Gottschalk), Betty Roadman (Mrs. Wheeler), Ann Summers (Miss Summers), also Tiny Jones, Eileen O'Malley, Lorna Dunn, Cyril Ring

Synopsis: Beautiful, erratic Jacqueline Gibson, owner of a New York City cosmetics firm called La Sagesse, disappears. Her sister, Mary, a student at Highcliffe Academy, sets out to find her. She interviews Mrs. Redi, new owner of La Sagesse, and Frances Fallon, an assistant. They suggest that Mary investigate a room Jacqueline rented in Greenwich Village

Not all of Val Lewton's celebrated psychological thrillers were "hits." His fourth, *The Seventh Victim*, inspired as much antipathy as did any of the Josef von Sternberg-Marlene Dietrich collaborations. Bad timing worsened the situation, for wartime moviegoers demanded the light, escapist entertainment which dominated the production schedules at all the studios. Horror pictures of the more traditional sort were, for some, as exhilarating as a Betty Grable musical, but so deeply philosophical and morbid a work as *The Seventh Victim* was about as welcome as the guest in red at Prince Prospero's *bal masque*. Even the critics—many of whom professed a desire to watch more weighty fare—turned up their noses, several going so far as to admit they were confused by the story and the less alert ones noting that the title had nothing to do with the picture. The fact remains, though, that *The Seventh Victim* is a masterpiece of film noir—and the title, for that matter, could hardly be a more straightforward summation of the goings-on.

"This picture's appeal, like that of its predecessors, is based on three fundamental theories," Lewton said in a studio press release. "First is that the audience will people any patch of darkness with more horror, suspense, and frightfulness than the most imaginative writer could ever dream up. Second, and most important, is the fact that extraordinary things can happen to very ordinary people. And third is to use the beauty of setting and camerawork to ward off audience laughter at situations which, when less beautifully pho-

over the Dante Restaurant. Mary breaks into the room to find it empty but for a hanging noose and, beneath it, a chair. She visits the Missing Persons Bureau and the morgue without avail. She meets Jacqueline's lover, Gregory Ward, a young lawyer. Ward, who had rented the room for Jacqueline, says that she seemed happy living there "in a world of her own fancy."

At her hotel, Mary meets Irving August, private detective, who believes Jacqueline is a prisoner at La Sagesse. That night, Mary waits fearfully outside in the darkness while August searches the cosmetics firm. August emerges, an expression of horror on his face, and falls dead at Mary's feet with a knife in his back. Mary flees the neighborhood, finally boarding a subway express. Two men in the car are holding up what appears to be a drunken companion. When the car lurches, the "drunk" man's hat falls off, revealing the face of Irving August. Mary runs to another car and returns with help, but the men have gone.

Jacqueline's analyst, Dr. Judd, tells Ward he needs money to take to Jacqueline's hiding place. Ward gives Judd the money, but Judd will not comment further. Judd offers to take Mary to Jacqueline. They go to an empty room. Judd leaves suddenly, and Mary catches a glimpse of Jacqueline at the door. Two men arrive, claiming to be detectives hired by Ward, whom they know as Jacqueline's husband.

At the Dante Restaurant, Ward tells Mary he kept the marriage a secret for reasons of his own. Jason Hoag, a poet, approaches them with an offer to help. Hoag takes them to a party at the apartment of Natalie Cortez, a former ballerina, coldly beautiful and missing an arm. Judd is there, but still he refuses to divulge anything.

Hoag learns at the public library that Mrs. Redi and Judd have checked out books on religious history including information about the Palladists, a devil-worship cult whose symbol—a triangle contained in a parallelogram— is identical to the La Sagesse trademark. Mary goes to La Sagesse to learn more about Mrs. Redi. Later, while showering, Mary sees the shadow of Mrs. Redi on the curtain; she is told to return to Highcliffe and ask no further questions because Jacqueline killed Irving August by mistake and is in danger of being connected with the crime.

The Palladists gather at Natalie Cortez's home to decide what must be done about Jacqueline, who they fear has betrayed them to Judd and endangered their safety by killing the detective. Six members who had betrayed the cult all were coerced into suicide. The same fate is decreed for Jacqueline; murder will be resorted to only if she refuses.

Judd gathers Jason, Mary, and Jacqueline in a room above the Dante, where Jacqueline tells how she joined the Palladists in despair and then tried to break free, whereupon she was imprisoned at La Sagesse. Thinking August was a cultist come to kill her, she stabbed him. Next morning, despite protective efforts, the Palladists capture Jacqueline and take her to the Cortez apartment, where she is urged to drink poison. Finally, at midnight, Jacqueline is freed and begins a fearful walk through deserted streets. Leo, a knife-wielding cultist, follows. The assassin turns back when Jacqueline encounters a group of actors en route to a cafe. Judd and Jason go to the Cortez place and tell off the Palladists, who include Mrs. Redi, Frances Fallon, Natalie Cortez, a La Sagesse chemist named Joseph, and other respectable-looking people.

Jacqueline returns to her old lodgings. In the hallway she meets Mimi, a drab neighbor, who fears her imminent death from consumption. Jacqueline tells her she must not await death. They go to their respective rooms while, in another room, Mary and Gregory reveal their love for one another. Mimi emerges from her room, dressed now in flashy clothing, going out "to live." The sound of a falling chair is heard from behind Jacqueline's door.

The Seventh Victim - Mary Gibson (Kim Hunter) tells Miss Lowood (Ottola Nesmith) and Miss Gilchrist (Eve March) that she must leave school.

tographed, might seem ludicrous."

The press release also engaged in a bit of implicit nose-thumbing at the competition, Universal, quoting Lewton to the effect that "Up to the advent of the new RKO horror school, the characters in the run-of-the-mill 'weirdies' were usually people very remote from the audiences' experiences. European nobles of dark antecedents, mad scientists, man-created monsters, and the like cavorted across the screen. With the thought that it would be much more entertaining if people with whom audiences could identify were to be shown in contact with the strange, the unusual, and the occult, we made it a basic part of our work to show normal people—engaged in normal occupations—in our pictures."

The Seventh Victim has fewer "normal" types than most other Lewton films, inasmuch as it is set in Greenwich Village, where rather unusual folk tend to congregate. The orphaned heroine—beautifully played by Kim Hunter, David O. Selznick's 20-year-old "discovery," in her film debut—invites attention, being a highly sympathetic innocent, a modern Jane Eyre. Most of the cultists are superficially ordinary types, such as one might expect to meet in any large city, although there are hints of lesbianism in the female-dominated cult (anything stronger than a hint would have been quashed by the Hays Office), and a couple of the male members seem less subtly deranged than others. The overall impression is that of misfits who feel betrayed by life and have turned to evil.

DeWitt Bodeen wrote the first story treatment of *The Seventh Victim* based upon Lewton's idea concerning a series of murders in an oilfield in Los Angeles. Lewton next sent the writer to New York to conduct research for a forthcoming script to be called *Curse of the Cat People.* While there, Bodeen received a letter from Lewton saying that his draft of *The Seventh Victim* had been scrapped and that Lewton and Charles O'Neal were working on a different approach. A subsequent letter instructed Bodeen to try to attend a Satanist meeting in New York City. Through the efforts of RKO's New York office, Bodeen was admitted as a silent observer at a cult meeting. He found the members to be predominantly older men and women who knitted and sipped tea while casting spells against Hitler. They seemed unexceptional—but for some basic flaw that made each one embrace evil. When Bodeen returned to Hollywood, he found the O'Neal script partly done but contributed some important details including realistic villains who add an unusual flavor. His cultists bear no resemblance to the robed, Latin-chanting fanatics depicted in other films about Satanism (cf. *The Black Cat*) and in fact anticipate the worshippers in the William Castle-Roman Polanski *Rosemary's Baby* (1968).

Prominent among the cultists, and establishing most effectively the idea of intelligent but twisted malcontents, are the one-armed former dancer, played with great style by Evelyn Brent; the melancholy Frances, given the proper note of despair by Isabel Jewell; and the mannish Mrs. Redi, invested with a slowly mounting malevolence in Mary Newton's performance. Ben Bard's characterization seems the grim sort of fanatic one finds in the vanguard of extremist political groups—a man who smiles often but without humor.

Tom Conway, curiously, repeats his role from *Cat People* even though the Dr. Louis Judd character was

The Seventh Victim - *Gregory (Hugh Beaumont), Dr. Judd (Tom Conway), Mary, and Jason (Erford Gage) listen to Jacqueline's (Jean Brooks) story.*

The Seventh Victim - Jacqueline almost meets death at the hands of Leo.

And all my Pleasures are like Yesterdays.

This picture marks the directorial debut of Mark Robson, who edited the previous Lewton films. A wise choice with respect to both artistry and financial consciousness, Robson brought the picture in within its budget inside of twenty-four days. Robson directed four more pictures for Lewton before his own "graduation" (like that of his predecessor with the Lewton unit, Jacques Tourneur) to bigger productions. Lewton's commitment to "beauty of setting and camerawork" had a willing and able practitioner in Nick Musuraca, who photographed five of the

killed in the climax of that first Lewton film. He is in this instance a more sympathetic character, although he is again paying court to another man's wife and there is a suggestion of hidden menace in his cynical, smooth performance. That the fascinating Elizabeth Russell also appears in a role which possibly identifies with her memorable scene in *The Cat People* further suggests a "prequel." Hugh Beaumont (a Methodist preacher who financed his ministry with acting roles) deadpans the part of the lawyer married to a girl who obviously has no interest in him, and Erford Gage lends little credence to the part of an unsuccessful poet who equates himself with Cyrano (as did Val Lewton). Lou Lubin is splendid as a sleazy, nervous private detective—a tragicomic role that anticipates the all-too-brief appearance of Walter Matthau in *Mirage* (1965), a worthy

descendant of the Lewton formula pitting everyday people against overpowering intrigue. Mme. Marguerita Sylva, celebrated operatic star of the turn of the century, is cast appropriately as a once-famous singer, and Chef Milani, a famed culinary expert on radio, is equally at home as the proprietor of the Dante Restaurant.

What most poignantly haunts the memory is Jean Brooks' portrayal of the confused, suicide prone Jacqueline. Her exchange with the dying wallflower played by Elizabeth Russell is both gentle and harrowing. The character of a fragile beauty doomed by her own irreconcilable distraction is so perfectly realized by Brooks as to strike a painful chord in the breast of anyone who has known such a person. It is she who embodies the John Donne quotation which opens and closes the film:
I run to death, and death meets me as fast.

Lewtons; Musuraca's exquisite compositions and chiaroscuro help immeasurably to carry the unrelenting mood of lurking evil. There is one interesting, undetectable optical composite in the picture: only the left side of the hallway outside Jacqueline's apartment was constructed and the other half was printed in for certain scenes.

A question exists as to how much more powerful *The Seventh Victim* might have been before the final editing; Bodeen felt the film suffered because several key sequences were cut from the release version.

Quality of sound matches that of photography, with long silences shattered by sudden noises—a cat topples a garbage can during one tense moment, and in another taut scene an off-screen peal of shrill laughter cuts through the ominous quiet—and subtly integrated music of a superior kind.

Bluebeard

1944 PRC Pictures, Inc.
Director: Edgar G. Ulmer
Producer: Leon Fromkess
Associate Producer: Martin Mooney
Original Story: Arnold Phillips and Werner H. Furst
Screenplay: Pierre Gendron
Musical Composition and Orchestration: Erdody
Production Design: Eugen Schufftan
Production Manager: C. A. Beute
Assistant Director: Raoul A. Pagel
Art Director: Paul Palmentola
Assistant Art Director: Angelo Scibetta
Set Decorations: Glenn P. Thompson
Sound Engineer: John Carter
Master of Properties: Charles Stevens
Director of Photography: Jockey A. Feindel
Wardrobe: James H. Wade
Coiffures: Loretta Francel
Makeup: Milburn Moranti
Supervising Film Editor: Carl Pierson
Marionettes: Barlow & Baker
Running Time: 73 minutes

Cast: John Carradine (Gaston Morell), Jean Parker (Lucille), Nils Asther (Inspector LeFevre), Ludwig Stossel (Lamarte), George Pembroke (Inspector Ranard), Teala Loring (Francine), Sonia Sorel (Renee Clarmont), Henry Kolker (Deschamps), Emmet Lynn (Le Soldat), Iris Adrian (Mimi), Patti McCarty (Babette), Carrie Devan (Constance), Anne Sterling (Jeanette)

Synopsis: In Paris in the last century, the puppet master Gaston Morrell leads a bizarre secret life: Between engagements for his marionette Faust, he paints haunting portraits of the beautiful women who fall for him; these are placed pseudonymously through a conniving broker named Lamarte. The agent exercises control through his knowledge that Morrell feels compelled to strangle every woman who poses for him. Morrell is the "Bluebeard" for whom the Surete searches—so named after the folk tale about a serial killer of women.

Morrell's tolerant mistress, the singer Renee Claremont, grows more jealous than usual when he attempts a flirtation with Lucille, a modiste. Morrell strangles Renee

On a chance encounter in a New Mexico coffee shop thirty years ago, John Carradine warmed to an opportunity for conversation. The grand-manner actor recited Shakespeare at length—to the amused puzzlement of the local regulars—and inventoried for us a handful of his more fondly remembered assignments from the almost 100 pictures he had graced during the thirty-one years prior to our meeting. His hard-luck Preacher Casey of *The Grapes of Wrath* (1940) was mentioned, of course, in part as his prelude to a gag about a grouchy-ghost story he called "The Gripes of Wraith." He cited his Abraham Lincoln impersonation in *Of Human Hearts* (1938) and his Aaron to Charlton Heston's Moses in *The Ten Commandments* (1956), as well as such generous slices of ham as *The Invisible Man's Revenge* (1944) and the *House of Frankenstein/House of Dracula* outings (both 1945) had allowed him. Carradine was touring Southwestern community playhouses at the time; upon returning to Hollywood, he would begin work on *The Man Who Shot Liberty Valance* (1962).

"Another one I have a great deal of affection for," said Carradine, "is a little period piece called *Bluebeard*. It's a variant on my 'madman' type, and more restrained than I usually come across. Now, I work most commonly just to keep myself working, with the predictable consequence that I have accumulated a sizeable body of work from which comparatively few jobs stand out. I believe *Bluebeard* stands out most admirably."

The visionary director Edgar G. Ulmer must be held largely responsible for the quality Carradine perceived in *Bluebeard*. Ulmer by 1944—his brilliance scarcely diminished after a decade of estrangement from the major studios—had become known as a maker of tightly budgeted independent features and short subjects; he was often at the helm of Yiddish and Ukrainian language and African American ensemble attractions for segregated theatrical exhibition.

Ulmer had alienated the brass at Universal Pictures suicidally early in his career because he had wooed and won the wife of producer Max Alexander, nephew of Universal's president, Carl Laemmle. Universal, in turn, had subjected Ulmer's masterpiece, *The Black Cat* (1934), to sacrificial scissoring in appeasement of that year's aggressive new tide of censorship.

Ulmer seems to have been bound sooner or later to develop a film from the legend of Bluebeard, European folklore's seducer and slayer of one woman after another. Ulmer's departure from Universal left his slated adaptation of *Bluebeard*—from a story by Gordon Morris, in which Boris Karloff was to star—unproduced. Ulmer fared marvelously with the topic at a substantially lesser studio and with a star player whose presence at the time suggested a younger, more saturnine Karloff. In John Carradine, Ulmer found an actor with a seldom-explored delicacy of manner that renders this Bluebeard's crueler instincts all the more disturbing. The thunderous Carradine voice is so thoroughly subdued here that when the killer reveals, "I was a very ambitious youth, and extremely sensitive," not long before his undoing, the effect is more convincingly saddening than intimidating.

Producers Releasing Corporation and its imposing PRC Pictures logotype are remembered chiefly today with mock fondness among a growing community of "bad cinema" devotees whose chief pleasure lies in belittlement. Such PRC releases as *Devil Bat* (1941), with Bela Lugosi, and *The Black Raven* (1943), with George Zucco, are familiar entries on the rosters of so-called "turkeys," but in fact the studio's output suffers more greatly from low-budgetitis than from ineptitude. No one can accuse a PRC of being a bore—a truer criterion for "bad" film.

During its span of less than a decade, PRC resolved often to partways with its Poverty Row origins and "strike out for a better trade," as *The Hollywood Reporter* interpreted the studio's ambitions in 1944. *Bluebeard* was begun with the usual 10-day schedule and tiny budget, but studio chief Leon Fromkess, after seeing the first two days' rushes, ordered a substantial increase in budget and a few more days of shooting time. Such rallyings have a great deal to do with Ulmer's several years at PRC. Before *Bluebeard*, he delivered several pictures including the strange gangster drama *Tomorrow We Live* (1942), with Ricardo Cortez, and the exotic lost treasure thriller *Isle of Forgotten Sins* (a.k.a. *Monsoon*, 1943), with Carradine, Gale Sondergaard, and Sidney Toler. Subsequent Ulmer PRCs include *Strange Illusion* (a.k.a. *Out of the Night*, 1945), a curious modern-dress *Hamlet*, and *Detour* (1945), a recognized classic film noir. Designed to accommodate a maximum of brooding shadowplay by the pioneering European cine-

Bluebeard - The mad puppeteer, Morrell (John Carradine), realizes that his mistress, Renée (Sonia Sorel), knows too much to live.

matographer Eugen Schufftan—a 1940 immigrant who had just begun to establish himself in Hollywood but was barred by union regulations from his regular trade—*Bluebeard* is so polite a study in madness and menace as to render Carradine almost sympathetic. His character's torments register early on, when leading lady Jean Parker asks offhandedly, "What would Bluebeard want with me?" and Carradine replies, "I should think he might find you irresistible, Madamoiselle." Carradine had sufficient professional background in common with Schufftan (for both men had worked as portrait artists and sculptors) to make the portrayal of a working artist fit seamlessly into Schufftan's designs of a practical milieu. Dialogue at one point includes a discussion of lighting requirements for a portrait sitting.

The pictorial design encompasses a remarkable approach to capturing Carradine's face. Resisting the commonplace tactic of exploiting his angular features and overall height in sharply lighted straight-on and low-vantage shots, Schufftan and the official director of photography, Arthur "Jockey" Feindel, concentrated on the actor's expansive forehead and intense gaze in softly lighted high angles, achieving a soulful aspect. These values carry over into the gracefully understated dialogue—which helps to mute the broader coincidences of the screenplay—and into the delicate Leo Erdody orchestral score, whose prevailing strings and woodwinds instrumentation is punctuated with threatening passages from French horns and tympani. Erdody, who was well known as a radio symphony conductor, based his score, in part, on Moussorgsky's *Pictures at an Exhibition.*

The collaborative work of Ulmer

Bluebeard - *Leaving the unconscious Lucille (Jean Parker) on the floor, Gaston flees from the police.*

and Schufftan registers stunningly, comparing favorably with the more celebrated teamings of director William Wyler and cinematographer Gregg Toland. Schufftan, whose groundbreaking miniature background process is integral to Fritz Lang's *Metropolis* (Germany; 1927), worked prolifically on an international scale following *Bluebeard.* He eventually won Best Black-and-White Photography Oscar for *The Hustler* (1961).

Morell's puppets play an integral part in the picture, their portrayal of Gounod's *Faust* providing an apt complement to the plot enacted by the principals. Many of the puppet scenes are lighted and photographed in close quarters in such a way that they almost seem to be living performers.

Bluebeard is served almost passively by Swedish-born Nils Asther, ten years after his splendid show of villainy in *The Love Captive* (1934), as the Sureté inspector who allows the women to do practically all his work in bringing

Carradine to bay. Asther had his own impressive new turn as a bad guy that same year, as a scientist obsessed with rejuvenation in *The Man in Half Moon Street.* Jean Parker, who was about to begin several years' retirement from a declining career, appears younger than her thirty-two years as the resourceful dressmaker who responds to Carradine with more inquisitive determination than flirtatious attention.

Austrian stage veteran Ludwig Stossel—in a sharp departure from the genial Germanic type that he defined in *Pride of the Yankees* (1942) and cinched a generation later in a run of "Little Old Winemaker" commercials for television—makes a worthy villain-behind-the-madman as the manipulative art dealer who proves capable of violence when stealth fails him. Iris Adrian has an hilarious sequence—New York accent and all—as a snippy prostitute. Sonia Sorel (Mrs. Carradine at the time) does well as Morell's mistress.

The Soul of a Monster

1944 Columbia Pictures Corporation
Director: Will Jason
Producer: Ted Richmond
Original Screenplay: Edward Dein
Director of Photography: Burnett Guffey
Film Editor: Paul Borofsky
Art Directors: Lionel Banks and George Brooks
Set Decorations: Fay Babcock and Robert Priestley
Musical Director: Mischa R. Bakaleinikoff
Music Themes: Dr. Karol Rathaus, Mario Castelnuovo-Tedesco, George Anthiel, Nico Grigor, Ernst Toch, George Parrish, Daniele Amfitheatrof, Frederick Hollander, John Leipold, Robert Stringer, Ben Oakland and Gerard Carbonara
Incidental Music: *Boogie Woogie Special,* Saul Chaplin and Walter Samuels; *Ain't That Just Like a Man?,* Don Raye and Gene DePaul; *Spanish Rhapsody* and *The Mephisto Waltz,* Franz Liszt; *Sonata Number 8,* W. A. Mozart; *Ave Maria,* Franz Schubert; and *Awake My Soul,* G. F. Handel
Running Time: 61 minutes

Cast: Rose Hobart (Lilyan Gregg), George MacReady (Dr. George Winson), Jim Bannon (Dr. Vance), Jeanne Bates (Ann Winson), Eric Rolf (Fred Stevens), Ernest Hilliard (Wayne), Clarence Muse (Cafe Pianist), Al Hill (Waiter), Edith Evanson (Mrs Jameson), Ida Moore (Mrs. Kirby), Milton Kibbee (Driver), Harry Strang, John Tyrrell (Policeman), Al Cross (Crippled Man), Charles Sullivan (Man in Bar), Howard Negley, Byron Shores (Reporters)

Synopsis: The city is saddened at word of the imminent death of Dr. George Winson, eminent physician and philanthropist. At his bedside are his wife, Ann; his assistant, Dr. Vance; young clergyman Fred Stevens; and Winson's dog. Ann repulses all attempts to comfort her, saying, "If he were cruel, perhaps he could go on living. . . Monsters live, saints die!" When Stevens begs her to pray she ridicules him for his faith and instead offers up a prayer to Satan.

A coldly beautiful woman strides toward the Winson home. A speeding car appears to strike her, but she continues on, unharmed. A power line falls across her path, but she walks past, unheeding. Entering the house, the

Once in a great while at the major studios a low-budget producer dared to tinker with a bizarre, off-beat idea. Very few such efforts actually went into production. A few gained some attention—the Val Lewton pictures, for example. Most, however, were ignored by the critics or, if noticed at all, were subjected to ridicule. Such was the fate of *The Soul of a Monster* which the critic of *The New York Times* called "a cheap way to go nuts." One of two paperback books that evaluate old films now shown on television rates it as a "BOMB" while another omits it altogether.

Lest we over-react, it should be noted that *The Soul of a Monster* is hardly a classic film; but we feel it deserves a longer glance. It contains several points of interest, including sharp dialogue, neat directorial touches, imaginative photographic treatment, sophisticated utilization of music, and good ensemble playing by freelance artists George MacReady and Rose Hobart, backed by a modest but competent cast of contract actors. The story places strong emphasis upon religion (an unusual note outside of the Biblical epic films), being a modern-dress version of the Faust legend. Paramount later tried something along similar but larger-scaled lines with *Alias Nick Beal* (1949).

The working titles of *Soul* were *They Walk Alone* and *He Walks Alone.* The author of the original screenplay, Edward Dein, had co-written the script of *The Leopard Man* for Val Lewton. His other work included a number of low-budget mystery and horror pictures for RKO and Universal, among them the first and best of the Inner Sanctum Mystery series, *Calling Dr. Death* (1943). Will Jason, who directed the picture, was a noted song composer (*Isn't This a Night for Love?, Penthouse Serenade, If It Isn't Love, It Can Happen to You, Out of the Blue,* etc.), but a less well-known director. Most of his work consisted of second-feature musicals and comedies. For him *Soul* was a surprising step from his usual path; he probably considered it a misstep, considering its lack of acceptance.

woman orders everyone from the room, saying, "You called for me. He'll live, but not if he's left in the hands of self-appointed saviors and friends." Winson rallies after the arrival of the woman called Lilyan Gregg.

Winson recovers within six weeks, but not without cost: Ann tells Stevens that Winson has become "cruel, suspicious . . . he's like an animal." The faithful dog now fears its master; Stevens finds the animal stabbed to death with garden shears. One day, Lilyan states that her work is done and leaves.

Winson, Ann and Stevens attend a piano recital at the home of their friend, Wayne. Stevens buys Ann a corsage, but it shrivels at Winson's touch; the flowers spring back to life after they are thrown into a gutter. Winson exults as the pianist performs his requested "Mephisto Waltz" during the thunder and lightning of a gathering storm. Winson leaves abruptly in reply to a telepathic summons from Lilyan to join her in a basement cafe across town. Ann later confronts Lilyan at the latter's apartment and begs her not to take Winson from her. Lilyan replies, "It's the other way around, isn't it? You lost him, I saved him." Lilyan slaps Ann and orders her out; Ann realizes suddenly that Lilyan fears her.

Stevens, who has waited outside in the dark, sends Ann home in his car. He stays and watches. Winson arrives at the apartment. Lilyan asks him to bring her an icepick. She directs his attention to Stevens, calling him "one of the barriers between you and happiness." When Stevens leaves, Winson stalks him relentlessly through the dark streets. Stevens bends to retrieve a dropped object and looks up to see Winson looming over him with the icepick. Stevens' crucifix has fallen into view; at sight of it Winson recoils and flees.

Stevens finds Winson gulping a highball at the basement cafe. Stevens tries to reason with him that a man's time is allotted to him by a supreme force and that if a man buys time that is not his from another source he loses his soul. Winson leaves angrily, going straight to Lilyan. She calms his self-horror by explaining that man-made laws are "made to be broken . . . There comes a time in every life when the desire to kill someone becomes an obsession. Why not follow that desire?"

Returning to his practice with the worshipful Vance, Winson seems more eccentric than ever. An argument occurs in which Vance seizes Winson's

wrists and is horrified to realize that Winson has no pulse. Later, Winson receives an accidental scalpel wound to the arm; it causes no pain and does not bleed. Lilyan arrives and accuses Vance of plotting to steal Winson's practice. Stevens has a confrontation with Lilyan that leaves her trembling.

Vance receives an emergency call from an address across the street. Rushing outside, he is struck down by Lilyan's auto. Winson, assisted by a housekeeper, Mrs. Jamison, prepares to perform an emergency operation to save his friend. Vance asks for a local anaesthetic so he can watch. Winson hears Lilyan ordering him to destroy Vance. He halts, permitting Vance to die. Jamison accuses him of murder.

Indicted by a grand jury and freed on bond, Winson explains to Ann and Stevens that he tried to fight Lilyan's influence but was helpless. He goes back to Lilyan to buy back his soul while Ann goes to a cathedral to pray. Lilyan tells him "You begged for life; you didn't bargain for terms." He replies, "The truth is your poison." When Lilyan draws a gun, Winson closes in on her. She fires six bullets into his body before she falls from a high window and is crushed under the wheels of a truck. Her body resembles a broken marble statue.

The scene returns to Ann uttering her prayer to Satan, just before Lilyan's first appearance. Winson, regaining consciousness, halts her. "When I was a little boy, I read something in the Bible: 'For we struggle not against flesh and blood, but against principalities, against powers—against the rulers of darkness in this world.' Pray for me, Ann."

The Soul of a Monster - *Vance is fearful of Ann's prayer to Satan.*

The Soul of a Monster - *Mrs. Jamison (Edith Evanson) is horrified at George Winson's callous negligence as Vance lies dying.*

The picture opens with a printed prologue: *Into the lives of many come strange realities—Into the lives of others come equally strange dreams—weird dreams that shape and guide their destinies. You may have lived or perhaps dreamed the story you are about to see. To many of you it may be a grim reality: to others. perhaps just a dream.*

At the fade there is an epilogue: *For the man who walks with evil walks alone: he who walks with evil has no soul. no hope: he lives but a life without faith. and without faith. there is no life.*

The influence of Lewton is unmistakable. There are the pretentious foreword and afterword *à la* Lewton, plus substantial emphasis upon menacing

shadows. The long sequence in which the bedeviled doctor stalks the young parson at night through weirdly lighted streets is of a piece with the furtive pursuits of *Cat People* and *The Seventh Victim.* Fraught with both explicit and implied danger, the sequence is punctuated with startling interruptions such as a sidewalk elevator which rises noisily behind the intended victim, the lights and rumblings of an elevated train (cleverly suggested rather than shown conventionally), and the sudden intrusion of a policeman.

Dein's dialogue, while occasionally preachy and overly pretentious, is sometimes reminiscent of his work in *The Seventh Victim.* There is a reference

to an ambulance siren as "the cry of a distressed city." The opening scene, in which the grief-crazed wife rebukes the solicitous preacher, seems almost a reply to the dressing down given the Palladists in the Lewton film: "Prayers are cheap, Fred. Why didn't they *work*? Because there's nothing behind them . . . Someone once put them down so stupid fools like you would have something to cling to." Told she's turning her back on God, she replies, "Yes, I am, because I want my husband to live! I've never prayed to the Devil. I was told of his horrors—he was something to hide from, he was destruction . . . Maybe he's been done an injustice." She turns to gaze into the fireplace. "If there is another power, whoever you are, wherever you are, I beg of you: save him." A surge of stormclouds and surreal images underscores her blasphemy.

The nightmare begins and ends with effective montages that include transitory glimpses of negative film changing to positive images (the first and last appearances of Rose Hobart), eccentric camera tilts, and superimposed storm clouds. Classical piano music is introduced intelligently into the tense private recital sequence, with subtle arrangement of Liszt's works to suit the action; as a thunderstorm rages outside, MacReady cries, "It's nature's music, isn't it? It ought to make a wonderful background for *The Mephisto Waltz!*" Liszt's daemonic score has never sounded more otherworldly than while being underscored by the thunderstorm.

Rose Hobart appears at the piano in another disquieting scene. A boogie-woogie piano solo with the marvelous black actor-composer, Dr. Clarence Muse, seen all too briefly at the keyboard, adds dramatic irony to the meeting of Erik Rolf and MacReady in the basement café. There is much background scoring, most of it adapted from the studio stock catalog.

The tight budget—about $80,000—is well concealed for the most part; the sets are adequate, and the high-grade photography and optical effects impart slickness almost throughout. A too simple dissolve is used to show dead flowers returning magically to life, but how many features made in a two-week schedule could indulge time-lapse photography? There are loose ends aplenty, but these are fairly explicable in terms of Heaven- and Hades-born miracles and an ending

The Soul of a Monster - *Winson turns against his supposed benefactor, Lilyan.*

which reveals the bulk of the film to have been a dying man's nightmare. Actually, the ending is ambiguous, with the viewer left to make his own decision whether MacReady is going to die or recover.

Rose Hobart, without assistance of unusual make-up, other than a coiffure that *suggests* concealed horns, is coldly effective as the visitor from Hell. MacReady, whose obscurity at the time belied his mastery at chilling the blood, brings a masterful understatement to the role of the good doctor who dreams he has become a walking dead man. The other principals—Erik Rolf, Jim Bannon, Jeanne Bates—were veterans of radio drama, and their voices in particular are memorable.

Rolf, as the energetic young holy man, is especially fine in a role that could have become unbearably pompous in less expert hands.

It was standard procedure in the Columbia B-unit to assign well known veteran cinematographers to each project with the idea that they could give help and sage advice to the often inexperienced directors. Burnett Guffey had only recently become a director of photography when he was given *Soul* although he had enviable credits as an operative cameraman for many a top cinematographer. His work in *Soul* is remarkable, creating an atmosphere of the fantastic on ordinary backlot streets and in standard knocked-together stage sets.

The Mad Ghoul

1943 Universal Pictures Co., Inc.
Director: James P. Hogan
Producer: Benjamin Pivar
Executive Producer: Joseph Gershenson
Screenplay: Brenda Weisberg and Paul Gangelin
Original Story: Hans Kraly
Director of Photography: Milton Krasner
Art Directors: John B. Goodman and Martin Obzina
Sound Director: Bernard B. Brown
Technician: Jess Moulin
Set Decorations: R.A. Gausman and A.J. Gilmore
Musical Director: Hans J. Salter
Film Editor: Milton Carruth
Gowns: Vera West
Assistant Director: William Holland
Song Adaptation for *All For Love* (from *Minuet in G*, W. A. Mozart) and *Our Love Will Live* (from *Piano Concerto in A*, P. I. Tchaikovsky); Milton Rosen,
Lyrics; Everett Carter, *I Dreamed I Dwelt in Marble Halls*; M. W. Balfe
Running Time, 65 minutes

Cast: David Bruce (Ted Allison), Evelyn Ankers (Isabel Lewis), George Zucco (Dr. Alfred Morris), Robert Armstrong (Ken McClure), Turhan Bey (Eric Iverson), Milburn Stone (Macklin), Andrew Tombes (Eagan), Rose Hobart (Della), Addison Richards (Gavigan), Charles McGraw (Garrity), Gus Glassmire (Caretaker), Lillian Cornell (Miss Anker's Singing Voice), Gene O'Donnell (Radio Announcer), Lew Kelly (Stagehand), Gibson Gowland (Detective), Isabel LaMal (Maid), Hans Herbert (Attendant), William Ruhl (Stagehand #2), Bess Flowers and Cyril Ring (Theater Patrons)

Synopsis: Chemistry professor Alfred Morris finds his interests veering into conflict when he discovers an ancient civilization's formula for bringing about a state of living death. Privately, Morris lusts after Isabel Lewis, whose career as a singer is about to blossom. Isabel's possessive fiancé, Ted Allison, happens to be a collegiate assistant to Dr. Morris in whose service Ted is to spend the lull between semesters.

Isabel, anxious for a respite from Ted's

Whoever said arrogance is an inverse function of competence must never have caught George Zucco's act. In his mastery of a narrow range, the Manchester-born character man could radiate a confidence to rival Errol Flynn, a calculating obsessiveness on a par with Lionel Atwill, and a full-of-himself calibre of stubborn pride that dresses up even such lesser efforts as *The Black Raven* (1943) and *Fog Island* (1945). Portly and balding, Zucco addressed the camera with a matinée idol's bearing and spent a twenty-year career in film as a dependable—typically villainous—scene stealer. His striking profile and huge, radiant eyes abetted the thefts, and so did his nuanced readings of predatory dialogue.

Zucco's big set piece in *The Mad Ghoul* is a polite drawing room scene, well removed from the film's grislier business. "Don't you suppose that I know how a woman should look at a man when she loves him?" the fifty-seven-year-old Zucco asks of the twenty-five-year-old Evelyn Ankers while her boyish fiancé, David Bruce, is away momentarily. Having convinced her to admit she wants out of the engagement, Zucco presses the issue: "It's perfectly natural, now, that you should turn to a more sophisticated man . . . who knows the book of life—and can teach you to read it." Ankers's agreeable response dovetails exquisitely with Zucco's escalating come-on to create a sequence that almost could have been lifted from one of the period's sophisticated "screwball" comedies. She is agreeing to matters quite apart from what he is hinting, and his arrogance renders him as vulnerable as her innocence renders her.

Other choice Zucco lines pepper the screenplay, "This is my private universe," he beams as Bruce enters the laboratory, but he conveys the gathering menace impressively enough with brooding

The Mad Ghoul - Dr. Morris (George Zucco) takes over where Pierce left off.

smothering affections, is about to embark on a perfor-mance tour with accompanist Eric Iverson. She has inno-cently misinterpreted Morris's overtures as fatherly con-cern. Certain that Isabel can be his if Ted is put out of the way, Morris infects the youth with the life-in-death vapor. Ted is transformed into an emaciated figure of zombie-like obedience; his restoration to a semblance of normalcy requires a heart from a recently deceased donor. The first exhumation by Morris and Ted leaves the police baffled. Newspaperman Ken McClure asserts that "one thing is certain: You got a maniac to deal with . . . What would anybody want with just a guy's heart?"

Ted travels with Morris to meet Isabel on the concert trail. He begs that she marry him immediately, then col-lapses in exhaustion. Morris demands privacy as Ted reverts to a cadaverous state. A series of town-by-town grave robberies begins to shadow Isabel's tour. A cemetary caretaker is murdered and his heart is taken. Reporter McClure, intent on cracking the case, catches up with the tour and arranges to hide in a casket in an undertaking parlor. McClure gets the drop on Morris that night, but is stabbed from behind by Ted and becomes the latest mur-der victim in the string of heart-snatching episodes.

Police Sergeant Macklin pronounces Eric a suspect. Ted, comprehending at last that Isabel loves Eric, frees her from their engagement and begins to rebel against Morris's control. Ted succumbs once again to the scien-tist's will, however, and leaves on Morris's orders to "kill Eric, then yourself." As Ted exits the laboratory, Morris finds himself accidentally exposed to the vapor. He franti-cally attempts to halt Ted, who will not be stopped.

Ted interrupts a performance by Isabel and Eric, bran-dishing a gun, but police shoot him to death on stage as the concert hall clears in panic. He has left a note clearing Eric of suspicion.

Dr. Morris, pale and gaunt from inhalation of the chemicals, rushes to a cemetery, where he dies while clawing at a grave.

silence and clipped commands. Top-billed David Bruce, who seldom graced films of this genre, fits *The Mad Ghoul's* title role superbly. Robust and clean-cut when first seen, Bruce estab-lishes the doomed Ted Allison early on as an insecure, passive-aggressive sort in his suffocating attentions to Ankers, then begins rallying toward coura-geous assertiveness only after Zucco has caused his irreversible poisoning.

Mysterious looking Turhan Bey, a veteran of high-adventure chapter plays and mystery/horror features after only two years in Hollywood, has unac-countably little to do here as the pianist who becomes Ankers's sweetheart. Milburn Stone, likewise a thriller and adventure picture dependable (who eventually became Gunsmoke's gruff Doc Adams on television), keeps an unusually low profile as the policeman who considers Bey a suspect. Robert Armstrong, forever to be remembered as the overzealous showman of *King Kong* (1933), serves *The Mad Ghoul* memorably as an enterprising journal-ist whose plot to crack the case back-fires fatally. None of the players diverts much attention from Zucco, who rewards the opportunity to carry the picture with a forceful performance topped only by his Professor Moriarty

of *The Adventures of Sherlock Holmes* (1939).

Zucco's aloof elegance is com-p l e m e n t e d throughout by the Universal chillers' customary atten-tion to appropriate production design and the cine-matography of one of Universal's top men, Milton Krasner. To illustrate the inge-nuity with which

The Mad Ghoul - Moriss sends Ted on an errand of Murder.

the penury of a Pivar budget was dis-guised, the climactic sequence was pho-tographed on the *Phantom of the Opera Stage*. The camera sweeps the upper left side of the theater, showing the box seats filled with patrons, then pans down toward the stage, taking in the first several rows of the lower floor with patrons in every visible seat. The effect of a theater filled with dress extras is perfect. The only laughable aspect—unless some crank cares to pick apart the far-fetched yarn itself—is the big-nose/big-foot cartooning style of the "prehistoric" paintings with which

Zucco illustrates a lecture on ancient rituals.

Director James P. Hogan pursued two distinct careers in film, helming almost thirty features during the silent screen's final decade and then return-ing in 1936 after five years of accus-toming himself to talking-picture grammar and technique. He averaged four movies a year from that point, including many of the *Bulldog Drummond* and *Ellery Queen* outings, until his death in 1943. *The Mad Ghoul* was Hogan's final assignment; it was released a week after his death.

Dark Waters

1944 Dark Waters Productions, Incorporated
A Benedict Bogeaus Production
Director: André de Toth
Screenplay: Joan Harrison and Marian Cockrell
From the Saturday Evening Post serial by Frank and Marian Cockrell
Additional Dialogue: Arthur T. Horman
Associate Producer: Joan Harrison
Executive Producer: James Nasser
Directors of Photography: Archie Stout and John Mescall
Musical Composition and Orchestration: Dr. Miklos Rozsa
Production Associate: Arthur Landau
Assistant to Producer: Carley Harriman
Art Director: Charles Odds
Set Decorations: Maurice Yates
Film Editor: James Smith
Costumes: Rene Hubert
Sound Technician: Frank Webster
Assistant Director: Joseph Depew
Choreographer: Jack Crosby
Property Master: Kenny Wagner
Special Effects: Harry Redmond
Second Unit Director: John W. Boyle
Dialogue Director: Herbert Farjeon
Running Time: 89 minutes

Cast: Merle Oberon (Leslie Calvin), Franchot Tone (Dr. George Grover), Thomas Mitchell (Mr. Sidney), Fay Bainter (Aunt Emily), Elisha Cook, Jr. (Mr. Cleeve), John Qualen (Uncle Norbert), Rex Ingram (Pearson Jackson), Odette Myrtil (Mama Boudreaux), Alan Napier (Doctor), Eugene Borden (Papa Boudreaux), Eileen Coghlan (Jeanette), Nina May McKinney (Florella), Rita Beery (Nurse), Gigi Perreau, Peter Miles, Louise Kerbrat, Alice Kerbrat, Fleurette Zama, Diana Martin and Diana Dubois (Children)

Synopsis: During the Second World War, torpedo fire cripples a ship on which Leslie Calvin is escaping from Japanese invaders. The girl breaks down following her rescue, and a doctor suggests she stay with her relatives at Belleville Planation in Louisiana. In the swampy Cajun country, Leslie meets Aunt Emily and Uncle Norbert for the first time. Also living at the mansion are Mr. Sydney and Mr. Cleeve. Unable to shake the

An elite cast, a popular *Saturday Evening Post* serial story, and some unusual topical aspects made *Dark Waters* one of the most popular Gothic chillers of the World War ll era. It was produced independently by Benedict Bogeaus, a Chicago real estate broker who, in 1941, purchased the site of its production, the Metropolitan Studio at 1040 Las Palmas, in Hollywood. Production is as lavish as possible in view of wartime set-construction restrictions imposed by the government to conserve strategic materials. Most of the work was done at the studio, with process plates and inserts made at New Orleans, Three Rivers, St. Tamminy Parish, the Cherfuncta River, and the bayous of the Teche Country, seventy-five miles north of New Orleans. The second unit, headed by John Boyle, also made scenes using acting doubles for intercutting with close shots of the cast members. The swamp, constructed on three acres of the back-lot, included a tank in which landscape features were mounted on submerged dollies so the trees and foliage could be moved about for varied settings. The jungle area outside of the water measured 110 by 150 feet.

fear that she is losing her mind, Leslie is horrified to hear Norbert and Sydney discuss the possibility of sending her to a psychiatrist. She comes to depend upon the young local doctor, George Grover, for strength and assurance. She is intimidated, however, by the seemingly furtive actions of Florella, the cook, and Person, the handyman.

At a local theatre Leslie sees a newsreel of a torpedoing and, later, she thinks she hears voices calling her name. A ghostly voice trails her from the house. At the end of a bayou pier, Leslie considers ending her life with a leap into the water. Pearson appears and asks if she hears the voices. This revelation convinces her that somebody is trying to drive her mad. She begs Pearson to tell her what he knows of the mysterious Mr. Sydney, but as Cleeve approaches, the terrified servant tells her she is in danger and leaves with a promise to talk to her in secret the next day.

Failing to reach Grover, Leslie walks aimlessly through the woods and stumbles upon a corpse—Pearson. Back at the house, she is about to tell Emily when a chance remark by the latter reveals she is not really Leslie's aunt. Leslie phones Grover. He comes to the house and tells Leslie she is imagining things, handing her a prescription for a sedative. Leslie senses betrayal until, alone in her room, she finds a note on the prescription sheet saying the doctor believes her but pretended not to because Sydney was listening. Cleeve seizes Leslie and drags her to the plantation fieldhouse, where Sydney is waiting. Grover has been waylaid. Sydney reveals he murdered Leslie's kin and hired imposters, planning to drive Leslie to suicide so as to gain the estate.

Leslie and Grover are forced into a motorboat and taken into the swamp, where an "accident" is planned. Far from shore, Grover turns the tables. He and Leslie escape into the water, and Sydney tries to run them down. Cleeve is killed instead, and the intended victims reach shore. In the dark jungle, Grover disarms and captures Sydney. The lovers take their prisoner back to Belleville. The false aunt and uncle have fled.

The exterior of a ghostly, white two-story mansion, surrounded by moss-covered oaks and complete with winding drive, gardens, and verandahs, was based upon a well-known Louisiana house called *Homewood*, which had burned several years earlier. Eight rooms, entrance hall with winding stair, parlor, library, dining room, pantry, and three bedrooms were built on sound stages and dressed in Victorian and Georgian furnishings. These menacing settings are right for the story, which receives further impetus from a fine musical score, tricky lighting, and fog effects.

Principal photography is the work of two top cameramen, Archie Stout (whose usual specialty was the Western spectacle) and John Mescall (famed for the likes of *The Black Cat*). In the striking jungle and swamp shots, the shadows of foliage create frightening patterns. The interiors are no less disturbing. A scene deserving of attention has the camera explore Merle Oberon's room in minute detail while the lighting changes to show transition from night to day.

Director André de Toth had been a cameraman and director in Hungary before coming to America to escape

Dark Waters - *Merle Oberon and Alan Napier in a hospital scene being directed by André de Toth. The man with visor is cinematographer John Mescall.*

Dark Waters - Leslie, unnerved by strange noises, is calmed by Aunt Emily (Fay Bainter), Uncle Norbert (John Qualen) and Sydney.

the Nazis. He made a *Lone Wolf* series low-budgeter for Columbia, then was assigned by that company to a large-scale project, *None Shall Escape* (1944), which led to *Dark Waters*. Subsequent good assignments for him were *Ramrod* (1947), *The Other Love* (1947), *Pitfall* (1948), *Last of the Comanches* (1952), and the most popular of the three-dimensional films, *House of Wax* (1953). *Dark Waters* remains one of de Toth's better efforts in a career that declined during the Sixties.

Additional production expertise shows in the work of the British Joan Harrison, who had just bowed in as producer on the successful *Phantom Lady* (1944). Her contribution to *Dark Waters* is twofold, as associate producer and co-author of the screenplay. Harrison had assisted Alfred Hitchcock on some of his best films from *The 39 Steps* (1935) through

Saboteur (1942); she found increasing prestige after *Dark Waters*, handling several well-received features in the Hitchcock vein and later becoming producer of Hitchcock's television series.

Acting in *Dark Waters* is all that can be desired, with Merle Oberon doing a virtuoso job of conveying tension and mounting hysteria without over-playing. Thomas Mitchell, wearing pasty make-up and dressed in white, managed to be terrifying without raising his voice or indulging in impassioned histrionics. Franchot Tone is a convincingly intelligent hero. The supporting villains are splendid: Elisha Cook, Jr., in his specialty, the sneaking, hungry-looking henchman; Fay Bainter, in a turnabout from her usual motherly roles; and John Qualen, the downtrodden little man of many John Ford productions. Rex

Ingram, Nina May McKinney, and Alan Napier lend distinguished assistance in sympathetic roles.

For the most part, the melodramatics are of the well bred variety, with only an occasional shocker—a severed arm floating in the water, the dead face of a servant staring up from the undergrowth. The outstanding score by Miklos Rozsa is an important part of the film. Not only does Rozsa's distinctive music point up the drama of the nightmares and chases, but it also incorporates such Cajun culture sidelights as the "Fais Dodo," a dance performed by 150 extras in a well-placed respite from terrors. (The term *fais dodo*, which translates as "go to sleep," designates in rural Cajun tradition an all-night dance. The term applies to the practice of placing the children in a back room to sleep while the adults celebrate.)

The Missing Juror

1944 Columbia Pictures Corporation
Director: Oscar Boetticher, Jr.
Producer: Wallace MacDonald
Screenplay: Charles O'Neal
Story: Leon Abrams and Richard Hill Wilkinson
Director of Photography: L. William O'Connell
Film Editor: Paul Borofsky
Art Director: George Brooks
Set Decorations: George Montgomery
Musical Director: Mischa Bakaleinikoff
Musical Composition: George Parrish, Nico Grigor, Paul Sawtell, Mario Castelnouvo-Tedesco, Sidney Cutner, W. Franke Harling, Joseph Nussbaum, Ben Oakland, Dr. Karol Rathaus, John Liepold, Gregory Stone, Werner R. Heymann, Daniele Amphitheatrof, Frederick Hollander, Gil Grau, Gerard Carbonara, Arthur Morton and William Grant Still
Assistant Director: Ivan Volkman
Sound Technician: John Goodrich
Running Time: 65 minutes

Cast: Jim Bannon (Joe Keats), Janis Carter (Alice Hall), George MacReady (Harry Wharton), Jean Stevens (Tex Tuttle), Joseph Crehan (Willard Apple), Carole Matthews (Marcy), Mike Mazurki (Colly), Cliff Clark (Inspector), John Tyrrell (Sergeant Regan), William Newell (Wally), George Lloyd (George Szazbo), Forbes Murray (District Attorney), Charles Wilson (Mack), Edwin Stanley (Warden), Ernest Hilliard (Doctor), Harry Strang (Sergeant Newton), Edmund Cobb (Deputy), William Hall (Officer Garrett), Trevor Bardette (Pearson), Walter Baldwin (Sheriff), Alan Bridge (Ben), Sam Flint (Judge), Jack Gardner (Reporter), Stuart Holmes (Juror), Frank O'Connor (Engineer), Milton Kibbee (Witness), Charles Hamilton (Bailiff), also Victor Travers, Fred Graff, Danny Desmond, Cecil Weston, Nancy Brinkman, Shelby Payne, Pat O'Malley, Jessie Grans, George Anderson, Bud Fine, Pat Lane and Dell Henderson.

Synopsis: A car pulls onto the tracks by night at a suburban railroad crossing. A shadowy figure props the body of a man behind the wheel, then hurries away. A train hurtles into

Oscar (Budd) Boetticher, Jr. has become something of a cult hero, largely because of *The Bullfighter and the Lady* (1951), a series of seven fine Randolph Scott Westerns he directed during the late 1950s, and the bullfight film, *Arruza* (1972). Boetticher had been a bullfighter and an assistant director (the jobs have something in common) before he began his directorial career with Irving Briskin's B units at Columbia. His first effort on his own was a minor comedy-mystery in the Boston Blackie series, *One Mysterious Night* (1944). His second, *The Missing Juror* is a taut suspense yarn in which the neglected George MacReady (of *The Soul of a Monster*) advanced to the ranks of memorable screen villains. Rising conspicuously above humble origins, *Juror* attracted more attention than the usual double-bill second feature and assured MacReady of steady work portraying psychopathic intellectuals, including the plum role of Rita Hayworth's sadistic husband in *Gilda* (1946). It also led to Janis Carter's promotion to higher budget pictures and proved a worthwhile vehicle for Jim Bannon.

"I've seen 'THE MISSING JUROR' ...it's Terrorific!"

Suspense...murder...thrills to chill you and fill you with excitement!

A Columbia Picture
with
JIM BANNON · JANIS CARTER · GEORGE MACREADY · JEAN STEVENS
Screen Play by Charles O'Neal
Produced by WALLACE MACDONALD
Directed by OSCAR BOETTICHEn, Jr.

the car. Investigators find that the victim had been hanged before the car was demolished.

Newsman Joe Keats learns the murdered man was the fifth person to die among a jury which had condemned an innocent man to the gallows. Keats, who had covered the original story, convinces his editor, Mr. Apple, that the matter has the makings of a worthwhile series. As Keats dictates the background, the past comes to life:

The case opened with the murder of a woman and the accusation of her playboy-sweetheart, Harry Wharton. George Szazbo, a private eye, gave evidence that swayed the jury to find Wharton guilty. Keats had considered Wharton innocent and sought to no avail an angle that would save him from the gallows. The day before the sentence was to be carried out, Keats happened to be present when Szazbo was shot to death by gangsters. Szazbo's last statement, to Keats and before witnesses, was to give the name of the man who framed Wharton. At the eleventh hour Wharton was spared, but the long stay on death row had shattered his mind. He had developed a fixation that everything happened in combinations of twelve. Later, he was removed to a private institution. Soon after a visit from the jury foreman, Benson, fire broke out in Wharton's room. From the ceiling there dangled a smoking rope, and in the fire was found a charred body.

Now that Keats has put the case back into the headlines, two others of the jury die violently. Keats meets one member, Alice Hill, and her pretty friend, Tex Tuttle, and develops a fondness for Alice. He meets foreman Benson, who says he has been unable to sleep since the death of Wharton. Benson haunts police lineups, conjecturing how many innocent men are arrested and how many of the guilty escape. "Benson" is Wharton in disguise; the body in the asylum was that of Benson.

Keats and Wharton go to a bathhouse run by a giant named Colly. Wharton, secure in the effectiveness of his disguise, locks Keats in a steam room. Colly rescues Keats and Wharton dismisses the near-fatality as an accident. Pretending to hire her to decorate his new home, Wharton lures Alice to a nearby town. He meets her at night at a lonely train station and takes her to a house where a hangman's noose is attached to a rafter. He discloses his identity and tells her she must die.

Keats has solved the case, but now he is jailed by mistake in the small town. Apple arranges his release and Keats finds out where Alice has gone. He and an inspector hurry to the murder house. Police gunfire kills the madman, and Alice is safe in Keats's arms.

The Missing Juror - *Wharton's (George MacReady) madness is apparent to the warden (Ed Stanley), Apple (Joseph Crehan) and Keats (Jim Bannon).*

The Missing Juror - *The Inspector (Cliff Clark) tells Keats that the charred body in the morgue is that of Wharton.*

"I was just learning on those five pictures I directed at Columbia," Boetticher recalled for us in 1989. "Harry Cohn called them 'fillers'—they were put with more important pictures to fill out a double bill. They were made in twelve days for about $100,000. But *The Missing Juror*—that was the one I liked, the good one. I have fond memories of George MacReady, a fine actor and fun to work with. Janis Carter was wonderful—I believe she could have been a top star if she'd wanted to be. She was too nice and too smart to play the game. We tried a few things in *The Missing Juror* that worked."

Jim Bannon told us that "MacReady and Janis were fine, but I suspect that Bud had less trouble fighting *el toro* than trying to direct some of the actors in that film."

The original story, by Leon Abrams and Richard Hill Wilkinson, somewhat resembles two earlier Columbia chillers, *The Ninth Guest* (1934) and *The Man They Couldn't Hang* (1939). The script, developed initially as a mystery, is by writer Charles O'Neal, co-author of *The Seventh Victim* (and father of actor Ryan O'Neal, and grandfather of Tatum). The approach changes about halfway, though, with the revelation (to the audience only) of the killer's identity; suspense thereafter is maintained through audience knowledge of the danger hov-ering about Carter and Bannon.

Boetticher's direction has commendable forward momentum, wasting no time. Hardness of lighting, dramatic camera angles, and extensive musical scoring (most of it from Columbia's library) contribute to a menacing atmosphere that makes the ranch lot streets and the mad villain's machinations convincing. Notable among the supporting performances is that of the huge wrestler, "Iron Mike" Mazurki, as a masseur who quotes Wilde's *The Ballad of Reading Gaol* whilst giving MacReady his massage. Other sturdy support comes from Joseph Crehan, Cliff Clark, George Lloyd, Walter Baldwin and Al Bridge.

Guest in the House

1944 (a.k.a. *Satan in Skirts*) Guest in the House, Inc.

Director: John Brahm
Producer: Hunt Stromberg
Additional Uncredited Direction: Lewis Milestone and André de Toth
From the Hagar Wilde, Dale Eunson stage play
Adaptation: Elliott Paul and Ketti Frings
Director of Photography: Lee Garmes
Musical Score: Werner R. Janssen conducting The Janssen Symphony of Los Angeles
Art Director: Nicolai Remisoff
Associate Art Director: Richard Irvine
Supervising Film Editor: James Newcom
Film Editor: Walter Hanneman
Make-up: Ernest Westmore
Gowns: Natalie Visart
Assistant Director: Sam Nelson
Running Time: 121 minutes

Cast: Anne Baxter (Evelyn Heath), Ralph Bellamy (Douglas Proctor), Aline MacMahon (Aunt Martha), Ruth Warrick (Ann Proctor), Scott McKay (Dan Proctor), Jerome Cowan (Mr. Hacket), Marie MacDonald (Miriam), Percy Kilbride (John), Margaret Hamilton (Hilda), Connie Laird (Lee Proctor)

Synopsis: Evelyn Heath, a heart patient, is brought by her fiance, Dr. Dan Proctor, to his family's seacost home. She meets Dan's older brother, Douglas, a successful magazine illustrator; Douglas' wife, Ann, and young daughter, Lee; Aunt Martha; Miriam, a live-in model; and the servants, John and Hilda. The family is favorably impressed with Evelyn's shy sweetness. Dan and Evelyn are supposed to stay during Evelyn's recovery. On the first night, Evelyn wakes the household with screams of terror occasioned by the discovery of a pet canary in her room. Douglas, first to arrive at her bedside, unwittingly arouses Evelyn's desire.

Evelyn convinces Dan to return to work. She keeps to her room, playing often a recording of Liszt's *Liebestraum*, which unnerves the others. She plants suspicion that Miriam is undermining Douglas's marriage. Lee begins to emulate Evelyn's hypochondria. The canary dies unaccountably. No one suspects Evelyn is responsible for the venemous

Hunt Stromberg produced more than 100 films in twenty years as an MGM executive. He had won forty-five awards, including the "Fame" designation as 'Champion of Champions' Producer over a ten year period. Stromberg quit MGM in the spring of 1942, vowing to seek greater artistic freedom as an independent. United Artists contracted with him to make five pictures with an average budget of $700,000 each, with the releasing firm obligated to take part in financing. The arrangement had a good start: *Lady of Burlesque* grossed about $2 million. The second entry, *Guest in the House* was an artistic success but only mildly profitable, clearing about $50,000. Five subsequent box office failures brought a distinguished career to a dismal close.

In a telegram to United Artists, published as an advance advertisement in January 1944, Stromberg wrote:

"I will definitely go into production February 1st with *Guest in the House*. This is a sensational Broadway stage hit whose theme combines appeal of three of my most popular box-office champions, *The Thin Man*, *Night Must Fall*, and *Guilty Hands*. Elliott Paul, author of the famous bestseller *The Last Time I Saw Paris*, is now completing a most distinguished, exciting script. Will announce director next week. He's a top-notcher."

It was announced at the same time that Anne Baxter, a lovely young actress whose career was booming at Twentieth Century-Fox, was being borrowed to head "a notable cast." Paul's script got considerable doctoring by Ketti Frings, an excellent writer of dialogue, before production began. The result was only basically similar to the play, which ran fourty-five weeks on Broadway. The announced director proved to be, as advertised, a top-notcher: Lewis Milestone, who had made *All Quiet on the Western Front* (1930), *The Front Page* (1932) and *Of Mice and Men* (1939).

Milestone got *Guest* under way, but an attack of appendicitis cut short his work. André de Toth took over for about two weeks but was called to military duty. John Brahm was borrowed from Twentieth Century-Fox to complete the film—a wise

atmosphere, but a worldly-wise family friend, Hackett, figures her for a psychopath.

Lee, climbing a tree outside the studio, sees her father embracing a scantily clad Miriam to massage her stiff neck. The daughter believes they are having an affair. John and Hilda refuse to remain in a house with such goings-on. Ann orders Miriam out, whereupon Douglas storms into town and gets drunk. When Douglas returns in the small hours, Evelyn throws herself into his arms. Ann comes upon the scene, but Douglas defends Evelyn, believing she

was glad to see him only in a sisterly way. Ann takes Lee and leaves. Evelyn declares she loves Douglas, who at last sees the truth and rushes out to find Ann.

Aunt Martha realizes Hackett was right about Evelyn. She overhears Evelyn phone Dan with a message to come quickly. Fearing that Evelyn will destroy Dan, Martha plays upon the schemer's fear of birds, convincing her that the house is filled with them. Screaming in terror, Evelyn races outside and plunges over a cliff to her death. Freed of its malignant guest, the household soon returns to normal.

choice. Brahm had just completed a brilliant study of a psychopath, *The Lodger*. It is his Germanic style and Lee Garmes's unusual photographic technique which dominate *Guest*.

Anne Baxter, who seems unnervingly true to life as a manipulative bitch masquerading as an innocent, keeps the showy central role subdued except when bravura playing is called for. Her

grasp of the psychology involved—the use of ill health and soft-spoken shyness to disarm her intended victims—helps overcome her appearance as one too physically fit for a role more suited

Guest in the House - *Lee (Connie Laird), her mind poisoned by Evelyn, thinks the worst as she spies on Douglas (Ralph Bellamy) and his model, Miriam (Marie MacDonald).*

to, say, a young Ida Lupino. Ralph Bellamy's artist-hero is above critical reproach; toward the climactic moments he delivers one of the most convincing "drunk" scenes ever filmed.

The highly publicized beauty, Marie "The Body" MacDonald, graces the scene as a semi-intelligent model. Jerome Cowan seems a real person in his fine portrayal of a friend in need, and the austerity of the rockbound coastline is reflected in the faces and voices of the accomplished Aline MacMahon, Percy Kilbride (the future "Pa Kettle" of a successful series), and Margaret Hamilton. Scott McKay and the moppet, Connie Laird, are convincingly naive as they succumb to the wiles of the guest. Ruth Warrick—an Orson Welles "discovery"—matches Bellamy's realism as the victimized wife.

Strictly a sound stage creation, *Guest* was made on small but artistically impressive sets, with the exteriors of a New England coastline suggested by props, painted backdrops, and photographic enlargements. The house was difficult to light because it had low ceilings, but Garmes managed to create lighting so perfectly controlled as to sparkle like sunshine. The horror grows without recourse to Gothic props or freakish shadows. Wide-angle lenses, deep focus, and slightly low camera angles lend somewhat of a *Citizen Kane* look. Most scenes are enacted in an outwardly cheerful environment, which takes on ominous shadings unobtrusively as the guest's evil scheming becomes more and more evident. For the final breakthrough into madness, hard shadows and angular compositions take over, the clincher being a striking overhead shot of the plotter whirling about in terror. This scene may have been a homage to D. W. Griffith's celebrated scene of Lilian Gish trapped in a closet in *Broken Blossoms* (1920).

Werner Janssen's memorable score, built in part upon Liszt, deserves much of the credit for dramatic impact. Somewhat overlong for heavy drama, *Guest* is nonetheless an engrossing film, worthy of the producer of that pioneering classic of psychological horror, *Night Must Fall* (1936), the director of *The Lodger* (1944), and the photographer of *Zoo in Budapest* (1932).

Guest in the House - *Ann at last learns the truth about her guest, but her husband defends the girl against her accusations.*

The Great Flamarion

1945 Republic Pictures Corporation
Director: Anthony Mann
Producer: William L. Wilder
Screenplay: Anne Wigton, Heinz Herald and Richard Weil
Story: Anne Wigton
Based on Vicky Baum's character *Big Shot* from *Colliers' Magazine*
Photography: James S. Brown, Jr.
Film Editor: John F. Link
Production Manager: George Moskov
Sound: Percy Townsend
Art Director: F. Paul Sylos
Set Decorations: Glen B. Thompson
Musical Score: Alexander Laszlo
Music Supervision: David Chudnow
Songs: *Chita,* Faith Watson; *Lights of Broadway,* Lester Allen
Assistant Director: Raoul Pagel
Running Time: 78 minutes

Cast: Erich von Stroheim (Flamarion), Mary Beth Hughes (Connie Wallace), Dan Duryea (Al Wallace), Stephen Barclay (Eddie), Lester Allen (Tony), Michael Mark (Watchman), Esther Howard (Cleo), Joseph Granby (Detective), John R. Hamilton (Coroner), Fred Velasco and Carmen Lopez (Dancers), Tony Ferrell (Singer), Beverly Tyler and Martha MacVicar (Chorus Girls), John Elliott (Agent), Franklyn Farnum (Stagehand)

Synopsis: Performers in a Mexico City music hall hear a shot from backstage. A wounded man falls from the rafters. Tony, a trouper, recognizes the man as the Great Flamarion, once renowned as the world's greatest sharpshooter. Dying, Flamarion tells his story:

Flamarion lived only for his collection of guns and his nightly show. All this changed when the middle-aged marksman fell in love with Al Wallace's beautiful young wife, Connie. Al and Connie were stooges for the sharpshooting act. Connie led Flamarion to think she loved him when in fact she saw in him a means to end her unhappy marriage. Al had become an alcoholic. Connie was carrying on a secretive affaire with Eddie, a cyclist.

Connie persuaded Flamarion to kill Al during a performance, making it appear accidental. In San Francisco, Flamarion carried

William Lee Wilder, older brother of director Billy Wilder, left his native Vienna and pursued an industrial career in New York for twenty years before establishing his own motion picture company in Hollywood. His first production, *The Great Flamarion* was made at the Charlie Chaplin Studio and sold to Republic for its 1944-45 program. This workmanlike job is distinguished by the up and coming Anthony Mann's firm directing and splendid acting by Erich von Stroheim, Dan Duryea, and Mary Beth Hughes. *Flamarion's* quality and Continental style gained Wilder some following, but few of his other productions lived up to the promise of this entry.

Except for familiar faces and English dialogue, Flamarion strongly resembles a prewar German film. This suggestion dominates the

QUICK on the trigger —and QUICK to kill!

ERICH von STROHEIM
MARY BETH HUGHES

The Great FLAMARION
(GREAT WITH A GUN)
with DAN DURYEA · STEPHEN BARCLAY · A REPUBLIC PICTURE

out the scheme during an intricate routine in which Al weaved back and forth while Flamarion shot targets behind him. The coroner was convinced Al died as a consequence of his own drunken miscalculations. Connie and Flamarion agreed to meet in Chicago.

Flamarion waited hopelessly, unaware of the double-cross. At last, he set out to search for his betrayer, eventually finding Connie and Eddie performing at a cheap theater in Mexico City. Flamarion berated her for her treachery. Connie played up to him, pretending she loved him still, until she was able to reach his gun and shoot him. With ebbing strength, Flamarion strangled Connie.

script, the photographic technique, the music, and much of the acting. Stroheim's own touches are obvious, particularly in a perfectly played solo sequence in which he tidies up a hotel room for the never-to-come arrival of his paramour. These doings, which call to mind Stroheim's portrayal of an obsessed Broadway ventriloquist in *The Great Gabbo* (1929), would have been right at home in any of his own directorial efforts.

Hughes, thought too pretty to be assigned serious dramatic roles, comes through with a satisfyingly shrewish performance in this respite from the musicals and comedies in which she usually appeared. Duryea was a stage actor who had gained attention in several good supporting roles for Samuel Goldwyn. He is so affecting as the cuckolded drunkard that he rivals von Stroheim for scene stealing. Like director Mann, Duryea was bound for bigger roles in bigger pictures.

Critics and historians have largely ignored *Flamarion* except to cite it as an example of the "worthless" sort of films in which Stroheim was wasted after his blacklisting as a director. Von Stroheim, however, liked the picture.

"*The Great Flamarion.* in my opinion, has the sort of story which forecasts the motion picture of tomorrow," said the master. "It is realism at its best, and there are no concessions to hokum."

The Great Flamarion *Vaudevillians in a Mexican theater hear gunshots. At left is Beverly Tyler, the older man is Michael Mark, and Martha MacVicar (Vickers) is at right.*

Jealousy

1945   Republic Pictures Corporation

Director: Gustav Machaty
Producer: Gustav Machaty
Screenplay: Arnold Phillips and Gustav Machaty
Concept: Dalton Trumbo
Song: *Jealousy*, Rudolph Friml
Original Music: Hanns Eisler
Musical Director: Alexander Laszlo;
Director of Photography: Henry Sharp
Sound: Percival J. Townsend
Art Director: Frank Sylos
Set Decorations: Glenn P. Thompson
Film Editor: John F. Link
Assistant Director: Benjamin Kadish
Technical Advisor: Dr. Eduard Frischauer
Costumes and Hairdressing: Maria Ray
Running Time: 71 minutes

Cast: John Loder (Dr. David Brent), Jane Randolph (Janet Urban), Karen Morley (Dr. Monica Anderson), Nils Asther (Peter Urban), Hugo Haas (Hugo Kral), Holmes Herbert (Melvyn Russell), Michael Mark (Shop Owner), Noble (Expressman), Chissel ("Kid"), Dracula (Cat)

Synopsis: Alcohol and despair have warped the mind of Peter Urban, once a renowned author in Europe, now a war refugee seeking a new life in the United States. His American wife, Janet, becomes a cab driver to support him. Urban obtains a pistol and attempts suicide. Janet stops him and hides the weapon. Though Urban takes delight in emotional sadism, Janet tries to remain loyal.

Janet takes solace in the friendship of one of her fares, Dr. David Brent, a prominent Hollywood surgeon. They fall in love to the consternation of Brent's associate, Dr. Monica Anderson. Monica pretends to be happy for David. Urban contemplates murder.

Urban proposes to move to Mexico, but Janet refuses to go. Urban grows more and more abusive. Janet leaves the house and returns to find Urban dead, shot through the head. She is arrested for murder. Urban's devoted friend, Hugo, a fellow refugee, becomes deranged as a result of the murder; his testimony against Janet is a deciding fac-

Republic Pictures' forte was action. The little company at Studio City—the lot now houses CBS Television City—made better Saturday Westerns and serials than any other outfit. Occasional ventures into high budget works varied from the excellence of *Man of Conquest* (1938), *The Dark Command* (1940), and *The Quiet Man* (1952) to misfires like *The Fighting Kentuckian* (1949) and *Belle LeGrand* (1951). Less frequently, Republic emphasized artistic appeal, as in Orson Welles's fascinating but not entirely successful *Macbeth* (1948) and Gustav Machaty's no less interesting *Jealousy*. A proper niche for these films eluded the marketers; they were too highbrow for mainstream theaters and not enough so for the art houses. The "artsy" forays did bring Republic some unaccustomed critical notice, though, and they were inexpensive enough to minimize financial risks.

Czech director Machaty was much admired for the artistry of *Erotikon* (1929) and *Extase* (1932), the latter being the picture that brought Hedy Lamarr fame. He came Stateside during the late Thirties and made a rather good film for MGM, *Within the Law* (1939). He did not make another until *Jealousy*. His next—and last—was the German made *Suchkind 312* (1956). He died in 1963, having made only eleven features in thirty-one years. For *Jealousy* Machaty gathered a company dominated by European artists and craftsmen. (Several, including author Dalton Trumbo, composer Hanns Eisler, and actress Karen Morley, were blacklisted or worse in

Jealousy - Janet and David fall in love.

tor in her trial. While the jury deliberates, David and Janet marry. After her sentence to twenty years' impris- onment, David solves the crime by tricking Monica into revealing herself as the killer.

the hysterical House Un-American Activities investigations.)

The flavor is strongly European, although much of *Jealousy* was filmed on the streets and in small bars and cafés of Los Angeles in a naturalistic style. Characters are convincing because they lack the cinematic conventionality of being all good or all bad. The decaying writer, set forth splendidly by the sensitive Scandinavian, Nils Asther, arouses both pity and dislike. Hugo Haas, who later directed several American films in a style reminiscent of Machaty, is a kind-hearted, clumsy man who becomes a

paranoid menace. John Loder and Jane Randolph are admirable and long-suffering, yet they carry on an adulterous affair. Karen Morley is a dedicated humanitarian but on a personal level is willing to sacrifice two lives to secure what she wants. Machaty kept a Viennese psychiatrist on the set to advise the actors how they should react, and the result of this coaching is exacting and realistic.

The film sometimes lacks the dramatic timing needed to give it punch. At other times it seems exactly right, as in a scene in which Miss Randolph

suddenly realizes the food Asther is throwing to some gulls is poisoned. A subtle use of slow motion adds to the truth of the scene. Another poignant sequence is a Christmas gathering in the unhappy household.

To compound the convincing "bite" of the story, Henry Sharp's photography melds realism and the poetic for a unified style. The music, which Hanns Eisler founded in part upon a bittersweet title song by the popular operetta composer, Rudolph Friml, is sophisticated and modern.

Jealousy - *A melancholy Christmas season bodes ill for Janet (Jane Randolph), Hugo (Hugo Haas) and Peter (Nils Asther).*

The Madonna's Secret

1946   Republic Pictures Corporation
Director: William Thiele
Associate Producer: Stephen Auer
Photography: John Alton
Original Screenplay: Bradbury Foote and William Thiele
Film Editor: Fred Allen
Musical Director: Richard Cherwin
Musical Score: Joseph Dubin
Orchestrations: Mort Glickman
Song: *C'est Vous*, Al Newman, Richard Cherwin, and Ned Washington
Art Director: Hilyard Brown
Sound: Ed Borschell
Costume Supervision: Adele Palmer
Miss Patrick's Gowns: Howard Greer
Set Decorations: John McCarthy, Jr. and George Suhr
Special Effects: Howard and Theodore Lydecker
Make-up: Bob Mark
Paintings: A. S. Keszthelyi
Assistant Director: Lee Luthaker
Running Time: 79 minutes

Cast: Francis Lederer (James Harlan Corbin), Gail Patrick (Elle Randolph), Ann Rutherford (Linda "Morgan" North), Edward Ashley (John Earth), Linda Stirling (Helen North), John Litel (Lieutenant Roberts), Leona Roberts (Mrs. Corbin), Michael Hawks (Hunt Mason), Clifford Brooke (Mr. Hadley), Pierre Watkin (District Attorney), Will Wright (Riverman), Geraldine Wall (Miss Joyce), John Hamilton (Lambert), Tanis Chandler (Singer), Pat Flaherty (Policeman), Gino Corrado (Waiter), Frank O'Connor (Guard), Lee Phelps (Detective), also Alex Harrier, Anne Chedister, Edythe Elliott, Harry Strong, Russ Whiteman, James Carlisle, George Magrill, Jack Daley, Rose Plummer, Eric Feldary and Bob Alden

Synopsis: Roaming the Hadley Art Gallery, drama editor John Earl of the New York *Globe* stops, transfixed by a girl's portrait by James Harlan Corbin. The face is somehow familiar. Earl learns the model was Helen North, but the face is that of Madeline Renard, a Parisienne who drowned mysteriously in the Seine several years ago. The face also appears in other recent works by Corbin,

Here is the best of Republic's infrequent sorties into the European-style "art" film. Directed and cowritten by William Thiele (a Viennese who was a well-known director in pre-Hitler Germany and had moderate success in England and America), *The Madonna's Secret* tells a fairly conventional mystery tale in a manner that would do credit to Paul Wegener or Fritz Lang. In no way "freakish," it builds a brooding atmosphere through masterful chiaroscuro, decor that threatens to smother the actors, and a sustained concentration upon the sensitive, haunted features of Francis Lederer (another refugee from the Third Reich).

The story strays at times, there are some dull stretches of dialogue, and a New York newspaper critic is depicted as being even more foppish than the usual stereotype. Not a flawless film, it is nonetheless a superior one, rich in ideas and pictorial beauty—certainly a more personal work than such Thiele "hits" as *The Jungle Princess* (1937) and *Tarzan Triumphs* (1943). Its elegant music is by

an aloof, handsome man with haunted eyes. Earl follows Corbin that night to the Chat D'Or cafe. Earl informs him that he recognizes him as M. Corbeille, Parisian artist and lover of Madeline Renard, pointedly suggesting that Corbin knows more than he told of the model's death. Corbin keeps silent.

Helen North's fiance, Hunt Mason, demands of her, "Doesn't it burn you up that he always paints this other girl's face?" He storms away angrily. Helen goes to Corbin's Hudson River studio, where he lives with his mother, and tells him she resents his use of another's face. Realizing the girl loves him, Corbin promises he will henceforth paint her as she really is. Helen thrills at the magnificent portrait he paints of her, and as Mrs. Corbin serves refreshments the two discuss dinner plans. A baleful premonition prompts Corbin to break the date. His mother urges him to go lest Helen be hurt. Later that night, Corbin's motorboat heads upriver. Next morning, Helen's body is found, murdered as was Madeline Renard—drugged, then drowned. John Earl presents his theory to the police, and Lieutenant Roberts questions and releases Corbin and Hunt. Earl and Hunt resolve to see Corbin hang, bringing the victims's sister, Linda North, into their plan. As "Linda Morgan," she applies as a model. Corbin hires her. Linda's thirst for vengeance is tempered as she develops sympathy for the melancholy artist.

Beautiful Ella Randolph, a wealthy widow, commissions Corbin to paint her portrait. Linda's job is sidelined while Ella keeps Corbin occupied. Corbin and Ella become gossip-column fodder. Linda visits Ella and is told Ella and Corbin plan to marry. Mrs. Corbin consoles the heartbroken Linda. Ella suggests marriage to Corbin, who reacts in anger. Later, he tells Linda he fears he has a dual personality—he may have killed without knowing it. Linda contends he is innocent, and as the two declare their love the police break in and arrest Corbin. Ella Randolph has been murdered.

The district attorney cannot force a confession. As Corbin is led to his cell, Linda cries out that she will prove his innocence. Mrs. Corbin suggests Linda accompany her to the studio. She drugs Linda's coffee, and as the girl's consciousness ebbs, she tells her she "must go like the others," but her death, Mrs. Corbin says, will serve as proof of Corbin's innocence.

Corbin, meantime, is being questioned. Realization of his mother's involvement in the killings dawns on him. Mrs. Corbin is about to inject poison into Linda's arm when the police arrive. Fatally wounded, Mrs. Corbin tells her son that her desire to protect him drove her to kill the women who fell in love with him.

Joseph Dubin, who did most of his Hollywood scoring on Disney cartoons. The paintings integral to the story are by the Polish master, Alexander S. Keszthelyi, one of this century's finest portrait artists. The celebrated Lydecker brothers provide some well-done miniatures of the boathouse, motorboat, and the river. An unusual touch is a club sequence in which Tanis Chandler sings of love while a knife marksman outlines her in blades against a wall.

The "other woman" incarnate, Gail Patrick, is fine in a brief, flashy role as a predatory dilettante. Ann Rutherford is charming as the most sympathetic player. Linda Stirling shows abilities beyond what was usually permitted as Republic's serial queen. Leona Roberts' possessive mother role and John Litel's efficient detective are strong assets. Lederer takes most of the acting burden, though, and gives it his all. Whether seen sulking about his studio, exhibiting strained gaiety, tossing off drinks in the Continental manner, or sharing an impassioned romantic scene, the Czechoslovakian-born actor applies precisely the right ambiguity to make the spectator suspect him of being a crazed murderer while hoping he is not.

The Madonna's Secret - Corbin poses his new model, Linda (Ann Rutherford).

Dragonwyck

1946 Twentieth Century Fox Film Corporation

Director: Joseph L. Manckiewicz
Screen Adaptation: Joseph L. Manckiewicz
Executive Producer: Darryl F. Zanuck
Producer: Ernst Lubitsch (removed from credits)
From the Anya Seton novel
Music: Alfred Newman
Orchestral Arrangements: Edward Powell
Director of Photography: Arthur Miller
Art Direction: Lyle Wheeler and J. Russell Spencer
Set Decorations: Thomas Little
Associate: Paul S. Fox
Film Editor: Dorothy Spencer
Costumes: Rene Hubert
Make-up: Ben Nye
Special Photographic Effects: Fred Sersen
Choreography: Arthur Appel
Sound Supervision: W. W. Flick and Roger Heman
Property Master: A. E. Lombardi
Assistant Director: Johnny Johnston
Running Time: 103 minutes

Cast: Gene Tierney (Miranda Wells), Walter Huston (Ephriam Wells), Vincent Price (Nicholas Van Ryn), Glenn Langan (Dr. Jeff Turner), Anne Revere (Abigail), Spring Byington (Magda), Connie Marshall (Katrine), Harry Morgan (Kass Bleeker), Vivienne Osborne (Johanna), Jessica Tandy (Pegay O'Malley), Trudy Marshall (Elizabeth Van Borden), Reinhold Schunzel (Count de Grenier), Jane Nigh (Tabitha), Ruth Ford (Cornelia Van Borden), David Ballard (Obadiah), Scott Elliott (Tom Wells), Boyd Irwin (Thompkins), Maya Van Horn (Countess de Grenier), Keith Hitchcock (Mr. McNabb), Francis Pierlot (Dr. Brown), Edwin David and Selby Bacon (Dancers), John Challot (French Count), Virginia Lindley (Helena), Nanette Vallon (French Countess), Mickey Roth (Nathaniel), Jamie Dana (Seth), Betty Fairfax (Mrs. McNabb), Douglas Wood (Mayor), Steve Olsen (Vendor), Grady Sutton (Hotel Clerk), Charles Waldron (Minister),Gertrude Astor (Nurse), Larry Steers, Tom Martin, Wallace Dean, Arthur Thompson and Al Winter (Servants), Ruth Cherrington and Elizabeth Williams (Ladies),

I did a wonderful villain in a marvelous picture called *Dragonwyck.* I'd have to say it was my favorite."

—Vincent Price
(*Conversation with the Authors,* 1974)

Any time a work of fiction became a best seller, Darryl F. Zanuck, long the head of production at Twentieth Century Fox, would likely bid highest for movie rights. Among the many romantic novels Zanuck brought to the screen, *Dragonwyck* ranks high as a carefully made spectacle. Ernest Lubitsch produced, but did not direct the film—although his name was removed by his own demand from the titles and most of the advertising materials. (Vincent Price, who himself was not altogether comfortable with the treatment, relates that Lubitsch argued with Zanuck about the production.) *Dragonwyck* provided a directorial debut for the distinguished writer, Joseph Manckiewicz, its success carrying him on to such other memorable films as *A Letter to Three Wives,* (1949) *No Way Out* (1950), *All About Eve* (1950), *Julius Caesar* (1953), and *Suddenly Last Summer* (1959). The direction is deliberately paced, yet never dull.

A magnificent group of sets serves, in toto, as the manor house of the title. The "exterior" was built on one sound stage; the grounds were landscaped on a four-inch covering of earth to represent, at various points in the story, spring, summer, fall, and winter. The great hall, including a carved-oak staircase, filled another stage, and the bedroom wings took up a third. Arthur Miller, director of photography, said he experimented for weeks before production began,

Dragonwyck - *Miranda becomes devoted to Van Rijn's daughter, Katrine (Connie Marshall).*

Ted Jordan, William Carter, George Ford, Alexander Sacha, Nestor Eristoff, Trevor Bardette, Walter Baldwin, Robert Malcolm, Harry Humphrey, Tom Fadden, Arthur Aylesworth, Addison Richards and Clancy Cooper (Farmers and Townsmen)

Synopsis: The story is set in the Hudson River Valley in 1844. Miranda Wells braves the disapproval of her religious fanatic father to leave Connecticut for a job at Dragonwyck as governess to little Katrine Van Ryn. The innocent Miranda is awed by the grandeur of the major house and its master, the aristocratic Nicholas Van Ryn. He is territorial patron—a feudal landlord given eternal ownership of the land by the Dutch West Indian Tea Company. Miranda sorrows for Johanna, Nicholas's ailing wife, and senses sadness and tragedy. Nicholas explains the manor is haunted by the spirit of an unhappy Van Ryn wife of another generation. The tenant farmers gather on July 4 for the kermess, a tribute to the patroon. A riot erupts. Kass Bleecker tries to assassinate Van Ryn. Jeff Turner, a handsome young village doctor, foils the assault. That night, Nicholas chooses Miranda as his partner to lead the ball. Afterwards, Johanna begs Nicholas to join her on a trip to recapture their lost love. Nicholas promises to do so once Johanna recovers from her illness, and he sends her his favorite oleander plant. He retires to a private tower room.

Turner asks Nicholas to spare Bleecker's life. Nicholas consents if Jeff will stay the night and examine Johanna. Jeff finds Johanna suffers from a severe cold. Before morning he is summoned to her room and finds Johanna dead. Miranda flees Dragonwyck after Nicholas has asked her to marry him; he has not the decency to wait until after the funeral bells have stopped tolling. Nicholas follows her to Connecticut and tells her of his years of misery with Johanna and of his longing to have a son. Miranda, admitting her love, consents. In the spring they marry, much to the disappointment of Jeff, who also loves Miranda. Later, when Jeff confirms that Miranda is with child, Nicholas' joy is unconfined.

A son is born, but its heart is malformed; the infant dies at christening. Nicholas disappears into the tower for weeks at a time. Miranda at last dares enter and finds him maddened by drugs and superstition. A maid summons Jeff, who finds Nicholas threatening Miranda to whom he has given some oleander plants. Jeff overpowers Nicholas, then tells Miranda he feels Nicholas murdered Johanna with the poisonous plant and has marked Miranda for a similar fate. They go for help, and upon returning they find Nicholas on his patroon's throne conducting an imaginary kermess. Seeing Jeff, Nicholas raises a pistol and takes aim. A farmer shoots Nicholas, whose arrogance remains to his dying breath: "That's right— take off your hats in the presence of the patroon."

seeking to establish a lighting style to serve both romance and eeriness. This was achieved by simulating candlelight. Subtle changes in lighting make the photographic tone flow smoothly from one mood to another. Alfred Newman's brilliant score, with some of the most exquisite string passages ever heard on film, helps unify the somewhat rambling story.

The rambling nature itself, of course, helps disguise an unfortunate flaw in the editing of *Dragonwyck* —the unaccounted for disappearance of the child, Connie Marshall, who plays the daughter of the manor lord. Hers is a necessary part, being the factor that draws Gene Tierney to the estate at the outset, and yet the film, as released, fails to follow through with what becomes of her. Another major character, a strange servant played by Spring Byington, also vanishes inexplicably.

Dragonwyck was advertised as a vehicle for the lovely Miss Tierney, who had become one of the studio's lead-

ing stars since her debut there in 1940. Her performance fully justifies this emphasis; equally good is the distin-

guished Walter Huston, whose name heads the supporting cast despite the brevity of his role. Third-billed Vincent

Dragonwyck - *Young Dr. Turner (Glenn Langan) incurs the displeasure of Van Rijn.*

Dragonwyck - *After his wife's death, Van Rijn passionately declares his love for Miranda.*

the poem:

> From childhood's hour I have not
>   been
> As others were—I have not seen
> As others saw—I could not draw
> My passions from a common spring.
> From this same source I have not
>   taken
> My sorrow; I could not awaken
> My heart to joy at the same tone;
> And all I lov'd, I lov'd alone.
> *Then* in my childhood—in the dawn
> Of a most stormy life—was drawn
> From ev'ry depth of good and ill
> The mystery which binds me still:
> From the torrent, or the fountain,
> From the red cliff of the mountain,
> From the sun that round me roll'd
> In its autumn tint of gold—
> From the lighting in the sky
> As it passed me flying by—
> From the thunder and the storm,
> And the cloud that took the form
> (When the rest of Heaven was blue)
> Of a demon in my view

"Edgar Allan Poe wrote that," Price continued, "and it has to be one of the most revealing autobiographical poems ever written, for Poe was indeed born with a demon within." Price's affection for the picture notwithstanding, he observed, "Censorship was a problem then. We had to leave out some of the best things in the book, including the ending where Van Ryn reformed. We had to kill him instead, because evil must be paid for. I didn't know how I would die because Mr. Manckiewicz couldn't tell me. He thought an actor's knowledge of his fate would psychologically 'type' the performance." Production, Price said, "was . . . tremendously lavish. The set was gigantic, and we had an unusually long schedule, about five months. I loved it; it was in the days when pictures were really produced beautifully."

Price actually is dominant, however, as the aristocratic tyrant. In an exceptional performance, easily the best of a vibrant career, Price gains audience sympathy and hatred by turns through subtly disciplined shadings of character. He is convincing throughout as the romantic young man who wins the ingenuous heroine, as the cool murderer who cultivates deadly oleanders (assembled by the prop department from oleander blooms and foliage and the twisted branches of a manzanita), and as the crazed addict.

Price, in discussions with the authors, recalled *Dragonwyck* fondly: "A villain represents conflict, but he need not be a drag fellow. According to Aristotle, he can be a man of great culture and high station. That makes him more interesting because the audience is fascinated that such a person can come to this. Our job is to make the unbelievable believable; we have to con you into thinking maybe we could not be so bad as you think. [In *Dragonwyck*] I was an extraordinary villain named Van Ryn, who believed in survival of the fittest. Anything that didn't live up to his standards shouldn't live. I did a lot of research trying to understand him, and I finally found the key in the front of the book. Anya Seton quoted the poem *Alone,* in the foreword." Here Price gave an interpretation of

Decoy

1946   Monogram Pictures Corporation
Director: Jack Bernhard
Producers: Jack Bernhard and Bernard Brandt
Screenplay: Ned Young
Original Story: Stanley Rubin
Director of Photography: L. William O'Connell
Musical Director: Edward J. Kay
Art Director: David Milton
Film Editor: Jason Bernie
Sound Recording: Tom Lambert
Stylist: Lorraine MacLean
Production Manager: Glenn Cook
Make-up: M. Morante
Assistant Director: William Callihan
Dialogue Director: Ken Kessler
Special Effects: Augie Lohman
Set Decorations: Ray Boltz
Costumes: Lorraine MacLean
Running Time: 76 minutes

Cast: Jean Gillie (Margot Shelby), Edward Norris (Jim Vincent), Robert Armstrong (Frank Olins), Herbert Rudley (Dr. Lloyd Craig), Sheldon Leonard (Joe Portugal), Marjorle Woodworth (Nurse), Phil Van Zandt (Tommy), Carol Donne (Waitress), John Shay (Al), Ben Roach (Bartender), Rosemary Bertrand (Ruth), also Jody Gilbert, Wlliam Self, Betty Lou Head, Louis Mason, Ferris Taylor, Willlam Ruhl, Walden Boyle, Franco Corsaro, Madge Crain, Pat Flaherty, Donald Kerr, Harry Tyler, Austin McCoy, Richard Eiliott, Virginia Farmer, Ray Teal, Kenneth Patterson and Don MacCracken

Synopsis: Alive only through grim determination, Dr. Lloyd Craig staggers into the apartment of beautiful Margot Shelby and shoots her. Detective Joe Portugal arrives to find Craig dead and Margot gravely wounded. She tells how she caused four deaths:

Frankie Olins, Margot's lover, hid $400,000 taken in a bank robbery before his execution for killing a guard. Margot feigned love for gangster Jim Vincent and convinced him to join a scheme to remove Olins' body just after execution. She also pretended affection to lure the prison doctor, Craig, from the nurse he loved to help in the plan. The hearse driver was murdered during the body-snatching.

Craig administered methylene blue and arti-

A Monogram postwar victory—a picture that rises well above the characteristic potboiler status—is *Decoy,* a taut melodrama with gangsters, illicit love, murder, and a touch of science fiction.   Jean Gillie, an English dancer and actress for whom great things were predicted, is the femme fatale who holds the audience in thrall She comes as close to portraying sexual sadism as the censors allowed. Despite acclaim for her brilliant interpretation of a poisonous woman, the red-headed actress remained largely overlooked at the studios. She returned to England, where she died in 1949 without achieving the prominence her abilities merited.

Decoy's substantial cast includes the excellent Robert Armstrong, Edward Norris, Sheldon Leonard, and Herbert Rudley, as well as the gorgeous Marjorie Woodworth as a girl whom Rudley (in what must be considered a moment of insanity) casts aside in favor of the murderous Miss Gillie.

Photographic and technical expertise displayed in *Decoy* indicates the growing-up of Monogram from its status as a maker of "quickies." This is a remarkably risk taking show, structured around a flashback which is both good and bad. It permits a striking opening with Rudley resembling a walking corpse (the make-up is a bit overdone, but here it's effective) as he staggers into a filthy service station restroom and sees his ravaged features in a cracked mirror and later as he stalks his prey. The resurrection of Armstrong is a fantastic premise on which to hang such a hard-boiled show; the idea had been given some credence by experimentation with laboratory animals, and rumors that a big-time mobster was revived after *his* execution in this manner.

Director/co-producer Jack Bernhard had done some work at

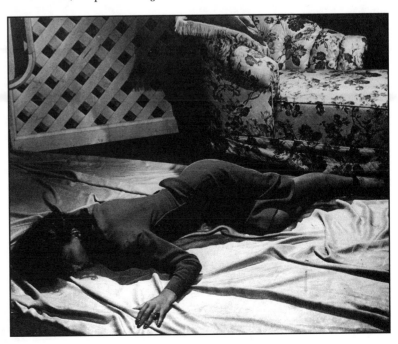

Decoy *- Margot (Jean Gillie) is found critically wounded.*

ficial respiration, counteracting the effect of the cyanide gas and restoring Olins to life. Olins gave Margot half of a map showing the location of the loot, but Vincent shot Olins to death and took his half of the map. Vincent and Margot set out after the money, forcing Craig to take them through police blockades. Vincent planned to kill Craig, but Margot ran Vincent down with the car. She and Craig found the cache, but as soon as Craig dug it up, Margot shot him and left him for dead. The money box is at Margot's side as she finishes her tale. After she dies, Portugal opens the box and finds in it a single dollar bill—Olins's joke from beyond the grave.

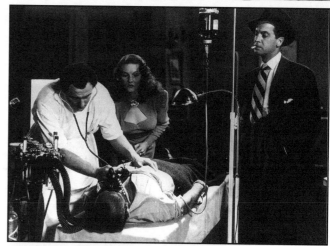

Decoy - *Craig works to revive Olins as Margo and Jim Vincent (Edward Norris) watch.*

Universal—including the popular *Man Made Monster* (1941)—before serving a wartime hitch. Upon his return he made *Decoy*, for which he received good notices, but this success led to little else of note. Scriptwriter Nedrick Young, a former actor, found his career blighted in the blacklisting that followed the House Un-American Activities hearings on Communist influence in Hollywood. Scenarist Stanley Rubin and actor Sheldon Leonard, on the other hand, rose to greater levels as movie and television producers. So did actor Bill Self, here in a small role, who became a top Television executive.

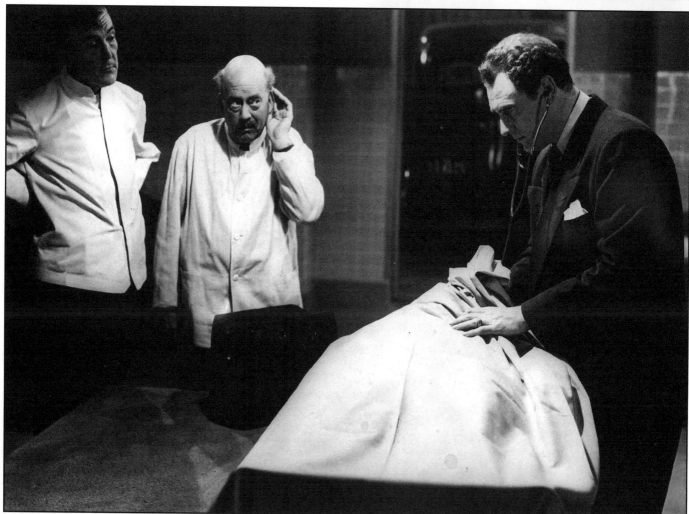

Decoy - *Morgue attendants(Louis Mason, Ferris Taylor) watch as Dr. Craig (Herbert Rudley) examines an executed man.*

The Dark Mirror

1946 International Pictures, Incorporated
Director: Robert Siodmak
Producer: Nunnally Johnson
Screen Adaptation: Nunnally Johnson
Based on the Vladimir Pozner serial
Executive Producers: Leo Spitz and William Goetz
Director of Photography: Milton Krasner
Musical Composition and Orchestration: Dmitri Tiomkin
Production Designer: Duncan Cramer
Special Photographic Effects: J. Deveraux Jennings and Paul Lerpae
Costumes: Irene Sharafl
Film Editor: Ernest Nims
Make-up: Norbert Miles
Hair Stylist: Mary Freeman
Sound: Fred Lau and Arthur Johns
Set Decorations: Hugh Hunt
Dialogue Director: Phyllls Loughton
Assistant Director: Jack Voglin
Running Time: 85 minutes

Cast: Olivia de Havilland (Terry Collins/Ruth Collins), Lew Ayres (Dr. Scott Elliott), Thomas Mitchell (Detective Stevenson), Richard Long (Rusty), Charles Evans (District Attorney Girard), Garry Owens (Franklin), Lester Allen (George Benson), Lela Bliss (Mrs. Didriksen), Marta Mitrovitch (Miss Beade), Amelita Ward (Photo-Double), Lane Chandler (Orderly), also William Halligan, Ida Moore, Charles McAvoy, Jack Cheatham, Barbara Powers, Ralph Peters, Rodney Bell, Lane Watson, Ben Erway, Jean Audren andJack Gargan.

Synopsis: A society physician is found in his apartment, knifed in the back. Detective Stevenson learns the victim had a date the night of the killing with Ruth Collins, who works at a newsstand in the lobby of the building where the doctor had his office. Stevenson thinks he has a case against her until he learns his suspect has an identical twin, Terry. One of the girls has an airtight alibi—but which? They have habitually substituted for one another on dates and jobs, and neither will reveal the truth. Lest he make a false arrest, Stevenson has Dr. Scott Elliott, a mental specialist, try to determine which sister is capable of murder. Both girls co-operate, and both seem to become

Though released as a Universal-International picture, *The Dark Mirror* is not a product of that company. Free agent Nunnally Johnson produced it in association with International Pictures, Incorporated; it was scheduled at first as an RKO-Radio release. With the merger in 1946 of Universal and International, the film became International's first contribution to the new combine. At sight of the finished product, director Robert Siodmak said, "This is it—my best to date." The point is arguable. The present writers consider Siodmak's earlier *Suspect* (1945), *The Spiral Staircase* (1945), and *The Killers* (1946) to surpass it in most respects. Still, *Mirror* is a charming chiller which managed to be novel even at a time when psychological melodramas were all the rage in Hollywood.

Johnson (whose writing credits include *The Grapes of Wrath*, 1940, *The Woman in the Window*, 1944, and *The Gunfighter*, 1950), provided a script with unusual twists, clever dialogue, and some well spaced humor. It is surprisingly naive at times, though, and lacks the agreeable earthiness found in most of his writing. The story moves rapidly and the German-trained Siodmak makes the most of the human touches inherent in an account of twins who seem a match, but for a hidden beast in one. Sets and photography are slick and romantic, and the suspense is achieved without obvious artifice.

Olivia de Havilland restrains both performances until the climax, when she pulls out all stops in depicting the mental disintegration of the evil sister. The concept is splendid as well as surprising inasmuch as the sweet faced actress was noted for her highly sympathetic portrayals (Maid Marian, for example, in *The Adventures of Robin Hood*,

The Dark Mirror *- A prominent society physician is found murdered in his apartment.*

romantically interested in Scott.

Ruth, the quieter sister, appears emotionally disturbed and experiences hallucinations. Terry is more aggressive and self-assured. Elliott becomes enamored with one of the girls, but their tricks confuse him as to which is which. One of them contemplates stabbing him in the back with a pair of shears. He feels one of the girls is in danger of being killed by the other. Actually, Terry is driving Ruth mad with drugs and flashing lights.

Elliott phones their apartment and asks for Ruth. Terry answers and pretends to be her twin. Elliott asks her to come to his office that night, but just after he hangs up the receiver, Ruth arrives. Stevenson helps Elliott lead Terry to believe Ruth has committed suicide. Triumphant in the belief, Terry acts the part of the good sister until she sees Ruth's reflection in a mirror; she flies into a murderous rage. Her innocence established before witnesses, Ruth finds solace in Elliott's arms as the authorities lead Terry away.

1938, and Melanie Wilkes in *Gone With the Wind*, 1939). Lew Ayres, back at work following a four-year Army stint as a chaplain's assistant, is a convincingly capable psychiatrist. Thomas Mitchell provides sturdy support as a rough-hewn detective. The special-effects scenes in which the twins appear together are among the most sophisticated of their kind, rivaled in the for-

ties only by those of Danny Kaye in *Wonder Man* (1945) and Bette Davis in *A Stolen Life* (1946). The use of complex separations, opticals, and traveling mattes enables the actress to roam the full breadth of the screen, cross in front of herself, walk arm-in-arm with her "twin," and even embrace herself. The effects are so flawless as to leave the impression there actually were two de

Havillands. Amelita Ward, a B-picture leading lady at Universal and RKO, was one of the twins; when the faces of both twins were in the same scene de Havilland's face was matted in with Ward's body.

A highly dramatic score by Dmitri Tiomkin points up the action a bit too much at times, but the music is generally effective.

The Dark Mirror - *Police are baffled as to which sister should be charged with murder.*

So Dark the Night

1946   Columbia Pictures Corporation
Director: Joseph H. Lewis
Producer: Ted Richmond
Screenplay: Martin Berkeley and Dwight V. Babcock
Based on an Aubrey Wisberg story
Director of Photography: Burnett Guffey
Film Editor: Jerome Thoms
Art Director: Carl Anderson
Set Decorations: William Kiernan
Sound Recording: Frank Goodwin
Musical Score: Hugo Friedhofer
Musical Director: M. W. Stoloff
Assistant Director: Chris Beute
Running Time: 70 minutes

Cast: Steven Geray (Henri Cassin), Micheline Cheirel (Nanette Michaud), Eugene Borden (Pierre Michaud), Ann Codee (Mama Michaud), Egon Brecher (Dr. Boncourt), Helen Freeman (Widow Bridelle), Theodore Gottlieb (Georges), Gregory Gay (Commissaire Grande), Jean del Val (Dr. Manet), Paul Marion (Leon Archard), Emil Ramu (Pere Cortot), Louis Mercier (Jean Duval), also Adrienne D'Ambricourt, Marcelle Corday, Alphonse Martel, Andre Marsandou, Francine Bordeaux, Esther Zeitland and Cynthia Gaylord.

Synopsis: A nervous breakdown threatens the Surete's finest detective, Henri Cassin, and he is sent to the village of St. Margot for a rest. The inn where he stays is run by Pierre Michaud and his wife. Their daughter, Nanette, is engaged to Leon Achard, a young farmer. Mama Michaud convinces Nanette to marry the rich, middle-aged detective instead of the handsome but poor youth. Nanette trains her wiles upon Henri, and they become engaged despite opposition from Pierre and Leon. At their announcement party, Leon declares no man will have Nanette but himself. Nanette and Leon disappear, and it is assumed they ran away together.

Several days later, the strangled body of Nanette is found. Henri can find no clues. Then Leon, the key suspect, is found, strangled as was Nanette. Under the body is a footprint. Henri makes a cast of it but finds no villager whose shoe matches.

A note in an eccentric hand warns Mama

Joseph H. Lewis learned the movie business from the bottom up, beginning as a camera boy at MGM, becoming chief film editor of the Mascot and Republic serials during the thirties, and directing second units and "quickie" Westerns and melodramas for several years. He served with the Signal Corps during the Second World War. Returning to Hollywood, Lewis made a good little *Falcon* picture at RKO (*The Falcon in San Francisco*, 1945) and won a berth as a contract director for the Briskin ("B") unit at Columbia. His first Columbia release, a mystery called *My Name Is Julia Ross* (1946), delivered so much artistry on a budget as to raise his status overnight. He made one more Briskin picture, *So Dark the Night* before being "kicked upstairs" to direct *The Jolson Story* (1946), the first of many highly regarded films to be directed by Lewis during the next dozen years including the celebrated *Deadly is the Female (Gun Crazy)*, (1949).

Though it shows the same expertise as *Julia Ross, So Dark the Night* attracted far less attention. It cannot match its predecessor for audience appeal, for the male lead is a short, middle-aged Hungarian usually seen in villain roles, and the only pretty girl in evidence is murdered early on. It also falls short in suspense, developing slowly with little action. It is in its own way a workmanlike job, however, with a memorable performance by Steven Geray as the detective unknowingly tracking himself. (The effectiveness of Geray's acting

So Dark the Night - *Inspector Cassin (Steven Geray) and Nanette Michaud (Micheline Cheirel) announce their bethrothal to the priest (Emil Ramu) and the girl's parents (Ann Codee, Eugene Borden).*

Michaud she will die next. Despite Henri's precautions, the strangler kills Mama. Back in Paris, Henri commissions an artist to make a reconstruction based on data he has deduced from the footprint. The sketch approximates Henri himself! He finds his own shoe fits the cast. Henri confesses to the Commissaire of Police, M. Grande. A psychiatrist finds that Henri is ostensibly sane by day but a crazed killer by night.

Escaping from his guards, Henri returns to St. Margot. M. Grande arrives just as Henri is strangling Michaud. A bullet saves Michaud. Henri, dying, looks at his reflection in the window and sees himself as he was, then as the killer. He smashes the glass and cries out, "Henri Cassin is no more. I have caught him and killed him."

was demonstrated by default in 1955, when the more celebrated Joseph Schildkraut played the same role in a *Lux Television Theatre* production, shown over the NBC network, with less happy results.) The other players do their jobs well.

The story is based upon a docu-mented *cause célèbre* of Europe during the mid-thirties. It is convincing and well dialogued. The sets, which had seen service in some elaborate war films, are properly dressed to suggest pre-war France, and the photography shows them well. Many shots are made through windows, so that the audi-ence, like Cassin, is an outsider. Most of the film is staged for depth. Hugo Friedhofer's musical score, conducted by Morris Stoloff, is outstanding. Interestingly enough, both Friedhofer and Stoloff won Academy Awards that year, for *The Best Years of Our Lives* and *The Jolson Story,* respectively.

So Dark the Night - Dr. Manet (Jean del Val) and Commissioner Grande (Gregory Gay) mourn the violent death of Cassin.

The Locket

1946   RKO-Radio Pictures, Incorporated
Director: John Brahm
Producer: Bert Granet
Executive Producer: Jack J. Gross
Original Screenplay: Sheridan Gibney
Director of Photography: Nicholas Musuraca
Music: Roy Webb
Musical Director: C. Bakaleinikoff
Special Effects: Russell A. Cully
Optical Effects: Linwood G. Dunn
Art Direction: Albert S. D'Agostino and Al Herman
Set Decorations: Darrell Silvera and Harley Miller
Film Editor: J. R. Whittredge
Sound Recording: John L. Cass and Clem Portman
Gowns: Michael Woulfe
Assistant Director: Harry D'Arcy
Dialogue Director: William E. Watts
Running Time: 85 minutes

Cast: Laraine Day (Nancy), Brian Aherne (Dr. Harry Blair), Robert Mitchum (Norman Clyde), Gene Raymond (John Willis), Sharyn Moffett (Nancy at ten), Ricardo Cortez (Bonner), Henry Stephenson (Lord Wyndham), Katherine Emery (Mrs. Willis), Reginald Denny (Wendell), Fay Helm (Mrs. Bonner), Helen Thimig (Mrs. Monks), Nella Walker (Mrs. Wendell), Queenie Leonard (Singer), Lillian Fontaine (Lady Wyndham), Myrna Dell (Thelma), Johnny Clark (Donald), Vivien Oakland (Mrs. Donovan), Nancy Saunders (Miss Whyatt), George Humbert (Luigi), Trina Varella (Luigi's Wife), Nick Thompson (Waiter), Connie Leon (Bonner Maid), David Thursby (Dexter), Tom Chatterton (Art Critic), Sam Flint (District Attorney), Tom Coleman (Steno), Virginia Keiley (Ambulance Driver), Wyndham Standing (Butler), Frederick Worlock (First Doctor), Henry Mowbray (Second Doctor), Cecil Weston (Nurse), Colin Kenny (Chauffeur), Leonard Mudie (Air Raid Warden), Pat Malone (London Bobby), Polly Bailey (Cook), Ellen Corby and Jean Ransom (Kitchen Girls), Keith Hitchcock (Orville), Gloria Donovan (Karen), Carol Donne, Martha Hyer and Kay Christopher (Bridesmaids), Ben Erway (Second Willis Butler), Mari Aldon (Mary), Charles Flynn,

A bizarre and artistic film by the imaginative John Brahm, *The Locket* was all but buried in the volume of psychological thrillers that followed World War ll. A pattern having been established, the critics were growing increasingly cold to such films, meting out the same harshness they had long accorded films about monsters and mad scientists. Nor was *The Locket* a popular favorite; many viewers reacted to its complex structure as they had to that of *Intolerance* (1916). However intolerant the response to it, though, *The Locket* is a virtuoso piece in which Brahm's gift for imagery takes full control. It is an equally fine showcase for the brilliant cameraman, Nick Musuraca, whose contributions to the genre in the Val Lewton horror films are definitive.

Sheridan Gibney's original screen story (originally titled "What Nancy Wanted"), unfolds as a flashback, within a flashback, within a flashback, set within a present day framing story! Brian Aherne's tale to Gene Raymond contains Robert Mitchum's story, which in turn

Only locked in their arms could she keep her sinister secret locked in her heart!

From one man's arms to another, she fled—trying to escape the evil memory of the tragic trinket whose strange power changed her life...destroyed her loves!

RKO PRESENTS

LARAINE DAY
BRIAN AHERNE
ROBERT MITCHUM
GENE RAYMOND in

The Locket

with
SHARYN MOFFETT · RICARDO CORTEZ · HENRY STEPHENSON
Produced by BERT GRANET · Directed by JOHN BRAHM · Written by SHERIDAN GIBNEY
RKO RADIO

Joey Ray, and Bob Templeton (Photographers), Broderick O'Farrell (Ministers), Dorothy Curtis (Maid), also J. W. Johnston, Allen Schute, Jacqueline Frost and Eddie Borden.

Synopsis: A posh party is in progress at the Willis home, where John Willis is about to marry Nancy. Dr. Harry Blair appears, uninvited, and demands to talk to John, saying he is a psychiatrist who was married to Nancy for five years. The angry groom consents at last to listen, and Blair tells his story:

Miami, 1938. Blair met and married Nancy. They were happy until one day an artist, Norman Clyde, approached Blair with word that an innocent man awaiting execution in Sing Sing could be saved only by Nancy. Blair agreed to hear him out, and Clyde presented this account:

Nancy had come to study in a life-painting class at Clyde's studio. Clyde and Nancy quarreled, and she left. He found her at a cafe and apologized. Later, Nancy brought a wealthy art patron named Bonner to consider Clyde's work. Bonner placed a painting by Clyde in a show, and as a result Clyde won an award. Mrs. Bonner, an invalid, bought the painting for a large sum. During a party at the Bonner mansion, Clyde learned Nancy had stolen an expensive bracelet from the Bonners. He confronted Nancy, and she told him this story of a childhood incident: Nancy Monks was the daughter of a housekeeper in a wealthy home. A jeweled locket disappeared during a party, and the coldly cruel mistress of the house blamed Nancy, then ten years old. After a vicious scene between the woman and the terrified child, Nancy's mother found the locket where it had fallen. Clyde found Nancy with the body of Bonner, who had been murdered. Clyde shielded her, and evidence pointed to a man who was convicted and condemned to die for the killing. Blair refused to accept Clyde's story, but after Clyde left, Blair began to worry. At last he asked Nancy about the incident; she replied with a lie, which he believed. After the execution had been carried out, Clyde came to Blair's office, seemingly calm. He repeated that the story he told was the truth, and then, as if to prove it, he leaped through a high window to his death. Blair and Nancy went to London, where they were houseguests of Lord and Lady Wyndham. Nancy admired the Wyndhams' fabulous collection of jewels. The Nazi blitzkrieg had begun, and when Blair's apartment was bombed, he found one of the Wyndham jewels in the rubble. Blair's mind snapped when he realized Clyde had told the truth, and he was committed to a mental asylum. Blair's complex story has run its course now, and John refuses to believe it. As the wedding ceremony proceeds, John's mother gives the bride a locket —it is the one Nancy was accused of stealing as a child, and it was John's mother who had accused her! Nancy walks to the altar as if in a trance, and as she stands before the assembly, she collapses. It is found that her mind has reverted to childhood. She is placed in an asylum, hopelessly insane.

contains Laraine Day's traumatic recollection. The moviegoer who settles in to watch after the picture is under way has little hope of picking up the threads. The transitions are garnished with the superb optical effects that had become an RKO trademark. A moody score by Roy Webb embellishes the visuals and helps unify the story elements.

Mitchum's suicide makes for an especially memorable scene. He leaves the doctor's office; the doctor hears the shattering of glass and rushes to the waiting room. The camera takes in the room and its several horrified occupants, then moves toward the smashed picture window, proceeds *through* the break, and tilts downward suddenly to show crowds gathering around a body on the sidewalk, far below. Although this appears to be one continuous shot, the various components of the sequence were brought together through ingenious optical work.

The Locket - Blair and Nancy in happier days.

The Locket - Norman's story to Blair is denied convincingly by Nancy.

Opticals also intensify the climactic scenes of the wedding and Laraine Day's final breakdown, giving a surreal quality through carefully planned distortions of images. This effect of distortion carries over into the soundtrack.

The actors respond well to Brahm's direction. Miss Day maintains a cool façade until the shattering climax, lending credibility to the premise that none of her victims can consider her anything but angelic. Brian Aherne is convincing as the self-assured psychiatrist driven to madness but determined to return and save others from his lethal wife. Robert Mitchum gives a robust interpretation of a working artist quite unlike the "ivory tower" stereotype. Gene Raymond is believable as a wealthy man bedazzled by beauty and false innocence. Katherine Emery chills the blood as a cruel society matron. Sharyn Moffett gives a sensitive portrayal of the misunderstood child, and Helene Thimig (the widow of Max Reinhardt) offers a touching cameo as the child's mother. Ricardo Cortez, Henry Stephenson, Reginald Denny, Fay Helm, and Queenie Leonard are among the highly professional players who add to the interest of this engrossing exercise in the macabre.

The Locket - A doctor (Frederick Worlock) tells Nancy that her husband is insane.

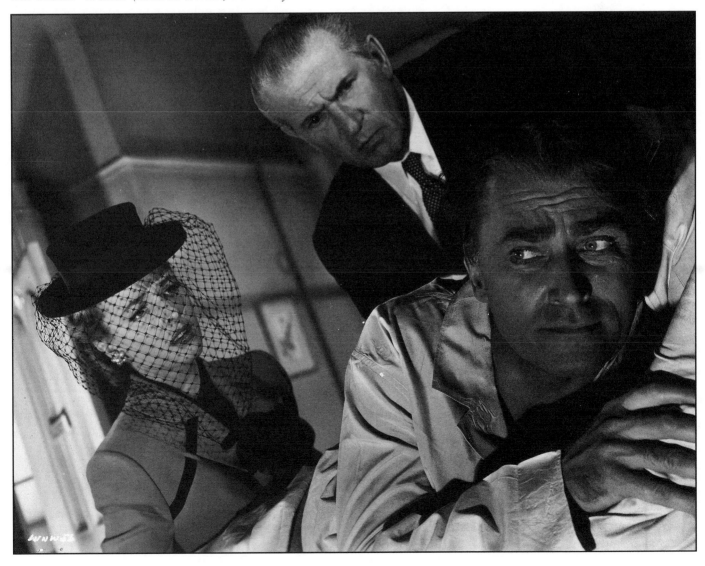

Ivy

1947 Inter-Wood Productions
Universal-International Pictures, Incorporated
Director: Sam Wood
Producer: William Cameron Menzies
Screenplay: Charles Bennett
From the Marie Belloc Lowndes novel *The Story of Ivy*
Director of Photography: Russell Metty
Music: Daniele Amfitheatrof
Art Directors: John B. Goodman and Richard H. Riedel
Set Decorations: Russell A. Gausman and T. F. Offenbecker
Film Editor: Ralph Dawson
Special Photography: David S. Horsley
Assistant Director: John F. Sherwood
Orchestrations: David Tamkin
Sound Director: Charles Felstead
Technician: William Hedgecock
Miss Fontaine's Gowns: Orry-Kelly
Hair Stylist: Carmen Dirigo
Running Time: 97 minutes

Cast: Joan Fontaine (Ivy), Patric Knowles (Roger Gretorex), Herbert Marshall (Miles Rushworth), Richard Ney (Jervis Lexton), Sir Cedric Hardwicke (Orpington), Lucile Watson (Mrs. Gretorex), Sara Allgood (Martha Huntley), Henry Stephenson (Judge), Rosalind Ivan (Emily), Lillian Fontaine (Lady Flora), Molly Lamont (Bella Crail), Una O'Connor (Mrs. Thrawn), Isobel Elsom (Mrs. Chattle), Alan Napier (Sir Jonathan Wright), Paul Cavanaugh (Dr. Berwick), Sir Charles Mendl (Sir Charles Craig), Gavin Muir (Sergeant), Mary Forbes (Lady Crail), Al Ferguson (Bailiff), Alan Edmiston (Harpsichordist), James Logan (Pilot), also, Lumsden Hare, Norma Varden, Matthew Boulton, Lydia Bilbrook, Harry Hays Morgan, Holmes Herbert, C. Montague Shaw, Gerald Hamer, Colin Campbell, Leon Lenoir, Jean Fenwick, Boyd Irwin, Wally Scott, Dave Thursby, Wally Scott, Claire duBrey, Art Foster, David Cavendish, Jack Boylan, Alberto Morin, Lois Austin, Herbert Clifton, Jack Perrin, David Ralston, Eric Wilton, Charles Knight, Schuyler McGuflin, Dave Dunbar, Herbert Evans, Manuel Paris, Harry H. Evans, Frank Tomlinson, Norman Ainslee, Ella Etheridge, Wyndham Standing, Clive Morgan, William Mind, John Peters,

Although she is best known for her great psychological horror novel, *The Lodger*, Marie Belloc Lowndes wrote other memorable tales of murder with emphasis more on the "why" than the "who." Foremost of these is *The Story of Ivy*, a 1928 novel, which reached the screen as a triumph of elegant production and pictorial design. The picture is a prime example of the elaborate films made in post World War II Hollywood. Given a 120-day shooting schedule and a budget of $1,500,000—of which $30,000 was allotted to a magnificent wardrobe for the central character—producer William Cameron Menzies and director Sam Wood were able to finish twenty days ahead of schedule, an accomplishment attributable to Menzies' careful predesigning of each shot, and to Wood's habit of directing long sequences without interruption after thorough rehearsals.

Wood's command of fine performances and Menzies' flair for design—he may well be the greatest production designer in the history of filmmaking—make for an impeccable movie. They had collaborated before as director and designer, their magnum opus being *Kings Row* (1941), another elegant horror tale. Screenwriter Charles Bennett invested *Ivy* with a remarkable balance between tension and

IVY is beautiful
IVY is lovely
IVY is EVIL...
to every man who loves her!

JOAN FONTAINE
Surpassing her performances in
"REBECCA" and "SUSPICION"

UNIVERSAL-INTERNATIONAL presents

JOAN
FONTAINE
PATRIC KNOWLES
HERBERT MARSHALL
RICHARD NEY

"IVY"

A Sam Wood PRODUCTION

with SIR CEDRIC HARDWICKE LUCILE WATSON ROSALIND IVAN SARA ALLGOOD
Directed by SAM WOOD • Produced by WILLIAM CAMERON MENZIES
Screenplay by CHARLES BENNETT • Based on the novel "The Story of Ivy" by Marie Belloc Lowndes • A UNIVERSAL-INTERNATIONAL PICTURE

Nigel Horton, Robert Hale, Elsa Peterson, James Fairfax, Robert Cory, Bess Flowers, Renee Evans, J.C. Johnson and Judith Woodbury

Synopsis: In London just after the turn of the century, Ivy Lexton is fed up with her weakling husband, Jervis, who has squandered his inheritance. She is superstitious and frustrated that a seer cannot tell her precisely what to expect. Proceeding recklessly to fashion her own fate, Ivy carries on a secret affair with a fashionable young physician, Roger Gretorex, who is unresponsive to her guarded hints that he should kill Jervis. Ivy steals poison from her lover's surgery and hides it in a secret compartment in the clasp of her purse. Jervis, who has become a heavy drinker, does not suspect Ivy is poisoning his brandy.

Her greed outstrips Gretorex' means; the wealthy Miles Rushworth falls readily under her spell. Rushworth gives Jervis a good job and moves the couple into a fine apartment.

When Jervis dies, Inspector Orpington suspects murder. Examination shows poison, and the substance is traced to Roger. The doctor, too much the gentleman to implicate Ivy, is indicted. Orpington, however, suspects Ivy, whose perjury incriminates Gretorex. It appears he will hang, but Orpington causes doubt to be cast upon Ivy. Scandalous disclosures cause Rushworth and the rest of her aristocratic circle to abandon her. Orpington finds the purse, with poison still hidden in the clasp, stowed in a grandfather clock. Ivy tries to flee and falls down an elevator shaft to her death.

Ivy - *Ivy is not happy in her marriage to the charming but weak Jervis (Richard Ney).*

Ivy - Ivy Lexton, the evil beauty of Mrs. Belloc Lowndes' "The Story of Ivy," is portrayed on the screen by Joan Fontaine.

pense cinema, notably in league with Alfred Hitchcock during 1934-40 on such memorable works as *The Man Who Knew Too Much*, *The 39 Steps*, *Young and Innocent*, and *Foreign Correspondent*. (The Bennett influence on Hitchcock carried over into the 1956 remake of *The Man Who Knew Too Much* for the story itself is a Bennett work). Conspicuous elements in the overall excellence of *Ivy* are the photography by Russell Metty and rich score by Daniele Amfitheatrof, who substituted a harpsichord, for the then-popular theremin, as a mood building solo instrument.

leisurely pacing, faithful to the novel's lavish amplification of an elemental and simply resolved tale. Bennett, also known for his novels and plays, scripted many influential examples of sus-

Ivy is a bit long, its almost languorous development being appropriate to the period and subject—but at the cost of some of the suspense that a snappier pace might have allowed.

Olivia de Havilland was originally scheduled to portray Ivy, but she balked at playing another murderess so soon after *The Dark Mirror*. Her sister, and then bitter rival, Joan Fontaine, stepped in willingly and proved ideal. Usually seen as a shy girl in such films as Hitchcock's *Rebecca* (1940) and *Suspicion* (1941) and Robert Stevenson's *Jane Eyre* (1944), Fontaine is very much the center of attention. Incidentally, she never liked the picture or Woods' direction. There is good support, particularly from Sir Cedric Hardwicke as a cold-eyed Scotland Yard man, from the genteel Mr. Marshall and from Richard Ney as a pathetic but likeable tippler.

An interesting sequence is a staging of the preparations for a flight of a primitive Curtiss-Wright aircraft across the English Channel. Also of note, a popular song, "Ivy" was written on commission by Hoagy Carmichael and used to promote the film, but is not heard as such on the soundtrack, although the song is based on a secondary theme in the score. It was recorded by such bigsellers as Dick Haymes, Woody Herman, Vaughan Monroe, and Jo Stafford.

Ivy - Lillian Fontaine, mother of Joan Fontaine and Olivia DeHavilland, appears as Ivy's friend, Lady Flora.

1530-53

The Queen of Spades

1949 Associated British-Pathé, Ltd.
Welwyn Studios
Produced by Associated British Picture
Corporation Limited
Distributed by Associated British-Pathé
Director: Thorold Dickinson
Producer: Anatole de Grunwald
From the Alexander Pushkin story
Screenplay: Rodney Ackland and Arthur Boys
Settings and Costumes: Oliver Messel
Assistant to Messel: Ann Wemwyss
Director of Photography: Otto Heller
Film Editor: Hazel Wilkinson
Music: Georges Auric
Musical Director: Louis Levy
Art Director: William Kellner
Production Manager: Isobel Parciter
Cinematography: Gus Drisse and Val Stewart
Sound: Frank McNaily
Dubbing: L. H. Shilton and Audrey Bennett
Assistant Director: John Gaudioz
Continuity: Marjorie Owens
Make-up: Robert Clarke
Hairdressers: Frank Cross and Betty Cross
Set Dresser: Phillip Stockford
Period Advisor: Dr. Baird
Wardrobe Advisor: W. Smith
Fabric Advisor: Scot Slimon
Furs by Dean Fields
Choreography: David Paitinghi
Running Time (England): 96 minutes

Cast: Anton Walbrook (Herman Suvorin),
Edith Evans (The Old Countess), Yvonne
Mitchell (Lizaveta Ivanova), Ronald Howard
(Andrei), Mary Jerrold (Old Varvarushka),
Anthony Dawson (Fyodor), Miles Malleson
(Tchybukin), Michael Medwin (Iliovaisky),
Athene Seyler (Princess Ivashin), Ivor Bernard
(Bookseller), Maroussia Dimetrevitch (Gypsy
Singer), Violetta Elvin (Gypsy Dancer), Pauline
Tennant (Young Countess), Jacqueline Clarke
(Milliner's Assistant), Yusef Ramart (Countess's
Lover), Valentine Dyail (St. Germain's
Messenger), Gordon Begg (General
Velchelnikoff), Gibb McLaughlin (Bird Seller),
Drusilla Wills (Old Servant), Aubrey Mallalieu
(Fedya), George Woodbridge (Vassili), Pauline
Jameson (Amayatka), Hay Petrie (Herman's
Servant), Brown Derby (Footman), Geoffrey
Dunn (Hair Dresser), Ian Colin, Clement
McCailin, John Howard, Aubrey Woods and

One of the most elegant of all British horror films is among the least known. Adapted from Pushkin's *The Queen of Spades*, the film was produced with loving care by Anatole de Grunwald and directed with superb attention to detail by Thorold Dickinson. As an example of telling a classic story in terms of moving pictures it bears favorable comparison with the adaptations of *Great Expectations* and *Oliver Twist* that David Lean directed during the same Golden Age of post-war British films.

The terrifying centerpiece of the show is the ancient Countess Ranevskaya as played by Dame Edith Evans, one of the last holdouts among the great English stage stars to appear in a talking picture. She is entirely convincing as a creature who has evaded death long after all her contemporaries have become dust. Helplessly frail, supported and fawned upon by a retinue of ladies-in-waiting, buried in layers of silken clothing whose rustlings become a motif of the film, she would seem to be an object more of pity than revulsion. There is, however, an aura of wickedness about this living mummy that cannot be denied.

The only player not overwhelmed by Dame Edith's presence is the brilliant Anton Walbrook, who delineates a demoniacally obsessed man worthy to rank with his better-known portrayal of the fanatical ballet master Lermontov in *The Red Shoes* (1949). Here, too, is a character who might be expected to gain one's sympathy: a poor man surrounded by rich aristocrats who throw money about like confetti. Instead he becomes more despicable with each moment, using

The Queen of Spades *- Yvonne is wooed passionately by the poor but ambitious Suvarin (Anton Walbrook).*

David Palenghi (Officers)

Synopsis: St. Petersburg, in 1906, is gripped by gambling fever. Young army officers, some of them wealthy aristocrats, spend their spare hours in casinos, gambling at the faro tables. An ambitious but poor Captain of Engineers, Herman Suvorin, watches avidly but never plays, fearful of losing his savings. Succumbing to the superstitions of the gamblers, he believes in the malefic influence of the queen of spades, and that any faro game can be won with a secret progression of three cards. In a rare old book Suvorin finds the story of how beautiful, young Countess Ranevskaya sold her soul in return for the secret of winning at faro. Learning that the Countess still lives he becomes obsessed with the idea of prying the secret from her. Winning the affections of Lizaveta, young companion of the Countess, he contrives to get into the palace and hide in the Countess's room. Later, when the ancient lady has been made ready for bed, Suvorin emerges and pleads for the secret. She is too terrified to speak. Then he threatens her with a pistol and she dies of fright.

Suvorin confesses everything to Lizaveta and flees, haunted by the staring dead eyes of his victim and a voice that seems to be saying, "The dead shall give up their secrets." While the funeral bells toll he visits the body as it lies in state and bends close to the face, hoping for a message. Then he runs away in horror. That night he is awakened by noises and a fierce wind that howls through the room. A silence falls, then he hears footsteps. The voice of the Countess tells him she forgives him and has been commanded to reveal the secret on condition that he marries Lizaveta. The secret: "Three, seven, ace."

Lisaveta spurns Suvorin and runs to Andrei, a young officer who loves her, telling him that Suvorin is insane and that he killed the Countess. Andrei searches for his former friend and finds him celebrating in a Gypsy night club. Slapping Suvorin's face, Andrei challenges him to a duel. Suvorin accepts and names the weapons: cards. Having made a deal with a notorious money lender, he lays 47,000 rubles on the table.

Suvorin wins the first game and the stakes go to 94,000 rubles. The winning card is three. He wins the second with seven, running the stakes to 188,000 rubles. At the climax of the third game he plays what he thinks is an ace. After it is too late he sees that it is the queen of Spades and its face is that of the Countess. Suvorin screams and goes hopelessly mad. As Andrei leads him away, he mutters, over and over, "Three, seven, ace three, seven, queen."

seduction, subterfuge and armed threat in his attempts to learn the Countess's secret. At last the girl who had loved him admits that when Suvorin asked her to marry him "it was like looking into the eyes of Satan."

The other players are good, particularly Yvonne Mitchell as the victimized girl, Ronald Howard as her true lover, Anthony Dawson as a cynical officer, Mary Jerrold and Athene Seyler as elderly confidantes of the Countess, and Ivor Bernard as a sinister bookseller. In the flashback sequence are notable performances by Pauline Tennant as the beautiful young Countess, Yusef Ramart as her faithless lover and Valentine Dyall as a minion of the necromancer, St. Germain. The voluptuous atmosphere

The Queen of Spades - *The Countess and Yvonne are accompanied to a concert by Andrei (Ronald Howard) and Feodor (Anthony Dawson).*

of a Gypsy dive frequented by Suvorin is enhanced greatly by the earthy beauty of the singer, Maroussia Dimetrevitch, and the dancer, Violetta Elvin.

Thorold Dickinson (1903-1984) had worked in films since 1926 as an editor and writer, but it wasn't until 1938 that he directed his first feature, *The High Command*. In the next dozen years he directed seven more features, including the excellent *Gaslight* and *Next of Kin* (1941), *Men of Two Worlds* (1950) and his last, *The Secret People* (1951). Then he left the industry to become a don at London University and devoted his life to education.

The Queen of Spades, which he took over after writer Rodney Ackland had begun directing, is probably his best of a fine lot. Much of the picture's effectiveness derives from the sets and costumes designed by Oliver Messel, assisted by William Kellner. Messel's early film work includes Douglas Fairbanks' last pictures, *The Private Life of Don Juan* and *The Scarlet Pimpernel* (1934), and *Romeo and Juliet* (1937). In 1945 his *Caesar and Cleopatra* placed him in the front rank of film designers. For *The Queen of Spades*, he created a Russia of rich, baroque decor that seems almost suffocating. The set is as prominent as the actors in the terrifying sequence where Suvorin returns to search the Countess's room while the eyes of the dead woman seem to follow him and scrutinize his every move.

Otto Heller's lighting brings out the drama inherent in the settings, and the almost ceaseless camera moves are smooth and unobtrusive. The musical score by the French composer Georges Auric, of *Dead of Night* (1945), *La Symphonie Pastorale* (1946) and *La Belle et la Bête* (1947) fame, is as redolent of Imperial Russia as a work by Tchaikowski or Borodin.

The Queen of Spades - *Confident of his forbidden knowledge, Suvarin plays his last hand.*

The Sign of the Ram

1948   Columbia Pictures Corporation
An Irving Cummings Production
Director: John Sturges
Producer: Irving Cummings, Jr.
Screenplay: Charles Bennett
Based on a Margaret Ferguson novel
Director of Photography: Burnett Guffey
Music: Hans J. Salter
Song: *I'll Never Say I Love You (to Anyone but You)*, Allan Roberts and Lester Lee
Musical Director: M. W. Stoloff
Art Directors: Stephen Goosson and Sturges Carne
Film Editor: Aaron Stell
Set Decorations: Wilbur Menefee and Frank Tuttle
Sound Director: Jack Goodrich
Assistant Director: James Nicholson
Make-up: Clay Campbell
Hair Stylist: Helen Hunt
Gowns: Jean Louis
Operative Cameraman: Gert Anderson
Script Supervision: Rose Loewinger
Grips: Ray Rich and Eddie Blaisdell
Stills: William Avery
Running Time: 84 minutes

Cast: Susan Peters (Leah), Alexander Knox (Mallory), Phyllis Thaxter (Sherida), Peggy Ann Garner (Christine), Ron Randall (Dr. Simon Crowdy), Dame May Whitty (Clara Brastock), Allene Roberts (Jane), Ross Ford (Logan), Diana Douglas (Catherine Woolton), Margaret Tracy (Emily), Paul Scardon (Perowen), Gerald Hamer (the Reverend Mr. Woolton), Doris Lloyd (Mrs. Woolton), Gerald Rogers (Station Master)

Synopsis: Young, attractive Sherida Binyon arrives at the St. Aubyn mansion, situated atop a cliff overlooking the Cornish Coast, to report as secretary to Leah St. Aubyn, a noted magazine writer. Sherida is surprised to learn Leah is confined to a wheelchair. Leah's poetry reflects an intense love for her husband, Mallory, and his three children by a former marriage. The family is no less devoted to Leah, who was paralyzed years before while rescuing two of the children, Logan and Jane, from the sea. Logan, now of age, is to wed his childhood sweetheart, Catherine Woolton, daughter of the village minister. Jane, the

Susan Peters had good reason to live in 1944. At twenty-three, her career was blooming, and she was happily married to writer-director-actor Richard Quine. A hunting accident on January 1, 1945, changed everything; a rifle bullet shattered her spine, paralyzing the lower portion of her body. For more than two years she struggled to resume her career. Help came at last from a surprising source: Harry Cohn, ostensibly the most despotic of movie moguls, approved her for the starring role in a high-budget film about a tyrannic, invalid matriarch. A press release attributed to Miss Peters related that she chose the story property herself ". . . because the central character, Leah, seemed real to me. At the beginning she is a sweet, thoughtful, kind girl who suffers an accident and afterwards is confined to a wheelchair. From then on, the fear of being left alone haunts her, and her affections become distorted. Possessiveness grows, and in order to keep those she loves close to her, she almost ruins the lives of everyone within her reach."

The courageous actress made the role such a tour de force of sub-

older daughter, is in love with Dr. Simon Crowdy. Teen-aged Christine seems almost pathological in her slavish love for Leah.

Leah's benevolence masks a malignant martyrdom. Her tyranny is so subtle it goes unnoticed by a family looking to her for strength and unity. Leah's well-concealed machinations cause a rift between Jane and Crowdy. Her psychological assaults upon Catherine drive the girl to attempt suicide. She sees that Mallory, however loyal, is attracted to Sherida, and inspires the unstable Christine to attempt poisoining Sherida. Mallory, after a talk with his contrite daughter, realizes his wife is insane. The truth laid bare, Leah wheels herself to the edge of the cliff. Before anyone can stop her, she plunges to her death.

tle villainy as to keep the rest of the noteworthy cast in her shadow. Its power transcending its "woman's picture" stereotype. *The Sign of the Ram* was both comeback and swan song for Peters, who died October 23, 1952, without making another film.

Shot almost entirely on sound stages in thirty-six days, *Sign* unfolds leisurely in tasteful, exquisitely lighted settings. The Charles Bennett screenplay (he wrote many of the Alfred Hitchcock classics) makes no concessions to sensationalism except for an attempt (straight from the popular novel) to explain Leah's despotism on the basis of astrology; it cites the characteristic which stargazers attribute to those born under Aries, the sign of the ram—an obstinacy of purpose that can lead to disaster.

The direction of John Sturges—his first of many top-of-the-line pictures after several years' apprenticeship in Columbia's low-budget division—is subtle and workmanlike. The studio's publicity desk termed Sturges *a believer in understated performances* (his expression:

The Sign of the Ram - *Mallory (Alexander Knox) is falling in love with Sherida (Phyllis Thaxter). This scene was photographed on the process stage; sea, sky and distant cliffs were back projected on a translucent screen.*

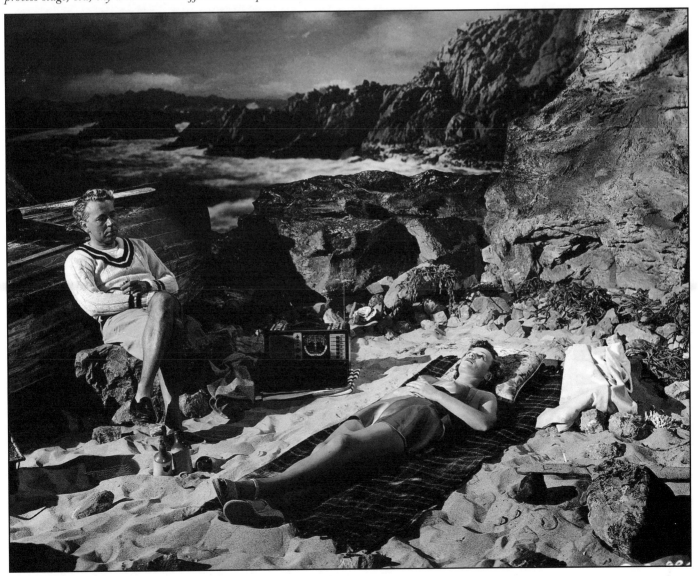

The Sign of the Ram - *An attempted suicide brings near-tragedy to the household. In this scene are Mallory, Sherida, Rev. Mr. Woolton (Gerald Hamer), Mrs. Woolton (Doris Lloyd), Logan (Ross Ford), Jane (Allene Roberts) and Dr. Crowdy (Ron Randell).*

The Sign of the Ram - *Susan Peters in her last screen role, as Leah.*

"inferential acting"). Sturges said he liked to "build an emotional scene carefully and let it be enacted with subtlety and a restraint that engenders reality. . . The strange events will have greater impact upon audiences if they are enacted in a way so natural that they appear likely to occur to anyone in the audience. As the drama builds and the characters are enmeshed, I hope the moviegoers will affiliate themselves with the characters, feeling what the people on the screen feel rather than merely watching what they show." Performances are fine throughout, with Alexander Knox, Phyllis Thaxter, Peggy Ann Garner, Allene Roberts, and Dame May Whitty standing out.

Hans Salter, longtime house composer at Universal, wrote the score; he began free-lancing after the Universal-International merger. The blending of music with sounds—the steady pounding of breakers and, in one sequence, the deep cracking of a thunderstorm—adds greatly to the suspense.

Behind Locked Doors

1948 (a/k/a *The Human Gorilla*) ARC
Eagle-Lion Films
An ARC Production
Released by the Eagle-Lion division of Pathé
Industries, Incorporated
Director: Oscar Boetticher
Producer: Eugene Ling
Screenplay: Malvin Wald and Eugene Ling
Original Story: Malvin Wald
Director of Photography: Guy Roe
Special Effects: George J. Teague
Art Director: Edward L. Ilou
Set Decorations: Armor Marlowe and
Alexander Ohrenbach
Musical Director: Irving Friedman
Film Editor: Norman Colbert
Sound: Leon S. Becker and Robert Pritchard
Production Manager: James T. Vaughan
Assistant Director: Emmett Emerson
Operative Cameraman: Lee Davis
Script Supervision: Richard Walton
Hair Stylists: Joan St. Oegger and Helen
Turpin
Make-up: Ern Westmore and Del Armstrong
Costumes: Frances Ehren
Grip: Charles Rose
Stills: Milt Gold
Running Time: 62 minutes

Cast: Lucille Bremer (Cathy), Richard Carlson
(Ross Stewart), Douglas Fowley (Larsen), Tom
Brown Henry (Dr. Porter), Herbert Heyes
(Judge Drake), Ralf Harolde (Hobbs), Gwen
Donovan (Madge Bennett), Morgan Farley
(Coppard), Trevor Bardette (Purvis), Dickie
Moore ("Kid"), Tor Johnson (Champ), John
Holland (Dr. Ball), Wally Vernon (Sign
Painter), Kathleen Freeman (Nurse), Tony
Horton (Sheriff)

Synopsis: Cathy, a San Francisco newspaper
reporter, tells private eye Ross Stewart she
knows where the fugitive Judge Drake is hiding. She proposes that Ross have himself
admitted to La Siesta Sanitarium and get evidence. Ross refuses until Cathy explains there
is a large reward. Posing as Cathy's mentally
disturbed husband, Ross is admitted after an
interview with Dr. Porter. He meets two attendants: the mild-mannered Hobbs and the
unpleasant Larsen. Ross soon ascertains that
somebody is living in locked and guarded lux-

Filmed in eight days on a tiny budget, *Behind Locked Doors* is a minor gem with plenty of sparkle. Oscar Boetticher's hard-hitting direction, convincing performances by a cast of thorough professionals, and the know-how of a veteran production crew make it a compact, satisfying chiller. The script wastes little time in establishing the hero inside the walls of a mental hospital—a forbidding enough clime even on a legitimate basis, but in this case one run by a crooked doctor and a sadistic attendant. From here to the last, the suspense never lags. There is no evidence of budget-cutting, and no spectacular settings are required for an adequate telling. Clever use of lighting imparts a claustrophobic milieu in which both sympathetic characters and menaces are trapped.

"I took the picture because it looked like fun—and it was!" Boetticher said. "How could I pass up a chance to work with Dick Carlson, my old Navy pal, and lovely Lucille Bremer—I loved every day of it. Carlson was just as good an actor as I knew he would be."

Lucille Bremer, the talented actress/dancer who had been Fred Astaire's leading lady at MGM, and Richard Carlson, whose intellectual aspect spared his youthful good looks from "juvenile" typecasting, give the central roles a cultured quality unusual in "quickie" productions. An unbilled and then unfamiliar Tor Johnson is terrifyingly effective as a huge, inarticulate homicidal maniac, his first and finest appearance in a role so often repeated as to muffle the impact of the actor's striking appearance. This characterization, powerful only in moderation, was so abused in the likes of *Bride of the Monster* (1956) and *Plan 9 From Outer Space* (1959) that it made

Behind Locked Doors - Cathy (Lucille Bremer) says so long to Ross (Richard Carlson) as Hobbs (Ralf Harolde) takes him away.

ury within the asylum.

Another room contains Champ, a crazed ex-wrestler of great size and strength. A grouchy patient, Purvis, angers Larsen, who takes the man from his room. When Purvis is brought back, brutally beaten, Ross suspects the man was thrown into Champ's room. Larsen subjects a youth known only as "the kid" to a cruel beating.

Ross spots Madge Bennett, the judge's lover, stealing into the suite. Ross sneaks matches to Coppard, a pyromaniac entrusted with cleaning up the hideout. Coppard sets a fire which routs the judge long enough for Ross to identify him. Larsen begins to suspect and locks Ross in his room. Hobbs tells Ross that "the kid" is his son; Hobbs only works at the sanitarium in order to look after him. Hobbs fears Larsen plans to kill Ross. Judge Drake questions Ross, who is then beaten by Larsen. Meantime, Cathy seeks help from Dr. Ball, the state psychiatrist, but Ball refuses. Larsen puts Ross into the room with Champ, who becomes homicidal when he hears a bell. Ross is beaten into unconsciousness. Cathy waylays Madge at gunpoint and forces her to exchange clothes. Disguised as Madge, Cathy gains entrance to the judge's suite and forces him to free Ross. Champ runs amok, giving Larsen a terrible beating. Dr. Porter shoots Champ to death. It appears that Cathy and Ross will be next, but at the penultimate moment the police arrive, summoned by Hobbs.

Johnson a clownish stereotype. Johnson, who died in the early 1970s, was in fact an intelligent and sensitive man whose imposing bulk contributed to a distinguished appearance in person. Elsewhere in the cast, Douglas Fowley excels as the cruel keeper, and Tom Brown Henry, Ralf Harolde, Morgan Farley, Trevor Bardette, and Dickie Moore (an *Our Gang* alumnus) may be singled out for strong characterizations.

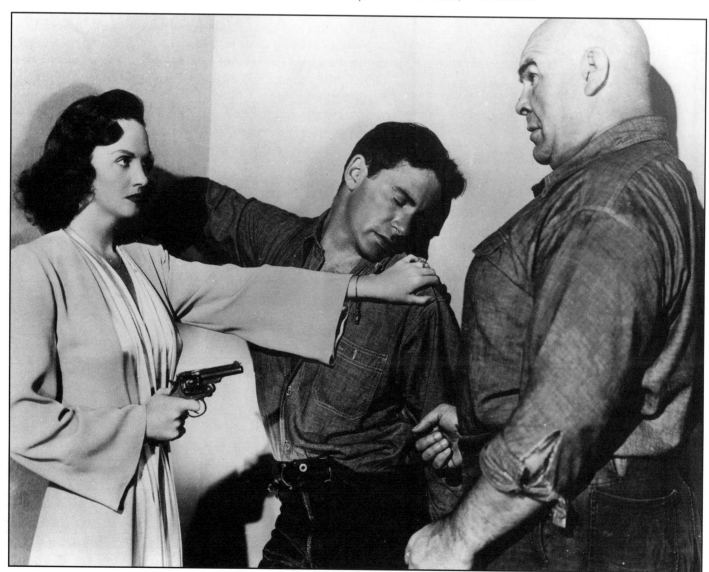

Behind Locked Doors - *An unbilled Tor Johnson makes a chilling appearance as a crazed pugilist.*

Obsession

1948 (U.S. Title *The Hidden Room*)
Independent Sovereign Films, Limited
Produced at Pinewood Studios
Presented by J. Arthur Rank
Distributed by General Film Distributors
American release via Eagle-Lion Films
Director: Edward Dmytrik
Producer: N. A. Bronsten
Screenplay: Alec Coppel, from his novel
Man about a Dog
Musical Composition: Nino Rota
Music Director: Louis Levy
Director of Photography: C. Pennington-Richards
Assistant Producer: Kenneth Horne
Art Director: Duncan Sutherland
Dialogue Director: Alec Coppel
Running Time, (England): 98 minutes (U.S.):
93 minutes

Cast: Robert Newton (Dr. Clive Riordan),
Sally Gray (Storm), Naunton Wayne
(Superintendent Finsbury), Phil Brown (Bill
Kronin), Monty (Himself), Ronald Adam
(Dogmatic Type—Club Scene), Michael
Balfour (First American Sailor), Betty Cooper
(Miss Stevens), Olga Lindo (Mrs.
Hampshire), Russell Waters (Flying Squad
Detective), Roddy Hughes, Allan Jeayes and
Lyonel Watts (Club Members), Christopher
Lee (Cop)

Synopsis: Dr. Clive Riordan is murderously
jealous. His beautiful wife, Storm, continually falls in love with other men. When she
comes home one night with American diplo-
mat Bill Kronin, Riordan kidnaps and chains
him in a bombsite cellar. "The intelligence of
a civilized husband is insulted," he maintains. He explains to his victim that he will
keep him alive and well until the hue and
cry have died, so if the police get on his
track he can abandon the murder plot and
produce Kronin unharmed. Toward the
happy day when he can finish the job,
Riordan brings each day a hot water bottle
filled with acid to dissolve Kronin's body.
The acid is collected in a bathtub out of
reach.

Storm's poodle, Monte, follows Riordan
to the cellar and Kronin grabs the animal.
Fearful to step within Kronin's grasp,

"There's one important thing *Obsession* did," director Edward
Dmytryk told us in 1978. "It helped kill a movement in
England that would have been terrible." The dedication this
comment reflects dates to 1923, when the Canadian-born Dmytryk,
at fifteen, started working after school at Paramount. He was a film
editor there at twenty-two, and a full-time director at thirty-one. He
had built a reputation as a maker of taut thrillers (*The Devil
Commands*, 1941, *Murder My Sweet*, 1945, and *Crossfire*, 1947) when he
ran afoul of the House Un-American Activities witch hunt. *Obsession*
is the first of several pictures he made abroad while he was blacklisted. Later he returned to America to direct *The Caine Mutiny* (1954),
Raintree County (1957), *The Young Lions* (1958), *Warlock* (1959), and
Mirage (1965).

As regards the role of *Obsession* in defeating a trend, Dmytryk said
that producer J. Arthur Rank "had bought a system of making pictures against process backgrounds called Independent Frame. It was
the best composite system in existence. But he had the idea of breaking down a story into exactly timed scenes and putting it on a con-
veyor belt, so to speak. A crew would go out and shoot all the backgrounds, and then they'd shoot the foreground action as interiors
with a simple foreground set, such as actors with a table and chairs.
Everything had to be timed to the second with a stopwatch and a little bell. It made it unbearable for everybody, but, in theory, a picture
could be made much more cheaply and efficiently.

Obsession - *Riordan makes his prisoner, Kronin (Phil Brown), comfortable
while he anticipates an acid bath ending to their rivalry.*

Riordan leaves the dog. Kronin trains the dog to pull the plug from the tub. Storm has become suspicious, and with the disappearance of Monty her fears increase. She brings in Superintendent Finsbury of Scotland Yard—a self-assured man who contends that "All murderers are amateurs"—but the C.I.D. man seems to make no headway. Meantime, the tub has filled, and Riordan decides the time is ripe to finish Kronin. He poisons the wife-stealer and is about to put him in the tub when Monty pulls the plug.

Finsbury and his men have kept on the trail, and they arrive in time to get Kronin to the hospital and save his life. Riordan is philosophical as he is led away to face the consequences.

"They work more slowly in England than they do in the States; the Hollywood crews are superior to any of the world, and they work together better. They were taking thirty-four, thirty-six, and forty-eight days to make their Independent Frame productions, and they thought they were doing great. For *Obsession*, we set a schedule of thirty days, stuck to it, finished on time, and had a much better film. They had scheduled a slate of twelve Independent Frame pictures and had made about four, but when they saw what we'd done, they gave it up. Not one of theirs was a success."

Obsession, which succeeds on all counts, is a curious, nonformula

Obsession - *Christopher Lee, destined for stardom, was an unbilled policeman in* Obsession.

Obsession *- Storm tells her suspicions to the eccentric Supt. Finsbury (Naunton Wayne).*

work—cleverly written, beautifully performed, and directed with skill. The major characters are somehow sympathetic even though one is a philanderer, another is a chronically faithless wife, and the third contemplates an acid-bath murder. These, plus a lackadaisical detective and a trained dog, are the performers of consequence in a story that gradually gains momentum until the suspense reaches a high pitch. The humor, if not black, is at least dark. While the story limits the settings, Duncan Sutherland's designs and sensible camera placements keep the scenery interesting. Another asset is a melodic dramatic score by Nino Rota, then Italy's most celebrated film composer.

Robert Newton and Phil Brown are on screen most of the time as kidnapper and victim. It is one of Newton's less fiery performances, and it may be his best. Few other actors could make so fiendish a character so winning. Dmytryk related that Newton "had a tremendous drinking problem. In fact, he had to post $20,000 bond on this picture. He was a sweet man when sober, but when drunk he was mean—very, very nasty. But he lasted through the picture, and on the last day of shooting he started at lunchtime to have some ale and was beginning to glow at five, when we finished." Brown, an American "method actor" who had played a psychopath in *Calling Dr. Gillespie* (1942) before his own blacklisting, is seen to great advantage here. Dmytryk, who considered Brown "a good actor, very technical and methodical," used him as an assistant on *Give Us This Day* (1949). Sally Gray is fine as the troublemaker. Naunton Wayne—providing high spots of British comedy in his teamings with Basil Radford in the likes of Alfred Hitchcock's *The Lady Vanishes (1939)* and Carol Reed's *Night Train to Munich* (1940)—does well as an amusing detective. The dog does its share of scene-stealing.

1951   Columbia Pictures Corporation
A Superior Films production
Director: Joseph Losey
Producer: Seymour Nebenzal
Associate Producer: Harry Nebenzal
Screenplay: Norman Reilly Raine and Leo Katcher
Additional Dialogue: Waldo Salt
Based on the 1931 Thea von Harbou, Paul Falkenberg, Adolph Jansen, Karl Vash, Fritz Lang screenplay
Director of Photography: Ernest Laszlo
Musical Score: Michel Michelet
Orchestra under the direction of Bert Shefter
Art Director: Martin Obzina
Set Decorations: Ray Robinson
Production Layout: John Hubley
Sound: Leon Becker
Re-recording: Mac Dalgleish
Make-up: Ted Larsen
Supervisor of Production: Ben Hersh
Assistant to the Director: Robert Aldrich
Editor: Edward Mann
Script Supervisor: Don Weis
Assistant to the Producer: Jorja Curtright
Running Time: 88 minutes

Cast: David Wayne (Martin Harrow), Howard da Silva (Inspector Carney), Luther Adler (Langley), Martin Gabel (Charles Marshall), Steve Brodie (Lt. Becker), Raymond Burr (Pottsy), Glenn Anders (Riggert), Karen Morley (Mrs. Coster), Norman Lloyd (Sutro), Walter Burke (MacMahan), John Miljan (Blind Vendor), Roy Engel (Regan), Benny Burt (Jansen), Lennie Bremen (Lemke), Jim Backus (Mayor), Janine Perreau (Little Girl), Robin Fletcher (Elsie Coster), Bernard Szold (Watchman), Jorja Curtright (Mrs. Stewart)

Synopsis: Lured by a charmer who plays a tune on a pennywhistle and buys her a balloon, Elsie Coster becomes the fifth child slain by a maniac at large in Los Angeles. A constant in the killings is that the culprit has taken the shoes of each victim. Inspector Carney, in charge of the manhunt, orders his second-in-command, Lt. Becker, to trace the whereabouts of each person cited on a list of recently discharged mental patients. The people listed include one Martin Harrow.

Harrow, alone in his lodgings, toys with

Comparatively few remakes stand out in an industry where such pictures are merely gratuitous. William Wyler's studied avoidance of schmaltz in *Hell's Heroes* (1930)—based on Peter B. Kyne's sentimental tale *The Three Godfathers*—sets it apart from not only two adaptations before but three after. John Huston weighed in formidably as a director in 1941 with the third filming in a decade of *The Maltese Falcon*, perceiving that Dashiell Hammett's exercise in detection and deception must possess grander possibilities than was found in either Roy Del Ruth's *Dangerous Female* (1931) or William Dieterle's *Satan Met a Lady* (1936). Henry Hathaway delivered in 1951 a Western that invites acknowledgment as a classic, *Rawhide* (a.k.a. *Desperate Siege)*, by rethinking the story told in George Marshall's *Show Them No Mercy*, a 1935 gangster thriller discussed earlier in this book.

A reappraisal of Joseph Losey's *M*, twenty years after Fritz Lang's imperishable 1931 German version, shows that it has a distinctive vision that transcends competence. The "new" *M* was widely reviled and repressed in its day because of its explicit handling of the psychosexual subject matter, not to mention a controversy over the radical-left political bearings of Losey, writers Norman Reilly Raine and Waldo Salt, actors Howard Da Silva, Karen Morley and several others. It was banned in eight states and several countries, censored

M - David Wayne as M finds satisfaction in fondling souvenirs of hls crimes.

the laces of his victims' shoes, plays his tin flute, and shapes in clay the image of his mother. He admires the figure, then crushes it. In another tense sequence he is seen stalking a bird, which escapes.

Enraged at the disruption of gangland activities brought about by Carney's investigation, mob boss Charles Marshall engineers a vigilante campaign to identify and dispose of the killer. Harrow begins stalking a sixth victim. The balloon vendor, a blind man from whom Harrow had purchased the gift for Elsie Coster, recognizes the melody of Harrow's pennywhistle and tips off an underworld member, who marks the letter M with a cue chalk on Harrow's back.

When the chalkmark gives him away, Harrow flees in terror. Marshall's gangsters find Harrow hiding in a storeroom in the Bradbury Building. They take him to the garage of Marshall's taxicab fleet. Subjecting the murderer to a mock trial, Marshall entrusts Harrow's defense to Langley, a hard-drinking, disgraced attorney. Harrow confesses, saying the city is too cruel to birds and children and that it was his mission to save them. He begs to be punished. Langley, shaken, turns on Marshall. The infuriated Marshall shoots the lawyer. The crowd rushes Harrow, but the police arrive in time to prevent a lynching.

when it wasn't banned, and picketed. Those controversies having faded in the two generations since its release, the film has suffered from a reputation as "almost an exact remake" and "an extremely minor film."

Elements in common with the original include the producer—New York native Seymour Nebenzal worked with Lang in Berlin until the Nazi rise to power prompted their departure in 1933—as well to the original screen story by Lang's wife, Thea von Harbou, and a storytelling moxie that makes each version's locale as crucial as the characters. In both versions the murders occur offscreen. The *Threepenny Opera*-like gangland fellowship of the original is reworked especially well into an American milieu of uneasy camaraderie among thieves. (Both Losey and Lang considered that the picture was weakened by the fact that the underworlds of Berlin and Los Angeles were entirely unalike.) Once more the voice of a mother calling for her missing daughter echoes in a stairwell, but otherwise the film is quite different visually, from its predecessor. Again a tune is rendered by the murderer in anticipation of his crime. In the Lang film the killer whistled Greig's "Hall of the Mountain King," while Losey's murderer plays on a pennywhistle an original tune written by the composer of the excellent, modernistic score, Michel Michelet.

Ernest Laszlo's cameras find in the intimidating vastness of Los Angeles—with the monolithic and cavernous

M - *The Murderer plays on his penny whistle while he buys his planned next victim (Janine Perreau) a balloon. John Miljan is the balloon seller.*

M - M seeks refuge In the cavernous Bradbury Building in downtown Los Angeles.

Bradbury Building as a centerpiece—as oppressive a setting as Lang's camera chief, Fritz Arno Wagner, had located in the 1931 *M*'s claustrophobic Berlin. Much of the action occurs in the then-decaying northern downtown area among the tall, wooden apartment buildings that stood on Bunker Hill above the Hill Street tunnel. A long sequence occurs on the now-extinct Angel's Flight, a tramway which lifted passengers up a steep hill. The streets, saloons, cafes, streetcars and a barber shop are used in important scenes.

Losey's adventurous embellishments on the spirit of the original story are somewhat countered by a loyalty to the letter of it. The departure has most notably to do with a film noir style which translates into a near documen-tary narrative approach and physical darkness that Losey and Laszlo ascribe to Los Angeles. Losey gave much of the credit for the look of the picture to John Hubley, an animator who made numerous conceptual drawings during production. But the quality of re-invention hinges most strongly on the title portrayal by David Wayne, a Broadway actor who brought a more advanced age, at thirty-seven, to the murderer's role than Peter Lorre had, at twenty-seven, in the Lang film. Longer than usual scenes were used throughout, with the most remarkable being Wayne's speech before the kangaroo court, done in one take with an immobile camera.

A brooding sadness anchors both performances, planting in the viewer a forbidden sympathy at odds with the response the situation demands. However, the energetically controlled rage Lorre conveyed, and which defined for years the cinema's vision of sexual psychopaths, gives way to Wayne's impression of apprehensive weariness. Wayne punctuates his fatigue with unnervingly explicit surges of erotic pleasure that cross his face when he fondles objects of his victims. On the wall in the background is a poster that asks, "Did you write to your mother?" Losey, some months before his death in 1984, told us that he intended Harrow as a mother-dominated closet homosexual who believed he was on a divine mission but was being crushed by a burden of guilt.

Perhaps because of the picture's forced obscurity, Wayne was not typecast as a psychopath in later roles. A thirteen-year veteran of the stage by the time he came to film in the 1940s, Wayne found in M "an intriguing test" of the range he had displayed in both leading and featured character assignments. Wayne made a career in both comedy and drama. (Peter Lorre was at work at the time on the remake of his only project as a director. In *Der Verlorene/The Lost One,* Germany, 1951), he portrayed a physician consumed by a killing urge. The paths of Lorre and Wayne crossed six years later, when the actors supplied pleasing relief in support of Jerry Lewis's tiresome star turn in *The Sad Sack.*)

Strong portrayals delineating tensions between the police and the underworld, combined with Wayne's dominant performance, create a triangle of inexorably shifting dimensions. Howard da Silva's boss cop is a study in surly efficiency, suggestive of a beefier and more driven Jack Webb. His counterpart among the lawless is the commandingly sinister Martin Gabel—an Orson Welles crony who is better remembered today as a "What's My Line?" television panelist than for his small variety of character parts on the big screen and long Broadway involve-

M - Carney (Howard da Silva) kneels over the murdered Langley (Luther Adler) while mobsters Pottsy (Raymond Burr), Riggert (Glenn Anders) and Marshall (Martin Gabel) watch Lt. Becker (Steve Brodie) and a policeman.

ment in acting and directing. Jowly Luther Adler makes much of the climactic kangaroo-court sequence, as the disbarred alcoholic lawyer. Steve Brodie is a suitably rugged No. 2 detective. Among the gangsters are some wonderful character actors: hefty Raymond Burr (long before he began his reign as TV's Perry Mason), sweaty Glenn Anders, the brilliant Norman Lloyd, and the nervous Benny Burt. Veteran actor John Miljan creates a memorable presence as the blind vendor.

Losey, a former critic who had helped in 1932 to make Radio City Music Hall a showcase for ensemble productions, studied under Sergei Eisenstein in Moscow before coming to American film in 1938 as a director, and occasional writer-producer of short subjects. His string of notable stage productions climaxed in a 1947 collaboration with the playwright and film theorist Bertolt Brecht on Brecht's *Galileo Galilei,* whose success led to a crack at

feature-film directing on the antiwar fable *The Boy with Green Hair* (1948). His five Hollywood pictures in three years— *M* was the third—averaged an efficient three weeks' shooting per title and signalled the arrival of a tremendous talent for pessimistic character-study drama, preoccupied with emotional vulnerability and social failings.

As *M* was coming into release, Losey was at work in Italy on *Imbarco a Mezzanotte/Stranger on the Prowl* when summoned to testify before the House Un-American Activities Committee. He declined the invitation lest production be snagged and returned to America following the shoot—only to learn he had been blacklisted. Denied work in Hollywood, he resettled in Great Britain, where he was obliged to work briefly under the pseudonyms Joseph Walton, Terence Hanbury, and Alec Snowden. His identity restored on *Time without Pity* (England, 1956), Losey gradually crystallized his interests and

abilities into a pretentious, overintellectualized style that has worked nicely on such imaginative oddities as *These Are the Damned* (England, 1961), *Modesty Blaise* (England, 1966), and *The Go-Between* (England, 1971), but also has contributed to the unwatchable self-indulgences of *Boom!* (England-U.S.; 1968) and *Figures in a Landscape* (England; 1970).

Its low profile and inaccurate reputation notwithstanding, the Losey *M* has proved influential among filmmakers concerned with the portrayal of destructive madness. It exercises particular bearing upon the overall tone and central portrayals of two pictures by William Lustig, the notorious *Maniac* (1980) and the more popularly well-received *Relentless* (1989). Shortly before his death in 1982, the comedian and aspiring dramatic actor John Belushi told interviewers of his intentions to take on the title role in a third filming of *M*.

THE VILLAINS STILL PURSUE ME

by *Vincent Price*

Good evening! Thank you, I'm delighted to be here. I have been lecturing for the past eighteen years all over the country, in about 250 colleges, 350 cities, and it's one of the most exciting things that I do, I think, because I get to meet people and to see people of all different kinds, particularly in the colleges, to meet people whose minds are growing and are excited by so many different things in the United States now. I went through all the periods of unrest, the sort of terrible upheaval of the past few years, when the young people were very, very nervous about what they were going to do and how they were going to do it. And they blamed it on a war. But really, they were bored. And I don't blame them for being bored because for the most part, the curriculum of the universities was so dead, so behind the times that it had no relationship to what was going on. And the young people wanted to be spoken to in their own time, in their own language. I don't blame them.

At first, I was going around the country on a sort of self-appointed mission, talking about the arts in America. I feel it's very important for Americans to know that this is the most creative art country in the world, that we are the most appreciative country in the world—in the world! Believe it or not! And a lot of you won't believe it: that we are musically the most aware people in the world, that we produce more great music, more great concerts, ballet, opera, everything, than any other country in the world. Also, we produce more art. We are the greatest art force in the world today. It is our dramatists and our novelists who have had the greatest influence on the world of that art today.

I got very involved in this mission, telling Americans how important they were in the world of art. I began to feel like that Salvation Army worker standing on the corner, beating a drum, who said, "Brothers and Sisters, I used to drink." And he beat his big drum. He said, "It started when I was a little kid. I'd take the heel taps out of my father's cocktail glass, and it got so bad that when I grew up, I drank a quart of liquor a day. And then, I saw the light, and now, I don't do that anymore." And he beat his big drum, and he said, "Brothers and Sisters, I used to steal. It started when I was a little kid. I'd pinch the pennies out of my brother's piggy bank. It got so bad that when I grew up, I lifted something from a big department store. And then,

I saw the light, and now, I don't do that anymore." He said, "As a matter of fact Brothers and Sisters, I don't do anything anymore but beat this damn drum!"

I really got kind of worried about this mission because people would come up to me and they'd say, "What else do you do? You go around, and yet, you must make a living. You can't make a living this way."

But I was up in a little town, at a little college in the state of Washington, and afterwards we had a question and answer period. And I suddenly said, "You know. I've been beating this drum for so many years now. I wonder if any of you would be interested in hearing anything about my career in movies, television and radio." And there was very nice applause, and I said, "And particularly, I wonder if you'd be interested in hearing about my favorite aspect of my career, villainy." There was a very nice hand, and I thought, well that gives me courage. I think I'll go and put together a lecture on villains.

So I went back to my motel, and I was just about to go to sleep when I heard a letter being stuck under my door. I got up and I opened the envelope, and I read. It was a charming letter from a teen-age girl. She allowed as how she and her friend had been at the lecture, and while they enjoyed the art lecture, they were very interested in my doing a lecture on villainy. So she wrote, "Just to give you courage, Mr. Price, I've written you a little poem, and I have included it in the letter." I read it, and I thought it was absolutely charming.

I wrote her a letter and said, "Thank you so much for your lovely letter and for the poem. May I read it to the people around the country as I do my lecture on villainy?" She wrote back and said, "Please, feel perfectly free to use it anywhere you want. Just send me my fee!" So I sent her a dollar, and here it is. It's called "Verses on Villainy," and it's dedicated to Boris Karloff and Vincent Price—the quick and the dead!

Anyone who should aspire to the throne of villainy
Should remember it involves immense responsibility.
Now, every villain has an image he must struggle to uphold,
One of eloquent dishonor handed down from days of old.

Take for instance, his apparel—top to bottom, front to back.
Disregard his favorite hue; tradition rules he dress in black.
Also, there are regulations pertinent to facial hair.
Be it in or out of fashion, something must be growing there.

Now, all his thoughts have been established to the very last detail.
Even as he dreams a scheme, he knows he's doomed to fail.
Never will he prove triumphant over those ordained to win;
For heroes have a secret weapon simply called the heroine.

Now, heroines are pretty creatures born without their wits intact;
They like to strain their vocal chords but seldom think and never act.
Imagine then the odds against a villain's victory.
Why to even stay alive, he must resort to treachery.

And so he lashes girls to railroad tracks and threatens them with mice
Neither one of which is thought to be considered very nice.
Now, for variety, he may concoct a lovely sort of bomb.
But to suit the hero's timing, all the fuses must be long.

For a villain is expected to behave obediently
According to the preference of our society.
Yet despite this, he is fortunate to have though they be few
Some worthy representatives personified by you.

There it is. I love it. I'll send her another dollar.

It's the same for all of us in movies. People come up to me, and they say, "Doesn't it bother you that a lot of people think of you as a villain—or in monster pictures, or horror movies, or whatever the Hell you want to call them?"

It doesn't matter. I've done a hundred and five pictures. Only twenty of them have been that kind of picture, but they've been very successful! And actually, if you think about it, everybody in movies is type cast. John Wayne is a cowboy and a bank salesman. Just remember that. I'm sure that most of the money in that bank is his. I am a villain. Cary Grant was a comedian. Robert Redford is Robert Redford. You know what I mean? We're all just that. That's what makes our fame. And you know, without fame, you really don't survive in this business. You've got to have some kind of identifying reputation. You must have it—really, truly. It's very important.

The other day, I had a proof of the fame that I have which is marvelous. I was sitting in an airport on my way somewhere, and a lady came up to me. I was sitting there minding my own business which I do pretty well. And she came up and stood in front of me and she said, "You are! Aren't you?"

And I said, "Oh, I don't know about that."

She said, "Oh yes, you are! Aren't you?" She said, "I know you movie actors. You don't like to be recognized. You are Boris Karloff. Aren't you?"

Well, I said—this is really true!— I said, "No, Madam, I promise you I'm not Boris Karloff."

She said, "Oh, come on! Why don't you admit it?"

I said, "I'm not Boris Karloff. He's dead."

She said, "He is? Well then, who the Hell are you?" And she left before I was able to tell her I was Christopher Lee!

But it really is quite extraordinary. People get you all mixed up. Fame doesn't mean a thing. It really doesn't.

I have played a lot of villains and I've enjoyed every one of them—well almost every one of them. They're great fun.

I lead a kind of double life. I'm really a pretty nice guy in person, I think. I'm a very good citizen. I vote. It doesn't matter what you vote for as long as you vote. And I am, I think, a very good parent. I'm practically a perfect example of planned parenthood. I have two children twenty-two years apart. That's the way to plan it! I'll tell you that. And I'm a very good husband. And I have been two or three times.

But I really love villains, and I love them for a lot of reasons which I'm going to try and explain to you tonight in this very serious lecture about villainy. First place, I love them because I feel that in playing villains, I'm connected with a group of actors whom I have greatly admired over the years—people who were really wonderful actors and I think some of the most memorable characters in movies and theater: Edward G. Robinson, Jimmy Cagney, Basil Rathbone, Peter Lorre, and my dear friend, Boris Karloff—wonderful people. I've worked with almost all of them, and they were really superb human beings, terribly nice people. Boris Karloff, with whom I've been confused so many times, I first met when I was doing a film called Tower of London. This was years and years ago, and I was playing the Duke of Clarence. I thought, gee whiz, you know, if I'm going to play villains—and I hope I get a chance to—I ought to change my name. I said, "Vincent Price—you know, that's such a pedestrian name. It sounds like I'm from Missouri, and I am!" Anyway, I thought—Boris Karloff, now, there's a really villainous name. As I got to know Boris, I found out that indeed he had felt the same way too and had changed his name. His real name was William Henry Pratt. I don't know whether you can believe it or not, but can you imagine William Henry Pratt in Frankenstein? Doesn't work—but Boris Karloff, oh what a glorious name!

Then, too, I love the villains because they last. They go on and on and on really. If you think of the hero, the minute he gets a double chin and bags under the eyes, and his hair recedes, he's finished, but not the villain. No! The more crinkled and crevassed he gets, the better you like him.

The other thing I love about villains is that they appeal to women. It's absolutely true, they have an enormous appeal to women. If you could get any woman in this audience to take a truth serum, she would admit to you that she thinks of her husband as a villain. It's absolutely true! When you were going steady, or whatever the expression was in the days when you were going with your future husband, you never sat down and told your girlfriend, "Oh, he was so sweet last night." No, no! You said, "Ohh boy, what he tried to do last night!" That's what you loved about him, all those wonderful little sort of evil things that he did. And then, you marry him and reform him, and that's the end of that.

There are many different kinds of villains, and I'm going to try to explain some of these different kinds. I did a picture once, a long time ago, that they show every once in awhile on television, It was all right. It was even a pretty good picture actually. It was called *The Bribe*. The thing that made the picture really outstanding was that there were three villains—three entirely different kinds of villains. Of course, there was the hero and the heroine. But first of all, there was John Hodiak. He was the sleek, black-haired villain with flashing eyes and teeth that went all the way around his head. Wherever, you looked at him, he had teeth. I don't know how it's possible. We've got a president like that now. Even on the back of his head he has teeth. And there was Charles Laughton, who was kind of chubby and cuddly and really sinister. And the third villain was the perfect, the suave, the debonair villain, myself!

The thing about these three different kinds of villains—very few pictures have three villains in them—was how they fit into the story. They fit into the story through the leading lady, the star. Before I tell you a bit about the plot and the three different kinds of villains, I want to pay tribute to this lady because she really was a star. I've played with some of the biggest stars in the business: the sex symbols, Jane Russell, Maureen O'Hara, Deanna Durbin, Lana Turner—a lot of them. But the only one who seemed to me to be really sexy was Ava Gardner. I can hear a few middle-aged sighs out there! Ava Gardner, oh gosh, every time I think about her, I just go limp. I'll never forget as long as I live that after the picture was over, the studio, MGM, kind of liked us, and so they gave a little party for us. They had a little orchestra, and we all had a chance to dance with Ava Gardner. I'll never forget. My turn came, and I took her in my arms, and she fit! It was like dancing with a warm, wet towel. If you haven't tried it, don't knock it; let me tell you—marvelous—what a wonderful woman!

In this film, at the beginning of the story, Ava Gardner was going steady with or was crazy about John Hodiak. That is, the one with the teeth. Then Charles Laughton came along and knocked off John Hodiak, and she sort of played along with Laughton for a while. Then, I came along, and I knocked off Charles Laughton, and she and I went steady for a while. Then, of course, what happens? Along comes the leading man, kills me, and who does she end up with? It was probably the biggest anti-climax in the history of movies. From Charles Laughton, John Hodiak, Vincent Price—she ends up with Robert Taylor. Can you believe it? What a bore! There it is, you see. These three men were terribly attractive to this very sexy lady. I just hope that the happy ending ended happily with Robert Taylor!

The villain is very necessary in the plot for a lot of reasons. I think a lot of people don't really stop to think how necessary the villain is. He is, in many instances, more necessary than the hero because his job is to keep up the suspense. If you know right off who the villain is, there is no suspense in the drama. Consequently, the villain's character has to be multifaceted. He has to be a man who keeps you guessing all the time. He can't just be this kind of predictable, ten, twenty, thirty villain, because you'd know who he was. You'd hiss him, and that would be the end of the drama. And so the villain has to hide under many disguises of charm, even of comedy. He can sometimes have the funniest part, and then end up in the really heavy role of the dastardly villain. He's a fascinating person.

Sometimes, I've been cast as a red herring in a movie because people will say, "Oh, if we cast Vincent Price in it, everybody will think he's the villain, and then, we can surprise them when it's somebody else." I did a picture one time, a circus picture. Peter Lorre and I were in it. And of course, everybody thought either one of us could be the villain. But we weren't the villains at all. It turned out to be Ricky Nelson! Believe me, that was a surprise. Nobody suspected him of being a villain or even an actor! But you know what I mean, you've got to keep people guessing.

The villain is the fellow who keeps up the most essential thing in all drama including the Bible, including all great works of literature—conflict—the conflict between good and evil. As long as there is good, there must also be evil. This is what the whole of the Great Book is about. This is what most great books, great novels, great stories, great plays are about—conflict! You can't have a story that is just about one good human being. You must have the conflict. Even in the story of Christ, there is the temptation of the devil. And without that temptation, there is no drama. That is what drama is based on—good and evil, conflict! Therefore, the villain has to keep up that conflict, sometimes more challengingly than the hero.

It's really fascinating. Think about some of the villains that you have seen in movies. They are the people who keep you, as I say, guessing right straight to the very end. Is he, or isn't he going to get away with it? You may know he's the villain, but he could possibly get away with it.

Now there seems to be a surge of a new kind of villain who does somehow or other seem to get away with it. *Marathon Man* was really a brutal and terrifying picture. While Dustin Hoffman's character wasn't the real villain of the piece, in the end he ends up murdering everybody and seemingly gets away with it. You know he isn't going to get away with it, but somehow, evil has to be paid off.

In the old days in movies, evil, the villain had to be apprehended by the law. This was a lovely conceit on the part of the censors, but of course, it didn't always work. In many of the great novels, the villain hangs himself, he gets caught by his own petard, but not by the law. But in movies at one time, the villain had to be caught by the law.

I remember doing a film once called *Dragonwyck* which I'll talk more about a little bit later. At the end of that film, this man, who was an extraordinary villain and a really extraordinary man, in a funny way justified himself. It was a wonderful scene that really would have made the movie a great, special gift, but because of the censorship, I had to be apprehended by the law. It was a terrible anti-climax for the people who had read the book, but that's beside the point.

The villain's acting challenge is what fascinates me, this thing of having to have different facets to your personality, comedy, all kinds of facets. You think about the villains, they keep you guessing. A wonderful villain today is a fellow named Bruce Dern, and he always keeps you guessing. Is he, or isn't he? He can be way overboard, or he can be very subtle. He must sometimes make the unbelievable, believable. He must sometimes make the despicable delectable, so that you enjoy it. Those are some of the subtleties of playing a villain. I think the main thing is that sometimes in very peculiar stories, and the villain sometimes comes out of very peculiar plots, his job is making it believable. In many of the science fiction films and horror films, whatever you want to call them, that I have done and that other people have done in the same genre that I work in, our job is this tremendous responsibility for trying to make the unbelievable believable. In the sort of modern drama that started with Marlon Brando and Jimmy Dean and those people, their job was apparently to make the believable, believable. But sometimes, I felt they made the believable unbelievable. I never met a man who talked like Marlon Brando. I never heard anybody who talked like that. I couldn't have understood him if I had heard him. But there was this idea that people were all very strange and very peculiar. But somehow or other, I think you have to be understood. The villain's job is to be understood for what he is trying to do—to keep up the conflict and the suspense of the picture.

I was not always a villain. I chose to be a villain. I started my career playing some of the "goodest" people in the world—boringly good people like Prince Albert in *Victoria Regina* with Helen Hayes. A wonderful part, a wonderful character, but the problem for the actor was that Prince Albert, while challenging, really was not very exciting. My main problem with playing a character like Prince Albert was that he was so good! He was called Albert the Good—God!

I'll never forget when I was very young and very excited, I was in London in a little production of this play before Helen Hayes ever did it. I had to find out something about Prince Albert, about his humanity. He was good! How do you play somebody who's just good? I read everything about him, and he was an ideal kind of human being. I finally did find out that there were certain elements of humanity in him—after all, he and Victoria had nine children—a certain amount of humanity required there! He was not above having a good temper, and he was a man who was not too kind to his son, Edward VII. He had frailties, and on those, you could hang a character, a cloak of acting.

A lot of you who are interested in the theater may never think of this, but one of the things about playing a historical character is trying to look like him. I had this problem with Oscar Wilde recently. But Prince Albert was somebody who really fooled me. Every time you see a picture of him or a statue of him or even on a tobacco can, there he is! And he's absolutely unbending and inflexible. The director in the play in London kept saying, "Mr. Price! Vincent, you know, you really do have the German accent. You look like Prince Albert, but you're a slob." I couldn't stand up straight that long. I really couldn't! The girl who was playing with me was four feet eleven inches, and I'd start the scene like this [standing straight], and I'd end up like this [bending over]. Anyway, I thought how can I get that posture, because that was what Prince Albert had. He was always like this!

I went over to the Victoria and Albert Museum to do some research, and I'll never forget it as long as I live because it's one of those silly little things that happen. I went up to the curator of the costumes there and I said, "I'm an American slob—actor!—an American actor, and I'm playing Prince Albert. Help me. How did he look like that?"

He said, "Well, it's perfectly easy, Mr. Price." He said, "I think I can help you. We have many of Albert's uniforms from the time that he was here in England, right from when he first came and married Victoria. And if you'd like to see them, I'd like to show them to you."

And I said, "That's fine."

He said, "We also have some of Queen Victoria's."

And I said, "No, Albert's will do for now." I went over, and he opened a big closet, and he pulled them out. Here were all Albert's uniforms. It looked like he was still in them.

I said, "Can I touch one?" I knew then why Albert was so unbending. There was a steel rod right from under his armpits to his hips. If he'd bent over, he'd have sprung right back into place! That's what held him up. I thought, well if that's the way Albert did it, then, I can do it.

I wound my way down to rehearsal that day. I went into an athletic store, a place where they sell things to athletes. And I bought one of those little half corsets that middle-aged men wear when they play golf to keep everything from falling out. I went in the men's room, and I put on this little corset, and I laced it up. And there I was—instant Albert!

I went down to the theater, and I started to rehearse the scene. And the director said," Ah now, Vincent, now, you have it. Now, you really look like Albert. You sound like Albert. You are Albert."

And I said, "Yes, thank you very much" and passed out cold.

About a half hour later, when somebody had enough sense to unbutton something other than my shirt, they found me in the Iron Maiden of Nuremberg and released me.

I learned an extraordinary truth from that thing, that corset. I did get some stays put into my clothes because they reminded me to stand up straight. Albert really wore those corsets; also, he had great military training. He was German, his presence was that. But he needed it. I needed it.

But what I needed most of all was to understand that acting is make-believe. It's a kind of double make-believe. It's making myself believe that I am Albert, or Oscar Wilde, or whomever I'm playing, and if I can make myself believe I am that character, then I can make you believe it. So it's a double make-believe. It's very, very important.

After Albert, I played a couple of other "goodies," really good people—difficult to play, difficult to find any kind of conflict in them, any kind of drama.

Finally, I looked around and I found a play called *Angel Street*, which maybe some of you saw as a movie many years later with Ingrid Bergman. It was called *Gaslight*. *Angel Street* was the play which I did on Broadway. And Jack Manningham was probably one of the meanest men I ever met.

Aristotle had a theory of drama. Now, this sounds like I'm digressing. And it's the story of my life; I digress. But part of Aristotle's theory of drama was that the villain, the man who must pay for his sins at the end of the drama, should not be a drab man. He should not be a skulking man. He should not be an ugly man. He needn't be the Hunchback of Notre Dame. He needn't be that kind of man. Actually, according to Aristotle, the villain should be a man of great nobility, of high birth, of wealth, of education, because Aristotle felt if that man has to pay for his sins—this educated, beautiful, noble human being—if he must pay for his sins, then, you and I, the hoi polloi, know that we must pay for ours.

Prince Albert was a noble man. The fellow in *Angel Street* was an ignoble man, and yet, there was a was a kind of nobility of badness about him. He was an ideal villain in a way. He believed in himself, in his own charm, in the fact that he could get away with anything. And he almost did. I'm going to tell you about this story of *Angel Street* because it's a fascinating story, and it changed my life. *Angel Street* is set in Victorian London about the year 1890. It's in a Victorian mansion, and when the curtain goes up, you see a Victorian living room with the fire burning and the gaslights flickering. On the couch is a rather arrogant, handsome man, very sure of himself. His fluttery wife, Bella, is flying around doing all those lovely things for him that you liberated women no longer do for us: bringing him his slippers and the paper. Jack Manningham is lying there, accepting it all as though it were his due. But you get a kind of clue from the dialogue that everything is not all sweetness and light in the Manningham household, that Bella has been kind of silly and kind of irresponsible.

Jack said, "But Bella, you know, my dear, you are much better. You aren't losing things quite as often. You haven't misplaced things as you usually do. And to reward you, I read in the paper here that your favorite actor is opening next week in London in the West End, and I'm going to take you to the theater."

Bella is hysterical with joy, a little too hysterical. She said, "Oh, Jack, if you do that, I promise I won't do all those terrible things. I promise you I'll keep my wits about me.

He said, "Well, that's fine, Bella. I'm going to take you to the theater." And he said, "By the way, Bella, what did you do with that watch that I gave you to take to be repaired?"

She said, "Oh, Jack, oh, you know, you gave me that watch, Jack. Just three days ago, Jack, you gave it to me. I took it, and when you left, I put it right in that drawer. And I've looked everywhere in this house."

Jack goes into a fit of temper, and he says, "Why am I taking you to the theater? You're just exactly as you were. You lose everything. You're losing your mind. Of course, I'm not going to take you to the theater now. I'm going out for my evening walk. And by the time I get back, you find that watch or else."

The poor lady is hysterical with frustration and heartbreak because she really thought that she'd been forgiven, and she wanders around the room. Behind the books, she finds a picture that he's accused her of taking down and hiding. She finds a grocery bill that he accused her of losing, and she finally just falls, collapses by the front door and is sobbing there. Jack has gone for his walk.

There comes a knock on the front door. She opens it, and a little man is standing there with a little cape and hat, and he says, "Mrs. Manningham?"

She said, "Yes, yes. What is it? What is it, please?"

He said, "I wonder if I might speak to you for just a moment."

She said, "No, please, please, not tonight. I'm not feeling well. Please, come back another time." And she shuts the door.

The little man says, "Just a minute, Mrs. Manningham. It will only take me a minute. May I talk to you?"

She says, "Well, come in. Come in quickly. My husband's out for his walk. He mustn't find you here. Come in."

So the little fellow comes in, takes his coat and hat off, and puts them down.

She says, "No! No! You mustn't do that. Now, you must leave."

He says, "But it's so hot in here, Mrs. Manningham." He puts his coat back down on the chair, and he starts to tell her a story. He is a retired sergeant from Scotland Yard, and he tells her a story that's really quite alarming, that here in this house where she, Bella, and Jack Manningham live, about five years before they moved in a horrible murder had taken place.

She said, "Why are you telling me this?"

And he said, "Well, Mrs. Manningham, I must tell you this because I have kept up an interest in this case. You see, this old lady who lived in this house—your house, Mrs. Manningham—was murdered right here in this very room, right where you're standing, Mrs. Manningham. Her body lay there. Her body was brutally ripped apart, and everything in the whole house was ripped apart. And the blood was all over there."

She said, "Please, don't tell me this. Please!"

He said, "Mrs. Manningham, I must tell you because I really want to know. You all have only lived here a little while, and I've waited until you were settled in. I want to know. Have you ever seen anything suspicious? Have people come to the door and talked to you—people you didn't know? Have you seen anyone standing across the street?"

She said, "No. Why?"

He said, "Well, you see, Mrs. Manningham, because the murderer was never caught, and because we discovered, through friends, that the old lady had a very famous collection of rubies, our theory is that perhaps the reason the house was so ransacked was that the man was looking for the rubies."

And she said, "No, I've never seen anybody. Now, please go because my husband is out, and when he comes back, he must not find you here."

Well, he goes on telling her more of his theories, and suddenly, while he's talking, the gaslight begins to grow dim, dim, dim. He says, "What's that?"

She said, "Oh, that's the gaslight. It happens every night, just exactly this same time. I'm sitting here, and the gaslight begins to grow dim."

He said, "Every night?"

And she said, "Yes, every night."

He said, "Every night at the same time?"

"Yes, every night at the same time, the gaslight grows dim."

He said, "Well, how do you explain it?"

She says, "Well, I've called the gas company. They say it's just the pressure. But don't worry about it."

So he says, "Every night at the same time? How do you know?"

And she said, "Well, you see, my husband is a very punctual man. Every night, exactly the same minute, he goes out and has his walk. And after he's been gone for about three or four minutes, the gaslight grows dim, and it stays that way for five or six minutes. And then, it starts to go up, and in three or four minutes, he comes back."

He said, That's very peculiar." He starts to tell her more about his theory, and she becomes really fascinated by this whole story. As they're talking, suddenly, the gaslight goes up.

She says, "There. You see? He'll be coming a back now in a minute. Now, you must go. Please, take your coat and hat. Go out the front door. Go to the right because he comes from the left, and hurry."

Well, the old fellow won't go. He starts talking to her, and finally, you hear a key in the front door. And the husband is coming back.

She says, "Now, he's here. Now, please! Take your coat and hat. Go hide in that closet in there. He never goes in there at night. After he's gone up to bed, I'll come and let you out."

So the old fellow takes his coat and goes and hides in the closet.

I don't know whether any of you have ever been to a New York opening night, but it's a disaster. The audience is dead. You have a feeling they don't know what they're doing. They're there for all the wrong reasons, but not this opening night!

That opening night, the audience had become so involved in this murder, in this extraordinary relationship between the husband and the wife and the detective, that when the old fellow took his coat and went and hid in the closet, the whole audience yelled, "You forgot your hat!"

I'm standing in the wings with the key in the door ready to come in. I turned to the stage manager. I said, "My God, they're alive!"

"You forgot your hat!"

So the old fellow comes out and gets his hat and goes back into the closet.

Anyway, it gives you an idea of the involvement that the audience had. To make the whole story short, I come back, and I accuse her of more things. Obviously, I'm the villain. Every night, I go out for my walk. I go around the block. I go up into the attic. I turn on the gaslight. The gaslight goes down. Then, I turn it off, and it comes back up. And I come back and come in. Finally, the detective catches me, and they find the rubies, and they put me in prison. That's the end of it; that's the plot.

The extraordinary thing was that opening night in New York, not only was the audience tense throughout the entire play, it probably was the greatest success of a play of its kind ever in the history of the American theater. And the audience—when Judith Evelyn, who played the wife brilliantly, came out, they screamed and yelled. For Leo G. Carroll, who played the detective, they cried "Bravo!" When I came out, the whole audience stood up and hissed. Oh, it was marvelous. It really was.

After that, I thought now, if I go to Hollywood and can find a good villain, maybe that will put me across as an actor, give me the identity that I want. I did a picture called *Song of Bernadette*, and I had a marvelous, marvelous role in it, but I wasn't a villain. I was the "heavy" in the picture, but I wasn't a villain. In a way, I was a villain because I was a politician but not really a villain.

But then I got a part, the ideal Aristotelian villain, in a film called *Dragonwyck*, a wonderful story by Anya Seaton which I did with Gene Tierney. This arrogant villain had everything in the world he wanted. He was educated, rich, owned a marvelous place on the Hudson River. And he had one thing which Jack Manningham didn't—his ego, his assurance of his own villainy. He had a belief in the survival of the fittest. He thought that anything that wasn't right should be destroyed. And one of the things, that wasn't right in his life, was his wife. So he thought he should destroy her. She had given him a daughter, but he needed a son to carry on his name. He had met Gene Tierney, and he thought that she would be a good mother for his son. His wife was getting fat and drinking too much, and he baked her a cake, and the frosting had ground-up oleander leaves, which are deadly poison, in it. Any of you want the recipe, I have it! But anyway, she died, he married Gene Tierney, and it was a lot better.

When I was studying for this part, I was trying to figure out where this man got this kind of arrogance, this kind of assurance. The extraordinary thing was he was not just a villain, like Jack Manningham—he wasn't a murderer! He was an educated, marvelous human being who just had an edge of evil. I read the book over and over trying to discover where Anya Seaton had gotten this character. Finally I looked in that place that we never look in, called the preface, and there it was! Seaton said that she had drawn the character of Nicholas Van Rynd from a poem called "Alone." Here is the poem, "Alone."

From childhood's hour, I have not been as others were.
I have not seen as others saw.
I could not bring my passions from a common spring.
From the same source, I have not taken my sorrow.

I could not awaken my heart to joy at the same tone.
And all that I have loved, I have loved alone.
Then, in my childhood, in the dawn of a most stormy life
Is drawn from every depth of good and ill the mystery which binds me still.

From the torrent of the fountain, from the red cliff of the mountain
From the sun that round me rolled with its autumn tint of gold

From the lightning in the sky as it passed me flying by
From the thunder and the storm and the cloud that took the form

When the rest of heaven was blue,
Of a demon in my view.
A demon in my view!
Never could I get it out of my view!

One of the great autobiographical poems of the world was written by Edgar Allen Poe who was indeed born with a demon in his view! Lots of people have been born with demons in their view. Poe's demon was genius, fortunately for us. But Hitler had a demon; Charles Manson had a demon. That's one kind of villain, that villain who is born with a demon in his view. Nicholas Van Rynd had a demon. He believed that anything that didn't, couldn't survive deserved to be destroyed or to die, and that is not humanity.

But some of the most fun villains that I've played have not been born with demons in their view. There have been people whom I think we understand much more readily because they're the kind of people who are villains either in spite of themselves or because life hurts them. We read about them all the time in the newspaper, about the fellow, the nice meek little man who lives down the street, and suddenly! he becomes a maniac. He destroys; he takes revenge. And it usually is revenge. Something hurts him, and he takes it out on other human beings. Somehow or other, we understand these people because they're the kind of people of whom we say, "There but for the grace of God, go I." They're the kind of people who just don't have the moral strength to go down the straight and narrow when "the whips and scorns of outrageous fortune" are attacking them.

One of the most fascinating of these fellows, that I played, was in a movie called *The House of Wax*. The audience watched it through those crazy 3D glasses—I loved it. My character, Professor Jarrod, was a nice fellow who had a little museum and a little talent for making beautiful figures of Marie Antoinette and Joan of Arc. One day, a man comes in and says, "Hey, Jarrod. You've got a good thing going here. Now, you and I'll go into business together. You'll add a Chamber of Horrors because you'd be good at making all those figures with blood and everything. And you'll clean up, and I'll be your partner. We'll make a lot of money."

Jarrod said, "I don't want that. Get out!"

So the fellow tried to convince him, and Jarrod was not about to be convinced, and so, he kicked the fellow out. The fellow was rather angry, and on the way, he dropped a match into a wastepaper basket, and—as happened in Hollywood two days ago—the House of Wax burned down, and in it, poor Mr. Jarrod, Professor Jarrod, was terribly burnt trying to save his beloved figures. Finally, the whole house crumbles in, and to all intents and purposes, he's dead.

I very rarely die the first time in these pictures. Sure enough, in the next scene, you see a new wax museum, and there's Professor Jarrod in a wheel chair because everybody knows he was in this terrible accident, looking just like himself: hands in gloves, with an assistant doing his sculpture for him. It's a new wax museum, and this time, the great attraction is the Chamber of Horrors. The Number One attraction in the Chamber of Horrors is a man hanging by the neck in an elevator shaft. When you look at his face, you see that it's the man who lit the match in the other wax museum. Well, that's one way to get rid of them—make exhibitions of them.

I used to have the best time when this picture was playing. It was one of the biggest moneymakers of all time, this picture. I used to go and sit in the back of the theater with those glasses on. Nobody could recognize me, and I'd preferably sit behind a couple of teen-age girls because their reactions were wonderful. They'd sit there with the popcorn. Once when the picture was over and I had fallen into a vat of wax, and the whole thing was burning up, the whole picture was over, I just leaned forward, and I said, "Did you like it?" Boom! They went right into orbit, these girls.

Not all villains are mean. I've played some lovable villains. Fagin in *Oliver*, he's a dear fellow. He keeps those little kids working—not a bad idea, let me tell you, with the cost of education these days.

One of the great villains who has always intrigued me is Iago in Shakespeare's Othello because he is really a born villain. Iago hates everybody. Especially, he hates Othello because Othello is so good, and that really "bugs" Iago, and so, he decides to destroy him.

When I was putting this lecture together, I looked for something in Shakespeare that kind of congealed this feeling of Iago. I couldn't find it. But one day, I heard the opera, and in the second act of Verdi's great opera, Otello, Iago sings a thing called "The Credo," in which he puts forth his creed. I got the libretto, and I translated it with a little help, and here it is—"The Credo" from the Second Act of Verdi's opera, *Otello*. I'm not going to sing it, so don't worry. He sings:

> I believe in a cruel God who has created me in his image
> And whom in hate, I name
> From some vile germ or atom base
> Am I born.
> I am evil
> Because I am a man.
> And I feel the primeval slime within me.
> Yes, this is my creed.
> I believe with a firm heart
> That whatever evil I think or do
> Was decreed for me by Fate.
> I believe that the honest man is but a poor actor,
> Oath in face and heart,
> And everything in him is alive,
> Tears, kisses, looks, sacrifices, honors.
> And I believe man to be the sport of an unjust fate
> From the germ of the cradle
> To the worm of the grave.
> After all this mockery comes death.
> And then? And then, death is nothingness.
> And heaven is an old wive's tale.

Iago, I like him—lovely fellow, Iago!

Not all of Shakespeare's villains were villains. Some of them were made villains by others. One of them in particular was made a villain by a woman. Probably one of the best ones in Shakespeare is a lady—Lady Macbeth. She had a husband who was rather timid, and she wanted him to be Chairman of the Board! I've always thought she might have been American, Lady Macbeth. Be that as it may, she talks Macbeth into killing off the people who stand in his way to the crown. Poor Macbeth kills one of them, and the ghost appears to him. Shakespeare gives Macbeth that healing antidote, a soliloquy. He says: "Come sealing night, scarf up the tender eye of pitiful day, and with thy bloody and invisible hand, cancel, and tear it to pieces, that great bond that keeps me pale."

Lady Macbeth catches him at it and says, "Oh, come off it, Macbeth! That ghost — 'tis the eye of childhood that fears a painted doll. My hands are of your color. But I shame to wear a heart so white!"

Not all of them are men!

Every actor longs to be in a classic film. I don't mean *The Ten Commandments*, or one of those. I mean a really well made film, a film that is so well made, so well acted, directed, photographed, written, everything, that it remains a classic. I think of one story about a very famous movie, one of those films that I was in and that I'm proud of, a film called *Laura*. Do you remember *Laura*? This is a fascinating story about evil, about villains. There were five of us in this picture: Gene Tierney, Dame Judith Anderson, Clifton Webb, Dana Andrews, and myself. When we were all sent the script, we all knew each other very well. We all called each other and said, "Darling, isn't it wonderful? We're going to be in this wonderful picture together. Isn't it marvelous? Darling, isn't it a wonderful script? And isn't it marvelous? And we're going to be with this darling director." It was repulsive.

So we got to the studio, and indeed, it was all darling. It was absolutely wonderful. The script was marvelous; the cameraman was marvelous. The director was wonderful; we were wonderful. And finally, after we'd been doing it for about a month, we got a call one Saturday saying, "When you come to work Monday, brush up on the first scene you did because everything has been scrapped!"

And we said, "But it was so darling! How is it possible that you scrapped it all?"

"Well," he said, "just be ready."

We got out there, and sure enough, everything was the same, but we were starting all over again. We had a new cameraman. But that often happens. We also had a new director. This time, it was a fellow named Otto Preminger. And we all started to work, and we all loved each other. We loved the script; we loved the new cameraman. We liked Otto. And finally, the picture was finished. We all went to see it together. It was extraordinary. It was ostensibly the same picture that we had done with the other director, or at least half done with him. But there was something added. Otto had imbued every single character in this play with an underlying evil. The other director had no knowledge of that, and we had played sort of surface characters. But the characters we were now belonged to that kind of upper crust of cafe society, if you know what I mean. The kind of people you know—Dee Dee is a nice man, and all his friends are the nicest people I know. I don't know any of those kinds of people. The people I know are evil.

And Otto Preminger said, "That's what I made all of you." It was really one of the extraordinary pictures of all time.

Some of the best villains, and non-villains but fascinating people, that I have found are in the stories of Edgar Allen Poe. They aren't really villains. They are people who're been put upon by life, and they're kind of sad people in a way, like Roderick Usher in "The Fall of the House of Usher." God, if you were locked in that house, you'd turn pale too; wouldn't you? And Prospero, in "The Masque of the Red Death," didn't do anything naughty really. He invited Death in for dinner, but I've been to a lot of dinner parties with Death, and sat next to him too, or eaten his cooking which is even worse. All these things are wonderful.One of the things that's really fun to do is to work. I really hate talking about this because these were people who were my close friends, and they've all gone now. But they were witty, wonderful men: Boris Karloff, Basil Rathbone, Peter Lorre. We did a picture one time, I think it was really one of the funniest pictures ever made. It was kind of a funny spoof on horror pictures called *Comedy of Terrors*. It had the greatest premise of any story ever told. This is the premise, period—it's a family of out-of-work undertakers! Now, what are you going to do? You've got to get a job. So whom do you kill? The richest man in town, so he'll have a big funeral.

The thing about playing these pictures that is really extraordinary is that you walk a tightrope right down the middle between comedy and terror. What I mean is, it's fine if we make somebody scream, and then they giggle. But God help us if they giggle and then scream! Some of them are really difficult to play. And we were very serious. Boris and I particularly had a marvelous time, because we'd say, "How can we scare them? What can we do? What's new?"

One day, I was doing a scene in *The Raven*. I had to walk down this long corridor, and I said, "Boris, I'm doing nothing. We've done all that a million times."

He said, "I've got an idea. We'll scare the men."

And I said, "What? Scare the men. What do you mean?"

He said, "There's one thing men are afraid of—cobwebs."

And I said, "What do you mean—cobwebs?"

He said, "Men hate cobwebs. Women just think you're a bad housekeeper, but men hate them. They stick. You know. They're awful."

So we rigged up this great big cobweb, and as I came down this corridor, I suddenly walked into this cobweb, and it went like that, so I looked like I had pantyhose over my boots.

Sure enough, when I went to the movie, when that scene came on and the cobwebs went like that, every man in the house went "Aghh -ghh -ghh!" But the women said, "Oh, why doesn't he keep the place clean?"

But we really had great fun, and don't think they aren't hard to play. I did a scene which was the most difficult scene I've ever had to do in my life, with one of the greatest actors who ever lived, Herbert Marshall, a great, great, great English actor, in a picture called *The Fly*. Now, you remember *The Fly*. It was such a success they made a sequel to it, which I wanted to call *The Zipper*, but they wouldn't—no sense of humor at all.

In *The Fly*, I was the good guy. My nephew was tinkering around with his home chemistry set, and he found that he could transport matter from one place to another. You know, all those marvelous light things and everything. So sure enough, he tries it on the "puddy tat." And the "puddy tat" is here, and then, it's there. So he thinks, I'll try it on myself. So he puts himself in—blr, blr, blrr—and he's there. What he didn't know was that in that one, there was a fly. When he transported himself from here to there, he ended up a man with a fly's head. Well, we swatted him.

But then, of course, there's a fly with a man's head. At the end of the picture, we looked for this fly with a man's head, and my little great nephew comes in and says, "Uncle, Uncle! We found that funny-looking fly out in the garden."

Herbert Marshall, who was the detective, and I, the good uncle, went out, and here sure enough is my nephew who is a fly with a human head. I don't know how many of you have nephews who are flies with human heads. I have one, I think.

But anyway, there he is, the little fly with the human head, in a great big spider's web, and this big spider goes jump and jump and jump. And a little voice is saying, "Help me! Help me!"

Herbert Marshall and I, two full-grown men, had to play a scene, a philosophical scene, deciding whether to let nature take its course and allow the spider eat the fly, or throw a rock and hit him and put him out of his misery, or catch him and put him in a jar and study him for science. We'd start to play the scene, and I'd say, "Well, Inspector."

And the little voice would say, "Help me!"

Then, Herbert would say, "Well, Monsieur, I think what we should—"

"Help me! Help me!" Finally, Herbert Marshall said, "Help you? The Hell with you. Help us."

It took us four hours to get a scene that should have taken us about ten minutes to do.

Wonderful things happen. I did a picture once called *The Haunted Palace*, and the director decided that every time I looked at a portrait of my grandfather, I should turn green. That's easy enough to talk about, but it meant that every time I looked at the portrait, I had to run out and put a little more green make-up on. Then, I'd look at the portrait and go back and put a little more green make-up on. He forgot to tell the lab that developed the film. And one day, the rushes were about four days late, and he called up, and they said, "We can't send this film back. Vincent Price keeps turning green all the time!"

One of my favorite villains is Richard III, Shakespeare's Richard III. But a terrible thing has happened to Richard III. About ten years ago, a woman started writing a book. Mystery writer Josephine Tey wrote a book called *Daughter of Time*, in which she practically proves that Richard III was the victim of one of the biggest publicity hoaxes in history, that he wasn't a villain, that he was a nice guy.

Why don't they leave him alone? Everybody's a nice guy.

It has now gone on and on and on, with more and more people trying to prove, and really almost proving, that Richard III was the victim of the king who followed him who blamed all of these terrible things on Richard. There's an extraordinary scene in Shakespeare's *Richard III* which is prophetic of this phenomenon. Before all these people started tampering with Richard's bad reputation, Shakespeare, that extraordinary genius of four hundred years ago, asked: was he a villain, or wasn't he a villain? There's a scene in the play where it's the eve of the Battle of Bosworth Field. Richard hears the news from his few remaining friends that Richmond is going to be there to do battle in the morning with a great host of warriors behind him. Richard's few remaining friends beg him to go into his tent, take off his armor, and have some rest. Richard goes in, takes his armor off, throws himself on his cot. He's about to doze into that wonderful limbo between sleep and wakefulness. Suddenly, the ghosts of all the people that he has murdered on his way to the throne appear to him: the little princes whom he smothered in the tower; his brother, Clarence, whom he drowned in a butt of wine; his best friend, Buckingham, whom he had beheaded.

Buckingham's ghost says: "Dream on, Richard. Dream on of bloody deeds and death. Fainting despair, despairing—yield thy breath."

Richard wakes up.

Have mercy, Jesu! Soft, I did but dream.
O coward conscience, how dost thou afflict me!
The lights burn blue. It is now dead midnight.
Cold fearful drops stand on my trembling flesh.
What do I fear? Myself? There's none else by.
Richard loves Richard, that is, I (am) I.
Is there a murtherer here? No. Yes, I am.
Then fly. What, from myself? Great reason why—
Lest I revenge. What, myself upon myself?
Alack, I love myself. Wherefore? For any good
That I myself have done unto myself?
O no! Alas, I rather hate myself
For hateful deeds committed by myself.
I am a villain; yet I lie, I am not.
Fool, of thyself speak well; fool, do not flatter:
My conscience hath a thousand several tongues,
And every tongue brings in a several tale,
And every tale condemns me for a villain.
Perjury, perjury, in the highest degree;
Murther, stern murther, in the direst degree;
All several sins, all us'd in each degree,
Throng to the bar, crying all, "Guilty! guilty!"
I shall despair; there is no creature loves me,
And if I die no soul will pity me.
And wherefore should they, since that I myself
Find in myself no pity to myself?

That's my kind of villain. Why don't they leave him alone?

Who is the greatest villain of all time? The Devil, the Superstar of Hell. I love the Devil. I've played a lot of devils, but the best of all devils, that I've played or ever read, is the one invented by George Bernard Shaw, a wonderful devil in a marvelous play called *Man and Superman.*

Right in the middle of it is a little scene which we took out and called "Don Juan in Hell." I toured the country with it, starting in San Francisco, with Charles Boyer, Cedric Hardwick, and Agnes Moorehead. In this little playlet, there are four people: the Commander; his daughter, Doña Anna; Don Juan, the great lover, and His Majesty, the Devil, the Super Host of Hell.

As the play opens, Don Juan, the great lover, is in Hell where you'd expect to find him. And you'd think he'd like it, he'd raised so much of it on Earth. But he's very upset, and he turns to the Devil, and he says, "I want to go to Heaven."

Now, the nice thing about George Bernard Shaw's Hell is that you can leave it any time you get tired of it. When Don Juan says, "I want to go to Heaven," the Devil says, "Well, please, my

Don Juan. Please, be my guest. Go to Heaven."

Shall I be frank with you and confess that men get tired of everything: of Heaven, no less than of Hell? All history is nothing but a record of the oscillations of the world between these two extremes.

He says, "I might as well tell you, and when you're as old as I am, I think I have a right to tell you, that I have a thousand times wearied of Heaven and a thousand times wearied of Hell, and that you will no longer imagine, please, that every swing from Heaven to Hell is an emancipation, or every swing from Hell to Heaven an evolution."

"The trouble with you earth people, Don Juan, is that you are uneducated and cannot appreciate my religion of love and beauty."

Then, Don Juan says, "Oh, my God! Oh, my God! That's the trouble. Hell is nothing but love and beauty. It's like sitting for all Eternity at the first act of a fashionable play, before the complications begin."

The Devil looks at him and says, "Go on. Go on, Don Juan."

He said, "Well, my dear Devil, in Heaven, you live and work instead of playing at pretending. There is the work of helping life in its struggle upward."

The Devil says, "Oh, I know, Don Juan. I know why you want to go to Heaven. Well, let me warn you about something. There are no beautiful women in Heaven. Now, up there, they're all dowdies. And they might as well be men of fifty."

And Don Juan says, "I know what you're talking about. You're talking about brainless magnificence of body. Aren't you? Well, brainless magnificence of body, my dear Devil, has been tried before. Things immeasurably greater than man in every respect but brains have existed and perished, for instance, the dinosaur and the pterodactyl. Where are they now? They are fossils in museums, but these things lived and wanted to live. But for lack of brains, they did not know how to carry out their purpose, and so they destroyed themselves."

The Devil, in the most beautiful speech almost in the modern theater, says, "And is man any the less destroying himself for all this boasted brain of his? Have you walked up and down upon the earth lately, Don Juan? Well, I have. And I have examined man's wonderful inventions, and I tell you that in the Arts of Life, man invents nothing. But in the Arts of Death, he outdoes Nature herself and produces, by chemistry and machinery, all of the slaughter of the plague, the pestilence, and the famine. When he goes out to slay, he carries a marvel of mechanism that lets loose at the touch of his finger all the hidden molecular energies and leaves the javelin and the arrow and the blowpipe of his ancestors far behind. In the arts of Peace, man is a bungler. Oh, I have seen his factories and the like with machinery a greedy dog could have invented had it wanted money instead of food. There is nothing in man's industrial machinery but his greed and his sloth. His heart is in his weapons. I could give you a thousand instances, Don Juan, but they all come down to the same thing. The power that governs the earth is not the power of Life but of Death."

Don Juan replies, "Oh, my dear Devil, you are taking man at his own evaluation of himself. Nothing would flatter him more than your opinion of him. He loves to think of himself as bad and bold. Well, he is neither the one nor the other. He is only a coward. But," says Don Juan, "you can make any one of these cowards brave by putting a single idea into his head."

The devil looks at him and says, "Oh, go to Heaven, Don Juan. I prefer to be my own master and not the tool of any blundering life force. I know that beauty is good to look at, that music is good to hear, that love is good to feel. I know that to be well exercised in these sensations is to be a refined and cultivated being. And I also know, Don Juan, that whatever they say about me, the Devil, in churches on earth, it is universally conceded in good society that the Prince of Darkness is a gentleman."

Thank you. You're a lovely audience. Thank you.

[Question from audience:] What do you think has made you successful, if you are, and what would you recommend young actors do?

I did a show the other day with Orson Welles; we both were in the theater together. I was in the Mercury Theater with him at the very beginning of his career. We both came to the conclusion that there's one thing to success in the profession of acting or theater of any kind, and in one word that is survival. It applies to almost all professions. But in our profession, you survive.

He said, "Well, you've done some lousy movies."

And I said, "You've done some lousy magic tricks." We had a wonderful time. But they are things that have made us survive.

The other day, I was on a talk show, and the host asked, "Why do you write all those books on art and cookbooks and everything?"

I said, "So I'll have something to talk about on your damn show! What am I going to talk about? I've run out of things to say about myself."

You do survive, and that's it. The young person who wants to go into the theater must understand that it's a tough business. I had a letter from a young kid the other day saying, "How do you justify the fact that you're in movies when you're so interested in art?"

I said to myself, "Now, wait just a minute. She wants to be an actress, and she doesn't believe that movies are an art form." So I wrote back and said, "You'd better get things straight right now. You'd better believe that movies are an art form because they are. It's one of the greatest art forms of our time."

But this girl was separating art, making it something too precious. Art is expression. Art is everything. Everything Picasso painted was not good, but he worked; he survived; he changed. Today we tend to be specialists. You can't be a specialist in a profession as large in scope as the theater. You must exercise all the time. There are hundreds of ways of doing it: in college drama, in local television, local radio. There are hundreds of ways of doing it. And it's just a question of always keeping at it and surviving in it, really. It's very tough to say, but there it is. That's it.

        Lo! 't is a gala night
Within the lonesome latter years!
An angel throng, bewinged, bedight
In veils, and drowned in tears,
Sit in a theatre, to see
A play of hopes and fears,
While the orchestra breathes fitfully
The music of the spheres

Mimes, in the form of God on high,
Mutter and mumble low,
And hither and thither fly—
Mere puppets they, who come and go
At bidding of vast formless things
That shift the scenery to and fro
Flapping from out their Condor Wings
Invisible Wo!

That motley drama!—oh, be sure
It shall not be forgot!
With its Phantom chased forever more,
By a crowd that seize it not,
Through a circle that ever returneth in
To the self-same spot,
And much of Madness and more of Sin
And Horror the soul of the plot.

But see, amid the mimic rout,
A crawling shape intrude!
blood-red thing that writhes from out
The scenic solitude!
It writhes!—It writhes!—with mortal pangs
The mimes become its food,
And the seraphs sob at vermin fangs
In human gore imbued.

Out—out are the lights—out all!
And over each quivering form,
The curtain, a funeral pall,
Comes down with the rush of a storm,
And the angels, all pallid and wan,
Uprising, unveiling, affirm
That the play is the tragedy, "Man,"
And its hero the Conqueror Worm.

—from Ligeia, "The Conqueror Worm," by Edgar Allan Poe.